The Routledge
in Philosophy of Education

The RoutledgeFalmer Reader in Philosophy of Education brings togᴜ   nge
of material to present an international perspective on topical issues in ⸝   of
education today. Focusing on the enduring trends in this field, this lively and informative
Reader provides broad coverage of the subject and includes crucial topics such as:

- philosophy and education
- the aims of education
- politics and education
- educational policy
- the moral dimensions of teaching.

With an emphasis on recent developments in philosophy and their relevance to
contemporary educational policy and practice, this book represents the research and
views of some of the most respected authors in the field today. Wilfred Carr also
provides a specially written Introduction which provides a much needed context to the
role of philosophy in the current educational climate.

This is an essential resource for students of philosophy and philosophy of
education who will find this Reader an important route map to further reading and
understanding.

Wilfred Carr is Professor of Education and Dean of the Faculty of Social Sciences at the
University of Sheffield.

Readers in education

The RoutledgeFalmer Reader in Higher Education
Edited by Malcolm Tight

The RoutledgeFalmer Reader in History of Education
Edited by Gary McCulloch

The RoutledgeFalmer Reader in Inclusive Education
Edited by Keith Topping and Sheelagh Maloney

The RoutledgeFalmer Reader in Language and Literacy
Edited by Teresa Grainger

The RoutledgeFalmer Reader in Multicultural Education
Edited by Gloria Ladson-Billings and David Gillborn

The RoutledgeFalmer Reader in Philosophy of Education
Edited by Wilfred Carr

The RoutledgeFalmer Reader in Psychology of Education
Edited by Harry Daniels and Anne Edwards

The RoutledgeFalmer Reader in Science Education
Edited by John Gilbert

The RoutledgeFalmer Reader in Sociology of Education
Edited by Stephen J. Ball

The RoutledgeFalmer Reader in Teaching and Learning
Edited by E. C. Wragg

The RoutledgeFalmer Reader in Philosophy of Education

Edited by
Wilfred Carr

Routledge
Taylor & Francis Group

LONDON AND NEW YORK

First published 2005
by Routledge
2 Park Square, Milton Park, Abingdon, Oxon OX14 4RN

Simultaneously published in the USA and Canada
by Routledge
270 Madison Ave, New York, NY 10016

Reprinted 2006, 2007, 2008

Routledge is an imprint of the Taylor & Francis Group, an informa business

Typeset in Sabon by
Newgen Imaging Systems (P) Ltd, Chennai, India
Printed and bound in Great Britain by
MPG Books Ltd, Bodmin

British Library Cataloguing in Publication Data
A catalogue record for this book is available from the
British Library

Library of Congress Cataloging in Publication Data
A catalog record for this book has been requested

ISBN 10: 0–415–34571–5 (hbk)
ISBN 10: 0–415–34572–3 (pbk)
ISBN 13: 978–0–415–34571–2 (hbk)
ISBN 13: 978–0–415–34572–9 (pbk)

CONTENTS

ACKNOWLEDGEMENTS

The following articles are reprinted with the permission of Taylor & Francis Journals, www.tandf.co.uk:

Robin Barrow, 'Inclusion vs fairness', *Journal of Moral Education*, 30, 3, 235–242, 2001.

Tomas Englund, 'Rethinking democracy and education: towards an education of deliberative citizens', *Journal of Curriculum Studies*, 32, 2, 305–313, 2000.

Maxine Greene, 'Imagining futures: the public school and possibility', *Journal of Curriculum Studies*, 32, 2, 267–280, 2000.

Max van Manen, 'Moral language and pedagogical experience', *Journal of Curriculum Studies*, 32, 2, 315–327, 2000.

Terence H. McLaughlin, 'Philosophy and educational policy: possibilities, tensions and tasks', *Journal of Education Policy*, 15, 4, 441–457, 2000.

Richard Pring, 'Education as a moral practice', *Journal of Moral Education*, 30, 2, 101–112, 2001.

Paul Standish, 'Ethics before equality: moral education after Levinas', *Journal of Moral Education*, 30, 4, 339–347, 2001.

Kevin Williams, 'The limits of aesthetic separatism: literary education and Michael Oakeshott's philosophy of art', *Westminster Studies in Education*, 25, 2, 163–173, 2002.

The following chapters have been reproduced with the permission of Taylor & Francis Books:

Eamonn Callan, 'The politics of difference and common education', in David Carr (ed.) *Education, Knowledge and Truth*, London: Routledge, pp. 145–158, 1998.

J. Mark Halstead, 'Liberal values and liberal education', in J. Mark Halstead and Monica J. Taylor (eds) *Values in Education and Education in Values*, London: Falmer Press, chapter 2, pp. 17–32, 1996.

Shirley Pendlebury, 'Feminism, epistemology and education', in David Carr (ed.) *Education, Knowledge and Truth*, London: Routledge, pp. 174–188, 1998.

James C. Walker, 'Self-determination as an educational aim', in Roger Marples (ed.) *The Aims of Education*, London: Routledge, chapter 10, pp. 112–123, 1999.

Christopher Winch, 'Autonomy as an educational aim', in Roger Marples (ed.) *The Aims of Education*, London: Routledge, chapter 7, pp. 74–84, 1999.

The following articles are reprinted with the permission of Blackwell Publishing:

Wilfred Carr, 'Philosophy and education', *Journal of Philosophy of Education*, 38, 1, 55–73, 2004.

Joseph Dunne, 'What's the good of education?', in P. Hogan (ed.) *Partnership and the Benefits of Learning*, Dublin: ESAI, pp. 60–82, 1995. Reprinted with the permission of the author.

Pádraig Hogan, 'The politics of identity and the epiphanies of learning', *Papers in the Philosophy of Education*, Annual Conference of the Philosophy of Education Society of Great Britain, New College, Oxford, 1997. Reprinted with the permission of the author.

Richard Smith, 'Paths of judgement: the revival of practical wisdom', *Educational Philosophy and Theory*, 31, 3, 327–340, 1999.

John White, 'Education, the market and the nature of personal well-being', *British Journal of Educational Studies*, 50, 4, 442–456, 2002.

WHAT IS THE PHILOSOPHY OF EDUCATION?

Wilfred Carr

I

This editorial introduction has three closely related and seemingly uncontroversial aims. The first is to answer some of the obvious questions that many of the book's potential readers may wish to ask about what the philosophy of education is and what it tries to achieve. The second is to show how the chapters in the Reader provide some understanding of the kind of questions that constitute the contemporary philosophy of education's research agenda. The third is to explain how the selected chapters represent the different ways in which these questions are now being addressed by some of the discipline's leading exponents.

Although these aims are easily stated they are not so easily achieved. For what is most striking about the contemporary philosophy of education is the range of diverse and often conflicting ways of understanding 'what the philosophy of education is' that those professionally engaged in the discipline now adopt. Far from there being a single agreed answer to the kind of questions that may be raised by this book's potential audience, the philosophy of education now offers a number of different and incompatible answers emanating from the different and incompatible philosophical traditions to which philosophers of education currently subscribe. On those rare occasions when representatives of one of these philosophical traditions – say, for example, Anglo-Saxon analytical philosophy of education – try to discuss their differences with the representatives of another – say, for example, the European hermeneutic tradition – the typical outcome is to be either dismissive ('what you do is not actually philosophy of education') or assimilative ('what you do is actually no different from what I do'). In either case the intractable disagreements about how the philosophy of education is to be conducted and understood continue to defy resolution and remain obstinately where they were.

The reason for this state of affairs is not hard to identify. Any attempt to assess the rival merits of the different philosophical traditions that now characterise the philosophy of education presupposes some independent evaluative standpoint from which one philosophical tradition can be judged to be rationally superior to another. But since there are no standards of rationality that are external to, or independent of, *some* philosophical tradition, it follows that there is no neutral way rationally to adjudicate between the rival philosophical traditions that the philosophy of education now employs. It is for this reason that the inability of philosophers of education to reach an agreement about how to characterise their discipline always extends to disagreements about how these disagreements are themselves to be characterised and understood. And it is for much the same reason that any argument in favour of one particular understanding of the philosophy of education is regarded as rationally conclusive only to those who already subscribe to the philosophical tradition from within which this argument is being advanced. For philosophers of education who subscribe to a different philosophical tradition, such an argument will be dismissed as nothing other than an expression of the very disagreement it claims to resolve.

But if there is no way rationally to resolve disagreements about how the philosophy of education is to be understood that does not itself embody and exemplify some particular philosophical standpoint, how is my editorial obligation to answer questions about 'what the philosophy of education is' be discharged? For one of the obvious consequences of my drawing attention to the incommensurability of the philosophical traditions employed by philosophers of education, is that any claim that the chapters included in this Reader convey a universally accepted view of the discipline is unlikely to receive anything remotely resembling unanimous assent. Another, less obvious, implication is that my portrayal of the contemporary philosophy of education as a discipline characterised by fundamental disagreement about its own nature and purpose, itself embodies a partisan philosophical standpoint and presupposes some particular philosophical tradition. What it also presupposes is a particular and equally partisan, historical understanding of how, over the past four decades, the philosophy of education has developed and evolved. How is this history to be written?

II

One way of writing the recent history of the philosophy of education in the English speaking world is as the systematic dismantling of the powerful position achieved in the discipline during the 1960s of what is known as 'analytical philosophy'. Though definitions of this kind of philosophy were often inadequate ('conceptual analysis', 'ordinary language philosophy', 'linguistic philosophy') they nevertheless pointed to its essential claim: that philosophy was a 'second-order' activity restricted to exposing and eradicating the incoherences and confusions inherent in the language through which our knowledge and understanding are embedded. By embracing this view of 'what philosophy is' the philosophy of education was able to define itself as a quasi-technical, value-free discipline primarily concerned with elucidating the meanings of basic educational concepts by analysing the logical conditions governing the terms used to express them. And by restricting itself to this narrow aim, the philosophy of education could present itself as a legitimate branch of academic philosophy that was no longer contaminated by values, politics or ideology but had matured into a respectable intellectual pursuit. One of the analytical philosophy of education's founding fathers announced his own allegiance to this view of philosophy in the following words:

> Philosophy...is above all concerned with clarification of the concepts and propositions through which our experiences and activities are intelligible – it is interested in answering questions about the meaning of terms and expressions.... As I regard it, philosophy...is not the pursuit of moral knowledge...it is rather...primarily an analytical pursuit.... Philosophy, as I see it, is a second order area of knowledge.... Philosophical questions are not about, say, particular facts or moral judgements but about what we mean by facts, what we mean by moral judgements.

(Hirst, 1974: 1–2)

By the end of the 1960s, as analytical philosophy of education became an established orthodoxy, so the writings of its principle architects and chief exponents began to provide it with its own canonical texts. The first of these was Isreal Sheffler's aptly titled '*The Language of Education*' (1960). But the most important were the publications of Richard Peters and Paul Hirst who, in a series of seminal works (Hirst, 1965, 1974; Peters, 1966a, 1973; Hirst and Peters, 1970), not only located the philosophy of education firmly within the analytical tradition, but also deployed a high level of intellectual power and technical skill in conducting the kind of philosophical analyses of educational concepts that the analytical tradition required. By far the most influential of these was Peters' book *Ethics and Education* (1966a) which offered 'a detailed analysis of the concept of education itself and the fundamental ethical and social principles on which the conduct and content of education could be coherently based' (Hirst, 1998: 9). Of similar importance was Hirst's paper '*Liberal Education and the Nature of Knowledge*' (1965) which provided a compelling epistemological justification for a liberal education based on seven (or eight?) forms of knowledge.

Although analytical philosophy of education was always portrayed by its protagonists as a value-neutral, 'second-order' activity, this should not be allowed to obscure how, by the mid-1970s, the works of Peters and Hirst had somehow managed to provide the philosophical basis for a value-laden, 'first-order' account of the purpose and content of education of precisely the kind that the methodological principles of analytical philosophy explicitly proscribed. According to this philosophy, the overriding purpose of education was with the development of reason through an initiation into 'intrinsically worthwhile activities' (Dearden *et al.*, 1972). It followed from this that

> The curriculum would be grounded in the recognition that certain activities were intrinsically worthwhile, rather than instrumentally opportune.... Of these worthwhile activities, a special educational importance attached to those informed by intelligent understanding of a diverse group of discreet forms of knowledge...which underlay...the rationality constitutive of personal autonomy.... Thus autonomy was...a primary educational aim (some would say the uniquely overriding educational aim) and respect for the autonomy of pupil or student was a major requirement in teaching.
>
> (Blake *et al.*, 1998: 5)

This apparent willingness of analytical philosophers of education to produce a substantive philosophical account of education from within the confines of a methodological perspective that denied any legitimacy to such an account, did not go unnoticed (Earwicker, 1973; Woods and Dray, 1973). Nor was it unusual. As Alisdair MacIntyre observed

> Analytic philosophy's strengths and weaknesses both derive from its piecemeal approach to philosophy, isolable problem by isolable problem.... What analytic philosophy gains in clarity and rigour it loses in being unable to provide decisive answers to substantive philosophical questions.... When analytic philosophers do reach substantive conclusions, as they often do, these conclusions only derive in part from analytic philosophy. There is always some other agenda in the background, sometimes concealed, sometimes obvious.... It is usually a liberal political philosophy.
>
> (MacIntyre, 1998: 259–260)

By the beginning of the 1980s, the evangelical enthusiasm of philosophers of education for analytical philosophy began to be tempered by a number of anxieties and concerns (Peters, 1983). Some of these stemmed from the apparent indifference of analytical philosophers of education to the historical, social and cultural context within which educational concepts are embedded. The inevitable consequence of this was that their philosophical analyses were constantly exposed to the accusation of offering a spurious logical necessity to interpretations of educational concepts that were both historically contingent and culturally specific. And it is precisely because it seemed to be conferring universal validity on whatever interpretation of educational concepts happened to be dominant in the prevailing cultural and political milieu, that analytical philosophy of education was also vulnerable to the suspicion that it was an inherently conservative form of philosophy that subserved (and rarely subverted) the political and educational status quo.

These suspicions were soon to develop into a catalogue of complaints that have been neatly summarised by Terrence McLaughlin. 'Criticisms of analytic philosophy of education' he writes,

> included inter alia: that it aspired to a spurious value-neutrality... was uncritical about its own values and assumptions... espoused... an untenable rationalism... was inherently conservative... read too much into what can legitimately be derived from a mere analysis of concepts... illicitly claimed a universal significance and value for certain ideals and values independent of all cultural and social contexts... and was of little use in relation to the determination of educational policy and practice.
>
> (McLaughlin, 2000: 446)

With characteristic perceptiveness, Alasdair MacIntyre has observed how 'the dominance of a position in philosophy is not so much a matter of how widely it is accepted as of how widely the need is felt *either* to defend *or* to attack it' (MacIntyre, 1983: 2). It is therefore testimony to the enduring dominance of analytical philosophy of education that, when confronted with its obvious inadequacies and failures, it has attracted both robust defence *and* hostile attack. The strategy most commonly deployed in its defence, however, has not consisted of the kind of rear guard action typically taken to preserve a status quo. Nor has it been based on a blanket refusal to accept criticisms of the assumptions, values and beliefs that analytical philosophy of education had uncritically presupposed. Instead it has been to insist that, far from being immutable or fixed, analytical philosophy is a 'continually evolving tradition' that 'since the 1980s has been... marked by much re-assessment and re-working of the most fundamental issues within the discipline' (Hirst, 1998: 16). As a result of engaging in this process of 'critical self-reflection', (ibid.: 15), analytical philosophers of education have now recognised the legitimacy of many of the criticisms of their original philosophical approach and have revised its aims, methods and scope in ways which enable it to overcome its previous weaknesses and limitations (Hirst, 1998; Hirst and White, 1998). By pursuing this strategy of critical reconstruction, analytical philosophy of education is now defended by its protagonists on the grounds that it has 'evolved' into a 'later phase' which 'while retaining a commitment to a broadly analytic approach... has been characterised by a broadening of approaches, canons and sensitivities and a move towards the more normative and practical concerns of applied philosophy' (MacLaughlin, 2000: 447).

The enduring strength of analytical philosophy of education is revealed not only by the extensive efforts that have been mounted in its defence but also by the severity with which it continues to be attacked. These attacks take a number of different forms and emanate from philosophical traditions as varied as Marxism, phenomenology, neopragmatism, hermeneutics, neoAristotelianism, critical theory and postmodernism. Though each of these tradition's particular point of attack may be different, they nevertheless all agree that the inadequacies of analytical philosophy of education are so deeply ingrained in the philosophical tradition within which it is embedded, that they cannot be eliminated save by abandoning the analytical tradition itself. In other words, they all share the conviction that it is only by removing the philosophy of education from the philosophical tradition within which it had originally been located, that fundamental questions about 'what the philosophy of education is' can begin to be adequately asked and the answers supplied by other philosophical traditions can be properly assessed.

The initial shots in this attack came from philosophers of education with an allegiance to the Marxist philosophical tradition and were aimed at exposing analytical philosophy of education's latent ideological character (Harris, 1979; Matthews, 1980). But of more significance was how, during the 1980s and 1990s, as the presuppositions of analytical philosophy were being brought under ever sharper critical scrutiny, some philosophers of education began to look to alternative philosophical traditions for the intellectual resources that would help them to identify the incoherence and errors of the analytical tradition and to forge a view of their discipline that was more congenial to their understanding of their task. In undertaking this search, philosophers of education were inevitably drawn to the writings of two 'post-analytic' Anglo-Saxon philosophers whose very different expositions of what has come to be known as 'the critique of modernity' were to be massively influential.

One of these was Alisdair MacIntyre who, in *After Virtue* (1981), launched a devastating attack on the separation of reason from morality that now characterises the emotivist culture of post-enlightenment modernity. Since MacIntyre regarded the analytical tradition as itself merely an expression of the culture of modernity, he has pursued his own project of reintegrating reason and morality by reviving the premodern Aristotelian philosophical tradition. This has led philosophers of education who have been influenced by MacIntyre's writings to deploy Aristotelian categories and concepts to explore a number of educational topics and themes. These include philosophical analyses of the nature of education as a 'practice' (Carr, 1987; Dunne, 1993) and the elaboration of a virtue-based approach to moral education that draws on Aristotle's ethical theory (Carr and Steutel, 1998).

The other post-analytic philosopher who has had a major impact on the philosophy of education is Richard Rorty who, in *Philosophy and the Mirror of Nature* (1979), critically deconstructed modern forms of philosophy (including analytical philosophy) and advocated instead a 'conversational' style of philosophy in which the modern pre-occupations with knowledge, rationality and truth are replaced by a more postmodern concern for understanding and edification. Rorty sometimes calls this style of philosophising 'hermeneutics' but he more often describes it as a late twentieth-century expression of the early twentieth-century American pragmatist tradition.

In articulating and defending his view of philosophy, Rorty draws heavily on the writings of John Dewey who he refers to as 'my principle philosophical hero' (Rorty, 1999: xii). Within the philosophy of education this has not only encouraged a re-assessment of the value and validity of the pragmatist tradition (Garrison and Neiman, 2003), it has also provoked a renewed interest in John Dewey's philosophical account of the role of education in a democratic society (Dewey, 1916) and its significance for any philosophical assessment of contemporary educational policies and practices (Carr and Hartnett, 1996).

As the writings of MacIntyre and Rorty began to penetrate the philosophy of education, so it became increasingly obvious that they had some affinity with the writings of two major philosophers who belonged to the hitherto neglected European philosophical traditions of hermeneutics and critical theory. One of these was Hans-Georg Gadamer whose radical reconstruction of hermeneutics has clearly had some influence on Rorty's view of philosophy (Gadamer, 1980). The other is the leading critical theorist Jurgen Habermas (1972, 1974, 1979) who, like MacIntyre, has located the source of the crisis of modernity in the modernist attempt to bring the social world under the control of an all embracing technical rationality. Also, like MacIntyre, Habermas has been concerned to show how the cultural and ideological condition of modern societies have made it impossible for the Enlightenment's emancipatory ideals to be realised or achieved. Since theses ideals were also educational ideals, Habermasian critical theory has had an obvious attraction for those philosophers of education who were looking for a philosophical perspective that attached a stronger role to the notion of 'critique' than analytical philosophy would permit. It is thus hardly surprising that the work of Habermas has been deployed within the philosophy of education to examine a number of educational issues including: the nature of educational theory and research (Carr and Kemmis, 1986), the philosophical basis of critical pedagogy (Gur-Ze'ev, 1999; Blake and Masschelein, 2003) and the significance for education of Habermas' critique of modernity (Blake, 1992, 1995).

There is, of course, a fundamental historical and cultural divide between the European philosophical traditions represented by Gadamer and Habermas and the Anglo-Saxon philosophical traditions to which both MacIntyre and Rorty belong. But despite their differences, they all tend to portray analytical philosophy as a legacy of post-enlightenment thought and thus as part of the problem of modernity rather than a source of its solution. And, by making the assumptions of post-enlightenment modernity more transparent and open to critical scrutiny, they prepared the ground for the arrival within the philosophy of education of that more radical response to the crisis of modernity commonly known as 'postmodernism'.

The difficulties involved in providing anything remotely resembling a satisfactory definition of 'postmodernism' are notorious. Indeed, one of the few generalisations that can be made about postmodernist thought is that it repudiates any suggestion that one way of defining it can be privileged over any other. But despite the vagueness and ambiguity surrounding its meaning, it is a characteristic feature of postmodernism to display a profound scepticism towards the fundamental presuppositions concerning rationality, knowledge and truth which constitute the epistemological foundations on which analytical philosophy of education has been erected. One of the radical implications of this kind of postmodernist scepticism is to repudiate any attempt to characterise the philosophy of education as an 'autonomous' discipline that can be separated from other educational disciplines such as sociology and history. Another is to ridicule any suggestion that the philosophy of education is a 'foundation discipline' providing the grounds on which rational educational policies and practices can be based. It is thus unsurprising that some analytically minded philosophers of education have given postmodernism a hostile reception (Carr, 1998). But other philosophers of education have seen postmodernism not as a threat to the continuing existence of their discipline, but as an invaluable resource for its future development. Drawing on the work of postmodernist writers as diverse as Lyotard, Derrida, Foucault and Levinas, these philosophers of education are now pointing the discipline in a number of different and exciting new directions (Standish, 1990; Peters, 1995; Blake *et al.*, 1998; Dhillon and Standish, 2000; Biesta and Egéa-Kuehne, 2001). Their assessments of postmodernism are often qualified and their views about its significance for the conduct of their discipline are not always the same. But despite their differences, these philosophers of education all acknowledge that postmodernism has seriously undermined many of their disciplines' most fundamental assumptions and, by so doing, has forced upon its practitioners an urgent need to engage in a critical dialogue aimed at radically revising their existing understanding of 'what the philosophy of education is'.

III

My interpretation of the recent history of the philosophy of education is, of course, neither impartial nor neutral. It is predicated on my belief that the developments that have taken place over the last forty years were due to a growing, if sometimes reluctant, admission of how, in the 1960s, the philosophy of education confined itself to an increasingly impoverished philosophical tradition whose inadequacies and limitations meant that the discipline was too narrowly conceived. However, the chapters in this Reader have not been chosen simply to endorse this historical verdict. They have been selected because, when read separately, they represent some of the different ways in which the inadequacies of limitations of earlier forms of analytical philosophy of education are being corrected and, when read collectively, they demonstrate how our understanding of 'what the philosophy of education is' is now being expanded and enriched by developments that are occurring in philosophy at large.

In the light of my historical narrative, it should come as no surprise to find contributors to the Reader disagreeing with each other, sometimes explicitly but often implicitly, about how the philosophy of education ought to be conducted and understood. Nor should it be surprising to find contributors who subscribe to different philosophical traditions examining the same educational issue in very different ways. This is particularly the case with the three chapters that make up Part I of the Reader which focus on fundamental questions about the purpose of the philosophy of education. In Chapter 1, Terrence H. McLaughlin examines 'the role which philosophy can and should play in relation to educational policy'. He argues that 'philosophy has a potentially important contribution to make to educational policy' but that there are some unexamined complexities – which he characterises as 'possibilities, tensions and tasks' – that need to be explored if this potential is to be realised. He therefore examines these complexities in some detail and considers the different ways in which philosophy may be related to the policy-making process, the kind of tensions intrinsic to this relationship and the specific tasks that need to be undertaken if philosophy is to make a fruitful contribution to educational policy. In conducting this examination McLaughlin acknowledges that 'different conceptions of philosophy give rise to potentially different conceptions of the contribution which it can and should make' and he confines his own discussion to a consideration of the contribution to be made by analytical philosophy.

In Chapter 2, I offer a very different interpretation of how philosophy is related to education. I argue that the root causes of the tensions and complexities that McLaughlin sees as preventing philosophy from making a positive contribution to educational policy are actually embedded in the presuppositions of analytical philosophy itself. In pursuing this argument, I conduct a historically informed analysis of the relationship between philosophy and education that reveals how the

Aristotelian philosophical tradition suggests the reconstruction of the philosophy of education as a species of 'practical' – as opposed to 'theoretical' – philosophy in which the 'tensions' that McLaughlin identifies between philosophy and education do not – indeed could not – arise.

Contemporary interest in Aristotelian philosophy should not be allowed to excuse Aristotle's explicitly dismissive attitude towards women. But the easy condemnation of Aristotle's views should not blind us to the possibility that some of our own philosophical approaches may themselves have an implicitly gendered nature and, in particular, may rest on a 'masculinist' epistemology. In Chapter 3, Shirley Pendlebury examines this possibility by assessing the extent to which feminist challenges to mainstream epistemology can be applied to the 'forms of knowledge' epistemology that informed the influential accounts of education, curriculum and teaching that were originally produced by analytical philosophy of education. In doing this, she focuses on feminist criticisms of the way in which the distinction between 'objectivity' and 'subjectivity' is treated within mainstream epistemology and calls for the philosophy of education to adopt an epistemological perspective that heeds the feminist call to 'take subjectivity seriously'.

Since the time of Plato, philosophers have been concerned with fundamental questions about the aims of education and the four chapters in Part II are intended to show how these questions are now being addressed by philosophers of education. Within analytical philosophy of education there has been a long-standing attachment to the educational aim of personal autonomy and, in Chapter 4, Christopher Winch, while remaining firmly within the analytical tradition, takes issue with the way in which this aim has usually been understood. Drawing a distinction between 'weak autonomy' – which is the ability to choose from a variety of socially approved and tolerated ends, and 'strong autonomy' – which is the ability to choose ends other than those that are socially approved, Winch argues that, in a modern pluralist democratic society, 'it is logically incoherent to suppose that a public education system could promote strong autonomy because to do so would undermine the assumptions and procedures on which that system is based'. He therefore insists that, in such a society, only 'weak autonomy' can be justified as a legitimate and realisable educational aim.

In Chapter 5, James Walker is, like many other contemporary philosophers of education, critical of the 'liberal rationalism' that informed early analytical philosophy's justification of autonomy as an educational aim. And, like Winch, he is critical of the way in which autonomy was taken to require 'a liberal education consisting of initiation into...putatively logically necessary forms of knowledge'. However, unlike Winch, he does not try to provide an alternative philosophical account of how the educational aim of autonomy should now be justified. Instead he 'outlines a philosophical case for self-determination as the fundamental educational aim which is consistent with contemporary theories of human development and knowledge about the conditions for optimal learning'. In making this case, Walker presents an account of self-determination that is communitarian rather than individualistic and is 'constituted by the dispositions to authentic self-expression, management of one's own learning and creation of the conditions for further enhanced self-determination'.

In Chapter 6, Pádraig Hogan also takes a critical attitude towards the efforts of analytical philosophers of education to uphold rational autonomy as an educational aim. But Hogan's concern is not so much with the particular arguments used by analytical philosophers as with their intrinsic dependence on the Enlightenment project of modernity – a project which postmodernism now regards as fundamentally flawed. He therefore draws on the work of Lyotard, Foucault and Derrida to show how 'the modernist ideal of rational autonomy is radically called into question by postmodernist standpoints'. He also endorses Gadamer's and MacIntyre's neoAristotelian insistence that 'the exercise of reason always takes place within a tradition and not in a rationally autonomous way which is independent of the influences that constitute each and every tradition'. And, drawing on the work of Richard Rorty, he presents an argument for re-constructing questions about the aims of education so that they focus on issues concerning personal identity and, in particular, on how the individual's sense of their own identity is something to be chosen and re-chosen rather than something that can be derived from a theory of human nature or disclosed through the acquisition of knowledge. For Hogan, then, the aim of education is to 'maximise the scope to choose and re-choose one's identity' and, in the final part of the chapter, he explains how what he calls 'epiphanies of learning' can contribute to the realisation of this aim by bringing about 'unexpected and unforced shifts in our understanding of ourselves'.

The philosopher of education who has done most to preserve and develop analytical philosophy's long-standing allegiance to the educational aim of personal autonomy is John White. One of the ways in which he has done this is by arguing that the core liberal value of personal autonomy rests on the more fundamental – and not specifically liberal – value of personal well-being (White, 1990). Another is by defending his commitment to autonomy against both external criticism and internal dissent (White, 1999, 2003). In Chapter 7, however, White does not try to justify this commitment but instead poses the question of whether the educational aim of 'well-being' is compatible with the aims and values of the market. He pursues this question by critically examining John O'Neill's attempt to justify the market on the basis of 'an individualistic objectivist preference-satisfaction notion of well-being' (O'Neill, 1998). On this basis, he outlines and defends an alternative 'non-individualistic subjectivist account of personal well-being' and suggests that educational institutions that pursued this notion of personal well-being would be driven by a set of values that would require the values of the market to be reassessed and, if necessary, altered, abandoned or discarded.

One of the untenable claims of early analytical philosophy of education was that it conducted inquiries that were independent of any particular political values or beliefs. Much has changed in the last three decades. Not only has analytical philosophy of education now conceded that it is, and always has been, firmly wedded to a particular version of liberal political philosophy (Hirst, 1998; White, 2003). There has also developed a growing interest in the political philosophy of education and, in particular, in the implications for educational policy and practice of liberal and democratic political theories (Gutmann, 1987; Carr and Hartnett, 1996; Jonathan, 1997). The three chapters in Part IV of the Reader reflect this interest.

In Chapter 8, Mark Halstead begins by recognising that, for the past thirty years analytical philosophy of education's approach to questions about educational values have typically begun with an analysis of the concept of education. In opposition to this, he argues that the best way to identify a society's educational values is by examining the political values of that society. He therefore conducts a philosophical analysis aimed at exposing the inter-connection between the values of a liberal society and the values of liberal education. He then goes on to show how the fundamental values that are endemic to most Western liberal societies – freedom, equality and rationality – not only support our understanding of liberal education. They also inform contemporary approaches to multiculturalism, citizenship education and 'education for democracy'. The chapter concludes with a discussion of the challenges posed to liberal education by the values of the market and by non-liberal communities.

One of the familiar claims of postmodernism is that the kind of liberal education that Halstead defends, not only promotes the values of a liberal society; it may also undermine and denigrate the values of other, non-liberal, societies and cultures. On this basis, some postmodernists have argued that education should no longer be based on a 'liberal politics' but on a 'politics of difference' which does not simply tolerate cultural diversity but also respects those cultures which reject liberal values and promote an alternative way of life. In Chapter 9, Eammon Callan, while acknowledging the force of the postmodernist critique of liberal politics, nevertheless insists that this does not fatally undermine the liberal political tradition or the kind of liberal common education it entails. Through a detailed critical analysis of Marion Young's influential postmodern critique of liberalism (Young, 1990), he concludes that while there is something true and important in the postmodern call for a 'politics of difference', this does not imply the abandonment of liberal education. But what it does imply is a need for serious collective discussion in which postmodern objections to the aims and content of liberal common education are taken seriously and the argument for education to take account of 'the politics of difference' can be adequately addressed.

In the 1960s and 1970s, it was quite common for analytical philosophers of education to be dismissive of the pragmatic philosophical tradition and to regard John Dewey's educational philosophy as 'obscure' and 'mistaken' (Peters, 1966b: 68). Today, however, Richard Rorty's reconstruction of pragmatism has led to an understanding of Dewey's analysis of the relationship between democracy and education that is not only consistent with the postmodern rejection of foundationalist epistemology, but also has major significance for our understanding of the educational needs of citizens in a postmodern democratic society. In Chapter 10, Thomas Englund shows how Rorty's neopragmatism provides the basis for an interpretation of Dewey's account of democratic education that differs from the interpretations given by the early twentieth-century educational movements of Progressivism and Reconstructionism. In his neopragmatic reading, Englund gives a central place to Dewey's idea of 'education as communication' and to its crucial role in creating a 'deliberative democracy' – a democracy whose citizens have been educated to participate in public discussion and debate, to understand different perspectives and to communicate their differences to those who may hold alternative points of view.

The four chapters in Part IV represent some of the different ways in which philosophy can contribute to the formation and critical assessment of specific educational policies. In Chapter 11, Joseph Dunne provides a philosophical dimension to the debate that followed the publication of the policy document '*Education for a Changing World*' in the Republic of Ireland. He does this by posing a fundamental philosophical question – 'what's the good of education?' – and outlining a conceptual context for interpreting and answering this question that is informed by Alisdair MacIntyre's Aristotelian account of the concept of 'practice'. From this Aristotelian perspective, the 'good' of education is internal to the practice of education and is pursued and achieved by practitioners striving to meet the standards of excellence central to this practice. In advocating educational policies that respect and acknowledge the integrity of education as a practice, Dunne does not so much make specific policy recommendations as offer an understanding of 'the good' of education that may help policy makers to appreciate what would count as a genuine *educational* reform.

In Chapter 12, Maxine Greene outlines the vision for public education in the United States that she believes ought to inform educational policy and curriculum reform in the twenty-first century. Central to this vision are the need for community – 'the coming together in the name of something to pursue'; and the contribution of the artist to human dialogue and conversation – 'the voice of the artist in imagining the possible'. Greene suggests that it is only the educational policies that are infused with this vision that will lead to the development of social imagination and the creation of an articulate democratic public.

The prominence given to literature and art in Greene's educational vision is something which Kevin Williams would no doubt applaud. However, in Chapter 13, he notes how the widespread belief that the educational significance of literature resides in its capacity 'to teach pupils something about life' stands in stark contradiction to the theory of literary education supported by the philosophy of Michael Oakeshott – a theory that precludes a teacher from making any direct connection between 'literature' and 'life'. By exploring the limits of Oakeshott's 'aesthetic separatism' Williams finds evidence for a more nuanced and defensible view of the role of literature in education.

In Chapter 14, Robin Barrow examines educational policies based on the principle of 'inclusion' that are now widespread in many educational systems. After drawing attention to the similarities between 'inclusion policies' and 'affirmative action' policies, he argues that, although a policy of inclusion may, in certain circumstances, be justified, it cannot be justified on the basis of a moral principle. Indeed, he maintains that the notion of inclusion is, at best, morally neutral and is likely, on many occasions, to offend the moral principle of fairness. He concludes by distinguishing empirical arguments for inclusion from would-be moral arguments and claims that there do not appear to be any compelling empirical arguments to support the widespread adoption of inclusion policies.

The educational discourse common to most modern Western societies tends to portray education as an instrument for achieving political and economic goals such as 'the national interest', 'good citizens' and 'the economic needs of society'. Within this discourse, teaching tends to be regarded as a technical means of producing the 'learning outcomes' that are conducive to the achievement of these goals and the idea of teaching as an intrinsically moral activity can hardly be entertained. The chapters that make up Part V of the Reader are concerned to expose the limitations and confusions infecting this discourse and to articulate an alternative language in which the moral dimension of teaching can be given a central place.

In Chapter 15, Richard Pring argues that although educational interest in morality has tended to be confined to the teaching of moral education, the connection between morality and education is much more fundamental. Indeed, he argues that education is itself a moral practice that can only be properly articulated, examined and understood through the kind of moral discourse that this understanding of education presupposes and requires. Our contemporary failure to recognise this, he maintains, means that education is becoming detached from its moral roots and teachers are being deprived of the coherent set of values that would enable them to confront, both morally and critically, the external pressures they now face to use education for political, economic and other non-moral ends.

Richard Smith is also concerned by the modern demoralisation of teaching which he believes to be in no small part due to the widespread impact of 'technicism' on the modern world. In Chapter 16, he argues that the ascendancy of technicism – and the consequent spread of technical and instrumental reasoning to all aspects of education – presents the philosophy of education with a formidable and important challenge: 'to develop richer more humane and, in the end, more educational conceptions of education'. In responding to this challenge, Smith outlines a view of teaching that is informed by Aristotle's account of practical judgement. Through a critical examination of some of the difficulties with Aristotle's original account, Smith formulates a modern interpretation of practical judgement that goes a long way to defending the moral dimension of teaching from the corroding and corrupting spread of technicism.

In Chapter 17, Max van Manen echoes many of the concerns expressed by Pring and Smith. He argues that 'the the most unfortunate fact about contemporary discourses and practices of education is that they have tended to become overly rationalistic, scientist, corporatist, managerial, and narrowly results-based'. And, like Pring and Smith, he believes that the most appropriate way for the philosophy of education to respond to this state of affairs is to develop a vocabulary for education that fully recognises the moral dimension of teaching. Van Manen explores the potential for creating such a vocabulary inherent in the language of 'care' that is now so prominent in the theoretical literature of education. However, as a phenomenological philosopher, van Manen is not so much concerned with how 'care' is understood conceptually or theoretically, as with capturing how 'caring' is actually lived and experienced in ordinary every day life. For this reason he explores the experiential subtleties of the moral vocabulary of care by drawing on literary and imaginative sources that can offer an understanding of the meaning of care that is 'unmediated by conceptualization'.

Paul Standish is not so much concerned with the moral impoverishment of contemporary educational discourse as with how the discourse of modern morality distorts our thinking about moral education. Common to this discourse is a conception of human being in which assumptions about equality are regarded as sacrosanct, values are somehow grafted onto an original subjectivity and ethics is regarded as a part-time business. In Chapter 18, Standish examines this discourse in the light of the work of two major postmodern philosophers: Jean-Francois Lyotard and Emmanuel Levinas. He explores Levinas' account of 'the primacy of ethics' – of my absolute responsibility in the face of the other – in order to reveal an idea of human being that, by invoking a sense of the importance of receptivity, releases the ethical from the limitations of moral reasoning.

References

Blake, N. (1992) 'Modernity and the problem of cultutral pluralism', *Journal of Philosophy of Education*, 29, 3–50.

Blake, N. (1995) 'Ideal speech conditions, modern discourse and education', *Journal of Philosophy of Education*, 29, 355–368.

Blake, N. and Masschelein, J. (2003) 'Critical theory and critical pedagogy', in N. Blake, P. Smeyers, R. Smith and P. Standish (eds), *The Blackwell Guide to the Philosophy of Education*, Oxford: Blackwell.

Blake, N., Smeyers, P., Smith, R. and Standish, P. (1998) *Thinking Again: Education after Postmodernism*, Oxford: Blackwell.

Biesta, G.J.J. and Egéa-Kuehne, D. (eds) (2001) *Derrida and Education*, London: Routledge.

Carr, D. (ed.) (1998) *Education, Knowledge and Truth: Beyond the Postmodern Impasse*, London: Routledge.

Carr, D. and Steutel, J. (eds) (1998) *Virtue Theory and Moral Education*, London: Routledge.

Carr, W. and Kemmis, S. (1986) *Becoming Critical: Education, Knowledge and Action Research*, Brighton: Falmer Press.

Carr, W. (1987) 'What is an educational practice?', *Journal of Philosophy of Education*, 21, 2, 163–175.

Carr, W. and Hartnett, A. (1996) *Education and the Struggle for Democracy*, Buckingham: Open University Press.

Dearden, R.F., Hirst, P.H. and Peters, R.S. (eds) (1972) *Education and the Development of Reason*, London: Routledge and Kegan Paul.

Dewey, J. (1916) *Democracy and Education*, New York: Free Press.

Dhillon, P. and Standish, P. (eds) (2000) *Lyotard: Just Education*, London: Routledge.

Dunne, J. (1993) *Back to the Rough Ground: 'Phronesis' and 'Techné' in Modern Philosophy and in Aristotle*, Illinois: University of Notre Dame Press.

Earwicker, J. (1973) 'R. S. Peters and the concept of education', *Proceedings of the Philosophy of Education Society of Great Britain*, 17, 230–259.

Gadamer, H.-G. (1980) *Truth and Method*, trans. G. Bardey and J. Cummings, New York: Seabury Press.

Garrison, J. and Neiwan, A. (2003) 'Pragmatism and education', in N. Blake, P. Smeyers, R. Smith and P. Standish (eds), *The Blackwell Guide to the Philosophy of Education*, Oxford: Blackwell.

Gur-Ze'ev, I. (1999) 'Towards a non-repressive critical pedagogy', *Educational Theory*, 49, 4, 437–456.

Gutmann, A. (1987) *Democratic Education*, Princeton, NJ: Princeton University Press.

Habermas, J. (1972) *Knowledge and Human Interests*, trans. J. Shapiro, London: Heinemann.

Habermas, J. (1974) *Theory and Practice*, trans. J. Viertel, London: Heinemann.

Habermas, J. (1979) *Communication and the Evolution of Society*, trans. T. McCarthy, London: Heinemann.

Harris, K. (1979) *Education and Knowledge*, London: Routledge and Kegan Paul.

Hirst, P.H. (1965) 'Liberal education and the nature of knowledge', in R.D. Archambault (ed.), *Philosophical Analysis and Education*, London: Routledge and Kegan Paul.

Hirst, P.H. (1974) *Knowledge and the Curriculum*, London: Routledge and Kegan Paul.

Hirst, P.H. (1998) 'Philosophy of education: the evolution of a discipline', in G. Haydon (ed.), *50 Years of Philosophy of Education*, London: London University Institute of Education.

Hirst, P.H. and Peters, R.S. (1970) *The Logic of Education*, London: Routledge and Kegan Paul.

Hirst, P.H. and White P. (1998) 'The analytic tradition and philosophy of education: an historical perspective', in P.H. Hirst and P. White (eds), *Philosophy of Education: Major Themes in the Analytic Tradition*, Vol. 1, London: Routledge.

Jonathan, R. (1997) *Illusory Freedoms: Liberalism, Education and the Market*, Oxford: Blackwell.

MacIntyre, A.C. (1981) *After Virtue: A Study in Moral Theory*, London: Duckworth.

MacIntyre, A.C. (1983) 'Moral philosophy: what next?', in S. Hauerwas and A.C. MacIntyre (eds), *Revisions: Changing Perspectives in Moral Philosophy*, London and Notre Dame: University of Notre Dame.

MacIntyre, A.C. (1998) 'An interview with Giovanna Borradori', in K. Knight (ed.), *The MacIntyre Reader*, Cambridge: Polity Press, 255–266.

McLaughlin, T.H. (2000) 'Philosophy and educational policy: possibilities, tensions and tasks', *Journal of Education Policy*, 15, 4, 441–457.

Matthews, M. (1980) *The Marxist Theory of Schooling*, London: Routledge and Kegan Paul.

O'Neill, J. (1998) *The Market: Ethics, Knowledge and Politics*, London: Routledge.

Peters, M.A. (ed.) (1995) *Education and the Postmodern Condition*, London: Bergin and Garvey.

Peters, R.S. (1966a) *Ethics and Education*, London: Allen and Unwin.

Peters, R.S. (1966b) 'The philosophy of education', in J.W. Tibble (ed.), *The Study of Education*, London: Routledge and Kegan Paul.

Peters, R.S. (ed.) (1973) *The Philosophy of Education*, Oxford: Oxford University Press.

Peters, R.S. (1983) 'The philosophy of education: 1960–1980', in P.H. Hirst (ed.), *Education Theory and Its Foundation Disciplines*, London: Routledge and Kegan Paul.

Rorty, R. (1979) *Philosophy and the Mirror of Nature*, Princeton, NJ: Princeton University Press.

Rorty, R. (1999) *Philosophy and Social Hope*, London: Penguin.

Scheffler, I. (1960) *The Language of Education*, Springfield, Il: Charles C. Thomas.

White, J.P. (1990) *Education and the Good Life: Beyond the National Curriculum*, London: Kogan Page.

White, J.P. (1999) 'In defence of liberal aims in education', in R. Marples (ed.), *The Aims of Education*, London: Routledge.

White, J.P. (2003) 'Five critical stances towards liberal philosophy of education in Britain', *Journal of Philosophy of Education*, 31, 1, 147–161.

Woods, J. and Dray, W.H. (1973) 'Aims of education – a conceptual enquiry', in R.S. Peters (ed.), *The Philosophy of Education*, Oxford: Oxford University Press.

Young, I.M. (1990) *Justice and the Politics of Difference*, Princeton, NJ: Princeton University Press.

PHILOSOPHY AND EDUCATION

CHAPTER 1

PHILOSOPHY AND EDUCATIONAL POLICY
Possibilities, tensions and tasks

Terence H. McLaughlin

Journal of Education Policy, 15, 4, 441–457, 2000

The nature of educational policy

It is helpful at the outset of our discussion to make a number of preliminary points about educational policy and policy making, which are relevant to the contribution which philosophy might make to them. Four preliminary points are of particular significance here.

First, what is an educational policy? In answer to this question, some writers stress the relationship between educational policies and politics, power and control (Codd, 1995: 1–2). Prunty (quoted in Codd, 1995: 1) defines educational policy making as 'an exercise of power and control directed towards the attainment or preservation of some preferred arrangement of schools and society'. Codd himself argues that 'educational policies are sets of political decisions which involve the exercise of power in order to preserve or alter the nature of educational institutions or practices' (ibid.). Prunty and Codd seem to imply that educational policies can be formulated only by those who exercise power and control and who are involved in politics in this sense. Is it not the case, however, that educational policies can be formulated by many bodies and agencies, including those who do not (either temporarily or otherwise) enjoy the exercise of relevant forms of power and control but seek merely to influence educational arrangements indirectly through (say) appeal to the electorate, lobbying of various kinds or the stimulation of general debate and discussion? The kinds of bodies and agencies one thinks of here include political parties in opposition, subject and teacher associations, 'think tanks' of various kinds and the like. A more sensitive characterization of the relationship between educational policy making on the one hand and politics, power and control on the other seems therefore to be required. What is central to the notion of an educational policy is that it is a detailed prescription for action aimed at the preservation or alteration of educational institutions or practices. However, an educational policy, and the related notion of 'educational policy making' can be used in either (i) power and control related or (ii) 'influence aspirant' senses and contexts.

Second, educational policies originate at different levels and contexts in the educational system and from a number of different agents and agencies ranging from national to school (and even to classroom level). There are different 'languages' of policy debate, which can be roughly labelled as 'official', 'professional', 'research' and 'popular' (McLaughlin, 1999a: 37–38).

Third, educational policies differ with respect to the scope of their content and application. One way of expressing these differences is to invoke various kinds of continuum on which policies can be located. One such continuum involves generality and specificity. At one end of this continuum are policies of a very general kind involving matters such as the aims of education and the structure of the educational system, whilst at the other end are very specific policies relating (say) to strategies for the teaching of particular topics within specific subjects. Another (related) continuum can be described as involving 'depth' and 'surface' characteristics. The 'depth' end of this continuum involves educational policies with clear philosophical implications and ramifications. Many current policies concerned with the general area of 'values education' fall into this category. At the 'surface' end of this continuum are educational policies, which are less apt for philosophical reflection. It is important not to assume, however, that 'generality' is uniquely associated with 'depth' and 'specificity' with 'surface' characteristics. General policies may not be suitable for philosophical reflection and specific policies may be rich in philosophical implication.

Fourth, it is useful to note the distinction between different (though interrelated) aspects of educational policy and policy making: (i) the process of educational policy making; (ii) the policy itself and (iii) the application and evaluation of the policy.

These four preliminary points have significance for the role which philosophy might play in relation to educational policy and policy making. Taken as a whole, the points caution against treating 'educational policy' in an unanalysed way if one is seeking to achieve a sensitive characterization of the contribution which philosophy might make to it. Considered individually, each point contains an insight worth noting. The first point urges alertness to the influence which power and control might have on proffered philosophical contributions to educational policy; the second point raises awareness of the different levels and contexts where such philosophical contributions might be made; the third point reminds us that not all educational policies are equally apt for philosophical illumination and urges us to reflect on how we might distinguish between those policies which do and those which do not properly invite philosophical attention, and the fourth point brings into focus the different aspects and dimensions of educational policy and policy making which philosophers might seek to contribute to.

Philosophy and educational policy: some preliminary considerations

The claim that philosophy is one of the reflective and critical resources, which should be brought to bear on educational policy if policies are to be coherent, justifiable and effective, invites attention to the precise nature of the contribution which philosophy might make in these matters.

At the outset, it is important to emphasize that the contribution which philosophy can offer is a modest one. This is for at least two reasons. First, philosophy is only one of the 'reflective and critical resources' relevant to educational policy. Second, reflection and criticism may be necessary for educational policy but it is not sufficient for its coherence, justifiability and effectiveness: the wide-ranging contingencies of circumstance and practice are highly salient and decisive. The modesty of philosophy must extend both to an acknowledgement that its contribution to educational policy is a partial one, and to an acceptance that its contribution must be offered in relationship and dialogue with other reflective and critical resources and with the contingencies of circumstance and practice. It should be noted that the contribution which philosophy may make to educational policy need not necessarily be a 'purely' philosophical one, but can (and sometimes should) be linked to, and form part of, reflective and critical contributions of a wider kind.[1]

One starting point for our investigation of the contribution which philosophy might make to educational policy is Amelie Oksenberg Rorty's remark:

> Fruitful and responsible discussions of educational policy inevitably move to the larger philosophic questions that prompt and inform them.
>
> (Oksenberg Rorty, 1998a: 1)

As it stands, this remark requires qualification in a number of ways. First, the remark should clearly not be interpreted descriptively, as referring to what actually happens in discussions of educational policy, but normatively, as indicating what should characterize discussions of this kind. Even interpreted in this way, however, as requiring that all policy discussion should move on to philosophical questions, the remark is not obviously true, in, for example, the case of educational policies with merely 'surface' characteristics. Second, it is not clear that all educational policies are 'prompted and informed' by philosophic questions. Educational policies with merely 'surface' characteristics are again a case in point here. Further, it is not clear that 'prompting' is the most accurate way of characterizing the relationship between philosophy and educational policy. Many policy discussions are prompted by severely practical considerations. Oksenberg Rorty goes on to claim that educational policy is blind without the guidance of philosophy (1998a: 2). This too seems overstated, in this case with respect to the necessary modesty which I have urged on the role of philosophy in these matters. The remark ignores the contribution, which other reflective and critical resources might make to educational policy including those arising from practical pedagogic and educational experience. The remark also underplays the continuity of philosophical reasoning and reflection with common sense. We all have some capacity to discriminate between sound and unsound reasoning, and to discern the need for clarity and justification.

A more well-grounded approach to discerning the proper contribution of philosophy with respect to educational policy is to focus upon the embeddedness of philosophical considerations in (many) educational policies. Many educational policies contain (to a greater or lesser extent) assumptions, concepts, beliefs, values and commitments which, if not themselves of a directly philosophical kind, are apt for philosophical attention. These elements permeate many educational policies, even if they do not amount to 'a philosophy of education' (cf. Carr, 1995: section 3), and are not articulated but remain implicit, embryonic and perhaps confused. These philosophically significant elements relate not merely to the 'content' of particular educational policies but also to broader matters relating to education and educational policy in general. The illumination which philosophy can bring is therefore wide ranging. For example, Israel Scheffler in his essay 'The Education of Policy Makers' (Scheffler, 1991: section 10) brings into focus why policy making cannot be reduced to merely technical considerations. Policy is made, he argues, in the context of '...multiple human activities, experiences, purposes, and needs' (p. 104) and so broad human understanding is required together with a grasp of matters of value and of the 'normative space' created by policy decisions.

The force of this point is that philosophical considerations do not need to be artificially brought to bear on educational policy. Such considerations are already implicit (and operative) within much policy. This is readily seen, for example, in policy-sensitive notions such as 'evidence based teaching'[2] and 'the knowledge creating school'.[3] Given that education is inherently value-laden, why is (educative) teaching seen as 'based in' rather than 'informed by' evidence? Why is the (educative) school seen as creating knowledge rather than (say) insight and commitment? The choice is therefore whether to make philosophical considerations in educational policy explicit and to aim systematically at achieving clarity and justification in relation to them, or to leave the elements unexamined and undisturbed. A choice to take the road of explicitness and systematic attention brings into focus the distinctive contribution of the philosopher, whose watchwords are clarity, perspective, warrant and vision.

Many philosophers have self-consciously sought to influence educational policy. One thinks here of major philosophers such as Plato and Dewey among others, and, in Britain, T.H. Green and the idealist philosophers of the late nineteenth century (on Green and the idealist philosophers, see Gordon and White, 1979). Amelie Oksenberg Rorty has recently outlined the practical effects on education of the thought of a number of philosophers, and the aspiration of much of this thought to have educational effects of this kind (Rorty, 1998b: section 1; cf. Almond, 1995: 3–4). Interestingly, she further argues that 'philosophy rings hollow' without attention to its 'educational import' (Rorty, 1998a: 2). A desire to inform practical policies of various kinds can be traced back to the origins of philosophy (see Warren, 1992). In addition to direct influence, philosophy contributes to, and influences, educational policy indirectly through the general intellectual and cultural climate:[4] secularism, pluralism, relativism, equality and the salience of market forces all have their philosophical progenitors.

All this is not to suggest, however, that the value of philosophizing about education should be judged solely in terms of its contribution to educational practice in general, and to educational policy in particular. There is some wisdom in R.K. Elliott's insistence that 'Philosophy did not free itself from domestic service to theology in order to become, in the sphere of education, little better than the oddjob man of pedagogy' (Elliott, 1986: 66). Harvey Siegel calls into question the suggestion that philosophers of education have a duty to attend to practical matters (Siegel, 1988; cf. Soltis, 1988). Nor is hestitation about interaction with the practical domain on the part of philosophers solely related to a concern with the value of the disinterested pursuit of truth for its own sake. Peters, for example, expresses doubts whether adequate and imaginative 'down to earth' work of a philosophical kind can be done unless the 'treatment', '. . . springs from a coherent and explicit philosophical position' (Peters, 1983: 55).

The nature of philosophy

Any attempt to gain a closer understanding of the distinctive contribution which philosophy can make to educational policy requires attention to how 'philosophy' is being understood. Philosophy, after all, is no one thing and different conceptions of philosophy give rise to potentially different conceptions of the contribution, which it can and should make to educational policy.

One prominent kind of philosophizing about education during the last forty years is locatable within the analytic tradition, associated with the pioneering work of Richard Peters and Israel Scheffler in the 1960s, and continued in a substantial body of work subsequently. The development of this tradition, specifically in the form of the discipline of 'philosophy of education', has been well charted in an extensive literature, as has the related methodological issues and disputes to which this development has given rise.[5]

'Analysis' has been described as

> ...the elucidation of the meaning of any concept, idea or unit of thought that
> we employ in seeking to understand ourselves and our world, by reducing it,
> breaking it down, into more basic concepts that constitute it and thereby
> showing its relationship to a network of other concepts or discovering what
> the concept denotes.
>
> (Hirst and White, 1998a: 2)

Analysis in this sense is concerned not merely with the meaning of beliefs, but
also with their justification and truth (ibid.). The 'connective' character of analysis
in this sense is worthy of emphasis: the investigation of '...how one concept is
connected – often in complex and ragged-ended ways – in a web of other concepts
with which it is logically related' (White and White, 1997: 2).

Whilst there are common elements across all phases of the analytic tradition in
philosophy of education it is possible to distinguish roughly an earlier and a later
phase (mirrored by comparable trends in philosophy generally), the earlier phase
subscribing to certain preoccupations and methodological commitments which have
come to be less prominent from the perspective of the broader focus and concerns of
the later phase.

In the early period, the analytical approach was applied to the clarification of
concepts distinctive to education (such as education itself, teaching, development
and indoctrination), and the delineation of philosophically interesting connections
between them; a critique of currently influential educational theories (such as
child-centredness) in terms of the philosophically problematic concepts and claims
they contained, and the application of philosophical analyses of educationally relevant concepts (such as knowledge, belief and emotion) and, more generally, of the
resources of epistemology, philosophical psychology, ethics and social philosophy
to educational concerns (Peters, 1966: Introduction; White and White, 1997: 6–7).

In retrospect, this earlier period has come to be seen as rather narrow in the
character and focus of its concerns and methodology. For example, this is apparent
in relation to the 'second-order' character of philosophical activity, which was
emphasized. On this view, the task of the philosopher is not to provide an answer
to any specific questions about (say) the aims and values of education, much less to
provide high-level 'directives for living'. Rather that task is seen in terms of the clarification of concepts, an exploration of the grounds of knowledge, the educidation
of presuppositions and the development of criteria for justification.

This earlier tradition in analytic philosophy of education was subjected to a
range of extensive criticisms. The criticisms included *inter alia*: that its approach
was inattentive to the history of philosophy, and in particular to the history of
concepts; that it aspired to a spurious value-neutrality with respect to its analyses
and commitments; that it was uncritical about its own assumptions and values
(including the view of human nature which it presupposed); that it espoused an
untenable rationalism; that its approach was inherently conservative politically,
socially and educationally; that it confined itself illicitly to 'second-order' clarification rather than the development of substantive arguments; that it read too much
into what can be legitimately derived from a mere analysis of concepts, espousing an
illicit 'essentialism' with respect to their meaning; that it implied that ordinary language use provides an unassailable court of appeal in determining meaning; that it
illicitly claimed a universal significance and value for certain ideals and values
independent of all cultural and social contexts; and that it was of little use in relation
to the determination and improvement of educational policy and practice.[6]

Whilst some of these lines of criticism are not without justification, it is important to be alert to the dangers of overstatement and even misunderstanding (see, e.g. Hirst, 1986). The claim that the approach sought to be value-neutral, for example, is only one example of the sort of misunderstanding which was evident in some quarters (ibid.: 17–18).

Dissatisfaction with this early analytic tradition was apparent even among those who retained allegiance to the analytic tradition in a broader sense. For example, writing in 1982, John White reported his frustration with the confinement of the role of philosophy to mere clarification. Rather than simply confine himself to clarifying the concept of an aim, he developed a substantive argument outlining what the aims of education should actually be (White, 1982: x–xi). For White, a concern for clarity had led merely to 'conceptual joustings' (ibid.: 6). Peters himself came to recognise the limitations of the 'early period', and drew attention to such shortcomings as the pedestrian, narrow, piecemeal, abstract and isolated character of much analysis and a failure to attend to the social and historical background and the view of human nature which the analysis presupposes (Peters, 1983). Peters' own recommendations for the future of the subject included a need to 'loosen up the analytic approach' (ibid.: 53).

It is important to note that this 'earlier' period in the analytic tradition in philosophy of education was not disconnected from educational policy. Peters himself edited two collections of philosophical papers which directly aspired to illuminate policy concerns (Peters, 1969, 1976) and much of the work which was undertaken in this period did, and was intended to have, policy implications.[7] John Wilson, for example, engaged in a sustained and sophisticated attempt to bring a detailed philosophical characterization of morality and the moral educated person to bear upon educational policy and practice (see, e.g. Wilson *et al.*, 1967; Wilson, 1990; McLaughlin and Halstead, 2000).[8] Hirst's 'forms of knowledge' thesis influenced certain policy documents on the curriculum, although not in ways which betrayed a clear understanding of the thesis which Hirst was actually arguing (Hirst, 1974: section 3; cf. 1993b). However, this 'earlier' period had its limitations with respect to its aptness for application to educational policy. One difficulty here was its emphasis on matters of 'second-order' clarification. As John White pointed out, those who are practically engaged in education are interested less in what the concept of an aim might be than in what the aims of education should be (White, 1982: 6). 'Second-order' preoccupations could lead to philosophers being perceived as ones who 'stand on the touch-line and jeer when the work is done' (Peters, 1983: 53). These difficulties were eased with the emergence of the greater breadth of focus and concern characteristic of the 'later' phase in the analytic tradition.

This 'later' phase, whilst retaining a commitment to a broadly analytic approach (in the sense that 'connective analysis' remains central), has been characterized by a broadening of approaches, concerns and sensitivities, and a move towards the more normative and practical concerns of 'applied philosophy'. The elements which are part of this development include a willingness to move beyond 'second-order' clarificatory concerns to develop substantive arguments in favour of particular positions; a lessening of concern for technicality; a willingness to engage with directly practical matters; a concern with 'thicker' and more substantive concepts such as those related to 'well-being' and the virtues; a concern to articulate the nature of the person, of human flourishing and of the place of reason in human life; a greater attention to the cultural and political frameworks within which concepts and educational practices are located; a central concern with ethics and political philosophy and a questioning of philosophical beliefs and forms of argument associated with the enlightenment.

Specific substantive concerns in this later period include the articulation of educational aims, values, processes and entitlement in a liberal democratic society (in which the development of the rationally autonomous individual and the liberal democratic citizen have figured prominently) (White, 1987a, 1995; White and White, 1997; Hirst and White, 1998a: 10–11). These developments have been influenced by, and have drawn upon, developments and trends in philosophy more generally, including neo-Aristotelian ethics, political philosophy and work on human well-being.

It is not difficult to see how this 'later' phase in the analytic tradition is more amenable to application to educational policy concerns than its earlier counterpart, with its freeing of the philosopher to make a less technical and a more flexible, substantive and tangibly constructive contribution to debate.

Although it is difficult to pin down the 'methodology' of the analytic tradition as a whole with any precision, a number of salient features can be safely identified. This tradition, with its characteristic emphases upon matters of meaning and justification, employs a recognizable style of argumentation. This form of argumentation is characterized by (amongst other things) the clarification of analysis of concepts, premises and assumptions, the consideration of counter-examples, the detection and elimination of defects of reasoning of various kinds, the drawing of important distinctions, a particular spirit of criticism and the structured development of argument. Central to the analytic tradition is an exploration of the conceptual schemes embedded in our everyday language in a form of analysis which is 'connective' in the sense indicated earlier, involving the elucidation of philosophically interesting connections and relationships between concepts. This, of course, does not imply that philosophers in the analytic tradition are interested only in language. What is at stake are our understandings, beliefs and values and these have transparent significance for human life generally. The analytic approach to philosophy of education is suspicious of unduly general statements and claims. It seeks a more fine-grained and detailed argument and debate in which attention to questions of meaning and justification act as an antidote to undue generality. The approach therefore tends to begin its work not from general statements or theories but from specific questions and problems, seeking their illumination, where appropriate, from the resources of broader philosophical argument.

In the present discussion, the analytic tradition in philosophy of education will be used as a point of illustration and reference throughout. It is important, however, not to overlook other traditions of philosophizing which are relevant to, and are brought to bear upon, education, such as those influenced by postmodernism. Although an extended treatment of these other traditions is impossible here, some attempt will be made to assess their significance for educational policy later in this chapter.

Philosophy and educational policy: possibilities

In exploring the possibilities which exist with regard to the relationship between philosophy and educational policy, it is useful to bear in mind parallel questions about the relationship between philosophy and educational research.[9] With regard to the relationship between philosophy and educational policy, a number of different but related modes and levels of relationship can be discerned.[10]

One respect in which the modes of relationship between philosophy and educational policy can be traced is in terms of a 'distance/proximity' continuum relating to the location of philosophizing *vis-à-vis* the policy-making process. At one end of this continuum is philosophizing conducted at some remove from policy making in universities and similar locations and yielding fruit in lectures, seminars, articles, books and other publications. Some of this work may be explicitly focused on educational policy.[11] This work, including its less obviously policy-focused elements, is available as resources for educational policy makers, although, as indicated at the outset, the context and 'climate' of educational policy making varies from time to time in the extent to which resources such as these are acknowledged and drawn upon. The effect which these resources have had on educational policy and educational policy makers, whilst difficult to judge, should not, however, be underestimated.[12] An obvious issue which arises here is the way in which these resources can be best mediated to policy makers. One response to this issue is to move philosophizing further along the continuum and closer to policy making itself. An interesting current development at the 'mid-point' of the continuum is an initiative of the Philosophy of Education Society of Great Britain in producing a series of policy focused 'IMPACT' pamphlets offering a philosophical treatment of contemporary policy issues which are launched in symposia involving policy makers and commentators as participants and respondents. At the time of writing, four pamphlets have been produced: on assessment (Davis, 1999), performance related pay for teachers (Luntley, 2000), equality and selective schooling (Brighouse, 2000) and post-16 training policy (Winch, 2000). Other pamphlets in preparation are dealing with topics such as the aims of the new National Curriculum, citizenship education and sex education. Also at the 'mid-point' of this 'distance' continuum are seminars and discussions of various kinds organized between philosophers and policy makers aimed at a sharing of perspectives and views. Seminars of these kinds have taken place on a number of policy-sensitive issues over the years such as spiritual and moral development and the aims of the new National Curriculum. At end of the continuum closest to policy making is the more direct involvement of philosophers in educational policy making itself through (say) membership of committees of enquiry. There are a number of examples here including Paul Hirst's membership of the Swann Committee (Great Britain Parliament House of Commons, 1985), Bernard Crick's role as Chair of the Advisory Group which produced recommendations relating to citizenship education (Qualifications and Curriculum Authority, 1998) and several other instances of philosophers working as members of policy-related groups at all levels including school level (cf. Elliott, 1994). Morwenna Griffiths has placed particular emphasis on philosophers and teachers working together closely (Griffiths, 1997, 1999).

Another element of the mode of the relationship between philosophy and educational policy concerns the differing aspects of the policy-making process on which philosophy might be brought to bear. Ham and Hill (quoted in Codd, 1995: 2–3) draw a distinction between 'analysis for policy' and 'analysis of policy'. 'Analysis for policy' contributes to the formulation of policy and takes two forms: 'policy advocacy' (which involves the making of specific policy recommendations) and 'information for policy' (which provides policy makers with 'information and data' relevant to policy formulation or revision). Philosophers can contribute to both, although in their case the 'information for policy' will take the form of offering (say) conceptual clarification. 'Analysis of policy', according to Ham and Hill, can also take two forms, 'analysis of policy determination and effects' (which examines the processes and outcomes of policy) and 'analysis of policy content' which examines 'the values, assumptions and social theories underpinning the policy process' (Codd, 1995: 3). Presumably, philosophers have a more obvious contribution to make to the latter, although they are not without a role in relation to the former, given Scheffler's point about the 'normative space' created by policy decisions.

Relevant to the mode of relationship between philosophy and educational policy is an important micropolitical issue about which communities of educationists should properly be engaged in philosophical work on the one hand and educational policy work on the other. Many of the points which Bridges makes about regrettable gaps which he sees between philosophers of education and educational researchers have application in the world of educational policy as well (Bridges, 1997, 1998a). It seems clear that policies of increasing collaboration between philosophers and educational policy makers should lead to an appropriate overlap of responsibilities and expertise here.

The notion of levels of relationship between philosophy and educational policy refers to the differing degrees of specificity with which philosophy can be focused on educational policy. At one end of a continuum here is work of a very general kind which may be concerned (say) with fundamental philosophical questions such as the aims of education, the nature and justification of moral education and an articulation and justification of principles such as equality of educational opportunity. Work of this generality is not without significance to policy makers, not least in providing a general background or 'framework' for their work. It is at this level that philosophers can offer a 'vision' to guide educational policy (cf. Pring, 1995a,b; Bridges, 1998a: 69–71; Fielding, 1999: 179–180). At a mid-point of this 'generality/specificity' continuum is work which engages in more detail in the critical assessment of practically significant educational assumptions and theories. At the most specific end of the continuum are analyses and discussions of current educational policies such as those offered by the IMPACT pamphlets and by philosophical journalism.[13] It is at these more specific levels of engagement that the role of the philosopher in articulating and probing concepts, values, assumptions and implications of particular policies comes particularly into play.

Before proceeding, it is useful to re-emphasize the complex interrelatedness of the differing modes and levels of relationship between philosophy and educational policy which have been delineated.

Philosophy and educational policy: tensions

Any sustained exploration of the relationship between philosophy and educational policy will uncover a number of tensions in the relationship. Some of these tensions arise from contingent factors such as the prevailing educational policy-making 'climate' of the day (see, e.g. Pring, 1995a).

In what follows, however, I shall be focusing attention on tensions which are more intrinsic to the relationship between philosophy and educational policy making because they arise from the very nature of the two partners involved.

Philosophy on the one hand and educational policy making on the other do not share the same aims, values, interests and priorities. One overly simple way of stating the differences here is to claim that educational policy, unlike philosophy, is not aimed at the elucidation of (say) truth or goodness but at the resolution of practical issues and problems. However, care is needed not to put this point in a way that presents educational policy making as a wholly technical exercise, without concern for values. The more precise and accurate point to be made here is that the concerns of educational policy are primarily practical (often including evaluative as well as technical matters) rather than theoretical.[14] As Scheffler puts it, the attitude of the policy maker is practical rather than 'reminiscent' or 'speculative' (Scheffler, 1991: 112).

One consequence of this is that there is a general tension in policy making between decision on the one hand and discussion and criticism on the other (cf. Scheffler, 1991: 115–116). Given practical constraints on decision such as time, policy makers can often engage only in a limited and practically focused amount of discussion and criticism. This has particular significance for the contribution which philosophy might make to educational policy. The nature of philosophy gives rise to tensions with the imperatives of limited and practically focused discussion and criticism in several ways. Philosophy is attracted to the non-instrumental exploration of complexity. The intrusion of philosophical considerations to a policy-making process may therefore not make decision making in relation to educational policy easier or even clearer, and may make it more difficult and opaque. Philosophy may seek to offer clarity and vision, but even where this is achieved it may serve to illuminate complexities, sharpen dilemmas, undermine grounds for practical compromise and encourage further discussion and argument rather than decision. As Scheffler has pointed out – 'self-consciousness' – '. . . increases the burden of choice and enlarges the perception of uncertainty', making the 'pervasive drive' to 'simplify', 'objectivify' and 'reduce' fully understandable (Scheffler, 1991: 107). Nor is clarity an unambigous good in policy making. Vagueness and ambiguity may have a lubricative and constructive effect here, as in other aspects of education (cf. McLaughlin, 1994: 458–460). Whilst points of this kind have significance for all the modes and levels of philosophical involvement with educational policy referred to in the last section, they have particular significance for philosophers closely involved in the policy-making process.

A related source of tension between philosophy and educational policy making arises from the question of the extent to which philosophical considerations can be properly made to 'bite' upon educational practice. An example of this tension can be drawn from the work of John Wilson in relation to moral education, which was referred to earlier. One of Wilson's central preoccupations is to offer a 'mapping' of the domain of moral education in which conceptual questions such as 'What is to count as morality, moral education and the morally educated person' are central (Wilson, 1990: 21ff., 1996: 90). Wilson claims that a clear answer to questions such as these, in the form of a 'map' or 'taxonomy', must be brought to bear upon, and in a sense, control, teaching, research and policy making in moral education if these activities are not to be misconceived and irrelevant. It is not enough, for Wilson, to speak in vague or general ways about what it is to be morally educated. We need to identify a precise set of qualities, attributes, skills, abilities and other features which are relevant to the area of the 'moral' and necessary for one who is going to take the area seriously (Wilson, 1990: part 3), and this conceptualization must be brought to bear on the work of teachers and policy makers. Whilst the ambition of applying a taxonomy of this kind to policy making seems intuitively plausible, it gives rise to a general problem I shall describe as 'taxonomic bite', where the difficulties which arise are not merely practical, but have a philosophical flavour to them. Complex questions arise in relation to the extent to which policy makers and others can be expected to secure and apply an appropriate grasp of the taxonomy both in its general and specific aspects. It is important for policy makers to achieve a correct understanding of philosophical arguments. The misunderstandings in relation to Hirst's 'forms of knowledge' thesis have already been noted. Wilson may, however, have over-estimated the accessibility of his taxonomy to teachers and policy makers, at least at the level of the detailed understanding, which he seeks on their part. Further, any taxonomy of this kind is going to contain significantly controversial elements and the extent to which any such proposal could achieve acceptance for the purposes Wilson seeks is open to dispute. Too much debate about the taxonomy would undermine its action-guiding function. Further, as John White rightly points out, our work in moral education cannot wait upon a definitive answer to the question of which theoretical account of morality is the correct one (White, 1990: 36–40).[15]

The problem of 'taxonomic bite' is related to a general uncertainty about the precise way in which philosophy can be brought to bear upon educational policy, which sustains the tensions, which have been noted. As Brenda Almond points out with reference to the notion of 'applied philosophy':

> ...philosophy is the most abstract of enquiries, perhaps even best defined as the investigation of problems that cannot be solved by empirical enquiry, while applied suggests a direct relationship with the world of facts that is belied by this understanding of philosophy.
>
> (Almond, 1987: 2)

What, then, is the precise role of the philosopher in a practical activity like policy making? For a range of reasons, the contribution of philosophy cannot be seen in terms of an 'expert' offering substantive conclusions or recommendations (on the general limitation of the notion of the philosopher as 'expert' with respect to practical questions see, e.g. D'Agostino, 1998). The notion of philosophy as offering a set of conclusions in search of application is deeply misconceived. On the other hand, as indicated earlier, a preoccupation with second-order clarification is similarly problematic. As Brenda Almond rightly insists, professionals are '...understandably, unable to hold their hand indefinitely from the plough while a perfect conceptual analysis of farming is sought' (Almond, 1987: 10). David Bridges sees such an approach as neglecting the more substantive role which philosophy might have in providing guidance, patronizing to the ability of non-philosophers to achieve clarity about language and concepts and over-confident about the possibility and coherence of achieving the sort of clarity about the meaning of concepts which is being sought (Bridges, 1997: 181–182).

It seems clear that the role of the philosopher as merely a critic is likely to exacerbate the sorts of tensions, which have been indicated. This gives rise to the question of the extent to which philosophers committed to a broadly 'postmodern' tradition in philosophy of education are able to respond to the need to offer more to the policy-making process than de-construction and problematization. An answer to this question requires a judicious understanding of the 'postmodern' tradition[16] in its relation to education.[17] Despite the origin of Lyotard's *Education and the Postmodern Condition* in a response to educational policy questions, it is perhaps unclear what a postmodern policy could be. The stimulative and provocative role of 'postmodernism' in relation to (say) matters of power, and the role of this tradition as a problematizing gadfly is prominent. Whilst the positive theses of 'postmodernism' are not devoid of educational implication (see, e.g. Blake *et al.*, 1998b) the extent to which a 'postmodern' perspective is compatible with easing the identified tensions is a matter for further reflection and exploration.

A further source of tension between philosophy and educational policy arising from the contrasting natures of the two activities may arise from the disinterestedness which is at the heart of philosophical enquiry, and which may be at odds with the aspiration of some policy makers to seek philosophical contributions under the aspect of providing legitimation for views arrived at on other grounds.

In addition, tensions may arise because of the 'positioning' of the philosopher with respect to the policy-making process, where this refers not merely to physical location but also to appropriateness of motive, commitment and solidarity. Griffiths captures something of what is at stake here in her criticism of philosophers who arrive in the manner of a 'raiding party' '...using education as one more example where their insights can be applied' (Griffiths, 1997: 198).

Philosophy and educational policy: tasks

If philosophy is to make a fruitful contribution to educational policy making, a number of tasks (both for philosophers and educational policy makers) emerge from the foregoing discussion.

Many of the points raised earlier give rise to readily specifiable tasks. Whilst philosophy needs to adopt a properly modest approach to the contribution it can make to educational policy, educational policy makers must acknowledge the extent to which the 'content' of their work, and the context in which it is undertaken, is saturated with assumptions, concepts, beliefs, values and commitments which, if not themselves of a philosophical kind, are apt for philosophical attention. Awareness of the differing modes and levels of relationship between philosophy and educational policy in its different aspects stimulates reflection on practical questions about the precise contexts in which dialogue between philosophers and policy makers can best be promoted, and about the precise kind of philosophical work, which is likely to promote this dialogue. One of the tasks here is surely that of transforming the general political climate so that it is amenable to, and supportive of, dialogue of this kind (on such an amenable and supportive climate in the case of the Irish Republic, see Hogan, 1995).

Some of the most interesting tasks, however, arise in relation to the tensions between philosophy and educational policy making, which were raised in the last section. Many of the tensions arise with particular significance for philosophers closely and directly involved in policy-making processes themselves. Here considerable practical judgement is called for on the part of philosophers.

In relation to tensions arising from the imperatives of limited and practically focused decision, philosophers must be able to make sensitive and sound judgements in relation to the following sorts of questions: How much philosophical illumination is needed by this policy-making process? What kind of philosophical illumination is needed and in relation to which matters? When should forbearance of philosophical influence be exercised in the interests of the imperatives of consensus and decision? When should a conceptualization or mode of presentation which is sub-optimal philosophically be accepted or even promoted for these kinds of interest?[18] How should a balance be struck between criticism and critique on the one hand and positive argument on the other? How much 'taxonomic bite' is it reasonable and practicable to expect in relation to policy matters, and how are 'best possible' solutions to be achieved?

The need for this kind of practical judgement on the part of philosophical participants in policy-making processes, which needs to take account, amongst other things, of the particular 'language' of policy making (McLaughlin, 1999a) which is being spoken and the complex empirical realities which intrude, is underscored by the realisation that philosophical contributions to such processes cannot take the form of the crude application of philosophical theories. DeMarco, for example, illuminates the limitations of attempts to apply abstract ethical principles to practical situations. The difficulties which arise here include the inherent abstractness of the principles in the face of inherent contextual complexity of the practical domain.

DeMarco's own preference is for a 'middle level' position between '...the excessive vagueness of moral principles and the provincialism of contextual judgements' (DeMarco, 1997: 292). Much of the wide-ranging general discussion of the proper relationship between theory and practice, and the need for teachers to possess a kind of pedagogic phronesis or practical judgement (McLaughlin, 1996b) apply also to the relationship between philosophy and educational policy making. Robin Barrow illuminates the capacity at stake here in terms of a practical form of 'philosophical competence' which headteachers of schools require (Barrow, 1976).[19] Perhaps the most important task for philosophers in these matters is to ensure not only that their abstract philosophical judgement is well formed, but also that they are well formed in philosophical and educational judgement of a practical kind.

Conclusions

In this chapter, I have sought to explore the role which philosophy can and should play in relation to educational policy.

Properly conceived, that role requires attention to a number of tasks, not the least of which concerns the role that philosophers must play in practical policy-making contexts if the fruitfulness of this contribution is to be achieved.

Acknowledgements

I am very grateful to David Bridges, Richard Smith and Paul Standish for helpful discussion of points discussed in this chapter and to Michael Fielding for his patient encouragement.

Notes

1 For this point in relation to philosophy and educational research see, for example, Bridges (1997, 1998a) (see also Soltis, 1988: 8–9).
2 See Hargreaves (1996, 1997) and Hammersley (1997).
3 Hargreaves (1999).
4 On the influence of Hegel, Fichte and Kant on the British idealist philosophers of the late nineteenth century who influenced education, see Gordon and White (1979).
5 See, for example, Peters (1966: Introduction), Wilson (1979), Feinberg (1983: section 6), Peters (1983), Jonathan (1985), Cooper (1986), Elliott (1986), Hirst (1986, 1993a, 1998), White (1987a,b, 1995), Soltis (1998), Evers (1993), Carr (1995: esp. Introduction, 1998), Kohli (1995: part 1), White and White (1997), Haydon (1998), Hirst and White (1998a,b: part I).
6 On these criticisms see the references outlined in section 2.
7 On this matter see White (1987a: 157–158). For a further example see White (1973).
8 For Wilson's account of philosophical methodology see, for example, Wilson (1979, 1986).
9 On these matters see, for example, Bridges (1997, 1998a,b) and Wilson (1998).
10 Cf. Soltis (1988: 10–12). For US literature on the relationship between philosophy and educational administration see, for example, Strike, Haller and Soltis (1988) and Haller and Strike (1997).
11 For some US work of this kind which might be unfamiliar to British readers see Strike (1981) (on the application of moral theory to desegregation) and Strike (1995) (on the application of discourse ethics to school restructuring).
12 On this matter, John White writes 'Over the last two or three decades philosophers have heard on various grapevines that their writings find their way on to the bookshelves of

HMI, local government officers, civil servants and even ministers at the Department of Education' (White, 2000: vii).
13 For related distinctions see White (1987b).
14 There are grounds for arguing that educational policy making should best be seen as kind of *praxis* on the same general grounds that Wilfred Carr adduces with respect to educational research (see Carr, 1997).
15 Cf. McLaughlin (1999a: 39–40).
16 For complexities in the use of the term 'postmodern' see Blake *et al.* (1998a).
17 On this see, for example, Beck (1994), Kohli (1995: part 1), Wain (1995), Burbules (1996), Blake (1996), Blake *et al.* (1998a) and cf. Carr (1998).
18 On the prevalence of 'lists' and rhetoric in educational policy documents see Blake *et al.* (1998: section 12).
19 On some related points relating to judgements of this general kind see White (1987a: 159–160).

References

Almond, B. (1987) *Moral Concerns* (Atlantic Highlands, NJ: Humanities Press International).
Almond, B. (1995) Introduction: Ethical Theory and Ethical Practice, in B. Almond (ed.), *Introducing Applied Ethics* (Oxford: Blackwell).
Barrow, R. (1976) Competence and the Head, in R.S. Peters (ed.), *The Role of the Head* (London: Routledge and Kegan Paul).
Beck, C. (1994) Postmodernism, Pedagogy and Philosophy of Education, in A. Thompson (ed.), *Philosophy of Education 1993* (Urbana, IL: Philosophy of Education Society).
Blake, N. (1996) Between Postmodernism and Anti-Modernism: The Predicament of Educational Studies. *British Journal of Educational Studies*, 44(1), 42–65.
Blake, N., Smeyers, P., Smith, R. and Standish, P. (1998a) *Thinking Again. Education After Postmodernism* (Westport, CT and London: Bergin & Harvey).
Blake, N., Smith, R. and Standish, P. (1998b) *The Universities We Need Higher Education After Dearing* (London: Kogan Page).
Bridges, D. (1997) Philosophy and Educational Research: A Reconsideration of Epistemological Boundaries. *Cambridge Journal of Education*, 27(2), 177–189.
Bridges, D. (1998a) Educational Research: Re-establishing the Philosophical Terrain, in G. Haydon (ed.), *50 Years of philosophy of Education. Progress and Prospects. Bedford Way Papers* (London: Institute of Education, University of London).
Bridges, D. (1998b) On Conceptual Analysis and Educational Research: A Response to John Wilson. *Cambridge Journal of Education*, 28(2), 239–241.
Brighouse, H. (2000) *Educational Equality and the New Selective Schooling*, IMPACT No. 3 (Philosophy of Education Society of Great Britain).
Burbules, N. (1996) Postmodern Doubt and Philosophy of Education, in A. Neiman (ed.), *Philosophy of Education 1995* (Urbana, IL: Philosophy of Education Society).
Carr, D. (1998) Introduction: The Post-War Rise and Fall of Educational Epistemology, in D. Carr (ed.), *Education, Knowledge and Truth. Beyond the Postmodern Impasse* (London: Routledge).
Carr, D. (ed.) (1998) *Education, Knowledge and Truth. Beyond the Postmodern Impasse* (London: Routledge).
Carr, W. (1995) *For Education. Towards Critical Educational Enquiry* (Buckingham: Open University Press).
Carr, W. (1997) Philosophy and Method in Educational Research. *Cambridge Journal of Education*, 27(2), 203–209.
Codd, J.A. (1995) Educational Policy as a Field of Philosophical Enquiry. Paper presented to the Annual Conference of the Philosophy of Education Society of Great Britain, Oxford.
Cooper, D.E. (1986) Introduction, in D.E. Cooper (ed.), *Education, Values and Mind. Essays for R S Peters* (London: Routledge and Kegan Paul).
D'Agostino, F. (1998) Expertise, Democracy and Applied Ethics. *Journal of Applied Philosophy*, 15(1), 49–55.
Davis, A. (1999) *Educational Assessment: A Critique of Current Policy*, IMPACT No. 1 (Philosophy of Education Society of Great Britain).

DeMarco, J.P. (1997) Coherence and Applied Ethics. *Journal of Applied Philosophy*, 14(3), 289–300.

Elliott, J. (1994) Clarifying Values in Schools. *Cambridge Journal of Education*, 24(3), 413–422.

Elliott, R.K. (1986) Richard Peters: A Philosopher in the Older Style, in D.E. Cooper (ed.), *Education, Values and Mind. Essays for R S Peters* (London: Routledge and Kegan Paul).

Evers, C.W. (1993) Analytic and Post-Analytic Philosophy of Education: Methodological Reflections. *Discourse: The Australian Journal of Educational Studies*, 13(2), 35–45.

Feinberg, W. (1983) *Understanding Education. Toward a Reconstruction of Educational Inquiry* (Cambridge: Cambridge University Press).

Fielding, M. (1999) Editorial: Taking Education Really Seriously: Two Years of Hard Labour. *Cambridge Journal of Education*, 29(2), 173–181.

Gordon, P. and White, J. (1979) *Philosophers as Educational Reformers. The Influence of Idealism on British Educational Thought and Practice* (London: Routledge and Kegan Paul).

Great Britain Parliament House of Commons (1985) *Education for All. The Report of the Committee of Inquiry into the Education of Children from Ethnic Minority Groups*, cm nd 9453 (London: HMSO).

Griffiths, M. (1997) Why Teachers and Philosophers Need Each Other: Philosophy and Educational Research. *Cambridge Journal of Education*, 27(2), 191–202.

Griffiths, M. (1999) Aiming for a Fair Education. What Use is Philosophy?, in R. Marples (ed.), *The Aims of Education* (London: Routledge).

Haller, E.J. and Strike, K.A. (1997) *An Introduction to Educational Administration. Social, Legal and Ethical Perspectives* (Troy, NY: Educator's International Press).

Hammersley, M. (1997) Educational Research and Teaching: A Response to David Hargreaves' TTA Lecture. *British Educational Research Journal*, 23(2), 141–161.

Hargreaves, D.H. (1996) *Teaching as a Research-based Profession: Possibilities and Prospects. Teacher Training Agency Annual Lecture* 1996 (London: Teacher Training Agency).

Hargreaves, D.H. (1997) In Defence of Research for Evidence-based Teaching: A Rejoinder to Martyn Hammersley. *British Educational Research*, 23(4), 405–419.

Hargreaves, D.H. (1999) The knowledge-Creating School. *British Journal of Educational Studies*, 47(2), 122–144.

Haydon, G. (ed.) (1998) *50 Years of Philosophy of Education. Progress and Prospects. Bedford Way Papers* (London: Institute of Education, University of London).

Hirst, P.H. (1974) *Knowledge and the Curriculum* (London: Routledge and Kegan Paul).

Hirst, P.H. (1986) Richard Peters's Contribution to the Philosophy of Education, in D.E. Cooper (ed.), *Education, Values and Mind. Essays for R S Peters* (London: Routledge and Kegan Paul).

Hirst, P.H. (1993a) Education, Knowledge and Practices, in R. Barrow and P. White (eds), *Beyond Liberal Education. Essays in Honour of Paul H Hirst* (London: Routledge).

Hirst, P.H. (1993b) The Foundations of the National Curriculum: Why Subjects?, in P. O'Hear and J. White (eds), *Assessing the National Curriculum* (London: Paul Chapman).

Hirst, P.H. (1998) Philosophy of Education: The Evolution of a Discipline, in G. Haydon (ed.), *50 Years of Philosophy of Education. Progress and Prospects. Bedford Way Papers* (London: Institute of Education, University of London).

Hirst, P.H. and White, P. (1998a) The Analytic Tradition and Philosophy of Education: An Historical Perspective, in P.H. Hirst and P. White (eds), (1998) *Philosophy of Education: Major Themes in the Analytic Tradition, Volume 1* (London: Routledge).

Hirst, P.H. and White, P. (eds) (1998b) *Philosophy of Education: Major Themes in the Analytic Tradition* (4 volumes) (London: Routledge).

Hogan, P. (1995) *Partnership and the Benefits of Learning. A Symposium on Philosophical Issues in Educational Policy* (Maynooth: Educational Studies Association of Ireland).

Jonathan, R. (1985) Education, Philosophy of Education and Context. *Journal of Philosophy of Education*, 19(1), 13–25.

Kohli, W. (ed.) (1995) *Critical Conversations in Philosophy of Education* (London: Routledge).

Luntley, M. (2000) *Performance, Pay and Professionals*, IMPACT No. 2 (Philosophy of Education Society of Great Britain).

McLaughlin, T.H. (1994) Values, Coherence and the School. *Cambridge Journal of Education*, 24(3), 453–470.

McLaughlin, T.H. (1999a) A Response to Professor Bridges, in D. Carr (ed.), *Values in the Curriculum* (Aberdeen: Gordon Cook Foundation).

McLaughlin, T.H. (1999b) Beyond the Reflective Teacher. *Educational Philosophy and Theory*, 31(1), 9–25.

McLaughlin, T.H. and Halstead, J.M. (2000) John Wilson on Moral Education. *Journal of Moral Education*, 29(3), 245–246.

Oksenberg Rorty, A. (1998a) The Ruling History of Education, in A. Oksenberg Rorty (ed.), *Philosophers on Education. New Historical Perspectives* (London: Routledge).

Oksenberg Rorty, A. (ed.) (1998b) *Philosophers on Education. New Historical Perspectives* (London: Routledge).

Peters, R.S. (1966) *Ethics and Education* (London: George Allen and Unwin).

Peters, R.S. (ed.) (1969) *Perspectives on Plowden* (London: Routledge and Kegan Paul).

Peters, R.S. (ed.) (1976) *The Role of the Head* (London: Routledge and Kegan Paul).

Peters, R.S. (1983) Philosophy of Education 1960–1980, in P.H. Hirst (ed.), *Educational Theory and its Foundation Disciplines* (London: Routledge and Kegan Paul).

Pring, R. (1995a) The Community of Educated People. *British Journal of Educational Studies*, 43(2), 125–145.

Pring, R. (1995b) Educating Persons: Putting *Education* Back into Educational Research. The 1995 SERA Lecture. *Scottish Educational Review*, 27(2), 101–112.

Qualifications and Curriculum Authority (1998) *Education for Citizenship and the Teaching of Democracy in Schools. Final Report of the Advisory Group on Citizenship* (London: QCA).

Scheffler, I. (1991) *In Praise of the Cognitive Emotions and Other Essays in the Philosophy of Education* (New York and London: Routledge).

Siegel, H. (1988) On the Obligations of the Professional Philosopher of Education, in W. Hare and J.P. Portelli (eds), *Philosophy of Education. Introductory Readings* (Calgary: Detselig Enterprises).

Soltis, J.F. (1988) Perspectives on Philosophy of Education, in W. Hare and J.P. Portelli (eds), *Philosophy of Education. Introductory Readings* (Calgary: Detselig Enterprises).

Strike, K.A. (1981) Toward a Moral Theory of Desegregation, in J.F. Soltis (ed.), *Philosophy and Education. Eightieth Yearbook of the National Society for the Study of Education*. Part 1 (Chicago: NSSE).

Strike, K.A. (1995) Discourse Ethics and Restructuring, in M. Katz (ed.), *Philosophy of Education 1994* (Urbana, IL: Philosophy of Education Society).

Strike, K.A., Haller, E.J. and Soltis, J.F. (1988) *The Ethics of School Administration* (New York: Teachers College Press).

Wain, K. (1995) Richard Rorty, Education and Politics. *Educational Theory*, 45(3), 395–409.

Warren, B. (1992) Back to Basics: Problems and Prospects for Applied Philosophy. *Journal of Applied Philosophy*, 9(1), 13–19.

White, J. (1973) *Towards a Compulsory Curriculum* (London: Routledge and Kegan Paul).

White, J. (1982) *The Aims of Education Re-Stated* (London: Routledge and Kegan Paul).

White, J. (1987a) The Medical Condition of Philosophy of Education. *Journal of Philosophy of Education*, 21(2), 155–162.

White, J. (1987b) Book Review: Philosophers on Education edited by Roger Straughan and John Wilson, *Journal of Philosophy of Education*, 21(2), 297–302.

White, J. (1990) *Education and the Good Life. Beyond the National Curriculum* (London: Kogan Page).

White, J. (1995) Problems of the Philosophy of Education, in T. Honderich (ed.), *The Oxford Companion to Philosophy* (Oxford: Oxford University Press).

White, J. (2000) Editorial Introduction, in M. Luntley (ed.), *Performance, Pay and Professionals*, IMPACT No. 2 (Philosophy of Education Society of Great Britain).

White, J. and White, P. (1997) The Analytic Tradition in British Philosophy of Education (unpublished).

Wilson, J. (1979) *Preface to the Philosophy of Education* (London: Routledge).

Wilson, J. (1986) *What Philosophy Can Do* (London: Macmillan).

Wilson, J. (1990) *A New Introduction to Moral Education* (London: Cassell).

Wilson, J. (1996) First Steps in Moral Education. *Journal of Moral Education*, 25(1), 85–91.

Wilson, J. (1998) Philosophy and Educational Research: A Reply to David Bridges *et al.*, *Cambridge Journal of Education*, 28(1), 129–133.

Wilson, J., Williams, N. and Sugarman, B. (1967) *Introduction to Moral Education* (Harmondsworth: Penguin).

Winch, C. (2000) *New Labour and the Future of Training*, IMPACT No. 4 (Philosophy of Education Society of Great Britain).

CHAPTER 2

PHILOSOPHY AND EDUCATION

Wilfred Carr

Journal of Philosophy of Education, 38, 1, 55–73, 2004

> It is one of the marks of a community of enquiry and learning that, while it cannot but begin from the standpoint of its own cultural and social traditions, what it is able to learn, in order to sustain itself, includes knowing how to identify its own incoherences and errors and how then to draw upon the resources of other alien and rival traditions in order to correct these.
>
> (Alasdair MacIntyre, 1998)

I

How is philosophy related to education and education to philosophy? This is my initial question and in trying to answer it I shall conduct an inquiry that proceeds through six stages. First, I shall describe how, in contemporary Western societies, philosophy no longer has much relevance to education and education has become insulated from philosophy. Second, I shall suggest that this situation may be due to limitations inherent in what we now understand the philosophy of education to be. Third, I shall argue that the only way to know if this suggestion can be made good is by producing an alternative history of the philosophy of education to that which currently exists. Fourth, I shall outline such a history in order, fifth, to argue that our inability adequately to relate philosophy to education or education to philosophy is a consequence of the fact that the contemporary philosophy of education has looked to the wrong place for its own intellectual ancestry. Finally, I shall suggest that it is only by recovering from history a view of the relationship of philosophy to education very different from our own that the reasons for the contemporary separation of philosophy from education and education from philosophy can be properly understood.

II

Within the academic culture of most modern Western societies the philosophy of education has now become an institutionalised and professionalised area of expertise with its own distinctive mechanisms for protecting itself from anything that would put its continuing existence seriously in question. It goes without saying that most of these self-protective mechanisms make use of rhetorical devices designed to convince the discipline's external audience of its significance for educational policy and its relevance to educational practice. But what also needs hardly be said is that such exercises in self-justification are increasingly being perceived as little more than contrived rationalisations designed to conceal the fact that the philosophy of education is now regarded by most members of the wider educational community as an inward-looking scholastic activity that, when judged by the most minimal criteria of practical relevance, makes little contribution to the formation of educational policy or the improvement of educational practice (Wilson, 2003). This is not to suggest that arguments emanating from the philosophy of education are *never* deployed to justify a particular educational policy or practice. But on virtually all the occasions when this happens, it is all too apparent that the philosophical argument is not being invoked because it offers a compelling justification for an educational standpoint such that a decisive refutation of the philosophical argument would lead to the abandonment of that standpoint. Instead, it is almost certainly being invoked in order to add a theoretical embellishment to the presentation of an educational standpoint that is being advocated for reasons that have little to do with its philosophical rationale.

Just as the philosophy of education has, in our culture, become practically ineffective, so education has become insulated from philosophy in at least two important respects. First, the modes of reasoning employed in the institutionalised arenas in which practically effective educational decisions are made rarely conform to the canons of rationality in terms of which philosophical arguments are typically conducted. Instead, policies are formulated and decisions are made on the basis of a process of reasoning that is rarely committed to following through the implications of rational argument and in which impersonal rational principles (commitment to truth, impartiality, respect for evidence and the like) are corrupted by a combination of irrational influences such as political expediency, vested interests and established power.

The second way in which education now insulates itself from philosophy is by conducting its debates through a mode of discourse which imposes constraints on the kinds of questions which can legitimately be debated and discussed and so ensures that neither the reasons for these constraints nor the questions they exclude can be explicitly formulated and become part of the educational debate itself. Amongst the questions that the contemporary educational discourse so excludes are, of course, substantive philosophical questions about the fundamental aims and values that should provide the intellectual basis for contemporary educational policy and practice. This does not mean that answers to these questions are not being provided by default. The discourse of educational debate is never neutral. However covertly and however implicitly, it always promotes some educational values and marginalises others.

Thus what we now have in most modern Western societies are two separate spheres of professional activity, both concerned to resolve issues central to contemporary educational debate. On the one hand, we have a small academic community of educational philosophers whose members examine these issues in accordance with the canons of rational inquiry but whose arguments and conclusions have little practical effect. On the other hand, we have a diverse group of politicians, policy makers, teachers and other educational professionals who make and implement practically effective educational decisions but do so in a way which generally lacks intellectual rigour and in which serious and systematic reflection on the fundamental philosophical standpoint that informs their decisions is conspicuously absent. What has been the response of the philosophy of education to this state of affairs?

One typical response has been to insist that the philosophy of education is, like philosophy in general, an essentially theoretical activity and if this makes it practically irrelevant then we should decry relevance and instead extol the virtues of scholarly excellence. Another response has been to insist that philosophy of education is a form of 'applied', rather than 'pure', philosophy and hence to look for solutions to the problem of relevance through the development of more effective measures for enhancing the practical impact of the discipline on policy and practice. But what is most interesting about these two responses is what they have in common rather than what sets them apart. For what they both share is a reluctance to contemplate the possibility that the problem to which they are addressed may be entirely self-inflicted: that this may be precisely the kind of intractable problem we should expect to be engendered by the philosophy of education as it is now conducted and understood. In other words, it may just be that the problem of relating philosophy to education is deeply rooted in the conceptual foundations on which the contemporary philosophy of education has been erected and hence be nothing other than the entirely predictable outcome of a fundamental intellectual disorder internal to the contemporary condition of the discipline itself.

But if the philosophy of education is indeed the agent of its own educational impotence, how are we to know? If problems concerning the relationship between philosophy and education are endemic to the conceptual framework governing our understanding of the discipline, how are they to be resolved? They are to be resolved by philosophers of education displaying the kind of philosophical imagination that would enable them to put this framework in question by drawing on intellectual resources that are not available from within the framework itself. It is only by displaying the imaginative ability to stand outside their existing framework of self-understanding that philosophers of education can begin to find an external vantage point from which to transcend the boundaries imposed by this framework and so make the presuppositions inherent in their self-understanding more transparent and open to question. What I am going to suggest is that the intellectual resources that will most help to engender this new level of reflective self-consciousness are to be provided by a historical account of how the contemporary philosophy of education originated and evolved that is very different to that which currently exists. In short, what I am going to suggest is that the most appropriate way of identifying what it is about our current understanding of the philosophy of education that may be causing its isolation from education is to find new ways of interpreting its past.[1]

III

In Great Britain, the interpretation of the history of the philosophy of education that any new interpretation would need to replace still remains the historical narrative produced in the 1960s (Hirst, 1966, 1998; Peters, 1966a,b) in order to show how, in the past, the discipline had been based on an erroneous view of 'what philosophy is' and how it was only after it had embraced the revolution in philosophy that had occurred in the twentieth century that the philosophy of education became 'a distinct area of academic philosophy' (Hirst, 1998: 1). It thus recounts this history as a story of methodological progress and philosophical advance – a history of the achievements through which the philosophy of education, by 'drawing life and energy from developments in academic philosophy' (p. 15) had acquired a proper understanding of its task. Though definitions of this task were various, they all accepted the received philosophical wisdom of the time: that philosophy was 'an analytical pursuit... concerned with the clarification of the concepts and propositions through which our experiences and activities are intelligible' (Hirst, 1974: 1).[2] It is thus hardly surprising that this history is a history of how, by embracing this view of philosophy, the philosophy of education had liberated itself from the errors and confusions of its past and matured into a respectable academic discipline.

Philosophy always bears the mark of its passage through time and, since the 1960s, this view of the philosophy of education in the UK has undergone several internal reviews (Hirst, 1983; Peters, 1983) and has been subject to numerous external criticisms (e.g. Harris, 1979). But, although the original enthusiasm for analytic philosophy of education has, to some extent, evaporated, the historical under-standing of the discipline that it conveyed has not yet been replaced. As a result, philosophers of education who do not regard themselves as practising analytical philosophy still tacitly adopt a version of their discipline's history that incorporates some of the taken-for-granted presuppositions that have been inherited from analytic philosophy and that continue to shape their understanding of how philosophy is related to education.

One indication of the philosophy of education's reluctance to revise its histo-rical understanding is the conspicuous silence with which it has greeted James S. Kaminsky's *A New History of the Philosophy of Education* (1993). In this, Kaminsky sets out to 'settle the question of what the philosophy of education is, what work deserves the honorific title of philosophy of education and so on' (p. viii). To this end, he sets out to write 'a different and new history' (ibid.) which shows how 'contemporary influential accounts of the discipline's prologue which assume that the main antecedents to the emergence of twentieth century philosophy of education are to be found in the narrow history of philosophy ... can only be maintained by neglect-ing educational philosophy's important connections with social reform, social science and political action' (p. xiii). He therefore constructs a history of British philosophy of education designed to substantiate his central thesis: that it was the major intellec-tual, social and political movements that occurred in Great Britain during the late nineteenth and early twentieth centuries that 'in some sense created the educational discipline that we now know as philosophy of education' (p. xii).

A New History of Educational Philosophy is a fine book that goes a long way to demonstrating how the history of the philosophy of education in Great Britain is just as much part of British social history as it is of the intellectual history of Anglo-Saxon philosophy. But just as the orthodox history of the philosophy of education is too philosophical and insufficiently historical, so Kaminsky's history is not philosophical enough. It is therefore apt to underestimate the significance of two philosophical insights concerning the peculiar relationship in which philosophy stands to history. The first is captured by Hegel's well-known description of philos-ophy as 'its own time apprehended in thought': the insight that the form that philosophy takes in any given age is always influenced by, and intimately related to, the presuppositions embedded in the culture of that age. The second is, in effect, the dialectical opposite of the first and is captured by John Dewey's observation that, while 'philosophy is always a creature of its past', it is also, simultaneously, 'a creator of its future' (Dewey, 1931: 3–5). It is thus the insight that although philosophy is always passively constrained by the presuppositions embedded in the culture of which it is a part, it is also the discipline that reflectively exposes and critically revises these presuppositions and, by so doing, makes an active contribution to that culture's future evolution and development. For Dewey, as for Hegel, 'philosophy' and 'history' are dialectically related: each changes, and is changed by, the other.

So far, I have argued that any adequate appreciation of why the relationship between philosophy and education is so unsatisfactory requires us to replace our existing version of the history of the philosophy of education with a historical narrative in which it is recognised that the future development of the discipline depends on transcending and correcting the limitations of the present by transcending and correcting misunderstandings inherited from the past. However, if the point and purpose of this history is to enable us reflectively to reconsider our current understanding of the philosophy of education, to take what we *now* refer to as 'the philosophy of education' as its starting point would be to presuppose at the outset an answer to the very question at issue. But if we are to produce a history of the philosophy of education that avoids this Whiggish tendency to treat the past as a mere prelude to the present, what would be its starting point? What would a history of the philosophy of education be a history of?

IV

The history of philosophy is not the history of some unchanging human activity that has continued to display the same essential features throughout time. What philosophy is taken to be at any given time and in any given culture will vary such that part of what is involved in coming to understand a particular historical period or a particular culture is trying to grasp how, within that period or that culture, the notion of 'philosophy' is being used and understood. So one way of understanding the history and culture of twentieth-century Western societies is to note how it was only in this particular historical and cultural context that 'the philosophy of education' became the name of a separate, institutionalised and professionalised academic specialism characterised by its own internal arrangements, academic curriculum and canonical texts.

Once it is understood historically, the emergence of 'the philosophy of education' as an autonomous sub-area within academic philosophy will be construed as just one of the many historically contingent and culturally specific developments that occurred in twentieth-century philosophy. Others include the way in which philosophy, while continuing to retain many of its pre-twentieth-century sub-areas (logic, metaphysics, epistemology, ethics and the like), also introduced several new areas such as the philosophy of mind, the philosophy of language and the philosophy of action. To complicate matters further, the twentieth century also saw the emergence of a range of new branches of philosophy related to other academic disciplines – for example, the philosophies of science, law and history. Add to this the fact that new distinctions were drawn between 'pure' and 'applied' philosophy and between 'Anglo-Saxon' and 'European' versions of the discipline, and some of the peculiarly twentieth-century transformations that occurred in how 'philosophy' was conducted and understood become readily apparent.

But, of course, things were not always so. Up to the seventeenth century, 'philosophy' was simply the name for virtually all forms of serious intellectual inquiry and it was only with the onset of modernity and the emergence of modern science that various new disciplines began to detach themselves from 'philosophy' and declare themselves to be autonomous 'sciences' (MacIntyre, 1982). A distinction that was applied – and that survived as a central part of the European intellectual tradition until the seventeenth century – was the classical Greek distinction between 'theoretical' and 'practical' philosophy. Theoretical philosophy referred to those detached forms of inquiry that employed a purely contemplative form of reasoning (*theoria*) and that led to a priori knowledge of necessary, eternal and unchanging truth (*episteme*). For the Greeks 'theoretical philosophy' was pursued entirely 'for its own sake' and had no relevance whatsoever to everyday practical matters. For this reason, it was distinguished from 'practical philosophy' which aimed to develop and improve the kind of 'context-based' practical reasoning that was employed in the conduct of a wide range of morally informed human activities. The classical theoretical vindication of practical philosophy was, of course, provided by Aristotle whose *Nicomachean Ethics* articulated a range of conceptual distinctions that was to provide 'practical philosophy' with its major source of theoretical intelligibility and support (Aristotle, 1955).

One of the most important of these distinctions was between two modes of non-theoretical reasoning that the Greeks called *techne* (technical reasoning) and *phronesis* (practical reasoning). *Techne* is that mode of value-free 'means–end' reasoning appropriate to those productive human activities that the Greeks called *poiesis* – activities whose 'end' can be clearly specified in advance of, and hence known prior to, any practical means taken to produce it. But as well as reasoning about how most effectively to achieve some given end, individuals also characteristically engaged in forms of practical reasoning about how to act in a morally appropriate way. The Greeks called this form of practical reasoning *phronesis* and the kind of morally informed human practice to which it applied *praxis*. The range of such ethically based practices was extensive and included music, politics, medicine and, significantly, education.[3]

For Aristotle the 'end' of a practice is some ethically worthwhile 'good' that is internal to, and inseparable from, the practice and only exists in the practice itself. It follows from this that the 'good' that constitutes the 'end' of a practice cannot be 'made'; it can only be 'done'. It also follows that, in practical reasoning, 'ends' and 'means' stand in a reciprocal relationship such that reasoning about the 'good' which constitutes the 'end' of a practice is inseparable from reasoning about the action that constitutes the 'means' for its achievement. Reasoning about 'means' and reasoning about 'ends' does not therefore involve reasoning 'technically' about the former and 'theoretically' about the latter. They are two mutually constitutive elements within the single dialectical process of practical reasoning.

How is the capacity for such practical reasoning acquired? For Aristotle, practical reasoning is not a methodical, rule-governed skill that can first be taught 'in theory' and then applied 'in practice'. Instead, it is a capacity that can only be acquired by an individual who, in the course of being initiated into a particular practice, comes to understand that what she is doing is unavoidably directed towards the pursuit of some 'good' that is not related to the satisfaction of her own immediate needs and desires but is internal to the practice itself. But if she is to make progress towards the achievement of excellence in her practice, what the novice practitioner will also have to learn is a disposition to think and act on the basis of sound practical reasoning about what, in a particular concrete situation, would constitute an appropriate expression of this good. Aristotle called this disposition *phronesis*, and, unlike *techne*, it is not a skill that can be learned in isolation from, and then applied in, practice. Rather *phronesis* is a moral and intellectual virtue rooted in a natural human capacity 'to do the right thing in the right place at the right time in the right way' (MacIntyre, 1981: 141). As such it can only be acquired through practice and on the basis of practical experience.

Although *phronesis* is an indispensable prerequisite for good practice, it is not always sufficient. For even the most experienced practitioner will, in the course of her practice, be confronted by the need to find practically usable solutions to intractable problems that cannot be answered on the basis of the pre-reflective understanding that practice alone has supplied. For what the resolution of such problems demands of the practitioner is that she acquires the ability to transcend the limits of her existing practical knowledge and understanding in order to put her own pre-philosophical understanding of her practice to the question. Thus, just as it is only those who have first learned to identify the good internal to their practice, and then learned how to emulate its established standards of excellence, who can develop the capacity to reason wisely and prudently about how to realise this internal good, so it is only those who are already proficient in such practical reasoning – the *phronimoi* – who, when faced with a practical need to exceed previously established standards of excellence, are in a position to reflect philosophically on the limitations of the understanding of their practice that they have acquired on the basis of their practical experience. Teaching practitioners to confront the limits of their own self-understanding in this way is the central task of practical philosophy.

Thus what instruction in practical philosophy offers experienced and proficient practitioners is an initiation into a mode of reflective inquiry that will enable them to expose and examine the taken-for-granted presuppositions implicit in their practice in order that they may reflectively reconstruct their understanding of their practice and of how its internal good may, in their own practical situation, be more appropriately pursued. As such, practical philosophy does not at all depend on the kind of theoretical philosophy that provides a purely intellectual knowledge of the 'good' that constitutes the end of a practice. Nor is it a form of 'applied philosophy' offering expert guidance based on a body of impartial, independent philosophical knowledge about how this end is to be most effectively achieved. Still less does it claim to provide a theoretical elaboration of the 'method' of practical reasoning to which ordinary practitioners should conform. On the contrary, the whole *raison d'être* for practical philosophy is based on a clear recognition that notions like 'theory', 'application' and 'method' have no place in practical reasoning and thus play no meaningful role in a form of philosophy specifically intended to contribute to its development.

But if practical philosophy is a non-methodical form of inquiry that provides neither theoretical principles nor practical prescriptions, how does it relate to the practice that constitutes its object of study? If practical philosophy is concerned to protect and preserve the mode of reasoning already inherent in practice, what does it have to offer experienced and proficient practitioners? 'How' in Joseph Dunne's words, 'can practical philosophy actually be practical – in the sense of contributing anything that is not already within the compass of concrete practical judgement itself?' (Dunne, 1993: 160). What are practitioners taught by, and what do they learn from, practical philosophy?

What practitioners are initially taught by practical philosophy is that the practice in which they are engaged has a history and thus that they are the inheritors of a historical tradition which enshrines the goods internal to their practice and through which the largely unarticulated body of practical knowledge and standards of excellence implicit in their practice are conveyed. But as well as teaching practitioners to think about their practice historically, practical philosophy also teaches them that the understanding of their practice bequeathed to them by history and tradition is neither immutable nor fixed and that, in the course of the history of their practice, previously established modes of practical knowledge and understanding have been continuously re-interpreted and reconceived by previous generations of practitioners in order to find answers to the kind of practical questions that *they* had to face – questions which *they* could only resolve by reflectively revising and reconstructing the pre-reflective understanding of *their* practice that tradition had provided to *them*.

Thus what practical philosophy teaches practitioners is that the authoritative nature of the historical tradition in which their practice is embedded does not mean that the practical knowledge it supplies has to be mechanically accepted or passively endorsed. A tradition progressively evolves through a process in which, by striving to move towards the achievement of excellence in their practice, practitioners raise the prereflective practical knowledge inherited from tradition to the level of reflective awareness in order to transcend the limitations of what, within that tradition, has hitherto been thought, said and done. In this sense, practical philosophy is simply the name of that tradition of reflective philosophy that enables each generation of practitioners to make progress in achieving excellence in their practice and, by so doing, ensure that the tradition constitutive of their practice continues to develop and evolve.

The story of the demise and eventual collapse of the Aristotelian tradition of practical philosophy is, of course, just a part of the complex history of the transition from 'classical' to 'modern' philosophy that began in the seventeenth century (Toulmin, 1988, 1990). One of the key episodes in this history was the marginalisation and eventual rejection of Aristotelian modes of thought that began in the sixteenth century (MacIntyre, 1988). Another was the emergence of what is now described as 'epistemologically-centred philosophy', which was founded primarily, though not exclusively, on Descartes' search for the a priori foundations on which certain knowledge could be erected (Rorty, 1979; Toulmin, 1988; Taylor, 1995). But any adequate historical understanding of how and why the notion of practical philosophy could find no place within the vocabulary of twentieth-century philosophy of education cannot be confined to episodes in the history of modern philosophy. It also has to incorporate some explanation of how the social, intellectual and cultural climate of the early twentieth century created the conditions out of which our contemporary understanding of education *and* our contemporary understanding of the philosophy of education emerged.

V

When, at the beginning of the twentieth century, education began to emerge as a subject in the academic curriculum of many British Universities, it was widely accepted that the study of education should, at least in part, be a study of its philosophy and history (Tibble, 1966). In particular, it was argued that it was these two subjects that would equip educational practitioners with the intellectual resources to engage in historically informed philosophical reflection on the educational values that sustained their practice (Adams, 1928: 2–4). Thus in the first institutionalised expression of what we now call the philosophy of education, 'education' was still construed as a practice and the 'philosophy of education' was understood as a 'practical' discipline in which the presuppositions inherent in practitioners' modes of thought and action could be systematically identified and reassessed. However, in the dominant intellectual and cultural conditions of the first half of the twentieth century, it became increasingly difficult for *either* this conception of education *or* this conception of the philosophy of education to be sustained.

What seriously undermined this conception of education was the unprecedented level of institutionalisation that accompanied the rapid expansion of state schooling in the first half of the twentieth century. For one of the major effects of this process was to make it increasingly common to see education less as a 'practice' and more as a 'system' that had to be organised, managed and controlled so as to make it responsive to the political and economic demands of the modern industrial state. As a result, the most pressing problems facing educational practitioners were no longer the kinds of questions that, in its initial twentieth-century embodiment, the philosophy of education had sought to address. Instead, they were narrow technical questions about how the externally imposed goals set for the educational system by the state were most effectively to be achieved. In this climate, it was clearly imperative for the study of education to develop a new non-historical and non-philosophical form. What, therefore, emerged to replace philosophy and history as the intellectual basis for the study of education were forms of study and inquiry that were modelled on the logic and methods of natural science. In the first half of the twentieth century, behaviourist theories of teaching and learning, scientific approaches to educational management and administration, and technical models of curriculum appeared – all purporting to provide a body of scientifically verified knowledge about how established educational goals could be most effectively achieved (Richardson, 2002). By the early 1950s practical rationality had been replaced by technical rationality and education, and its dominant modes of theoretical discourse had become fully accommodated to the scientific spirit of the age.[4]

It goes without saying that the emergence of this 'scientific' approach to the study of education did not occur in a philosophical vacuum. It was legitimised and reinforced by a set of early twentieth-century epistemological doctrines that dominated Western thought in the first half of the twentieth century and that collectively constitute what is commonly called 'logical positivism'. One of the characteristics of these doctrines was their firm insistence that only the neutral sciences could provide an acceptable foundation for rational knowledge. Another was their deep-seated hostility to philosophical traditions that treated reflectively acquired self-knowledge as a legitimate epistemological category (Kolakowski, 1972). But the most salient feature of positivism's twentieth-century history concerns its changing cultural role. For although positivism's original philosophical advocates had presented it as a radical and culturally subversive philosophy that would liberate human thought from the dictates of ideology, this did not prevent it from itself being transformed into a dominant ideology – an uncritically accepted and all-pervading way of seeing the world that became embedded in twentieth-century social life and hence in the discourse, organisation and practice of education as well. David Cooper has designated this ideology 'naturalism' (Cooper, 1998: 30–32) but it is more appropriately referred to as 'scientism' (Habermas, 1972: 4). For the essence of this ideology was to sustain a culture in which scientific standards of rationality had been made normative for rationality as such. Such a culture not only took it as a self-evident truth that forms of reasoning that do not conform to the canons of scientific reasoning – for example, the forms of practical reasoning employed in morality, politics and education – should be excluded from the realm of rational discourse. It also legitimised what Cooper calls 'the dominant culture of philosophy' – the background assumptions that shaped the prevailing twentieth-century view of what philosophy is and how it is to be practised and understood (Cooper, 1998: 25–27). What characterised the philosophical culture, dominated by the ideology of scientism, was the assumption that scientific rationality no longer has to be justified against standards laid down by philosophy. On the contrary, philosophy has to be defined in accordance with standards of rationality laid down by science.[5]

In such a philosophical culture, it was only to be expected that there should become available an account of the philosophy of education in which this view of the relationships between philosophy and science was fully accepted and endorsed. This expectation was more than met with the publication, in 1957, of

D.J. O'Connor's *An Introduction to the Philosophy of Education.* In this O'Connor enlisted two of logical positivism's canonical texts – A.J. Ayer's *Language, Truth and Logic* (1946) and C.L. Stevenson's *Ethics and Language* (1944) – in order to dismantle the existing approach to the philosophy of education and replace it with a view that was consistent with the methodological and epistemological require- ments of 'contemporary philosophical analysis'. By invoking logical positivism's familiar doctrines – the fact/value and analytic/synthetic distinctions, and the verifi- cation principle – it was not difficult for O'Connor to show how, in the past, philosophers of education had made use of a whole range of philosophical beliefs and value judgements neither of which could be scientifically verified and both of which should be removed from the realm of rational inquiry. Nor was it difficult for him to argue that, if philosophy of education was to become a serious academic activity, then it had to recognise that science was the only legitimate source of 'first order' educational knowledge and that philosophy was a limited 'second order' analytical activity in which only questions about the meaning of 'first order' empirical beliefs and value-judgements were regarded as genuinely 'philosophical'.

O'Connor's aim was to show that the only way for the philosophy of education to become a genuine academic discipline was to rid itself of its existing conceptual confusions and methodological impurities, and reconstruct itself in accordance with the requirements of contemporary philosophical analysis. However, the offi- cially endorsed version of the discipline that, under the guidance of Richard Peters and Paul Hirst, was to gain widespread institutional recognition in the 1960s, refused to accept O'Connor's restricted view of the philosophy of education on the grounds that it was 'not concerned enough with what is educational' (Peters, 1966b: 67). Indeed, Paul Hirst insisted that since education is a value-laden practical activity, the philosophy of education must be concerned with 'determining the value judge- ments about what ought to be aimed at in education' (Hirst, 1966: 52) – a concern which could only be expressed by adopting a view of the philosophy of education that would accord philosophical legitimacy to the kind of questions that O'Connor had proscribed.

But, as O'Connor was to point out, if the philosophy of education was to insist on retaining its traditional concern with education as an ethically informed prac- tice rather than as an instrumental system for achieving externally established ends it was clearly obliged to reject the contemporary view of philosophy that he him- self had deployed to deny this concern any philosophical legitimacy (O'Connor, 1973: 53). However, far from doing this, both Peters and Hirst explicitly endorsed O'Connor's view of the philosophy of education as a second order analytical activ- ity with the limited task of 'criticism and clarification' (Peters, 1966a: 15; Hirst, 1974: 1–2). It was, of course, because of this reluctance to resist the demand to conform to the aims and methods of 'contemporary philosophical analysis' that analytical philosophy of education was, from the outset, continuously accused of addressing normative educational questions that contravened the value-neutral principles of analytical philosophy (Earwicker, 1973; Woods and Dray, 1973). But what, with historical hindsight, is now also clear is that the main reason why analytical philosophy of education displayed such reluctance was because it was just as much a victim of 'the dominant culture of philosophy' – and hence could no more avoid being contaminated by the cultural ideology of scientism than could the more explicitly positivistic view of the discipline proposed by O'Connor (Cooper, 1998: 32).

The subsequent inability of the philosophy of education to resolve the basic contradiction between 'value-free' philosophical analysis and the 'value-laden' questions to which the practical activity of education gives rise is no doubt part of the reason why, in the 1980s, it abandoned its confinement to analytical philosophy. But since doing this, it has not sought to reconsider the value or validity of the early twentieth-century understanding of the discipline that analytical philosophy of education had critically repudiated and replaced. Instead, the hegemonic dominance of analytical philosophy has now given way to such a multiplicity of different philosophical perspectives and traditions – hermeneutics, critical theory, pragmatism and postmodernism are just some – that there is now no longer any single account of 'what the philosophy of education is' that can command anything remotely resembling universal assent. But although some analytically minded philosophers of education may view these post-analytic developments with some consternation (Wilson, 2003), the idea that philosophy of education is a branch of academic philosophy has remained unchallenged, and the belief that the philosophy of education must conform to *some* tradition of theoretical philosophy is still unreflectively presupposed. As a result, post-analytical philosophy of education still conceives of its relationship to education as one of offering a detached theoretical commentary upon the activities and judgements of educational policy makers and practitioners, and the question of whether a form of philosophy whose avowed purpose is to guide a practical activity like education should be so dependent on *any* tradition of theoretical philosophy is rarely, if ever, asked. The extent to which post-analytical philosophy of education continues to neglect this question is thus a measure of the extent to which it continues to remain deeply infected by a 'culture of philosophy' in which non-theoretical forms of reflective philosophy have been discarded and the need for a mode of philosophy that would protect and preserve the integrity of education as a practice has been conveniently ignored.

Of course, to adherents of the perspective which sustains this understanding of the discipline, any suggestion that the philosophy of education may be something other than a species of theoretical philosophy will be all but incomprehensible and, while they may readily acknowledge that there are intractable difficulties concerning the discipline's impact on education, they will have no reason to believe that these difficulties constitute a serious refutation of the perspective to which they subscribe. But once this perspective is brought into critical confrontation with the perspective afforded by the Aristotelian tradition of practical philosophy, some interesting insights into our contemporary understanding of how philosophy is related to education and education to philosophy begin to emerge.

What, first, emerges is that the Aristotelian tradition is able to offer an understanding and explanation of the discipline's practical sterility that contemporary philosophy of education cannot provide for itself. It is able to do this in so far as it is able to show why the separation of philosophy from education that everybody now deplores is actually endemic to the contemporary view of the philosophy of education as a branch of academic philosophy that can be undertaken in isolation from educational practice and conducted in a theoretical and practical context different from the theoretical and practical context to which it is supposed to apply. Since, from an Aristotelian perspective, 'education' is not some kind of inert phenomenon to be isolated, analysed and theorised about, to construe the philosophy of education as a form of theoretical philosophy – as a species of *theoria* guided by *episteme* – is simply to transform educational problems into philosophical problems and thereby assimilate the preoccupations of the educational practitioner to those of the theoretical philosopher. Indeed, from this perspective, it is precisely because our contemporary understanding of the discipline has been derived from a view of 'what philosophy is' that is unconstrained by any detailed consideration of 'what education is' that it is now confined to a form of philosophy in which the nature of its relationship to the practice that it is supposed to be 'the philosophy of' is never adequately articulated or defined. And it is precisely because it is now restricted to forms of theoretical philosophy which deprive education of its essentially practical character that contemporary philosophy of education now has so little practical effect.

But as well as providing an explanation of why the contemporary philosophy of education is practically ineffective, the Aristotelian perspective also offers some understanding of why, in our culture, education has become insulated from philosophy. For just as the philosophy of education has treated the educator's practical need reflectively to discuss the ends of their practice as synonymous with the philosopher's need to develop theoretical accounts of 'the aims of education', so the contemporary removal of education from the sphere of practice has virtually eliminated discussion of the ends of education from the official agenda of educational debate. Technologisation, institutionalisation and bureaucratisation – those core embodiments of the ideology of scientism – effectively ensure that education is now construed as a species of *poiesis* guided by *techne,* and hence as an instrumental activity directed towards the achievement of externally imposed outcomes and goals. In a culture that has subordinated the excellence of practice to institutional effectiveness, it is only to be expected that educational debate will be reduced to a mundane technical debate in which non-technical questions about how to achieve excellence in pursuing the goods internal to education are no longer asked.

VI

How is philosophy related to education and education to philosophy? What I have argued is that the contemporary philosophy of education lacks the resources to frame an adequate answer to this question and that the only way to rectify this situation is to replace our current version of the history of the discipline with a version that can provide us with an understanding of this relationship that the contemporary philosophy of education cannot provide for itself. In particular, I have argued that the history of the discipline that currently exists – a history that is largely confined to twentieth-century developments in academic philosophy – insulates us from those aspects of the past that would help us to identify and overcome the limitations of our contemporary understanding of the philosophy of education by helping us to understand how the emergence of the philosophy of education in the 1960s was not just the historical starting point for our present understanding of how philosophy is related to education, but also the end point of a much longer historical period during which this relationship had been portrayed in a very different way.

In pursuing this argument, I have sketched the bare outline of a historical narrative that has been written from the standpoint of a philosophical tradition with which the contemporary philosophy of education shares very little and which, therefore, differs from the orthodox history of the discipline in several crucial respects. For example, it acknowledges that any history which simply recounts those intricate and abstract philosophical arguments by means of which twentieth-century philosophy of education was originally vindicated will always underestimate the extent to which those arguments were themselves part of a much broader and more complex process of cultural change and hence always underestimate the extent to which the contemporary philosophy of education is just as much a product of historically contingent cultural factors as of any changes to the internal logic of academic philosophy.

What also distinguishes my alternative history is that it refuses to treat 'the history of philosophy' and 'the history of education' as two separate histories, and so refuses to remain blind to the suggestion that the transformation of education from an ethically informed practice into a system of schooling, and the transition within the philosophy of education from practical philosophy to theoretical philosophy, were not two unrelated events but mutually dependent parts of the single historical process through which our conception of education *and* our conception of the philosophy of education were simultaneously transformed. Indeed, it is only by constructing a historical narrative in which these two histories are recognised as interdependent parts of one ordered totality that it has become possible to appreciate how these twentieth-century changes to how 'education' and 'philosophy' were interpreted and understood were mutually reinforcing expressions of a culture dominated by the ideology of scientism: a culture in which practical rationality had been assimilated to scientific rationality and the conception of education as a species of *praxis* could no longer be expressed.

What, finally, is distinctive of my reconstructed history is that 'the philosophy of education' has not been treated as the name of an academic discipline that only emerged in the mid-twentieth century but as a historically evolving and culturally embedded practice whose practitioners can only adequately answer the questions they now face concerning their discipline's relationship to education by reflectively recovering the historically sedimented presuppositions taken for granted in their existing practice. It is therefore no accident that my attempt to confront these questions has itself turned out to be an exercise in 'practical philosophy' and thus to exemplify, however imperfectly, the kind of philosophy of education it has sought to recover and revive.

Thus the main conclusion to be drawn from my inquiry is not just that the Aristotelian tradition enables us to spell out a conception of the philosophy of education for which our current problems about the relationship of philosophy to education would not – indeed could not – arise. Nor is it that it offers an external perspective that is able to illuminate how these problems are due to incoherences inherent in our dominant contemporary conceptions of the discipline. Rather, it is to suggest that any satisfactory resolution to these problems will only be achieved by the philosophy of education's proficient and experienced practitioners – its *phronimoi* – displaying a willingness to test their own convictions and beliefs about 'what the philosophy of education is' through critical encounter with a philosophical tradition which some of them may initially find incoherent and to which others may be implacably opposed. It is thus to anticipate a debate about the relationship between philosophy and education in which some old certainties would be abandoned and some new questions would be addressed. Is the purpose of the philosophy of education to articulate and defend the integrity of education as a practice? If so, can our understanding of education as a practice remain intelligible once we have discarded the Aristotelian concepts of *phronesis* and *praxis*? How in a modern educational context, can the philosophy of education contribute to 'the development of *phronesis*...as an abiding disposition'? (Dunne, 1993: 369). Should our efforts to develop a less practically impoverished understanding of the philosophy of education be informed by the work of those contemporary philosophers who, despite their differences, have all appealed to the Aristotelian philosophical tradition not only critically to expose the practical impoverishment of modern moral and political philosophy, but also to revive the notion of practical philosophy in a way that would make it appropriate to the modern world (Gadamer, 1967, 1980, 1981; Bernstein, 1971, 1983, 1991; Habermas, 1972, 1974; MacIntyre, 1981, 1988, 1990, 1998; Williams, 1985; Toulmin, 1988, 1990; Taylor, 1995; Miller, 1996; Nussbaum, 1997)?

To propose that questions like these should now be seriously confronted by the philosophy of education is, of course, to reiterate the basic philosophical principle enunciated by Alasdair MacIntyre in my opening quotation: that we will only be able to expose any incoherences and errors in our own philosophical self-understanding by bringing our convictions and beliefs (or as Gadamer would say our 'prejudices' and 'prejudgements') into critical confrontation with the claims of an alien and rival tradition of philosophical inquiry. What I have tried to show is that by being prepared to learn from the Aristotelian tradition of practical philosophy, by treating it with imagination and sensitivity and by interpreting it in the best possible light, we can begin to engage in a critical dialogue about the present condition and future prospects of the philosophy of education which is neither constrained by the presuppositions of conventional thinking nor foreclosed by the exigencies of existing practice. It thus turns out that the end point of my inquiry is to do little more than identify the starting point from which philosophical dialogue and debate about the relationship of philosophy to education and education to philosophy ought to begin.[6]

Notes

1 The view of the relationship between philosophy and its history running throughout this chapter owes much to the contributions of Charles Taylor, Alasdair MacIntyre and Richard Rorty to Part 1 of *Philosophy in History* (Rorty, Schneewind and Skinner, 1984; see also Bernstein, 1991).

2 This view of philosophy is virtually identical to the view of Richard Peters who, in *Ethics and Education* had described the philosopher as someone engaged in 'the disciplined demarcation of concepts, the patient explication of the grounds of knowledge and the presuppositions of different forms of discourse' (Peters, 1966a: 15).

3 My discussion of Aristotle's account of the relationships between practice, practical reasoning and practical philosophy draws on a number of resources. Of particular value have been: Joseph Dunne's excellent exposition of Aristotle's discussion of *phronesis* and *techne* (Dunne, 1993, Part 2: *Phronesis and Techne in Aristotle*); Gadamer's various attempts to demonstrate the contemporary relevance of Aristotelian practical philosophy (Gadamer, 1967, 1980, 1981, 1993); and Alasdair MacIntyre's efforts to retrieve and reinstate the Aristotelian tradition of practical reasoning (MacIntyre, 1981, 1988, 1998).

4 This kind of close affinity between a prevailing view of education and the prevailing mode of theoretical discourse that serves to articulate that view has often been noted by educational historians. Brian Simon, for example, has insisted that any explanation of why psychometry dominated educational theory during the 1920s and 1930s 'needs to be sought not only in the history of ideas but also in the actual circumstances of the time which called insistently for theories which legitimised the hierarchical system brought into being from 1902 ... There appears to be a clear relationship between the economic and social conditions ... of the interwar period ... and the dominant theory legitimising and lubricating this system' (Simon, 1983: 78–79).

5 Jurgen Habermas has identified scientism as 'the most influential philosophy of our time ... It means science's belief in itself: that is, the conviction that we can no longer understand science as *one* form of possible knowledge but must identify knowledge *with* science' (Habermas, 1972: 2).

6 The ideas and arguments expressed in this chapter have been extensively discussed with Pádraig Hogan and Joseph Dunne. Also, the account I provide has been extensively revised in the light of their detailed and invaluable comments on an earlier draft. For this I offer them my gratitude and thanks.

References

Adams, J. (1928) *Educational Theories* (London, Ernest Benn).

Aristotle (1955) *The Nicomachean Ethics*, trans. J.A.K. Thomson (London, Penguin).

Ayer, A.J. (1946) *Language, Truth and Logic* (London, Gollancz).

Bernstein, R.J. (1971) *Praxis and Action* (London, Duckworth).

Bernstein, R.J. (1983) *Beyond Objectivism and Subjectivism: Science, Hermeneutics and Praxis* (Oxford, Blackwell).

Bernstein, R.J. (1991) 'Philosophy, History and Critique', in: R.J. Bernstein (ed.), *The New Constellation* (Cambridge, Polity Press), pp. 15–30.

Cooper, D.E. (1998) 'Educational Philosophies and Cultures of Philosophy', in: G. Haydon (ed.), *Fifty Years of Philosophy of Education* (London, Institute of Education), pp. 23–40.

Dewey, J. (1931) *Philosophy and Civilization* (New York, Moulton, Bach & Company).

Dunne, J. (1993) *Back to the Rough Ground: 'Phronesis' and 'Techne' in Modern Philosophy and in Aristotle* (Illinois, University of Notre Dame Press).

Earwicker, J. (1973) R.S. Peters and the Concept of Education, *Proceedings of the Philosophy of Education Society of Great Britain*, 7, pp. 239–259.

Gadamer, H.-G. (1967) Theory, technology, practice: the task of the science of man, *Social Research*, 44, pp. 529–561.

Gadamer, H.-G. (1980) Practical philosophy as a model of the human sciences, *Research in Phenomenology*, 9, pp. 74–85.

Gadamer, H.-G. (1981) 'What is practice?: the conditions of social reason', in: H.-G. Gadamer (ed.), *Reason in the Age of Science*, trans. F.G. Lawrence (Cambridge, MA, MIT Press).

Habermas, J. (1972) *Knowledge and Human Interests*, trans. J. Shapiro (London, Heinemann).

Habermas, J. (1974) *Theory and Practice*, trans. J. Viertel (London, Heinemann).

Harris, K. (1979) *Education and Knowledge* (London, Routledge & Kegan Paul).

Hirst, P.H. (1966) 'Educational Theory', in: J.W. Tibble (ed.), *The Study of Education* (London, Routledge & Kegan Paul).

Hirst, P.H. (1974) *Knowledge and the Curriculum* (London, Routledge & Kegan Paul).

Hirst, P.H. (1983) 'Educational Theory', in: P.H. Hirst (ed.), *Educational Theory and its Foundation Disciplines* (London, Routledge & Kegan Paul).

Hirst, P.H. (1998) 'Philosophy of Education: The Evolution of a Discipline', in: G. Haydon (ed.), *Fifty Years of Philosophy of Education* (London, Institute of Education), pp. 1–22.

Kaminsky, J.S. (1993) *A New History of Educational Philosophy* (London, Greenwood Press).

Kolakowski, L. (1972) *Positivist Philosophy* (Harmondsworth, Penguin).

MacIntyre, A.C. (1981) *After Virtue: a Study in Moral Theory* (London, Duckworth).

MacIntyre, A.C. (1982) Philosophy and the Other Disciplines, *Soundings*, pp. 127–145.

MacIntyre, A.C. (1988) *Whose Justice? Which Rationality?* (London, Duckworth).

MacIntyre, A.C. (1990) *Three Rival Versions of Moral Enquiry* (London, Duckworth).

MacIntyre, A.C. (1998) 'Practical Rationalities as Forms of Social Structure', in: K. Knight (ed.), *The MacIntyre Reader* (Cambridge, Polity Press), pp. 120–135.

Miller, B. (1996) *Casuistry and Modern Ethics: A Poetics of Practical Reasoning* (Chicago, IL, University of Chicago Press).

Nussbaum, M.C. (1997) *Cultivating Humanity: a Classical Defence of Reform in Liberal Education* (Cambridge, MA, Harvard University Press).

O'Connor, D.J. (1957) *An Introduction to the Philosophy of Education* (London, Routledge & Kegan Paul).

O'Connor, D.J. (1973) 'The Nature and Scope of Educational Theory', in: Q. Langford and D.J. O'Connor (eds), *New Essays in the Philosophy of Education* (London, Routledge & Kegan Paul).

Peters, R.S. (1966a) *Ethics and Education* (London, Allen & Unwin).

Peters, R.S. (1966b) 'The Philosophy of Education', in: J.W. Tibble (ed.), *The Study of Education* (London, Routledge & Kegan Paul).

Peters, R.S. (1983) 'The Philosophy of Education', in: P.H. Hirst (ed.), *Education Theory and its Foundation Disciplines* (London, Routledge & Kegan Paul).

Richardson, W. (2002) Educational Studies in the United Kingdom 1940–2002, *British Journal of Educational Studies*, 50(1), pp. 3–56.

Rorty, R. (1979) *Philosophy and the Mirror of Nature* (Princeton, NJ, Princeton University Press).

Rorty, R., Schneewind, J.B. and Skinner, Q. (eds) (1984) *Philosophy in History* (Cambridge, Cambridge University Press).

Simon, B. (1983) 'History of Education', in: P.H. Hirst (ed.), *Educational Theory and Its Foundation Disciplines* (London, Routledge & Kegan Paul).

Stevenson, C.L. (1944) *Ethics and Language* (New Haven, CT, Yale University Press).

Taylor, C. (1995) *Philosophical Arguments* (Cambridge, MA, Harvard University Press).

Tibble, J.W. (1966) 'The Development of the Study of Education', in: J.W. Tibble (ed.), *The Study of Education* (London, Routledge & Kegan Paul), pp. 1–28.

Toulmin, S. (1988) The Recovery of Practical Philosophy, *The American Scholar*, 57(3), p. 354.

Toulmin, S. (1990) *Cosmopolis: the Hidden Agenda of Modernity* (New York, The Free Press).

Williams, B. (1985) *Ethics and the Limits of Philosophy* (Cambridge, MA, Harvard University Press).

Wilson, J. (2003) Perspectives on the Philosophy of Education, *Oxford Review of Education*, 29(2), pp. 279–283.

Woods, J. and Dray, N.H. (1973) 'Aims of Education – a Conceptual Enquiry', in: R.S. Peters (ed.), *The Philosophy of Education* (London, Oxford University Press).

CHAPTER 3

FEMINISM, EPISTEMOLOGY AND EDUCATION

Shirley Pendlebury

In David Carr (ed.) *Education, Knowledge and Truth* (1998),
London: Routledge, pp. 174–188

Hesitant forays

The feminist challenge to mainstream epistemology and related approaches in philosophy of education has been warmly welcomed by some and cursorily dismissed by others. Still others find themselves blowing hot and cold – supporting the feminist project in spirit, yet concerned about too radical a repudiation of 'masculinist' tools of philosophical analysis. In this chapter I consider whether, how and at what educational cost recent feminist work in epistemology serves to challenge those liberal approaches to education that rest on 'forms of knowledge epistemology'.

Of course, there is more than one feminist position and within each more than one challenge to mainstream epistemology. Similarly, there is no homogeneous feminist philosophy of education and, apart from some of Jane Roland Martin's essays (e.g. Martin, 1981), little sustained feminist criticism of forms of knowledge epistemology in education. Nonetheless, philosophers working from a range of feminist perspectives do give grounds for challenging the kinds of educational and epistemological claims canonized in the three influential volumes edited by Dearden *et al.* (1971), and by their heirs. What held this group together was not common consent to Hirst's forms of knowledge thesis but the view that the constitutive aim of education is the development of reason and understanding. Proper attention to reason and to the nature of human knowledge seemed to promise objective curriculum choices unhampered by fashion, ideology or politics. This optimism and its supporting arguments were a far cry from the naive empiricism of so much of what passed – and still passes – for a science of education. While Hirst and colleagues celebrated reason, they gave neither the emotions nor morals short shrift; they regarded objectivity as a matter of inter-subjective agreement, facts and values as interdependent and language, meaning and truth as bound up with one another.

How far can feminist challenges to 'masculinist' epistemology be taken as challenges to forms of knowledge epistemology in education? I undertake this appraisal with trepidation. Three predicaments fuel my anxiety. Personal though they may seem, they also take us to the heart of current concerns in feminist epistemology and so suggest an agenda for the chapter.

For a start I do not believe it is possible to undertake any appraisal whatsoever without some recourse to the tools of traditional philosophical analysis; yet the strongest feminist challenge to epistemology consists precisely in a rejection of these analytical tools. Some form of argument, for instance, seems to me to be indispensable. On the face of it, this drives me to one of three equally unsatisfactory choices: either I use some of the rejected analytical tools to show that the 'radical position' is tenable, or I use them to show that it is not, or I simply assume (without offering any reasons) that it is untenable or tenable, in which case I will have refused the invitation to appraise the position.

Second, little of my previous scholarly work – in philosophy, curriculum or teacher education – has been written from an explicitly feminist standpoint. Does this not disqualify me from undertaking the assigned task? After all, an editor of a collection on contemporary issues in philosophy of science would not normally invite a contribution from someone who had done no work in the field; nor would it do for me to declare like Sojourner Truth 'Ain't I a woman?', as if being a female person guarantees epistemic authority on matters of feminist theory. If I use tools of 'masculinist epistemology' and write from a perspective developed outside of an active participation in feminist theory-making, both method and standpoint are bound to be suspect.

Finally, a single chapter is too confined to permit a deep, textured and context-sensitive account of a full range of feminist work in philosophy of education. While space permits a brief taxonomy, mere taxonomies are tedious and misleading, taxing the patience of readers already familiar with the field and making false promises to those who are not. Dictates of clarity, economy and rigour suggest instead that I take some claims and submit these to critical scrutiny. Yet this route not only involves taking sample claims out of context and presenting them as if they were the whole story, it also offers the easy temptation to laud, bolster or bash a group of straw women and so escape the more daunting task of responsible critical appraisal.

Even as these predicaments impede my project at its start so they set an agenda for its progress. The first arises from too easy a slide into 'blind' logic, coupled with dismissive presuppositions about what is entailed in rejecting the methods of traditional epistemology. A more substantial account of feminist challenges to 'masculinist epistemology' may dissolve the predicament. The second predicament is not merely personal for it points to a controversy about whether and how a knower's subjectivity is relevant to an appraisal of her knowledge claims. It raises the question 'Who knows or claims to know?' and, in education, the related question 'Who may come to know?', a question concerning whether and how a learner's subjectivity is pertinent to acquiring knowledge. The third marks a controversy about whether and when, without risk of distortion, claims to knowledge can be detached from their context and from the conditions and purposes of their production.

Indelible tracks

Which aspects of traditional philosophical analysis are primary targets for feminist repudiation? Answers range from 'the lot' to concerns about how philosophical analysis construes the nature of reason and objectivity, how it construes or ignores the identity of the knower and how it construes or ignores the nature of emotions. 'The lot' is surely an absurd answer, one which undermines the very possibility of a strong feminist project and sounds an obituary for education. For the moment I shall set aside this extreme position and focus on four targets of repudiation, all of which parade under the banner of what Lorraine Code labels '*S*-knows-that-*p*' epistemologies (Code, 1996: 191).

Feminists have challenged:

1   The view that assumes an isolated unencumbered knower, a view that is both a-topic and a-chronic, that is, from nowhere and no time (e.g. Nelson, 1996; Walker, 1996).
2   The view that assumes the identity of the knower is irrelevant and thus ignores subjectivity (e.g. Harding, 1991; Code, 1996).
3   The view that assumes rigid conceptions of rationality and objectivity and thereby excludes emotion both from the domain of discovery and from the domain of justification (e.g. Rose, 1994; Jaggar, 1996).
4   The view that assumes that knowledge is knowledge of objective reality (e.g. Haslanger, 1996).

Each line of repudiation incorporates a concern with subjectivity, as may be seen in the following counterclaims (some actual, others possible):

1   Knowledge claims are perspectival; they are always made by someone, or some epistemic community, at some time.
2   The identity of claimants is crucial to a proper assessment of knowledge claims, regardless of whether the claimants are individuals or an epistemic community.
3   Both our sensitivities and our senses are vital to what we claim to know and how we justify our claims. Love and hate, pride and prejudice, passions of heart and mind, jealousies and jeopardies may all impinge on justification as well as discovery. Memories of time past may do as much as clean reason, if not more, to shape our intellectual habits and pursuits.
4   There is no way of reaching the world except through our conceptual apparatus. Different epistemic communities have different conceptual apparatuses. How we come at the world is partly a matter of who we are and where we belong.

We should not be surprised that subjectivity is so strong a theme in feminist criticism of mainstream epistemology. Feminists of many different stripes argue that subjectivity-blindness perpetuates 'the hegemony of masculinist epistemology'. Putting subjectivity into the picture is thus an important feminist project. In its most robust version the project takes subjectivity as central both to the logic of discovery and to the logic of justification.

What happens to objectivity in this project, in its robust version especially? How, if at all, is it possible to give due regard to subjectivity without collapsing into subjectivity? More to the point for present purposes, how is it possible in educational practice to give subjectivity its due without ditching, or at least seriously compromising, critical understanding and justification – without ditching education itself, some might wonder. (These are obvious questions for anyone who takes the constitutive end of education to be the development of reason. Give up this conception and it may seem that education is under no deep threat from the feminist project. Yet it will not do to take too simple a line here. As I shall argue later, some ways of putting subjectivity back into the picture are as much a threat to the feminist educational project as they are to any other educational project, just as other ways of putting subjectivity back into the picture are vital to sustaining teaching as a practice in which learners matter, not only for what they know and may come to know, but also for who they are and the kind of world they inhabit.

Without a much fuller picture of what is intended, it is risky to take a stand either for or against the project of putting subjectivity back into the picture.)

An intriguing response is that objectivity and, we might add, critical understanding and education, *are not possible unless subjectivity is taken into account.* Lorraine Code follows this line, as an attack on and a corrective to mainstream epistemology or '*S*-knows-that-*p* epistemologies'. Whatever their differences, both coherentism and foundationalism are '*S*-knows-that-*p* epistemologies' because they share the assumption that 'the places *S* and *p* can be indiscriminately filled across an inexhaustible range of subject-matters' and 'knowledge worthy of the name must transcend the particularities of experience to achieve objective purity and value neutrality' (Code, 1996: 194). No doubt some readers will flinch, as I did, at this crude caricature, now made even cruder in my minimalist sketch. Rather than questioning Code's account of mainstream epistemology, I shall consider what she proposes instead and examine some educational implications of her proposal.

Against '*S*-knows-that-*p* epistemologies' Code proposes an account that requires as much attention to the nature and situation of *S* as traditional epistemologists commonly apply to the content and justification of *p*. The circumstances of *S* are taken to be central to logic of discovery as well as to procedures and logic of justification and evaluation. How so? Just as there are no dislocated, disinterested observers so there is no homogeneous 'we' in whose name philosophers may speak, Code argues, following a line that is neither new nor uniquely feminist. Arguments against the view from nowhere abound within mainstream epistemology as well as in its counter currents and side eddies, as do arguments against singularity. A feminist version goes like this: traditional epistemology operates from a position of presumed political innocence but is an artefact of 'a small, privileged group of educated, usually prosperous, white men' whose circumstances enable them to believe that 'they are materially and affectively autonomous, and to imagine that they are nowhere and everywhere, even as they occupy an unmarked position of privilege' (Code, 1996: 197). Any artefact bears the marks of its makers, so the point of feminist criticism is not to censure traditional epistemology for its male traces. Rather, it is to debunk the objectivist ideal: 'if the ideal of objectivity cannot pretend to have been established in accordance with its own demands, then it has no right to the theoretical hegemony to which it lays claim' (p. 200).

To reject the objectivist ideal is not inevitably to go down the slippery slope of subjectivism. The slide is prevented by a realistic commitment to achieving empirical adequacy in the pursuit of knowledge, with the proviso that this is taken as involving a situated analysis of both the knower and the known. In short: objectivity requires taking subjectivity into account. What does this mean, especially for education? I shall take two routes towards an answer: one via an analysis of objectivity, the other via some feminist work in education.

Tethered by reality

Suppose that objective theories, observations, claims and methods of inquiry are those constrained either by the facts of the matter or by some non-arbitrary criteria and so are not determined by our wishes about how things ought to be. To illustrate: I may wish that my body did not limit the range of things I might choose to do; but wishes aren't horses and no amount of begging or wishful thinking could coax my body to sprout wings and fly. The fact of the matter is that I am not a winged creature, whatever my flights of fancy.

In supposing that objectivity requires non-arbitrary criteria – that is, some world independent of ourselves – we need not presuppose that an objective theory or observation springs from or yields a god's eye-view; nor need we presuppose value-free inquiry or foundational certainty. These are distinguishable claims, not a take-it-or-leave-it package deal. So long as standards for the non-arbitrary are not set impossibly high, there is no inconsistency in requiring non-arbitrary criteria for objectivity and contending that all human practices – theoretical or otherwise – are perspectival, value-governed and vulnerable to vicissitude.

To borrow a distinction from the work of the feminist philosopher of science Helen Longino (1990): some of the values governing a practice stem from its constitutive ends; others from contextual ends.[1] If the constitutive aim of a practice – scientific inquiry, for instance – is to produce reliable theories, then, ideally, the practice will be regulated by a truth principle and by such epistemic values as explanatory power, coherence, consistency and evidential fit. Yet contextual goals and values, both virtuous and vicious, may also guide scientific practice.

For example, environmental research may be shaped by a concern for social justice (clean air for all and not only for those who can afford to live and work beyond the reach of belching factories and flatulent exhausts) or by a demand, covert perhaps, to cover the tracks of greed and negligence. In the latter case, contextual concerns appear to override the epistemic values which constitute and sustain the practice. So, too, might they in the former case – for data may be doctored in good causes as well as bad. Yet there may be nothing so blatant as data-doctoring in either case. What counts as evidence depends not only on the relationship between a theory or hypothesis and a state of affairs but also on the background beliefs and related values, constitutive and contextual, of the epistemic community concerned. Acceptable hypotheses are never determined by epistemic values alone, for background beliefs always involve contextual values – or so one line of feminist argument goes.

So we return to the idea of artefacts bearing their makers' fingerprints. Strong objectivity (Harding, 1991), or taking subjectivity seriously, requires us to look for these fingerprints, not to erase them – for they are indelible – reminding ourselves that impartiality is impossible. Every view is a partial view and permanent partiality is definitive of all our theories, observations and claims (Haraway, 1990; Harding, 1991). But this brings us full circle: Is a commitment to permanent partiality not the start down the slippery slope of subjectivism?

Much depends on how we understand the notion of permanent partiality. A weak reading, Miranda Fricker (1994) suggests, takes permanent partiality as an expression of the situated nature of knowledge, whereas a strong reading takes permanent partiality as an epistemological ideal. On the weak reading, permanent partiality is a methodological imperative for the knowing subject to place herself within the critical field and be open to how her own situation may influence her beliefs. Or, to put the matter in communal rather than individual terms, permanent partiality may be read as an injunction for an epistemic community to place itself within a critical field of reflection. To say that permanent partiality is an epistemological ideal is to say, crudely, that the more partial the view, the more reliable the beliefs issuing from it. The danger here is that once partiality of perspective is presented as epistemologically desirable, there is no justification for halting its progress:

> this has the devastating consequence that there is no way of justifying the maintenance of any shared belief-system without committing a pernicious act of coercion: the eclipsing of the perspective or potential perspective of some

person or group. Without a shared belief-system we clearly cannot sustain the minimal realism which I have argued is necessary to feminist politics...nor can we maintain norms for belief; nor sustain any systematic self-critical practice.

(Fricker, 1994: 102)

Strong permanent partiality seems to rule out the possibility of education. For now, I shall accept the weak reading, although not quite with warts and all.

The notion of situated knowledge is closely related to the idea that evidence and justification depend on contextual as well as epistemic values. Knowers and would-be knowers are all always somewhere – at once enabled and constrained by their locations and their position in relation to other epistemic subjects. But there are very different ways of characterizing this 'somewhere', which is seldom singular. More often than not we are situated in multiple, overlapping communities and social positions. One such 'some-where' is the place of the subjugated (women, ethnic minorities, slaves, children and other legally defined minors). For some feminists, this view from below has special epistemic authority.

Two considerations compel me to reject the presumption in favour of the view from below: one concerning its sweep, the other concerning its consequences for the practice of education. While the view from below may be the most telling view for some kinds of knowledge claims, it cannot be so for all. More seriously, in education, granting special epistemic authority to the view from below leads to the absurd, albeit perhaps seductive, idea that pupils have epistemic authority over their teachers. But education cannot get off the ground unless we grant *teachers* some sort of epistemic authority and unless we recognize *pupils* as being capable of coming to know.

Safe homes and disappearing acts

What might it mean to take subjectivity seriously in education? Or to put it in more formal, analytical terms: What is involved in paying as much attention to S as to p in locutions of the form 'S knows that p'? Who is S in an educational situation? Teachers or learners or those about whom they learn? Individuals or epistemic communities?

I approach these questions via a brief critical discussion of two sets of feminist challenges to mainstream education, each of which echoes aspects of feminist challenges to mainstream epistemology. One – apparently gentle and humane – falls under the rubric of caring and seems to some of its critics to control through cosy domestication; the other – a pedagogy assertive in intent and motivation – is designed to disappear at the moment of its own performance. Both caring theory and performative pedagogy take subjectivity seriously in ways that may undermine the enabling conditions for education; nonetheless each is rich in insights into educational practice and its dilemmas.

Caring theorists (see, e.g. Martin, 1981, 1992; Gilligan, 1982; Noddings, 1984, 1992) challenge liberal education on at least four counts. For a start they argue that the declared universalism of liberal education is not universal at all since its singular ideal of an educated person assumes the person to be male. In emphasizing the 'masculine virtues' of rationality and the disinterested pursuit of knowledge, the liberal ideal is seen to cast women either as uneducated and feminine or as educated but failed women. Second, caring theorists argue that reason- and justice-based frameworks for education ignore the fact that reason and justice require caring, at least as their complement if not as their ground. Third, they reject both instrumental and generalized conceptions of care: caring and other 'private sphere' values are not limited to performing a service on behalf of justice and other 'public sphere' values; nor can pupils' needs be determined outside a personal relationship where the teacher attends to the particularities of each pupil. Like knowing, caring is situated and it is a primary not a parasitic virtue. In education, caring is no pedagogical sweetener but the very ground of curriculum meaning and value. This brings us to a fourth challenge. Caring theorists reject both disciplinary-based and content-saturated curricula. Instead, curriculum should have its basis in what Jane Roland Martin (1992) has called the three Cs of care, concern and connection, and not in bodies and bits of knowledge.

In several respects these challenges to liberal education match the feminist challenges to mainstream epistemology I listed earlier in the chapter. To wit: there is no disinterested view from nowhere from which teachers can properly see what their pupils need in order to flourish; a pupil's identity is a crucial consideration in founding and sustaining a pedagogical relationship; care and love are central to the content as well as the processes of teaching and learning. Caring theorists take subjectivity seriously by requiring teachers to respect and nurture what is special in each pupil and to nurture in pupils an attitude of respect and care for others.

Even so, from the vantage of feminist epistemology, caring theorists turn a blind eye to crucial aspects of subjectivity by failing to place themselves and their ideas in the critical field. They ignore their own and pupils' subjectivity by neglecting to ask what trust and caring mean when teachers and their pupils belong to different ethnic groups or social classes; when, to quote Audrey Thompson's example, 'the teacher is Anglo and the students are Ute, or the teacher is middle-class and the students from poor families' (Thompson, 1997: 338). Caring theory thus fails the test of strong objectivity in so far as it takes the meaning of caring for granted.

Also, although caring theorists criticize liberal education for its rationalism, their arguments for a homelike school seem to rest on the notion of a school as an idealized home, a 'rationalised, purified environment' where teachers become surrogate mothers (Thompson, 1997: 337). Here, too, caring theorists may stand accused of failing the test of strong objectivity because they seem to ignore the role that one version of a caring ethic has played in sustaining a social order inimical to women's empowerment. In short, despite their professed feminism, caring theorists take subjectivity seriously in ways that put the feminist project at risk.

What of the educational project more broadly conceived? Does caring theory promote or impede education? By singling out individuals for attention, perhaps it pays too little heed to the importance of sustaining and invigorating epistemic communities, their practices and their bodies of knowledge. Education, in my view, is centrally a matter of getting people to care about practices that might otherwise have meant nothing to them, a matter of getting them to care about evidence and justification as well as about other people. It is partly a matter of socializing them into traditions and practices so that they might, in time, use the language of those practices to criticize, advance and perhaps overturn them; as well as a matter of habituating character through critical and disciplined practice for the purpose of nurturing practical reasoning.[2] But I am casting ahead. I shall pick up and offer some defence for this position in the final section of the chapter.

Feminists who advocate performative pedagogy reject traditional teaching as well as the standard views of reflective teaching and critical pedagogy on the grounds that all presuppose the possibility of one self coming to know and understand other selves (see, e.g. Phelan, 1993; Orner *et al.*, 1996).[3] In their view, such 'inter-subjective' understanding between teacher and learners can be accomplished, if at all, only at the cost of reducing the historical and embodied richness of self to one who is present in the classroom in the form of a rational argument. Here the teacher maintains superficial order by banishing all other aspects of self to a private world, outside the classroom. Feminist teachers who reject the discourse of reason face the challenge of giving full play to learners' expressive selves and yet exerting sufficient authority to meet feminism's normative ideals, ideals that require the teacher to alter the learners' perceptions and concerns.

How is it possible for a teacher to change her pupils' perceptions without either imposing her own views or silencing theirs and without exacting a class of pared-down selves? Through enactment not teaching, through performance not argument, say the advocates of performative pedagogy. Performative pedagogy honours the 'situatedness' and 'contingency' of learners' responses by opening ways for their personal meanings to emerge in a series of exquisite pedagogical moments that leave no visible trace and can neither be planned nor repeated. Hence the description: a pedagogy for disappearance (Phelan, 1993). It aims to elicit personal responses not coherent understanding, multiple readings not singular arguments or teacher-led dialogue. As one line of feminist attack on the discourse of reason, it opens the closet of the 'private' and allows outlaw emotions out. ('Pandoras all', a nervous rationalist might brand these feminists of performative bent. Be that as it may, the principle of multiple readings also allows for a Pandora whose remaining hope is not to recall the pestilential emotions and trap them once more beneath the lid of authority but rather that they might go into the world and shake up reason's tyranny.)

Performative pedagogy calls on the teacher to see her own slippery position, to be aware and wary of her own authorial and authoritative positioning. It takes subjectivity seriously through a radical turn to specificity, an ever-shifting play of relationships, perspectives and voices where, if anyone has authority, it is the learner – and then only at the moment of expression. Learner-centredness here rests on an apparent presumption in favour of the view from below – apparent because it involves something of a pretence by the teacher and because there is no singular view from below, but many.

Taking subjectivity seriously in this way thwarts the very project it intends to quicken and undermines the constitutive goods of teaching. How so?

For a start, without normative benchmarks, anything goes. By treating all voices and views as equally valid, Carmen Luke (herself a feminist) argues, the feminist teacher risks a dangerous sameness: 'Views and voices from everywhere and every body potentially are views and voices from nowhere and no body' (Luke, 1996: 291). If anything goes, then changing learners' perceptions becomes a matter of chance and if the teacher has a role at all, it is to play stagehand to happenstance. Here teaching would seem to be thoroughly luck-dependent, leaving the teacher without resources to establish the enabling conditions for fulfilling the definitive ends of her practice (cf. Pendlebury, 1995).

Authority of some sort is among the enabling conditions for teaching to accomplish its ends and sustain its goods. This is a formal point and in no way presupposes agreement on the substantive goods of teaching. In her critique of performative pedagogy, Yael Shalem (1997) argues for the importance of what she calls pedagogical authority. Roughly, the argument runs as follows. Every teacher worth her salt conducts some kind of epistemological labour to bring learners into a working relationship with the traditions and practices that inform the curriculum. Save by luck, performative pedagogy can accomplish neither its feminist nor its educative ends without the teacher selecting and sequencing texts and other artefacts to be presented for students' responses. Like it or not, this epistemological labour puts the teacher in a position of pedagogical authority in relation to the learner. For it is the teacher who selects the pedagogical entry point into a tradition and who casts ahead, listening attentively for points of resolution to signify the end of a pedagogical episode.

Of course, a teacher can't plan or replicate an exquisite pedagogical moment any more than she can make the moon rise over the sea on a cloudless night. Yet it is these moments that teachers long for and cherish. Neither longing nor planning can ensure them. Preparation of the right kind may invite them. In order to thrive, teaching surely needs attentive planning as well as situational attunement; discipline as well as imagination and insight; serendipitous and intimate moments as well as controlled activities and respect for privacy; responsive teachers as well as responsive learners. Caring theory and performative pedagogy remind us, in rather different ways, of some of these requirements and the impediments to meeting them. They remind us of the role of the expressive self in learning, of the many contradictions of classrooms as contexts for education, of the difficulties of teaching across difference, of the fact that human flourishing requires much more than a bloodless pursuit of knowledge for its own sake. But it would be a bad mistake, I think, to remember these things at the cost of forgetting the crucial place of reason, evidence and disciplined inquiry in education.

Human flourishing and habitable epistemic communities

At the start of the previous section I asked what it might mean to take subjectivity seriously in education. Or, to put the question in formal and rather restrictive terms: what is involved in paying as much attention to S as to p in locutions of the form 'S knows that p'? An answer depends partly on who is taken as S – the teacher, the pupils, or the subjects of study (Emily Dickinson, the colonizers of Africa, the author of this or that historical text). Caring theory and performative pedagogy are examples of feminist approaches that attend to the subjectivity of learners and teachers in ways which, I have argued, thwart the feminist project and underplay or threaten the enabling conditions for education and teaching.

So: can we heed the feminist call to take subjectivity seriously without compromising education? And are there ways of taking subjectivity seriously in ways that support with the constitutive ends of teaching? I want to say a resounding 'Yes' to both questions and to add that not taking subjectivity seriously in the right ways may be as thwarting to education as is taking it seriously in the wrong ways.

My defence of these claims rests on an assumption that education is centrally – although not solely – concerned with opening ways for people to become members of one or more epistemic communities. I take this concern to be a constitutive end of education and of educative teaching. I draw my conception of an epistemic community from two sources: some recent work in feminist epistemology (e.g. Nelson, 1993; Walker, 1996) and Alasdair MacIntyre's notion of a practice (MacIntyre, 1984). No doubt some readers will find the two sources somewhat incongruous. So be it. What I offer here is a provisional sketch of a promising idea, not a definitive or detailed account of a fixed or pure position.

An epistemic community is a group that shares and maintains resources for acquiring and developing knowledge. Resources include procedures for qualifying and disqualifying evidence, a language of description, other conceptual tools and a critical mass of practitioners who have the virtues (or habits of character and mind) necessary for sustaining the community and its definitive practices. All would-be knowers are situated in epistemic communities. What we know depends inextricably on the shared knowledge, concepts, standards and practices of the various epistemic communities to which we belong. Active and fully-fledged members of an epistemic community will reconstruct their prior understandings on the basis of current standards and evidence, revising if need be their views about who knows what and how. Other members stagnate, holding on to the comforts of long cherished beliefs despite new and compelling evidence to the contrary. Still others are newcomers who may gradually come to know the ways of the community or who may hover at its periphery, feeling anxious or alien.

A central concern of education, I have suggested, is to provide access for membership in a range of epistemic communities, to give people a taste for typical practices and to help them acquire some of the disciplined ways of doing things within those communities. In so doing, education also helps to constitute selves. This is not to say that we are nothing without education. People are already always members of some or other epistemic community. Taking subjectivity seriously in educational practice is partly a matter of taking account of current memberships and how these might enable or constrain access to other epistemic communities. This is why it is fitting to ask 'Who claims to know? And under what conditions and in what company does she so claim?'. Quite simply, in a teaching situation, how one assesses a knowledge claim (or its functional equivalent) depends very much on how old the claimant is, what concepts she has, what counts as everyday knowledge for her – and, of course, the kinds of reasons she offers for her claim. For example, a child who can use Dienes blocks to show how she solved a mathematical problem also shows that she has a sense of how to justify her claims mathematically, even though she does not yet have (and may never have) the kind of language and theoretically rich arguments that mark a fully-fledged mathematician. Notice that this way of taking a learner's subjectivity seriously is not a matter of 'anything goes'.

There is an additional way in which subjectivity is pertinent to educational practice. Feminist epistemologists have argued that strong objectivity requires us to take subjectivity seriously. This suggests a teaching desideratum: when a teacher introduces pupils to a novel, an historical text, the causes and effects of volcanoes or the relationship of form and function in organisms, part of her task is to help them to see what part other people have played in generating these artefacts and facts. So we return to the importance of evidence and justification and debates about them. We also return to the idea of an epistemic community, of a group of practitioners who have special ways of going about their business but who nonetheless are vulnerable to challenge and criticism. Alasdair MacIntyre (1984) makes a similar point, I think, in his claim that to enter a practice is to enter into a relationship with its practitioners, present and past, especially those who have extended the reach of the practice through their achievements.

The idea that all would-be knowers are situated in epistemic communities whose standards, concepts, goods and practices both constrain and enable the knowledge and experiences of their members assumes that, in some sense, knowledge and our experience of the world are socially constructed. Nothing in the assumption commits us to the view that there are no facts of the matter. Nor does the claim that there are many overlapping epistemic communities mean that all have equal footing. Epistemic communities that are worth sustaining through education should be both reliable and habitable. I take these as normative criteria. If the collective wisdom and standard procedures of an epistemic community lead us to act in ways that are self-defeating through illusion, ignorance, false beliefs or sheer pig-headedness about what is possible and what is not, they are not worth sustaining. Although the term 'epistemic community' may not have featured in the work of Paul Hirst and his colleagues and intellectual heirs, I think they did much to explore and analyse the features of reliable epistemic communities and the educational conditions for sustaining them. Feminist writers – in education, epistemology and ethics – remind us, in a myriad of ways, that the quality of our lives is affected by the kinds of epistemic and moral communities of which we are members.

Notes

1 The distinction between constitutive and contextual ends is similar to Alasdair MacIntyre's distinction between the internal and external goods of a practice (MacIntyre, 1984).
2 I am assuming a rich conception of practical reasoning, of the sort described in many of Martha Nussbaum's essays (e.g. Nussbaum, 1990).
3 My discussion of performative pedagogy owes much to the work of my colleague Yael Shalem.

References

Barwell, I. (1994) 'Towards a defence of objectivity', in Kathleen Lennon and Margaret Whitford (eds), *Knowing the Difference: Feminist perspectives in epistemology*, London and New York: Routledge: 79–94.

Code, L. (1996) 'Taking subjectivity into account', in Ann Garry and Marilyn Pearsall (eds), *Women, Knowledge and Reality: Explorations in feminist philosophy*, London: Routledge: 191–221.

Dearden, R.F., Hirst, P.H. and Peters, R.S. (eds) (1971) *Education and the Development of Reason*, London: Routledge and Kegan Paul.

Fricker, M. (1994) 'Knowledge as construct: Theorising the role of gender in knowledge', in Kathleen Lennon and Margaret Whitford (eds), *Knowing the Difference: Feminist perspectives in epistemology*, London and New York: Routledge: 95–109.

Gilligan, C. (1982) *In a Different Voice: Psychological theory and women's development*, Cambridge, MA: Harvard University Press.

Haraway, D. (1990) 'A manifesto for cyborgs: Science, technology and socialist feminism in the 1980s', in Linda Nicholson (ed.), *Feminism/Postmodernism*, New York and London: Routledge: 190–233.

Harding, S. (1986) *The Science Question in Feminism*, Milton Keynes: Open University Press.

—— (1991) *Whose Science? Whose Knowledge? Thinking from Women's Lives*, Milton Keynes: Open University Press.

Haslanger, S. (1996) 'Objective reality, male reality, and social construction', in A. Garry and M. Pearsall (eds), *Women, Knowledge and Reality: Explorations in feminist philosophy*, London: Routledge: 84–107.

Jaggar, A. (1996) 'Love and knowledge: Emotion in feminist epistemology', in Ann Garry and Marilyn Pearsall (eds), *Women, Knowledge and Reality: Explorations in feminist philosophy*, London: Routledge: 166–190.

Longino, H. (1990) *Science as Social Knowledge: Values and objectivity in scientific inquiry*, Princeton, NJ: Princeton University Press.

Luke, C. (1996) 'Feminist pedagogy theory: Reflections on power and authority', *Educational Theory* 46(3).

MacIntyre, A. (1984) *After Virtue*, London: Duckworth.

Martin, J.R. (1981) 'The ideal of the educated person', *Educational Theory* 31(2): 97–109.

—— (1992) *The Schoolhome: Rethinking schools for changing families*, Cambridge, MA: Harvard University Press.

Nelson, L.H. (1996) 'Epistemological communities', in Linda Alcoff and Elizabeth Potter (eds), *Feminist Epistemologies*, New York: Routledge.

Noddings, N. (1984) *Caring: A feminine approach to ethics and moral education*, Berkeley, CA: University of California Press.

—— (1992) *The Challenge to Care in Schools: An alternative approach to education*, New York: Teachers College Press.

Nussbaum, M. (1990) *Love's Knowledge: Essays on philosophy and literature*, Oxford: Oxford University Press.

Orner, M., Miller, J. and Ellsworth, E. (1996) 'Excessive moments and educational discoures that try to contain them', *Educational Theory* 45(4): 71–91.

Pendlebury, S. (1995) 'Luck, responsibility and excellence in teaching', in James W. Garrison and Anthony G. Rud (eds), *Gaps in the Educational Conversation*, Albany, NY: SUNY Press.

Phelan, P. (1993) *Unmarked: The politics of performance*, London: Routledge.

Rose, H. (1994) *Love, Power, Knowledge: Towards a feminist transformation of the sciences*, Cambridge: Polity Press.

Thompson, A. (1997) 'Surrogate family values: The refeminization of teaching', *Educational Theory* 47(3): 315–339.

Walker, M.U. (1996) 'Feminist skepticism, authority and transparency', in Walter Sinott-Armstrong and Mark Timmins (eds), *Moral Knowledge? New readings in moral epistemology*, Oxford: Oxford University Press: 267–292.

PART II

THE AIMS OF EDUCATION

CHAPTER 4

AUTONOMY AS AN EDUCATIONAL AIM

Christopher Winch

In Roger Marples (ed.) *The Aims of Education (1999)*,
London: Routledge, pp. 74–84

A major theme in the liberal project of the definition and justification of education has been the selection of autonomy or rational autonomy as an aim.[1] The purpose of this chapter is to argue: first, that although there are no a priori grounds for making autonomy a non-trivial educational aim for all societies, there are good grounds for thinking that some form of autonomy has to be an aim of public education in democratic societies; second, that if it *is* accepted as a non-trivial educational aim, then it is quite compatible with a wide variety of different forms of educational practices and curricula; and third, that there are, contrary to the views of many liberal thinkers, grave problems about adopting strong autonomy as an educational aim. In effect, the liberal educational project as it has tradition-ally been conceived of exclusively as a form of academic education cannot be sustained if autonomy conceived of in a broad sense is a primary educational aim. I will also argue for a minimal sense of autonomy, which is usually ignored by the advocates of autonomy as an educational aim. By a minimal sense of autonomy is meant the degree of independence necessary to fulfil any other aims of education, whatever they may be.

There can, however, be little quarrel with autonomy as a minimal aim of education. If education in any society is, broadly speaking, about the preparation of children for adult life, and adults need to be more independent than children, then it is unavoidable that autonomy in this minimal sense is an aim of any educa-tional process, since children need to be prepared for independent life as adults and education is, in a developed society, one of the main routes, if not the only one, for achieving it. Perhaps 'minimal' is the wrong word here in any case, since it is no trivial matter to be able to make a living, raise a family and play some role in the running of the affairs of a community. Indeed, any education that failed to prepare children for these things would, on the broad definition above, have failed, since it would not, in any meaningful sense, have prepared someone for adult life.

But many of the supporters of autonomy as an educational aim would not regard the 'minimal' definition of autonomy as educationally important. The achievement of autonomy is, for them, a much more significant matter than the ability to function as a member of society. It could include the achievement of rationality or the ability to formulate and carry out a life plan.[2] Some writers in the liberal analytical tradition of the philosophy of education would question whether independence or minimal autonomy is an *educational* aim at all. They would prefer to say that it is a worthy aim but a worthy aim of *schooling* rather than of education.[3]

How can one justify the division of activities that prepare people for adult life into various subconcepts that include *education* and *schooling*? Granted that there are some activities, such as buying a house in which to raise a family, which are not educational in any remote sense, but which are a preparation for adult life, it is not clear that one can separate vocational preparation, religious instruction or safety training from another set of activities called 'education'. It is not clear – that is, unless one accepts a certain definition of education which excludes those activities from its scope. But there is no good reason for doing this unless we are already persuaded that the proposed definition of education is the one to be accepted. But this is what is at issue.

One final point: the context of this discussion is the modern, pluralist democratic type of polity rather than traditional, authoritarian or totalitarian systems. It is taken for granted, therefore, that citizens in such a society are entitled to question at least some of the values on which the society is based. Educating someone in such a society in such a way that they have a basic understanding of how it works, therefore, involves getting them to understand that *some* at least of the values on which the society is based are open to questioning. This much is implied by the 'minimal' conception of autonomy in such societies, since it is a necessary part of citizenship in a democratic society that one understands this. This is not, however, true of all societies and even in some democratic societies there are more limits on what can be legitimately questioned than there are in others.

Autonomy and the complexity of society

A complex society requires a division of labour as well as a set of common knowledge, assumptions and practices. Not everyone can do everything and everyone can only do a limited number of things really well. Because of these constraints, public education systems have to find a way of ensuring that common knowledge, assumptions and practices, as well as a huge variety of specialised occupations, are present in society. This seems to imply that schooling has to make children literate, numerate, reasonably knowledgeable about a core of basic geographical, historical, political and scientific facts and has to give them the wherewithal for some degree of functional specialisation in employment.[4] The parts of society are, therefore, unavoidably *interdependent*. Whatever independence people develop is to be exercised within the framework of a common interdependence if society is not to fragment into a mass of individuals, each of whom can only pursue their individual aims through constant friction with others who may be pursuing contrary goals. These reflections suggest three things. First, that people have to be independent to a certain degree in order to function in a society that expects individuals to work, raise families and take part in the democratic process. Second, since independent action involves association with others, there needs to be a common core of rules, concepts, assumptions and propositions that allow such association to take place without too much misunderstanding. Third, since a complex society requires a division of labour, the preparation that each individual has for adult life cannot be identical. These are the constraints that surround any attempt to specify autonomy as an educational aim in a complex society.

So what do they imply for the specification of autonomy as an educational aim? It seems, as we have already noted, that some degree of autonomy is implied by reflecting on the nature of education in any society, and this degree of autonomy not only requires, but implies, a degree of dependence on others.[5] Furthermore, in a modern democratic society, *some* degree of autonomy about ends as well as means seems to be implied by the foregoing discussion. Beyond this, it is difficult to see how autonomy could be the *exclusive* educational aim. The reason for this has already emerged: any complex society has a number of goals and requires some degree of division of labour in order to function. At the very least, education has to prefigure that division in its own aims, making children aware of the requirements of employment, family life and citizenship, for example, even if it does not, within the schools, actually *prepare* them for these roles.[6] Education has a number of aims, none of which entails more than independence. That, at least, is our provisional conclusion.

Education, autonomy and politics

So how is it possible to specify autonomy as a legitimate and realisable educational aim? And, if it is, what sense of autonomy is meant? In order to answer these questions, it is first necessary to look at the way in which educational aims ought to be determined, for it is only by looking at this process that it will become possible to distinguish between legitimate and illegitimate ways of specifying them. It has been a commonplace since the time of Aristotle that political societies embody various interests which are often in conflict and need to be accommodated.[7] Instead of warfare, pressure, persuasion and compromise are the ways in which different interests seek to pursue their ends within a framework that is not mutually destructive of the interests of all.

There is, however, a problem. All these interests will have ethical commitments, and there is something conceptually incoherent about the supposition that these could be the subject of compromise. Insofar as moral values partly constitute a person's identity and core of their personality, they are not something that can be negotiated away. Were they to be so, this would be a *prima facie* reason for taking them to be something else, like judgements of fashion rather than of moral value. But if this is so, then how could it be possible to accommodate different interests that involved different and mutually incompatible values? The problem is a particularly pressing one for the issues under consideration, since the aims of education are precisely the sorts of things that could reasonably be supposed to embody moral values. If some forms of autonomy are incompatible with some forms of interdependence or dependence, then how can all these be legitimate educational aims without provoking conflict?

The answer lies in accepting the integrity of personal values but coming to some arrangement concerning their implementation in the public sphere. In this way, citizens are not expected to compromise their values (which is an incoherent idea), but to negotiate about the nature and extent of their *implementation*. The public values that a society adheres to ought, to a large extent, to reflect this process of negotiation and compromise.

Public education will have, among its aims, the promotion of those values or at least the promotion of values consistent with them. It is natural to think of a compromise about values resulting in the adoption of a plurality of desirable or at least acceptable values, and that public education would tend towards the promotion or at least the informing of young people about them. A democratic society committed to the promotion, or at least tolerance, of a variety of values would normally allow its public system of education to give future citizens choice over which values to adopt and which ways of life expressive of those values to follow.

For example, a society would probably wish to promote the value of mutual cooperation and would thus educate future citizens to become socially useful and productive members of their communities.[8] But there are many different ways of doing this: through paid employment, through voluntary work, through the pursuit of domestic life and so on. Even within these categories there are many choices to be made (e.g. between different forms of employment), and within a lifetime choices may be made about whether to work in paid employment or to leave work to bring up a family or to retire and engage in voluntary work. It is thus evident that, within the set of values promoted or tolerated, there are numerous and difficult choices that each individual has to make in order to promote both personal and social well-being, and education would, at the very least, provide some of the tools to make these choices.

However, *independence* in the sense outlined above could not be sufficient for the fulfilment of aims which involve the kinds of choices required. Someone could be independent in this sense and yet live a life of complete heteronomy, having all the major decisions in life taken by someone else. It is probably more accurate to say that independence is a necessary or near necessary condition for living a life which involves successfully making the kinds of choices alluded to above. So education in a democratic society seems to entail that something stronger than independence ought to be a primary educational aim, and a natural candidate for such an aim is that individuals should be properly equipped to make those choices that allow them to be both happy and productive members of society. They should, in one relatively uncontroversial sense of the term, become autonomous.

So far, the argument has established that a public education system has good reason to promote a variety of different goals in life which its citizens can autonomously choose from. This conception of autonomy is sometimes known as 'weak autonomy' and is contrasted with 'strong autonomy'.[9] It is worth noting that weak autonomy is a form of autonomy about ends; it does not *prescribe* ends or only allow choice regarding the means to achieve those ends: it invites citizens to choose from a variety of approved and tolerated ends. It incorporates minimal autonomy, and thus entails that someone who is weakly autonomous nevertheless understands that *some* at least of the values on which their society is based are properly open to questioning and that they have some responsibility for choosing which values to adopt. The conclusion we have now reached is a stronger one than that reached at the end of the previous section.

But this is not sufficient for the proponent of *strong autonomy* who tends to be sceptical about the idea of an imposed common good that lies behind the set of values that a public education committed to weak autonomy supports. It will be my argument that not only does weak autonomy not commit itself to any developed notion of a common good, but is the most liberal conception of autonomy that is consistent with the idea that education is, in some sense, about promoting both social and human flourishing.

Strong autonomy as an educational aim

What do advocates of strong autonomy suggest? We have seen that they, like weak autonomists, support the idea that citizens should be able to choose their own route through life. Unlike weak autonomists, however, they would prefer not to prescribe a set of ends from which the citizen would be entitled to choose. The weak autonomist is not committed to the idea that society itself should not be strongly autonomous; that is, that it cannot choose and promote those ends which it determines – indeed, the stance of weak autonomy as it has been outlined here suggests that the values that a society wishes to promote and tolerate are a matter of negotiation among citizens. The citizens, though, are constrained by the *outcome* of that process of negotiation. Neither are weak autonomists concerning education necessarily committed to the view that individuals should not be strongly autonomous; they can, in consistency, say that an individual should be free to choose to live a life that meets with the disapproval of most of society. Indeed, weak autonomists might even concede that a child might be *educated* to be strongly autonomous in some circumstances (see the next section). What they cannot concede is that a *public education system* should have strong autonomy as one of its aims.

Most strong autonomists would argue that strong autonomy is a legitimate aim for a public education system. The argument could go along the following lines. In a democracy, it is no part of society's remit to tell people what kind of life they should adopt. Citizens have rights which cannot be violated; among the most important of these is that of choosing what kind of life they should lead. These rights impose a duty on society to respect them, and it follows that public educa-tion, as an agent of society, should also respect those rights. This seems to entail that a public education system should at least not *proscribe* strong autonomy as an educational aim. However, if one of the major aims of education is to allow young people to make informed choices, then schools can hardly avoid pointing out that there is a wider range of choices available than those approved of by society. If it is one of the aims of public education to allow citizens to make informed choices, then it is a *duty* of the system to ensure that future citizens be given the where-withal to do so. Since the ability to make informed choices in the widest possible sense is the ability to choose ends unchosen by society itself, then it is tantamount to strong autonomy. Acceptance of citizen's rights appears, therefore, to entail that a public education system has the *duty* to adopt strong autonomy as an aim.

The flaw in this argument results from a misinterpretation of the premiss that individuals have inviolable rights to choose what kind of life they should lead. This principle must be subject to some limitation if it is not to lapse into incoherence. Since individual rights have implications for the rights of others, they impose duties on those others. In particular, the duty of A not to violate the rights of B is entailed. Therefore individuals can only have rights which do not themselves violate the rights of others. Not even a strong autonomist can, therefore, take the view that *any* social value is subject to question. It would not be open to a strong autonomist to say that *as a matter of right* it is allowable for someone to choose aims that involve constraining the rights of others, because, unless one distin-guishes between the degree of rights of different citizens, the proposal would render the claim to such rights incoherent. *A fortiori*, it would not be allowable for a public education system to pursue such aims since they would compromise the weak autonomy of some citizens.

Furthermore, *public* education systems are funded by citizens for the purpose of realising certain aims that have been mutually agreed. Typically, in a democratic society, this will include a range of aims to do with culture, citizenship and occupa-tion, together with the aim that citizens should be weakly autonomous. Funding is usually given on the basis of an understanding that it be put to use in carrying out the purpose for which it was initially allocated, in this case to pursue a variety of educational aims, which include, as one of them, the recognition that some values at least, are susceptible to doubt and criticism. It could not be the case that such a system allowed *all* values to be subject to doubt and criticism for two reasons.

The first has just been alluded to; were the proposition that people's rights are not to be violated to be questioned, then weak and even minimal autonomy would come under threat. The second is that an aim would be promoted which had not been sanctioned as a result of the process of negotiation alluded to earlier, since an outcome of any negotiation of that sort would be that a finite set of aims would be promoted which would in turn lead to the promotion and toleration of a finite set of values, rather than a questioning of all of them. Third, the proposing of strong autonomy would suggest that the system by which a consensus about aims is arrived at would no longer be stable, thus undermining the basis on which strong autonomy as an aim could legitimately emerge. When held as a political aim, strong autonomy in its strongest form, which suggests that all socially held values are no more than non-mandatory options, is a position that contains the seeds of its own incoherence.

Autonomy in a stronger sense than independence emerges as a necessary condition of choosing among societal ends (independence does not entail this condition – one could independently pursue someone else's chosen end). But the aim of independence entails a richer and more diverse set of aims than does weak autonomy by itself. If independence is to be achievable, the aims of education must include some form of preparation for work, for family life and for citizenship. Weak autonomy would allow one to choose the right mix of these aims for different phases of life.[10]

Strong autonomy and the aims of independent education

Strong autonomy is, quite possibly, a legitimate aim for an individual in a democratic society. Many such societies tolerate views which are inimical to the values and assumptions on which the society is itself based, even if they do not actively promote them. Provided that the holding of such views is compatible with non-violation of the rights of fellow citizens, then it may be tolerated. However, where strong autonomy entails that the *pursuit of certain chosen ends* violated the rights of other citizens, then there are grounds for legally curtailing it. This is not an exclusive feature of strong autonomy; any action, even if it results from the activity of a weakly autonomous or merely independent person, is subject to the same constraint. But we have seen that it is logically incoherent to suppose that a public education system could promote strong autonomy because to do so would undermine the assumptions and procedures on which that system is based.

On the face of it, this constraint does not apply to non-publicly funded education; if a group of parents were to decide to finance an education for their children that promoted strong autonomy, then those who were educating their children would, on the accountability criterion mentioned earlier, be *obliged* to pursue that aim. Furthermore, the only negotiation about aims that would need to take place would be among those who were providing the resources for the education in the first place and, if these could agree on strong autonomy as an educational aim, that would seem to be the end of the matter.

But this brings us to another aspect of accountability that has not so far been touched upon. So far the discussion has proceeded as if it were purely a matter of finance. But our interests in our fellow citizens extend beyond our concern as to how they spend our money; their behaviour in other respects affects our well-being. If others in our society fail to flourish or flourish in an inappropriate way, then this has repercussions for us. The interests of others affect us more directly as well, through the allocation of positional goods; if there is a desirable position in society which can be filled by only a limited number of people, then whoever fills it other than oneself affects one's own ability to fill it.

Traditionally, parents have educated their children independently for one of four principal reasons. First, to enable them better to acquire coveted positional goods such as jobs and status (the British public schools exist largely to fulfil this purpose); second, to provide a secure *grounding* which, they fear, cannot be provided by what they see as a decadent public education system; third, to promote *heteronomy* of ends (schools dedicated to various forms of confessionally based religion are an example; independent Catholic schools in France exist largely because of the secular nature of French public education). Fourth, they exist to promote various forms of strong autonomy (like the 'progressive' independent schools found in Britain, such as Summerhill or Dartington Hall).

For the reason mentioned above, no society could be indifferent to the existence and nature of an independent education sector, but the question arises as to whether or not it would wish to regulate or even restrict its operation. There is no one answer to this question; one major issue is that of parental rights – to what extent should parents be the interpreters of their children's long-term interests? Should they be allowed to educate them in such a way, for example, as to promote strong heteronomy? Alternatively, should they be allowed to promote very strong autonomy when it is felt that strongly autonomous individuals might undermine social cohesion? In a democratic society, any decision to restrict parental rights has to be made as part of a balance of judgement as to the damage to civil society and to democratic values of such a decision. Even within a Lockean framework of thinking about children's rights, there is much scope for differences of opinion on these matters.[11]

What does seem clear, however, is that if we grant that parents cannot be strongly autonomous in relation to the upbringing of their children, then there may come a point when society may wish to place limits on the education that they provide, or enter into some form of negotiation with such parents as to what aims they might choose that would be compatible with the aspirations of the rest of society.[12] The point applies as well, of course, to parents who choose to educate their children in such a way as to promote strong heteronomy, although in many cases there will be considerations of religious freedom which will need to be taken carefully into account in any such process of negotiation. If, though, it is accepted that people as citizens in a democracy have further interests in the well-being of their fellows than purely financial ones, then, however they educate their offspring, that will have an impact both on the society and on the individuals within that society. If politics is about the negotiation and accommodation of differing and sometimes conflicting interests, then the aims of independent education are a matter of legitimate political interest, no matter that it be funded independently of the rest of society.

Conclusion

We started with the notion of accountability in public education systems as a financial consideration; is the money spent on education being spent in accord with the negotiated aspirations of social partners? This led us to the view that, although independence and autonomy in relation to a range of ends is likely to be an aspiration for the education of children in democratic societies, a form of autonomy that encouraged people actively to question or undermine the institutions which allow such negotiation of the spending of public money would not be tolerated unless the society was already sceptical about the value of its democratic institutions. A healthy and self-confident democratic society would, then, quite properly be unwilling to prescribe strong autonomy as an educational aim.

There is more, however, to accountability than finance. If we all have interests in society, then the behaviour of others, including the way in which they educate their children, is going to affect those interests. If some, at least, of our rights are grounded on our interests, then we have rights to enter some form of negotiation with parents who wish to educate their children independently, as to what aims they may choose for their children's education.[13] Their freedom to choose strong autonomy as an educational aim will thus be a matter for negotiation. What the fine detail of the outcome of any such negotiation should be is a matter for different societies and is beyond the scope of this chapter. That there should be such negotiation is what I have been seeking to establish.

Similar considerations of non-financial accountability apply in the public sector of education; the negotiation of aims must take into account the ramifications of the pursuit of certain aims on different interests. But to say that is to say no more than that the negotiation of aims for public education is more than just a matter of whether or not such aims can be afforded; it is a question of how to balance the interests of different groups and individuals in order to bring about outcomes that are satisfactory to all.

Notes

1 See, for example, J.P. White, *The Aims of Education Restated*, London: Routledge, 1982; *Education and the Good Life*, London: Routledge, 1990; R.F. Dearden, *Means and Ends in Education*, London: Routledge, 1984.

2 R.S. Peters, *Ethics and Education*, London: Allen & Unwin, 1966; P.H. Hirst, *Knowledge and the Curriculum*, London: Routledge, 1974; J.P. White, *The Aims of Education Restated*, London: Routledge, 1982.

3 Cf. R. Barrow, *Common Sense and the Curriculum*, Harvester Wheatsheaf, 1981; see pp. 26ff.

4 It is not sufficiently realised that this is an *epistemic* rather than a political constraint. Since the learning of some facts and skills presupposes mutual understanding, those facts and skills that are necessary to mutual understanding need to be learned first. Cf. E.D. Hirsch, Jr, 'The primal scene of education', *New York Review of Books* XXXVI(3): 29–34.

5 The idea that autonomy and heteronomy are incompatible opposites seems to be a consequence of Kantian theorising about ethics, with its deterministic view of the phenomenal world. Rejection of this rigid framework allows us to get a clearer view of the relationship between autonomy and heteronomy. See I. Kant, *Groundwork of the Metaphysic of Morals*, available in H.J. Paton, *The Moral Law*, London: Hutchinson, 1948.

6 For a sensitive discussion of this issue, see H. Entwistle, *Education, Work and Leisure*, London: Routledge, 1970.

7 Cf. Aristotle, *The Politics*, especially Books III and IV, edited by Stephen Everson, Cambridge: Cambridge University Press, 1988.

8 Note that this does not entail any particular view about the nature of the common good, but expresses a minimal condition for a self-sustaining form of mutual association and interdependency.

9 Cf. J.P. White, *Education and the Good Life*, London: Routledge, 1990, p. 102; R. Norman, ' "I Did it My Way": some thoughts on autonomy', *Journal of Philosophy of Education* 28(1) (1994): 25–34.

10 In this sense it would allow young people to form a life plan, which is one of the requirements of autonomy drawn attention to by J.P. White, *Education and the Good Life*, London: Routledge, 1982.

11 J. Locke, *Second Treatise of Government*, London: Dent, 1924 (first published, 1690). See chapter VI.
12 There is nothing unusual in the idea that the independent sector should be regulated; the issue here is whether or not the aims of independent education should be subject to some form of regulation.
13 For a discussion of interest-based accounts of rights, see D.N. McCormick, *Rights in Legislation*, available in P.M.S. Hacker and J. Raz (eds), *Law, Morality and Society*, Oxford: Oxford University Press, 1977.

References

The references are to: John Stuart Mill, *On Liberty*, chapter 2; Immanuel Kant, *Critique of Judgement*, First part, Second book; David Hume, *Enquiry Concerning Human Understanding*, section 10; René Descartes, *Rules for the Direction of the Mind*, Rule 3; and for Socrates on the examined life, Plato, *Apology* 38A. The image of the cave appears in Plato, *The Republic*, Book 7.

CHAPTER 5

SELF-DETERMINATION AS AN EDUCATIONAL AIM

James C. Walker

In Roger Marples (ed.) *The Aims of Education (1999)*, London: Routledge, pp. 112–123

Implicit in every educational decision is a fundamental choice. Are students, of whatever age, to be enabled to become more self-determined in their learning? Or are they to be disempowered, their learning subjected to the purposes and presumed interests of others, whether government, industry, educational institutions or indeed students' own parents and families?

The second option is not only morally and politically questionable; it is also, arguably, self-defeating. Economic prosperity, political stability and family harmony are likely best served by a population of human individuals capable of spontaneous self-expression, independence of thought and autonomous decision making. Unless our young people are becoming more self-determined and capable of communicating their views and knowledge and awareness of the problems of our world and our societies, then education in the twentieth century will have largely failed to deliver. Meeting the need for self-determination of our children and young people in the twenty-first century is a precondition for, not in competition with, meeting the needs of government, economy and society. At any rate, this can be argued, and would strongly support an educational philosophy highlighting self-determination as an educational aim.

Be that as it may, in this chapter I outline a philosophical case for self-determination as *the* fundamental educational aim, a case which is consistent with contemporary theory of human development and knowledge about the conditions for optimal learning. I present an account of self-determination as constituted by the dispositions to authentic self-expression, management of one's own learning, and creation of the conditions for further, enhanced self-determination. Since the third disposition, I shall argue, entails creating the conditions for enhancement of others' self-determination, my account of self-determination is communitarian rather than individualistic. In as much as self-determination is an aim for educators and educational institutions, educational policy and practice will be geared to the fostering of each of these three dispositions. Students will acquire the capacities for each and education will provide environments conducive to the development of each.

Education for self-determination does not entail the use of any particular educational method. Which methods facilitate self-determination, and in what respects, are matters for further inquiry. Direct instruction, for example, serves some purposes but inhibits others; likewise, inquiry learning, groupwork and so on.

On the other hand, it is also important not to confuse the issue of particular methods with the more general methodological question of whether self-determination as an educational aim is best pursued by methods which, taken together, reflect self-determination as a procedural principle, encouraging students to act in self-determined ways. I argue that the pursuit of the aim requires adoption of the procedural principle; that the conditions for the development of self-determination are the same as the conditions for its exercise. In education this means the creation of free associations of people in learning communities.

Self-determination, freedom and autonomy

In contemporary English-language educational philosophy there has been little or no discussion of self-determination as an educational aim. (I am not aware of any treatment in another language.) There has, on the other hand, been considerable discussion of the related issues of freedom and autonomy in education. This may be explained by the philosophical ancestry of relevant problems and theories prominent in contemporary philosophy of education. For instance, *liberty*, an Enlightenment ideal, has persisted for two centuries of liberalism of all forms, particularly as applied to individual liberties, including human rights. *Autonomy* has a more specific history deriving, in contemporary moral, political and educational philosophy, from the work of Kant, whose primary concern is the moral autonomy of the responsible moral agent, and its relation to the moral law, or *nomos* (Kant, 1956). An autonomous person wills his or her own moral law, just as a *polis* in ancient Greece itself (*autos*) made its own laws (*nomoi*).

Isaiah Berlin provides another way of understanding autonomy and liberty, characterising two different but related forms of freedom or liberty (he uses the words interchangeably) as 'positive' and 'negative'. The latter, negative liberty, 'is involved in the answer to the question "What is the area in which the subject – a person or group of persons – is or should be left to do or be what he is able to do or be, without interference by other persons?"' Whereas positive liberty (or autonomy) 'is involved in the answer to the question "What, or who, is the source of control or interference that can determine someone to do, or be, this rather than that?"' (Berlin, 1969: 121–2).

Following Berlin's characterisation, we may say that when the source of determination on one's doing or being is oneself, one is self-determined and possesses positive liberty in Berlin's sense. One controls, and influences, oneself. Two questions arise: what is the self? and what is self-determination – is it inherited or acquired, and if acquired, how? If the conditions for the development of self-determination are identical to the conditions for its exercise, then freedom from control or interference is one of those conditions. It then becomes critical to know which aspects of the individual are to be free or controlled by others: thoughts, desires, actions – or all of these?

It is on this issue that educational philosophers of 'the London school', particularly Richard Peters, Paul Hirst and Robert Dearden, have been influential in thinking about personal autonomy among contemporary philosophers of education. Their view, which I call 'liberal rationalism' (Walker, 1981) holds, following Kant, that one's autonomy depends on the exercise of one's reason, in which one is aware of rules as alterable conventions which structure one's social life, subjecting them to reflection and criticism in the light of principles, such as impartiality and respect for persons (Peters, 1973: 124). This is not a matter of following one's own desires, but of freely accepting the discipline of the principles of reason, which include moral principles transcendentally deduced, in the manner of Kant, from the nature of reason itself (Peters, 1966). Thus, when Dearden says 'a person is "autonomous" to the degree that what he thinks and does cannot be explained without reference to his own activity of mind' (Dearden, 1972: 453), by 'explanation' he does not mean causal explanation; he means an account of conscious, rule-governed thought where outcomes are determined by reasons the person has for beliefs and actions. The development of reason does not occur in the natural world of cause and effect: reasons are not causes, and explanation by reference to reasons is logically distinct from causal explanation which cannot account for purposive, rule-following action (Peters, 1958). We understand human action through the conceptual schemes of common sense, not science. Indeed, causal explanation in psychology applies properly only to the 'limbo of lapses' from genuinely free, self-determined action. Empirical psychology is relegated by Peters to the exploration of this limbo (Peters, 1969).

Liberal rationalism locates the development of reason, and therefore of personal autonomy, in a liberal education consisting of initiation into and mastery of putatively logically necessary forms of knowledge (Hirst, 1965; Hirst and Peters, 1970). The historical context of this view is significant. The connection between personal autonomy and forms of knowledge was made, during the *floruit* of liberal rationalism some thirty years ago, with a view to more than a philosophy with implications for the curriculum and an argument for the professional authority of the educators who are masters of the forms of knowledge. There were polemical purposes as well. Armed with their rationalist doctrine of autonomy as a function of mind, and a radical distinction between mind and emotion, the liberal rationalists attacked 'progressivist' notions of autonomy which emphasised the self-expression of the child and required conditions of liberty (negative freedom) for this to develop, thus taking a position contrary to my suggestion that there is an equivalence between the conditions for development and exercise. In his preparation for an attack on the equivalence view of progressivists, Peters (1973: 119) rejected 'the presupposition implicit in the writings and practices of educators...that some desirable state of mind or character trait will be best developed by an institution whose workings reflect the principle, which is thought desirable when personalised as a character trait'.

For the liberal rationalist answer is there is a development/exercise dichotomy rather than a development/exercise equivalence. Elsewhere I have argued that this position, commonly adopted in our schooling systems, is logically unsustainable (Walker, 1984). This does not mean that students do not accept the authority of a teacher, nor that the teacher does not need to exercise control. It raises the question of when authority should be exercised through control. I argue that this is so when it is necessary for securing the conditions for the development of self-determination, and that this can only be so when there is agreement between student and teacher. If so, the educational institution promoting self-determination as a desirable principle will always reflect that principle in its own workings.

As to the question of the nature and identification of the self, in the liberal rationalist theory of personal autonomy, 'the self who owns and rules in the autonomous life', as Eamonn Callan puts it, 'is located in the reflective powers of the individual, as opposed to whatever might seem to fix identity prior to rational reflection'. Other views locate the self elsewhere. For example, Callan (1994: 35), followed by Aharon Aviram (1995: 63) identifies a voluntarist view, evident (for instance) in the thought of David Hume, for whom personal autonomy is evident in the 'unhindered expression of the will and desires'. The role of reason, for

Hume (1959) is to be slave of the passions. Rousseau's view in *Emile* (Rousseau, 1969), reflected in certain versions of educational progressivism, is similar. There is no sense to the idea that self-expression can or should be rationally regulated.

Callan (1988, 1994) and Aviram (1995) canvas a third possibility, voluntarist-rationalism, an earlier version of which is found in John Stuart Mill (1954). Whereas Mill holds the self's desires to be innate and organised by the autonomous person into a rational pattern and life plan, for Callan desire is socially embedded, if not determined; but for both of them what is constitutive of the self precedes rational reflection (see also Lindsey, 1986).

Self-determination, authenticity and the self

The theory of self-determination I advocate includes, but goes beyond, what is understood by the various theories of personal autonomy. In particular, it espouses a compatibilist account of the determination of free human action, the classical advocates of which are Locke, Hume and Mill (Flanaghan, 1984: 48), the predecessors of contemporary naturalism in philosophy and philosophy of education (Walker, 1996). Human freedom, in both of Berlin's senses, is compatible with causation, and free actions are to be explained causally. Free action is not uncaused; it is determined by certain types of cause present in the conscious mental life of the person, including beliefs and desires, reason and emotion. What are these self-determined causes, then, and how is the self to be understood? To develop a satisfactory answer to this question we need, contrary to the liberal rationalists, to blend our philosophising with relevant psychological theory and research. Research on personality and cognition is particularly important.

First, consider the identification of the self. One way to approach this is to differentiate the self from the non-self, both within and outside the human person. Some aspects of our personality are self-determined and some other-determined. In a review of psychological theory and research on personal identity differentiation and maintenance, Polster (1983) draws attention to the capacity of the individual to differentiate between characteristics of one's own self and characteristics of other selves, to be able to draw a boundary between the former and the latter. The point is not that the boundary is never crossed, that characteristics of others are not taken on and assimilated into the self – on such an account no learning from others as models, a universal feature of human growth and development, would be possible – rather that, somewhat analogously to consuming healthy food rather than poison, what is absorbed promotes the well-being of the self rather than debilitating or destroying it (Whitfield, 1993: 1–2). Moreover, the self grows and changes throughout life (autonomously rather than heteronomously, in political–legal language) in a self-determined fashion.

In this respect both versions of voluntarist-rationalism just discussed are, although on the right track, a little one-sided. Mill's view that the authentic desires of the self are innate is half true: there is no reason that desires cannot be authentically acquired in a way which honours and succours what is innate. Likewise Callan's assertion of the necessary social embeddedness of all authentic desires cannot account adequately for what is innately unique to each of us. Incidentally, it is not necessary that we are able to distinguish the innate from the acquired in all cases – that would be to re-run the tortured heredity/environment, nature/nurture debate. Rather, what is necessary is to establish social relationships and educational processes which enable the individual person to be aware of what is conducive to self-determined growth and to decide, accordingly, what action to take.

There is a range of psychological theories suggesting different ways of describing self-identity differentiation and maintenance. For example, developments from ego psychology through to object relations theory (Guntrip, 1973) are in agreement that healthy development of the self begins with the infant child's initial separation of self from parents and independent exploration of the environment. This is a gradual process which is stunted if for some reason the child becomes trapped in 'all or nothing' thinking ('splitting') – for example, that saying no is always bad – rather than sometimes good and sometimes bad – but advanced if the latter lesson is learned, along with the correlative independent behaviour (Kohut, 1971).

The sense of self necessary for self-determination is learned in the first place in the family if there is a sensitivity and practical support for identity differentiation and independent exploration. For self-determination to take root and flourish during childhood, a social setting, a community of individuals modelling self-determination, beginning with the family and extending beyond, is required. Eventually, after the child discovers the main similarities between self and others, during adolescence the individual moves to separate from parents and family, the successful autonomous achievement of which is a condition for adult independence and intimate relationships. There is also considerable clinical evidence that the capacity to understand and manage the boundary between self and others is a critical factor in determining both individual and family health and avoidance of illness (Minuchin, 1974). Psychotherapists are working within a conceptual framework which stresses the integrity of the self and prevention or reversal of processes of fusion of self with others. In each of these stages and situations there is an equivalence between the conditions for development of self-determination and for its exercise.

Some psychologists, echoing the distinction between authenticity and inauthenticity, have distinguished between a 'true self' and a 'false self' (or ego) (Whitfield, 1993: 54–9). I operate from my true self when I set my own boundaries, determining, aware of my beliefs and desires, what I will absorb and what not. The decisions and actions involved range all the way from saying 'yes' or 'no' – 'yes' to offers to assist me in pursuit of my goals and 'no' to invasions of my privacy – to active involvement in emotional, intellectual and professional relationships with others which either enhance or detract from my capacity for self-determination. If, as a child, I have believed my survival to be dependent on subjecting myself to the unwelcome incursions of my parents or others, whether extreme such as incest or subtle such as implied denigration of my integrity, and this subjection becomes an established strategy for relating to others, my self-determination, although present in the original decision, is compromised by the consequences, and establishes a false, or other-determined, self. Unless I re-establish my authentic or true self as my driving force, my chances of enhanced self-determination across the various spheres of my life are diminished. Even though I may become highly self-determined in one sphere of my life, such as the intellectual, to the extent that I am unable authentically to express my true self in my activities and relationships my self-determination is limited.

The self-determined learner in a learning community

Given this understanding of the consequences of the child's suppression of his or her authentic responses, desires and beliefs, it follows that a condition for the continuing development and exercise of authentic self-expression is trust between adult and child. Trust takes root when the adult respects the child's wishes and seeks agreement for joint adult/child activities, such as formal educational processes. An agreement is a relation between individuals, whether or not they enter it individually or collectively. It may be explicit and formalised, or implicit in the relationship itself. Where the relationship is one of mutual trust and respect, there will be little or no need for explicit formal agreements, especially when there is a prior, under-pinning agreement to a role relationship, such as teacher/student; although sensitive and effective teachers will constantly monitor the state of trust and consent between them and their students.

Self-determined learning can occur only in a situation where there is agreement to participate (Walker, 1995). Where there is no agreement, there is no self-control in respect of the learning itself. A student in disagreement with a teacher may well exercise self-control, in the sense of self-discipline, by restraining negative emotional reactions which are not in their own interest. This self-discipline is indeed self-determined: it is geared to survival, and acknowledges the power structure of the unfree situation. This self-control, however, masks, through suppression, relevant aspects of the student's true self and so hinders authentic self-expression.

The liberating power of education comes from agreements between people to learn together. Keeping these agreements, in turn, requires self-control and social control. The situation must be maintained and people not keeping the agreement prevented from destroying the creative partnership between those who do. This may require coercion on the part of the teacher or indeed of other students (contrary to the libertarian view of freedom and autonomy for which the liberal rationalists rightly criticised some progressivists – Walker, 1981). Every teacher has the responsibility to impose control in such a situation, where the prior right is created by agreement from all, including the student who has broken the agreement. To enter an agreement is to make a commitment, to oneself and to others. The commitment to oneself is one of honour; it is a basis for self-respect. It is a moral act, a promise. The commitment to others recognises the mutual need to support each other in our individual self-determination, and is the basis for creation of community.

From this it is evident that agreement to community, based as it is on recognition of each other as individuals – that is, valuing authenticity by embedding the conditions for its expression in social practice – is necessary for there to be hope for the future, *within that social situation*. If there is no agreement to community, the result will be despair, whether it is expressed as alienated resignation, or resistance and rebellion reflecting the belief that the only hope for self-determination lies in escaping from the present situation. The classrooms in our schools reflect countless examples of each kind of response. A condition for self-determination is the enhancement of the conditions for further self-determination.

This requires commitment to and caring for each other. The communitarian view I am putting is to be distinguished from views which oppose community to autonomy, seeing autonomy as detached separation from others (e.g. Stone, 1990) or as undermining our capacity to care for each other (Cuypers, 1992). (For a critique of these views, see Morgan, 1996.) Thus it is a mistake to believe that it is not possible to love another person and still retain one's autonomy because of the supposition that the autonomous person would preserve a degree of distance from all such emotional attachments, and any attachments formed would have a somewhat provisional nature and be constantly subject to critical scrutiny and review. Such versions of communitarianism are mistaken, confusing love with attachment. Love is care and commitment which might sometimes lead to breaking attachments where they compromise self-determination. As I have argued, it is not possible to exercise such care and commitment without maintaining healthy boundaries.

Community, based as it is on agreement, cannot be imposed; it has to be created by people working together. To create it they will need to learn about each other, to discover each other's true selves and support each other in expressing them. When students are readily and as a matter of course in agreement with their teacher, when there is a classroom community, there will be few 'discipline problems' and the students will spontaneously accept the teacher's authority. Teachers who know their students and their subjects well enough to create quickly such communities of agreement are often described as possessing 'natural authority', and this is an apt phrase. The authority is natural because it flows from the authentic expression of the students and the teacher. Such knowledge of students is commonly constituted of intuitive as well as formalised knowledge, and is expressed in affinity for and empathy with students.

This affinity is also a condition for effective communication, including the communication of the teacher's aims and purposes to the students. The educational purposes of the teacher and the school cannot be communicated effectively unless there is knowledge and appreciation of the purposes of the students. Moreover, very frequently students need to be assisted to discover, decide or formulate their purposes, whether they be quite specific and contextual ('What would you like to do this morning?') or long term and developmental ('What would you like to do when you leave school?'). When there is an understanding of each other's purposes and a framework of agreed classroom practice where these purposes can be cooperatively pursued, there is a flow of communication and learning, and a co-determination which is co-created out of a united set of self-determinations. When this is achieved, there is no need for the imposition of control by coercion. It is not that control is absent – that would be to equate control with coercion – but that control is exercised individually and collectively through the agreed social practices.

This requires skill, not just will, on the part of the teacher; and also on the part of students. The teacher's skill derives as much from mastery of the content of the curriculum as it does from knowledge and understanding of the students. The knowledge of subject matter is not crudely or simply applied to the teaching of the students. In teaching mathematics, for instance, affinity for the students means understanding how they think and the levels of understanding they have achieved. This is an epistemic synthesis which is at the core of the expertise of the successful teacher, and has been described by Lee Shulman (1987) as 'pedagogical content knowledge'. Shulman suggests that it is at the heart of teaching's professional knowledge base. It varies, of course, with the age and prior educational experience, and often with the gender and culture of students. Acquiring it requires formal learning as well as sustained practical experience working with students. Effectively mixing the two is a perennial problem for teacher education.

Research in cognitive science, particularly cognitive psychology, is now demonstrating how teachers' expertise consists in deploying pedagogical content knowledge to students' self-managed learning (Leinhardt and Smith, 1985; Leinhardt and Greeno, 1986), as they assist students to progress from the status of novice to expert in a range of curriculum fields. Thanks to recent syntheses of research by Perkins (1995) and Bruer (1993), we are now developing an understanding of how self-determined learning in one field can be built into more empowered learning overall. Similar thinking in organisational psychology is demonstrating how the points I have been making about community translate into successful management of organisations, including schools (Senge, 1992; Argyris and Schön, 1996).

No teacher is perfectly skilled, and no learning community is perfect. (If this were the case there would be nothing to learn.) There will be occasions when a teacher's affinity fails, and occasions when students do not sustain their commitments to each other and the teacher. This is not only a normal feature of healthy community life, but itself an essential condition of self-determined learning. Community has to be constantly recreated, and self-determination, never an all-or-nothing affair, strengthened and developed. Problem solving, trial and error, learning from mistakes, testing hypotheses and discovering what we want to do individually and together, are at the heart of education, as they are at the heart of science. The difference between a learning community of self-determined individuals and a coercive, alienated situation is that in the former there is agreement that it is not only inevitable and acceptable that people make mistakes, but that it is desirable because this is a major way in which learning occurs. People will be detached about their errors, and welcome them as opportunities for further learning. There will be safety for people to reveal their lack of knowledge, their misconceptions, and their real level of skill. Needless to say, this has implications for assessment as well as pedagogy. It will be acceptable, too, for the teacher to make mistakes, and to be supported by students as fellow human beings in learning from them.

Self-determination: the fundamental educational aim

If this account of self-determination is sound, then self-determination is not only the fundamental outcome of educative learning and characteristic of educated people, but securing self-determined learning is also the fundamental procedural principle of well-directed education. This is as it should be, given the argument that the conditions for the development of self-determination are identical to the conditions for its exercise. The naturalistic position I am advocating inclines us, unlike the liberal rationalists, to look to science, as well as practical experience, to understand the causal basis for education for self-determination, and for the development of suitably effective pedagogy, curriculum and assessment, and professional education for teachers. Progress towards these achievements would be reflected in the choice, made in every educational decision, to the empowerment of our students and of their contribution to our social health and prosperity.

References

Argyris, C. and Schön, D.S. (1996) *Organizational Learning II: Theory, Method and Practice*, Boston: Addison-Wesley.

Aviram, A. (1995) 'Autonomy and commitment: compatible ideals', *Journal of Philosophy of Education* 29(1): 61–73.

Berlin, I. (1969) 'Two concepts of liberty', in *Four Essays on Liberty*, London: Oxford University Press.

Bruer, J.T. (1993) *Schools of Thought: A Science of Learning for the Classroom*, Cambridge, MA: MIT Press.

Callan, E. (1988) *Autonomy and Schooling*, Kingston, Ont: McGill-Queen's University.

—— (1994) 'Autonomy and alienation', *Journal of Philosophy of Education* 28(1): 35–53.

Cuypers, S.E. (1992) 'Is personal autonomy the first principle of education?' *Journal of Philosophy of Education* 26: 5–17.

Dearden, R.F. (1972) 'Autonomy and education', in R.F. Dearden, P.H. Hirst and R.S. Peters (eds), *Education and the Development of Reason*, London: Routledge & Kegan Paul.

Flanaghan, O. (1984) *The Science of the Mind*, 2nd edn, Cambridge, MA: MIT Press.

Guntrip, H. (1973) *Psychoanalytical Theory, Therapy and the Self: A Basic Guide to the Human Personality*, New York: Basic Books.

Hirst, P.H. (1965) 'Liberal education and the nature of knowledge', in R.D. Archambault (ed.), *Philosophical Analysis and Education*, London: Routledge & Kegan Paul.

Hirst, P.H. and Peters, R.S. (1970) *The Logic of Education*, London: Routledge & Kegan Paul.

Hume, D. (1959) *A Treatise of Human Nature*, London: Dent.

Kant, I. (1956) *Groundwork of the Metaphysic of Morals*, trans. H.J. Paton as *The Moral Law*, 3rd edn, London: Hutchinson.

Kohut, H. (1971) *The Analysis of the Self*, New York: International University Press.

Leinhardt, G. and Greeno, J.G. (1986) 'The cognitive skill of teaching', *Journal of Educational Psychology* 78(2): 75–95.

Leinhardt, G. and Smith, D. (1985) 'Expertise in mathematics instruction: subject matter knowledge', *Journal of Educational Psychology* 77(3): 247–71.

Lindsey, R. (1986) *Autonomy*, Houndmills: Macmillan.

Mill, J.S. (1954) *On Liberty, in Utilitarianism, Liberty and Representative Government*, London: Dent.

Minuchin, S. (1974) *Families and Family Therapy*, Cambridge, MA: Harvard University Press.

Morgan, J. (1996) 'A defence of autonomy as an educational ideal', *Journal of Philosophy of Education* 30(2): 239–52.

Perkins, D. (1995) *Outsmarting IQ: The Emerging Science of Learnable Intelligence*, New York: The Free Press.

Peters, R.S. (1958) *The Concept of Motivation*, London: Routledge & Kegan Paul.

—— (1966) *Ethics and Education*, London: Allen & Unwin.

—— (1969) 'Motivation, emotion and the conceptual schemes of commonsense', in T. Mischel (ed.), *Human Action*, New York: Academic Press.

—— (1973) 'Freedom and the development of the free man', in J.F. Doyle (ed.), *Educational Judgments*, London: Routledge & Kegan Paul.

Polster, S. (1983) 'Ego boundary as process: a systemic contextual approach', *Psychiatry* 46: 247–57.

Rousseau, J.J. (1969) *Emile*, London: Dent.

Senge, P.M. (1992) *The Fifth Discipline: The Art and Practice of the Learning Organization*, New York: Random House.

Shulman, L. (1987) 'Knowledge and teaching: foundations of the new reform', *Harvard Educational Review* 57(1): 1–22.

Stone, C. (1990) 'Autonomy, emotions and desires: some problems concerning R.F. Dearden's account of autonomy', *Journal of Philosophy of Education* 24(2): 271–83.

Walker, J.C. (1981) 'Two competing theories of personal autonomy: a critique of the liberal rationalist attack on progressivism', *Educational Theory* 31(3–4): 285–306.

—— (1984) 'The development/exercise dichotomy', in C.W. Evers and J.C. Walker (eds), *Epistemology, Semantics and Educational Theory* (Occasional Paper 16), Sydney: University of Sydney Department of Education.

—— (1995) 'Self-determination in teaching and learning: an essay review of W. Louden's *Understanding Teaching*', *Curriculum Inquiry* 25(1): 101–10, 115–16.

—— (1996) 'Practical educational knowledge: a naturalist philosophy of education', in D.N. Aspin (ed.) *Logical Empiricism and Post-empiricism in Philosophy of Education*, London: Heinemann.

Whitfield, C. (1993) *Boundaries and Relationships: Knowing, Protecting and Enjoying the Self*, Deerfield Beach, FL: Health Communications.

CHAPTER 6

THE POLITICS OF IDENTITY AND THE EPIPHANIES OF LEARNING

Pádraig Hogan

Papers in the Philosophy of Education, Annual Conference of the Philosophy of Education Society of Great Britain, New College, Oxford, 1997

Introduction

I am continually intrigued by attempts to ground the philosophy of education in a conclusive theory of human nature. I also remain doubtful however about what such attempts claim to achieve. In the history of Western philosophy, figures like St Augustine and Rousseau, Plato and Thomas Hobbes, come to mind as exemplars of theories of human nature which are, respectively, grim or optimistic in outlook, metaphysical or scientific in character. Now it might be claimed that such theories should scarcely concern us today, that they are really things of the past; matters of historical interest only in a post-metaphysical age. And clearly they *are* things of the past, but perhaps more importantly, things *with* a past; a past moreover which is newly alive and well where much of philosophy itself has now entered a post-analytic, or a post-modern age. Witness for instance the call made in a retrospective essay by Richard Peters (in his 1984 contribution to *Educational Theory and its Foundation Disciplines*): 'Above all, philosophy of education is in need of a more explicit theory of human nature' (p. 51). Witness also the prolific writings of philosophers like Alasdair MacIntyre, whose major and lesser works since the early eighties have amply furnished that for which Peters called. MacIntyre did this by accomplishing a robust rehabilitation of Aristotelian rationality; one with decisive import for the conduct of most contemporary human practices, including that of educating a public.[1] MacIntyre sees his own theory as one for a post-virtuous age. In North America, witness the resurgent metaphysics underlying such controversial works of the late twentieth century as Mortimer Adler's *The Paideia Proposal* (1982) and Allan Bloom's *The Closing of the American Mind* (1987).[2]

Notwithstanding their obvious differences in idiom and philosophical sophistication, such efforts to re-establish authority and influence for theories of human nature share at least two important features. The first of these is a toleration of diversity which is both informed and circumscribed by a more important emphasis on uniformity where human self-understanding is concerned. The second is a view of education which gives pride of place to a canonical curriculum through which the desired uniformity of self-understanding might be promoted. The practical significance of these points is that they encourage practices which entertain strong proprietorial designs on the emergent identities of learners. They tend to invest such practices with an acceptability, a sense of traditional *gravitas* and an accompanying sense of normative rightness. In this way, a pedagogical context is established where acquiescent responses are affirmed more so than ones that are questioning in a radical sense, where the more substantial requirements of pluralist democracy are somehow bypassed or unheeded.

Earlier versions of this picture are quite familiar to us from the history of education, as indeed are the criticisms of it in more recent decades in the arguments of the many upholders of rational autonomy as an educational aim.[3] But I want to argue that both the traditional accounts inspired chiefly by human nature theories and the more recent ones springing from Enlightenment currents of rational critique are problematic. More particularly, I want to argue that attempts to escape both kinds of difficulty by some of the more notable of today's postmodernist approaches serve to confound an already intractable issue, not least because they fail to engage constructively with education as a practice. Finally, and on a more promising note, I want to reclaim from their eclipsed origins a few distinctly Socratic insights that are not concerned with anything as problematic as a theory of human nature, and to review their import for educational attitudes and practices. I hope to show that attitudes and practices proceeding from an original Socratic inspiration (as distinct from Platonist and metaphysical inspirations) anticipate some of the more incisive insights of twentieth-century practical philosophy. I am also keen to show that such reclaimed insights, when considered afresh with some recent philosophical insights, are singularly promising and defensible in their engagement of the emergent identities of learners in the educational settings of contemporary pluralist societies.

Identity as the denial of difference

For most of the thousand-year ascendancy of Christendom and its institutions in Western civilisation (roughly 800–1800) the chief task of education, or more precisely its declared *telos*, was seen as evangelical. This was the task of shaping the identity of a fallen creature to the image and likeness of godliness, while establishing in the learner's understanding both the certainty of God's existence and that of the learner's own unworthiness of God's redeeming grace. In practical terms this meant that the identity of each person was already ordained, in all essentials at least, by the precepts and pronouncements of religious authority. To claim against such authority any rights such as the right of each individual to be different, the right to assert that difference through dissent, and the right to live that difference without fear of discrimination, would be an offence. It would amount to making a claim against what was seen as a divinely ordained order and would place the claimant promptly in a position of heresy, or worse.

By contrast, one of the chief characteristics of pluralist societies in the modern West is the tendency to contest, or even to dismiss, any world-view or doctrine which claims the status of objective truth and which binds its followers to obedience. It is precisely in this critical tendency that the legacy of the Enlightenment – its assertive temperament and its modernist ideal of rational autonomy – remains most influential. And because Enlightenment currents of thought view reason as autonomous and prejudice of any kind as a blemish, they are slow to recognise any prejudices in their own standpoints, or in their own appraisals of the world-views of a previous age. Where reason is championed as autonomous, standpoints which take a more accommodating view of authority and tradition fall in for particular criticism. Proprietorial rights or designs on the minds and hearts of learners would thus be seen here as illegitimate: as the imposition of an alien identity on the young and the curtailment, explicit or otherwise, of young learners' capabilities of attaining rational autonomy. Not surprisingly then, the conceptions of self-understanding and identity in the writings of the most influential of classical philosophers are a regular target for criticism from upholders of the modernist legacy of the Enlightenment. Briefly, examples of such criticism, most notably of the standpoints of Plato and Aristotle, might run as follows.

Plato's arguments in *The Republic*, and also in his *Laws*, provide the most well-known example of a metaphysical theory of human nature with comprehensive prescriptions for how education is to be conceived and conducted. Here the issue of human identity is pre-figured in all essentials by the form (ιδεα) of the Good. The question of identity, in other words, is definitively answered, rather than engaged in a manner that remains open to contrasting interpretations. The answers themselves then become embodied as imperatives of educational effort; embodied, that is, in rituals and 'noble myths' which seek to effect a transformation of the *polis* and its inherited culture. The main differences recognised by this scheme of Plato's are differences of intellectual capacity, on which hierarchical differences of occupation and self-understanding are built – Guardians, Auxiliaries and ordinary citizens. For instance, of the third class here Plato writes: 'For the mass of men does not self-control largely consist in obedience to their rulers, and ruling their own desire for the pleasures of eating, drinking and sex?' (*Republic*, 389e) Plato, of course, challenges some accepted discriminations based on gender and social rank in his attempt to define a new order of things.

For all Aristotle's criticisms of Plato's form of the Good, his own conception of education answers the question of identity in a manner which seems even less tolerant of differences than the provisions laid down by Plato. In book VIII of his *Politics*, for instance, Aristotle argues as follows:

> And since the *polis* as a whole has but a single aim (*telos*), it is plain that the education of all must be one and the same, and that the supervision of this education must be public and not private, as it is on the present system, under which everyone looks after his own children privately and gives them any private instruction he thinks proper. Public training is wanted in all things that are of public interest. Besides, it is wrong for any citizen to think that he belongs to himself. All must be considered as belonging to the *polis*: for each man is a part of the *polis*, and the treatment of the part is necessarily determined by the treatment of the whole.
>
> (*Politics* VIII, i)

The opening sentence of the passage suggests that there is but a single identity for everyone in the *polis* and that this must be imposed on all. This seems to be confirmed by the two final sentences, which apparently make the citizens the property of the *polis* and its rulers. And of course to later generations of Western Christendom, proprietorial conceptions of this kind found a new application: baptism into the church signified entry to a spiritual *polis* – a 'city of God' in St Augustine's words – where church authorities enjoyed custodial powers over the souls, and thus the actions, of the baptised.

To the critical spirit of Enlightenment however, the passage I have quoted from Aristotle's *Politics* – no less than Plato's prescriptions in the *Republic* – is significant chiefly as an example of the authoritarian spell cast by classical philosophy over the conduct of life and learning in Western civilisations. Yet if such critical judgement can be suspended for a moment, evidence of a more subtle kind might then be able to present itself from Aristotle's arguments. We might thus begin to glimpse something of the kind of reclamation I referred to in my opening remarks, although here in the case of Aristotle rather than Socrates. For instance, it must be recalled that, for Aristotle, the 'one aim' for the *polis* as a whole is happiness, or flourishing (ευδαιμονια), in its citizens. It must also be remembered that this happiness is not something passive. Aristotle describes it, at its best, rather as a conscious *activity of the soul* in accordance with goodness. (*Nicomachean Ethics* I, vii; *Politics* VII, xii) When we recall moreover the rather intimate scale of the *polis* as a city-state, 'belonging to' a *polis* loses most of the anonymous starkness of being owned by the state. Thus, on a more sympathetic, but also a more searching interpretation of Aristotle, 'belonging to the *polis*' could be rephrased as follows: identifying actively with one's own civic community, with the traditions and customs of one's locality; or in other words, being identified as a person belonging to a community with a distinct *ēthos* – a strong sense of its traditions and its collective identity.[4]

But from the standpoint of rational autonomy, the criticism can still be made that such identification of self with community is mainly a matter of conformity; that ancestral concepts such as *polis, telos, ēthos* and *belonging* signify not an emancipation but rather an uncritical acquiescence in the patterns of identity which one's traditional upbringing held forth as acceptable, to the neglect or exclusion of other possibilities for self-understanding. Such acquiescence might therefore be regarded as an indoctrination of a more intractable kind; an unquestioned schooling in strongly held 'essentials', with the likely consequence of closing off of any real possibility for an emancipation of one's self-understanding.

But the emancipation envisaged by modernist ideals of rational autonomy is radically called into question by postmodern standpoints, springing mainly from the influence of Nietzsche. Such standpoints, most notably that of J.F. Lyotard in *The Postmodern Condition*, detect in the 'project' of emancipation a 'grand narrative' that seeks to legitimate 'consensus' and that 'does violence to the heterogeneity of language games'.[5] On postmodern accounts, emancipation is alleged to be no less exclusionary than the premodern forms of authoritarianism that the critical philosophical efforts of modernity saw themselves as overcoming. Arguments of this kind feature not only in the writings of Lyotard but also in much of the work of Michel Foucault and in the earlier writings of Jacques Derrida.[6] One of the more daring cases of such argument however, has been made by Richard Rorty in his major work *Philosophy and the Mirror of Nature* and in subsequent writings.[7] This presents a radical case not for emancipation of self-understanding through rational autonomy, but for maximising the scope to choose and to re-choose one's identity. Rorty's critique is directed not so much against traditional patterns of schooling and upbringing, but against most of the Western traditions of philosophy itself, including those which have provided the foundations for schooling of every kind.

Identity, learning and choice

Like Nietzsche, Rorty is unsympathetic to any suggestion – metaphysical, epistemological or other – that there are objective truths to be known by the human mind. And this includes the suggestion that human beings have anything like 'a common essence'.[8] For Rorty, there are only alternative sets of descriptions, just as for Nietzsche, there were just alternative interpretations, or perspectives. Rorty sees epistemology as a successor discipline to metaphysics. It seeks to discard those certainties of its predecessor that are unscientific, but also to salvage others which it thinks can be grounded for once and for all by reason. Kant's philosophy, for instance, included in this latter category the formal principles of morality, which presented human reason with a 'categorical imperative': 'Act only on that maxim through which you can at the same time will that it should become a universal law' (*Critique of Practical Reason* 33). But in Rorty's view, all such efforts to salvage or reconstruct some enduring concept or principle which might apply universally to humankind as such, or which might act as a unifying end or *telos*, remain a pursuit of illusions:

> The dominating notion of epistemology is that to be rational, to be fully human, to do what we ought, we need to be able to find agreement with other human beings. To construct an epistemology is to find the maximum amount of common ground with others. The assumption that an epistemology can be constructed is the assumption that such common ground exists.
>
> (*PMN* 316)

It is just this assumption that Rorty is keen to undermine, so his critique of epistemology provides not only the recommendation to give up the quest for certainty. Much more radically, Rorty calls for abandoning the search for any truth which might be a candidate for universal acceptance. Rorty's dismissal of epistemology then is much more than a dismissal of the claims to certainty which epistemology seeks to establish on behalf of reason. Rather it involves the further step, or more precisely the further leap, of dismissing any claims which would say of humans that they share some essential characteristic worthy of universal respect and dignity. Rorty frequently employs a witty irreverence to dispose of the attempts of metaphysics and epistemology to represent human identity, or 'personhood', as something distinctive, or unique. In one such passage, where he seeks to minimise the differences between human and non-human entities, he draws on Sartre's distinction between *en soi* and *pour soi*, (viz. *en soi* as being in its totality and *pour soi* as the being of human consciousness and its desires) and argues as follows:

> In a sufficiently long perspective, man may turn out to be less δεινός (terrible) than Sophocles thought him and the elementary forces of nature more so than modern physicalists dream. To see this point it helps to bear in mind that there are plenty of occasions on which we do well simply to ignore the *pour-soi* of human beings. We do this in the case of particularly dull and conventional people, for example, whose every act and word are so predictable that we 'objectivize' them without hesitation.
>
> (*PMN* 352)

So the question now confronts us: what kind of conception of personal identity, or selfhood, informs Rorty's reflections? Rorty's answer to this is to present a curious argument which separates consciousness, or 'inner life' from reason,[9] and to claim that once this separation is carried out, personhood can be seen for what it is: 'a matter of decision rather than knowledge, an acceptance of another being into fellowship rather than a recognition of a common essence' (*PMN* 38). This means that one's sense of identity is not to be understood as something that is *disclosed*, whether through the fruits of reflection on moral teachings, or on one's relations of trust with a community, or through any enduring knowledge that comes from experience. Rather it is *chosen*, and *re-chosen*, in much the same way that Nietzsche held that one's 'values' must not be appropriated through intercourse with a tradition but must in each case be *created*. Where the 'will to power' (as driving force) supplied Nietzsche's *übermensch* with some kind of criterion for creating his values, Rorty seems to find something parallel in what he calls 'conversation'; or more precisely, in the effort to 'keep the conversation going rather than to find objective truth' (*PMN* 372, 377). On this account then, it seems that personhood would be primarily associated with one's capacity to participate in the conversation, as would any decision to admit another being into fellowship.

From what has just been said it is hardly surprising that the kind of conversation Rorty has in mind is not just any conversation. In the first place, Rorty takes over Michael Oakeshott's metaphor 'the conversation of mankind' and presses it into new service to describe a kind of intercourse which is actively concerned *not* with the search for 'objective truth', but rather with the 'project of finding new, better, more interesting, more fruitful ways of speaking'. Second, it is in this project that Rorty sees the educational, or as he prefers to call it the 'edifying' purpose of philosophy (*PMN* 359–360). In keeping with his charge that 'objective truth' wrongly assumes for itself a 'privileged description' of the way things are, he recommends 'edification' as a conversion from any kind of 'objective truth' loyalties, or *telos* loyalties, to a different kind of outlook. This latter outlook is one which holds that endless sets of alternative descriptions of human selfhood are possible, and that keeping the conversation open means pursuing these possibilities ever anew and preventing the pursuit from 'degenerating' once again into a situation where 'objective knowledge' asserts its supremacy. For such supremacy, in Rorty's view, does violence to the diversity of *different* discourses; it invariably attempts to 'commensurate' what is 'incommensurable'; it imposes a hierarchy in the order of being and knowledge, by presuming to adjudicate between the claims of alternative sets of descriptions and by conferring on some more ontological status (viz.: a higher place in the hierarchy) than others.

The educational significance of the arts and the sciences lies, for Rorty, not in contributing to any such hierarchies, but in the endless ability of these pursuits to show us new ways to 'remake' ourselves, to 'redescribe' ourselves, to 'become different people' (*PMN* 359) as we give our energies to reading, to writing, to study and to conversation. In his later writings moreover, he reserves this purpose to higher education while insisting on a more conformist 'socialisation' function for primary and secondary education.[10] Expectations that Rorty's novel thoughts on 'remaking ourselves' might yet betoken something or even something philosophically promising for a student's emergent sense of identity are mistaken. The 'remaking' in question – despite Rorty's depiction of it at one point as 'becoming new beings' (*PMN* 360) – turns out to be something quite commonplace:

> The sense in which human beings alter themselves by redescribing themselves is no more metaphysically exciting or mysterious than the sense in which they alter themselves by changing their diet, their sexual partners, or their habitation. It is just the same sense: viz., new and more interesting sentences become true of them.
>
> (*PMN* 351)

One can hardly fail to be struck by the absence of criteria of justification in Rorty's arguments on 'redescribing ourselves'. But the absence is not accidental.

In his later work, *Contingency, Irony, and Solidarity*, Rorty identifies himself as a liberal ironist: a person who holds the liberal view that 'cruelty is the worst thing we do', but who also 'faces up to the contingency of his or her most central beliefs and desires'.[11] He calls this central set of beliefs and desires one's 'final vocabulary' and insists that there is no noncircular way of justifying it. Rorty declares that liberal ironists 'do not think of reflection as being governed by criteria'. He goes on to explain: 'Criteria, on their view, are never more than the platitudes which contextually define the terms of a final vocabulary currently in use.'[12] Acknowledging that 'metaphysicians' might call this a capitulation to relativism, Rorty responds by drawing a sharp distinction between the ironist's private sense of identity and her public liberal hopes. The most that philosophy can do he claims, is to accommodate these to each other, not to synthesise them. While redescription would become the imaginative task of the self in the private sphere, one would also acknowledge that one's commitment to solidarity in the public sphere was a commitment to something that was no more than a 'fortunate happenstance creation of modern times'.[13]

The contrast could scarcely be stronger with traditional conceptions of identity, or with the rationalist conceptions of identity championed by the Enlightenment and its pluralistic legacies. Traditional conceptions of identity sought – chiefly by coercive means – to provide the self with outlooks which retained their unquestioned authority over the course of one's lifetime. Modernist conceptions of identity had an educational purpose that was equally long term and steadfast, though in this case the inspiring ideal was that of promoting to full maturity the power of critical reason. Postmodern conceptions of identity-as-choice, or as redescribing oneself, provide us with just the reverse: a conception of selfhood which, despite initial appearances of combining a pluralist conception of identity with an enduring sense of freedom, offers little by way of coherent criteria for the exercise of choice itself. In this central respect, and unlike its traditionalist and modernist predecessors, identity-as-choice remains largely susceptible to the sweep and sway of the transitory and the episodic.

Self-understanding and the epiphanies of learning

The explorations of the preceding sections bring home to us just how implicated the question of personal identity is with the complex interplay of educational influences, and just how intractable the justification of education is in universal terms. Yet the attempt to make progress in seeking such a justification is not an impossible one. And an important premise of my argument is that it is precisely this attempt, rather than the attempt to furnish definitive theories of human nature, that holds the more promising and more practical prospect for the philosophy of education. But progress here calls for a line of reasoning which acknowledges the impasses in the conflicting approaches we have been considering and which indicates a different path for thought and action if these are to be overcome. Let us first briefly review the impasses.

In contemporary democratic societies the traditional view that a person's sense of identity is something which can in large part be imposed, or 'transmitted', cannot easily evade the charge of indoctrination. On the other hand, conceptions of identity-as-chosen present a picture of individual autonomy which finds it more than difficult to escape the charge of arbitrariness, and which pays too little regard to the inherent biases of rationality or to the necessary features of social life and civic welfare. I propose to call now on a long-eclipsed Socratic line of argument – identity as unforced disclosure – to identify a pathway that is educationally fruitful and that does not encounter these difficulties. But this may provoke a few objections. First, one can anticipate objections from those – many of whom are teachers who see themselves as anything but 'postmodernists' – who still might invoke a Rorty-type argument. It would go something like this: In very many cases the effort to uncover something original or distinctive in the emergent identity of each learner is a waste of time and effort. Those who make this kind of objection may instance as proof of their case those plentiful pupils who show little or no promise in school, or who are 'particularly dull and conventional people', or 'whose every act and word are so predictable that we "objectivize" them without hesitation'. Others might invoke a Lyotard-type argument, claiming that the very notion of 'disclosure' of identity is a totalitarian one: that it presupposes some kind of missionary 'metanarrative', or grand presumption, that the life of each individual has a meaning waiting to be discovered, a *telos* waiting to be fulfilled.

I believe that objections can be dealt with by the fresh path for thought and action I have just referred to. In the space available I can only sketch briefly the initial steps on this path, and indicate something of their practical import. The tenor of the path itself is identified by combining two key points, which can be summarised as follows. The first is the point that human understanding always takes place *within* a historical context, or tradition. The second is that forms of teaching and learning which are candidates for defensibility in a universal sense are indeed a practical possibility, but that they are more a matter of epiphany than a matter of transmission.

In relation to the first of these points, most philosophers in the English-speaking world will be familiar by now with MacIntyre's argument that the exercise of reason always takes place within a tradition, and not in a rationally autonomous way which is independent of the influences that constitute each and every tradition. And a much more fully developed form of this insight can be traced through the hermeneutic themes in the works of Heidegger, Gadamer, Ricoeur, among others. But many may be surprised that the possession of a much earlier form of the insight can be discerned in the educational practices of Socrates, as documented in the early, or non-metaphysical works of Plato. They occur, for example, in the often dramatic bringing-to-light of the limitations of human understanding itself, of the ineluctable play of prior influences in the sequences of learning, un-learning and *re*-learning recorded in Dialogues such as *Protagoras, Euthyphro, Apology, Crito, Republic Bk.I.*

It is not difficult to see how the quest for certainty that marks most of the history of Western philosophy from Plato onwards had the effect of eclipsing this Socratic insight. The very subject matter of both metaphysics and epistemology helped to obscure it. To put the point of the insight in educational terms, Socrates was aware that both his interlocutors' arguments and his own arose from contexts that were influenced and constrained by perspective. That is, they were influenced by preconceptions, presuppositions, prejudices, predispositions. More importantly, he also seems to have been aware that the effort to overcome these 'deficiencies' in understanding could never achieve 'real wisdom' as he called it.[14] Though such efforts might produce candidates for our beliefs and convictions which were much more worthy in a universal sense than the existing ones which they challenged, these more enlightened beliefs and convictions, though deeply held, could themselves never be more than provisional. They would not constitute a 'final vocabulary', to use Rorty's phrase. They would rather remain open to further argumentation, criticism and revision.[15] Hence the importance Socrates gave to learning as an unfinishing search, jointly undertaken by learners whose pre-dispositions were tempered and disciplined by the virtues appropriate to undertaking such a search.

Such virtues would arise from an acknowledgement of the partiality and incompleteness of even the most accomplished human understanding, and would thus have an educational character from the start. They would include: a continual attentiveness to our own prior influences as these are brought to light in exchanges with others; a recognition of the partiality of even our best efforts to understand; an appreciation of the necessity for listening in a disciplined way to the voices of plurality – for instance as presented to us in encounters with others and with different fields of study; an evaluative eye for the propensities and patterns which disclose themselves in our own responses; in short, an ever alert acknowledgement of the possibilities and limitations which constitute our own way of being human among others, which disclose the character of own sense of selfhood, or identity.

Bearing these issues in mind let us now examine the second of the two points, the importance of epiphany in the experiences of learning. I would like to introduce the notion of epiphany not so much in the biblical sense, but more in the sense given to the word by James Joyce, and expanded upon by Charles Taylor in his major study *Sources of the Self: The Making of the Modern Identity* (1989). Joyce appropriated the word epiphany from religion for his own artistic purposes. In his biography of Joyce, Richard Ellman describes the Joycean connotations of the word as follows:

> The epiphany was the sudden 'revelation of the whatness of a thing', the moment in which 'the soul of the commonest object...seems to us radiant'. The artist, he felt, was charged with such revelations, and must look for them not among the gods but among men, in casual, unostentatious, even unpleasant moments.
>
> (Ellman, *James Joyce*, p. 83)

Taylor discerns a special significance in Joyce's use of the term epiphany, and grants it a wider sense in relation to our experience of works of art. In *Sources of the Self* he writes:

> What I want to capture with this term is just this notion of a work of art as the locus of a manifestation which brings us into the presence of something which is otherwise inaccessible, and which is of the highest moral and spiritual significance; a manifestation, moreover, which also defines and completes something, even as it reveals.
>
> (p. 419)

An epiphany in a work of art is therefore something essentially different from art as mere representation, or copy of something else. It is something essentially more than Plato, for instance, was prepared to allow in his description of art as imitation (*mimesis*). To be brought into the presence of something that is otherwise inaccessible, in the sense described by Joyce and Taylor, is not to escape – nostalgically or otherwise – from the everyday and the ordinary. It is rather to see the everyday and the ordinary from a new perspective; to have one's relation to one or other aspect of the everyday transformed by an unforeseen recognition, and invested with a new significance. The work of art evokes a mood, un-covers an insight, sets forth a previously familiar world in a way charged with a meaning previously undetected.

One of the most striking examples in writing of what an epiphany means in the experience of works of art is given by Martin Heidegger in his reflections on a painting by van Gogh of an apparently familiar and unremarkable object – an old pair of boots. The boots are so worn and battered that they are hardly worth a second glance. Their usefulness as equipment shows nothing of the promise or sturdiness of a new pair of boots. They are precisely the kind of object which, from an everyday perspective in modern society, would already be thrown out as rubbish. As Heidegger writes:

> A pair of peasant shoes and nothing more. And yet – From the dark opening of the worn insides of the shoes the toilsome tread of the worker stares forth. In the stiffly rugged heaviness of the shoes there is the accumulated tenacity of her slow trudge through the far-spreading and ever uniform furrows of the field swept by a raw wind. On the leather lie the dampness and richness of the soil. Under the soles slides the loneliness of the field-path as evening falls. In the shoes vibrates the silent call of the earth, its quiet gift of the ripening grain and its unexplained self-refusal in the fallow desolation of the wintry field.

Far from being a mere imitation, or a projection of 'aesthetic' insights into the work, the work itself here summons our attentions and invites us to dwell awhile with it. Far from any nostalgia or escapism, the work evokes remembrance and educates us by re-presenting us with what in our everyday experience has been passed over; that is, by re-presenting the familiar in an unforeseen and newly intelligible way. The work thus embraces us within the stay of the world which it opens up; a world which is in greater or lesser degree already familiar, but is now also newly intelligible; where the familiar and the yet unfamiliar are held in a mingling play. So, far from being 'objectivized' in Rorty's sense, and thus rendered scarcely worthy of serious attention, the ordinary and the everyday receive here a special significance. They now suggest themselves as areas where many epiphanies might blush unseen. So also, it is worth adding, might the '*pour soi*' of 'dull and conventional' pupils.

Epiphanies bring about unexpected and unforced shifts in our understanding of ourselves, of others, and of humankind's common lot. They may identify and call forth – in ourselves and others – abilities and aptitudes of which we were scarcely aware. In the experiences of teaching and learning epiphanies may enable us to identify with and share in aspects of a cultural inheritance that previously seemed remote, forbidding or irrelevant. On the other hand, they may bring us face to face with shortcomings and limitations that had remained undiscovered, or else denied, in our experience. Either way, epiphanies are interruptions of the kind of learning which is routine and unreflective in character. They are, in the fullest sense of the phrase, what we mean when we say 'learning from experience', or 'learning through experience'. They call attention, first and foremost, to the *quality of what is actually experienced*. They are, in a special way, the means by which one's own most potentials are uncovered and appropriated. In short, they are unforced disclosures and affirmations of identity.

Experiences which become routine, but without the element of critical reflection, are ever likely to produce what we call 'creatures of habit'. In this kind of experience, whether in teaching and learning or in any other walk of life, anything having the quality of an epiphany is likely to remain overlooked. That is not to say that such experience is without merit. Rather it is to suggest that teaching and learning here become dominated by practices which may well produce impressive grades, but which frequently bypass the heart of what particular encounters with one or other tradition of learning have to offer. The practice of teaching and learning, as an epiphanic art, calls then for a reflective refinement of understanding and a subtle attunement of sensibility. Just as van Gogh's painting may appear to many as nothing more than a dull and uninteresting pair of boots, so also may many pupils and students appear to teachers and educational authorities as no more than dim, or indifferent, or disruptive. So if the epiphanies of the everyday are to play their proper part in how learners come to understand the qualities, potentials and limitations that are peculiarly their own, then it is necessary that the understanding of teachers is attuned in the first place to the occurrence and the possibilities of epiphany itself in the experiences of learning. It is also necessary that teaching embodies practices which discern and build on epiphanies in a coherent way.[16]

Conclusions

In summarising some of the main points of my account here, I will also try to capture their import for the attitudes and practices which are most appropriate to the conduct of teaching and learning in circumstances of cultural diversity. (a) Because our human efforts to understand are inescapably constrained by perspective, each of us will always understand incompletely, and in some degree differently. (b) In each case then, our understanding is constituted by a partiality, in both senses of the word (bias and incompleteness); a partiality that cannot finally be overcome during our lifetimes. (c) But we needn't be simply at the mercy of this partiality. Our understanding can, through disciplined, co-operative and sustained efforts in any field of study, become *more* complete even if it can never become absolute. (d) On the other hand, the partiality inherent in understanding can quickly become more divisive and intractable (for instance through overt or unnoticed conceit, partisanship, ethno-centrism, sexism, narcissism, etc.) depending on how our efforts to understand become engaged, sustained and schooled during our lives. (e) To realise the best in ourselves as human learners is therefore to become aware that we *are* a dialogue,[17] whose possibilities can be taken up ever anew, or declined, or bypassed, or even smothered. (f) This awareness discloses certain virtues which are particularly appropriate wherever teaching and learning are attempted. (g) To practise these virtues in ways which enable pupils and students to discover through their studies the strengths and the limitations that are unique to each of them is to treat the issue of personal identity more as a matter of epiphany than of imposition, of disclosure than of conformity. (h) This also involves building an *ēthos*, where an emergent commitment to learning goes hand in hand with a sense of belonging to a community of learners. Such a community, being the fruitful outcome of accomplished teaching, is one where differences are not only acknowledged. They are also explored in such a way that they enlarge the context of our knowledge, enrich our appreciation of diversity and progressively discipline all judgement that is human and finite.

Notes

1 The works by MacIntyre I have in mind here are *After Virtue* (1981), *Whose Justice? Which Rationality?* (1988) and *Three Rival Versions of Moral Enquiry* (1990), all published by Duckworth, London; and also his essay 'The Idea of an Educated Public' in *Education and Values*, edited by Graham Haydon (London: University of London Institute of Education, 1987).

2   Mortimer J. Adler, *The Paideia Proposal: An Educational Manifesto* (New York: Macmillan, 1982) and Allan Bloom, *The Closing of the American Mind* (New York: Simon and Schuster, 1987).

3   The book *Education and the Development of Reason* (Dearden *et al.*, 1972) contains a number of articles inspired by the rational autonomy theme. This book became a central point of reference for two decades or so in the world of English-speaking philosophy of education.

4   The passage I have quoted from Aristotle makes him appear in quite a poor light to modern eyes, especially if they are coloured by Enlightenment presuppositions. For an insightful account of Aristotle's relevance to the educational concerns and practices of our own day, see Dunne (1993).

5   Lyotard (1992), pp. xxiii–xxv, 65–66.

6   See, for instance, Michel Foucault, *Power/Knowledge: Selected Interviews and Other Writings 1972–1977*, edited by Colin Gordon (New York: Pantheon, 1980). See also Derrida (1972, 1978). For an incisive exploration of postmodern currents of thought in the philosophy of education, see Nigel Blake, Paul Smeyers, Richard Smith and Paul Standish, *Thinking Again: Education After Postmodernism* (Westport, CT: Bergin & Garvey, 1998) and also their more recent *book Education in an Age of Nihilism* (London and New York: Routledge, 2000).

7   Richard Rorty, *Philosophy and the Mirror of Nature* (Oxford: Basil Blackwell, 1980).

8   *Philosophy and the Mirror of Nature*, p. 38; also p. 361. Rorty differs from Nietzsche in some important respects, not the least of which is the following. Despite his insistence that there are no such things as facts, only interpretations, Nietzsche still seeks to establish his doctrine of the will-to-power as something which applies universally to humans as such. This amounts to a metaphysics of human nature – that humankind has an 'essence', namely to strive for power.

9   *Philosophy and the Mirror of Nature*, p. 38. For Rorty, 'consciousness' seems to be almost exclusively Cartesian, namely a kind of awareness presided over by reason, but which employs reason firstly to doubt everything that can be doubted, except the consciousness of one's own existence, and secondly to seek a secure and permanent foundation for all enquiry. But this conception of consciousness is now something of a straw man. Rorty's attempt to deprive 'consciousness' of its status in relation to reason would be confronted with a much more daunting task were he to take as his target a strong contemporary conception of consciousness (for instance Heidegger's). Such a conception doesn't have to prove that there is a world external to the self, but is aware that the self's existence is, inescapably and from the start, a being-*among-others* which involves a continual interplay of the rational and the irrational. Such a conception of consciousness describes much more closely than Descartes' does, what actually occurs in human experience and also calls attention to the error in Rorty's attempt to divorce consciousness from reason. This divorce appears in a somewhat modified form as an irreconcilable rift between the private and the public in Rorty's later work *Contingency, Irony, and Solidarity* (Cambridge: Cambridge University Press, 1989).

10 See, for instance, Rorty's 'Education as Socialization and as Individualization' in his collection of essays *Philosophy and Social Hope* (London: Penguin, 1999), pp. 116ff.

11 Richard Rorty, *Contingency, Irony, and Solidarity* (Cambridge: Cambridge University Press, 1989), p. xv.

12 Ibid., pp. 73–75.

13 Ibid., p. 68.

14 See especially *Apology*, 23.

15 Richard J. Bernstein offers a detailed exploration and defense of a practice of the kind I have described here in his *book Beyond Objectivism and Relativism* (Bernstein, 1983).

16 Much of Michael Oakeshott's discussion of learning and teaching in his different writings comes close to acknowledging the occurrence and significance of epiphany in learning: for example, school as a place where 'the learner is animated, not by the inclinations he brings with him, but by intimations of excellence and aspirations he has never dreamed of; here he may encounter . . . questions which have never before occurred to him; . . . here he may learn to seek satisfactions he had never yet imagined or wished for' (Oakeshott, 1972). But Oakeshott's deep conservatism, his apparent reluctance to grant the learner any decisive standing as a moral agent, his disinclination to allow 'inclination' itself to

join forces with the 'intimations of excellence'; these betray a very one-sided, though very imaginative, conception of teaching and learning in schools.

17 This formulation is Gadamer's. It is paraphrased from a short passage which reads as follows: 'We are seeking to approach the mystery of language from the conversation that we ourselves are' (*Truth and Method*, p. 340). 'Wir suchen von dem Gespräch aus, das wir sind, dem Dunkel der Sprache nahezukommen' *Wahrheit Und Methode* (Fourth edition, Tübingen: J.C.B. Mohr – Paul Siebeck, 1975) p. 360. The German word Gespräch, can be translated either as dialogue or conversation. This passage introduces one of the most significant claims in all of Gadamer's writings. This is the claim that it is through the to-and-fro of conversation – and more especially the kind of dialogue which seeks to understand the other party in the fullness of his or her otherness – that what is most significant about being human is disclosed. The third part of *Truth and Method* explores this claim in detail, and is accordingly titled 'The Ontological Shift of Hermeneutics Guided by Language'.

Bibliography

Adler, Mortimer J., *The Paideia Proposal: An Educational Manifesto* (New York: Macmillan, 1982).

Aristotle, *Politics*, translated by T.A. Sinclair, revised with an Introduction by T.J. Saunders (London: Penguin, 1981 edition).

Augustine, *De Civitate Dei (The City of God)* (London UK and Cambridge, MA: Heinemann and Harvard University Press – Loeb Classical library 1957–1972).

Bernstein, Richard J., *Beyond Objectivism and Relativism* (Oxford: Blackwell, 1983).

Blake, Nigel, 'Modernity and Cultural Pluralism', *Journal of Philosophy of Education*, Vol. 26, No. 1, 1992, pp. 39–50.

Bloom, Allan, *The Closing of the American Mind* (New York: Simon and Schuster, 1987).

Derrida, Jacques, *Margins of Philosophy*, translated by Alan Bass (Chicago, IL: University of Chicago Press, 1972).

Derrida, Jacques, *Writing and Difference*, translated by Alan Bass (London: Routledge & Kegan Paul, 1978).

Dunne, Joseph, *Back to the Rough Ground – 'Phronesis' and 'Techne' in Modern Philosophy and in Aristotle* (Notre Dame: University of Notre Dame Press, 1993).

Ellman, Richard, *James Joyce* (Oxford: Oxford University Press, 1983).

Foucault, Michel, *The Foucault Reader*, Paul Rainbow (ed.) (London: Penguin, 1991, 1984).

Gadamer, Hans-Georg, *Truth and Method* (*Wahrheit und Methode* 1960), translated by Garrett Barden and John Cumming (London: Sheed and Ward, 1975).

Gadamer, Hans-Georg, *The Idea of the Good in Platonic–Aristotelian Philosophy*, translated with an Introduction by P. Christopher Smith (New Haven, CT: Yale University Press, 1986).

Heidegger, Martin, *Being and Time*, translated by John Macquarrie and Edward Robinson (Oxford: Blackwell, 1973).

Heidegger, Martin, 'The Origin of the Work of Art' in *Poetry, Language, Thought*, translated and introduced by Albert Hofstadter (New York: Harper and Row, 1975).

Lyotard, Jean François, *The Postmodern Condition: A Report on Knowledge*, translated by G. Bennington and B. Massumi, with a Foreword by F. Jameson (Manchester University Press, 1992 edition).

MacIntyre, Alasdair, *After Virtue: A Study in Moral Theory* (2nd ed. 1985); *Whose Justice? Which Rationality?* (1988); *Three Rival Versions of Moral Enquiry* (1990). All published by Duckworth, London.

MacIntyre, Alasdair, 'The Idea of an Educated Public' in *Education and Values*, Graham Haydon (ed.) (London: University of London Institute of Education, 1987).

McLaughlin, T.H., 'Peter Gardner on Religious Upbringing and the Liberal Ideal of Religious Autonomy', *Journal of Philosophy of Education*, Vol. 24, No. 1, 1990, pp. 107–125.

Oakeshott, Michael, 'Education: The Engagement and its Frustration' (1972) published in *The Voice of Liberal Learning: Michael Oakeshott on Education*, Timothy Fuller (ed.) (New Haven, CT: Yale University Press, 1989).

Peters, Richard S., 'Philosophy of Education' in *Educational Theory and its Foundation Disciplines*, P.H. Hirst (ed.) (London: Routledge & Kegan Paul, 1983).

Plato, *The Dialogues of Plato*, translated by B. Jowett (New York: Random House, 1937 edition, two volumes).

Rorty, Richard, *Philosophy and the Mirror of Nature* (Oxford: Basil Blackwell, 1980).

Rorty, Richard, *Contingency, Irony, and Solidarity* (Cambridge: Cambridge University Press, 1989).

Taylor, Charles, *Sources of the Self: The Making of the Modern Identity* (Cambridge: Cambridge University Press, 1989).

CHAPTER 7

EDUCATION, THE MARKET AND THE NATURE OF PERSONAL WELL-BEING

John White

British Journal of Educational Studies, 50, 4, 442–456, 2002

A key aim of education is to help students to lead personally fulfilling lives. The aim has to do with *the pupil's* well-being, not – at least, not initially – with his or her moral responsibilities towards other people.

The moral aims of education also have personal well-being at their core. If children are brought up to be morally sensitive to others' needs and interests, it is the well-being of these others to which they must attend. So at the heart of both the prudential and the moral aspects of education is the notion of individual flourishing.

In this chapter I will be focusing on the former – on education insofar as it aims to help those being educated to lead flourishing lives. (I am not assuming that this aim is entirely separate from education's moral aims. Whether a flourishing life from a prudential point of view must contain an altruistic element is an issue I shall leave open at this point.)

In England and Wales it is only since 2000 that the government has laid down for schools, in any detailed way, what their aims should be. These include 'personal' aims to do with helping the pupil to lead a flourishing life. Before 1988, aims were in the hands of schools and teachers. The year 1988 saw the introduction of the National Curriculum, but despite its complicated programmes in specific subjects it came with next to nothing in the way of overall aims attached to it – a mere two lines. The post-2000 National Curriculum is very different. The new *National Curriculum* handbook begins with a four-page statement of aims and underpinning values. In the original draft of this (QCA, 1999), the first of these values mentioned is 'a belief in education as a route to the well-being and development of the individual'. (This became somewhat more complex in its final version (DfEE/QCA, 1999: 10), but the basic notion is still the same.)

What, then, is personal well-being? What is it for an individual to lead a flourishing life? This is an ancient philosophical question. The fact that it is shows how essential philosophy is for educational policy. If foremost among the values which underlie a national education system is the well-being of the individual, policy-makers need to be able to say what that well-being consists in – and this plunges them immediately into issues of great depth and complexity that go back to Plato.

A condition of personal flourishing is that, by and large, one's basic needs are met. No one can lead a fulfilled life without food or shelter or money. What a fuller list of such needs would be – to what extent, for instance, it should include health or liberty – is an issue I shall bypass here in favour of another question: what counts as a life of well-being given that one's basic needs are broadly met?

Here a core issue – and one of great significance for everyday educational decisions – is this. Can one draw up a reliable objective list of the components of personal well-being, components which apply to any human being whether they are attracted to them or not? Or is well-being a subjective matter, consisting in the satisfaction of those desires of the individual which matter most to him or her?

The significance of this distinction for education should be clear. Suppose we take some common elements among those contemporary philosophers who favour the objective view. A quick survey of leading writers reveals that most of the following items appear on list after list:

1   accomplishing things in one's life which make that life meaningful,
2   being self-directed or autonomous in the conduct of one's life,
3   knowledge and understanding,
4   the enjoyment of beauty,
5   deep personal relationships,
6   moral goodness,
7   sensual pleasures.

Suppose it could be conclusively shown that these are the main components of anyone's well-being. Educators would then have a good reason to steer pupils towards these things as ends in themselves. Not that all of them typically depend on institutionalised learning. Where schools *can* contribute to them, teachers have reason to be confident that, in equipping their charges with different kinds of understanding, with aesthetic sensitivity, with dispositions towards self-directedness and accomplishment, they are enriching their lives. They need not fear that they are paternalistically imposing ends which may be important to themselves, the teachers, but simply reflect their own subjective preferences. For on the account we are considering the values are universal components of human well-being.

This does not imply that teachers must lead pupils to believe that, come what may, they cannot turn their backs on any of the items, that is, that they must all continue to be involved in aesthetic and intellectual matters or deep relationships throughout their lives. For the existence of an objective list of personal goods is compatible with differences in the way individuals weight these goods. For some, for instance, aesthetic matters may be of maximum significance in their lives while intimate relationships count for much less. But at least these learners would have to adopt a certain attitude towards rejected or downplayed values: they would still have to come to see them as objective constituents of human well-being, valuing them as such when they see them highlighted in other people's lives, even though they do not highlight them themselves.

It is one thing to draw up allegedly objective lists of personal goods, another to *show* their objectivity. How far do lists merely reflect the subjective preferences of their proponents? G.E. Moore's (1903, chapter 6) ideal values – the pursuit of beauty and of personal intimacy – were those of the Bloomsbury group with which he was connected. In philosophy of education, the 'intrinsically valuable activities' favoured by R.S. Peters (1966, chapter 5) are those to do with the pursuit of truth, Peters's own master passion, rather than, say, the arts.

One reason for adopting a cautious scepticism towards objective lists is their potential significance, already mentioned, in shaping social, including educational, policy. If they are well-founded, state partiality towards, say, the worlds of academe or the arts, or towards an intellectually biased school curriculum may well be in order. But until such well-foundedness can be shown to exist, why should public policy favour the listed goods?

A challenge to the objective list view is the characterisation of personal well-being in terms of the satisfaction of an individual's major informed preferences. Personal good is now a function of an individual's desires – and not determinable independently of these as on the objective theory. *Major* preferences come into the picture, since any individual's desires are hierarchically structured and if a particular person attaches a lot of weight to the place of watching football in his life but much less weight to eating oysters, then his well-being is more a function of success in the former project than in the latter. *Informed* preferences are important, because even major desires can be based on illusion or insufficient understanding – for instance, wanting to be a famous poet while imagining that one is blessed with a poetic gift and knowing nothing about the craft and its traditions – and it would be odd for success in deluded activities of this sort to count towards one's flourishing.

What might be the educational applications of this subjective theory of the good? One application is this. In a liberal society we may assume that individuals will themselves choose which major informed preferences they wish to satisfy. A key aim of education here is to equip them for such choices. This entails providing them with whatever acquaintance is necessary with a wide range of possible intrinsic goods from which to make informed choices. Items favoured on most objective views – such as engagement in aesthetic activities – will be included, but they will not be privileged over other items. As on the objective view, individual pupils may reject or downplay such items as aesthetic activity. But they do not have to reject them for other objective list goods. If their major preferences are for the acquisition of material goods or others' recognition and they have no place for intellectual or other objective list pursuits, they can still lead a flourishing life if successful in attaining their preferred goals.

I would like to connect this discussion of the two perspectives on personal well-being with recent arguments by John O'Neill about well-being and the market. Here, as in the argument so far, my main interest will be in applications to education.

O'Neill's 1998 book *The Market: Ethics, Knowledge and Politics* examines notions of individual well-being embodied in various arguments in favour of the market. I will not run through them all here. The most defensible account in O'Neill's eyes turns out to be the subjectivist view I sketched above.

> Well-being can be identified with the satisfaction of fully informed preferences. The position allows for error but still holds that whether something is good for a person depends ultimately on what they would want or value. What is good for us is still determined ultimately by our preferences.
>
> (O'Neill, 1998: 47)

O'Neill's argument is interesting because, if one assumes a subjectivist framework on the flourishing life, it enables one to see education as much more intimately connected with the market than it is often taken to be. The two institutions are sometimes treated as mutually antagonistic, or at least in uneasy tension with each other. O'Neill's discussion suggests a wider perspective – of the education system as one branch of social activity working with other agencies, both public and private, in the pursuit of common ends.

A partial version of this ideal is familiar enough. Like other public services, the health service is intended to provide one necessary condition of a flourishing life – good health, just as the education service is intended to supply another – which includes acquaintance with possible options. The private sector, if sufficiently controlled, can also work towards the same end, providing the wealth necessary for personal flourishing as well as employment opportunities which enlarge a person's range of life-choices.

O'Neill shows – by implication – how a more radical version of this ideal is possible. The private sector is not now merely an agency, like the health service, for the satisfaction of *basic needs* – in its case, adequate wealth and material goods. The market can bring with it, too, an ethical conception of the *final ends* of human life. It locates these, in the most sophisticated version, in the satisfaction of fully informed individual preferences. As such, it is itself an educational vehicle, reinforcing in each of its everyday transactions this message about the *summum bonum*. Schools, universities and families are not the only, or even the most important, educational institutions. Neither are they champions of 'eternal human values' which stand opposed to the acquisitive values of the market. For schools and families and the market are, or should be, all working together in the same direction. They are all promoters of individual well-being, as conceived on the subjectivist theory. Schools, colleges and families open up new options, steering as clear as they can from paternalist privileging of some over others. The market, in opening up its own ranges of options to meet the consumer's autonomous preferences, reinforces the implicit messages about personal well-being that the educational bodies have been transmitting.

How adequate is the picture just presented?

A large part of the answer has to do with the adequacy of the subjectivist theory of personal well-being. This is O'Neill's chief target. He supports an objectivist view, founded on the commonalities of human nature. If he is right, what he calls the strongest justification for the market collapses and there is a strong case for basing educational aims on objective goods. If they were so based, the education system and the market would tug, after all, in different directions.

I will look at O'Neill's objectivism later. First, though, I would like to stay within the subjectivist framework and ask whether, *within this framework*, educational aims and the market could not still be at loggerheads.

Behind the *version* of subjectivism adopted by leading market theorists – that individual well-being (utility) resides in the satisfaction of one's major informed preferences – is the assumption that one's preferences are revealed in the choices one makes in the market place (Sumner, 1996: 115–116) This effectively rules out preferences which cannot be costed in monetary terms (p. 118). While it caters for my preferences for a Mercedes over a Volkswagen Golf, it cannot encompass the value I attach to my relationship with my wife over that with a colleague at work. The economists' narrow definition of well-being in monetary terms fits some of the ways we commonly think about the topic: if you are 'better off' than someone else, for instance, that means you have more money than them. But it fails to fit what we normally understand by 'flourishing'. This is partly because there is a whole range of goods that are left out – friendship, for instance, or self-understanding, aesthetic enjoyment of nature, personal autonomy or bodily pleasures. These are all goods that may be prized as making for a more fulfilled life, whether on a subjectivist or an objectivist account of well-being. It is also because the satisfaction of informed market-place preferences, in itself, may not count towards one's own well-being as normally understood: one may buy goods not for one's own benefit but out of some motive of altruism or obligation (Sumner, 1996: 120).

All this supports the thesis that within a *broad* subjectivist framework, that is, one not necessarily tied to choices in the market place, educational aims and the market could still be in tension. If the relevant aim of education in this context is to open up options from which students may select their preferences, on many of these options – aesthetic and intellectual enjoyments, say – no price can be put.

Even so, the education system and the market could *still* work together towards the same overall aim of helping people to satisfy their major informed preferences. The two agencies would be providing *different sorts* of intrinsically desired options: those that cannot be bought or sold, like aesthetic awareness or scientific understanding, and those which can, like owning a yacht. (If we include extrinsically desired goods, the education system can come even closer to the market: a student may seek scientific understanding as a commodity whose use can be sold in the vocational market place.)

If we are working within a broad subjectivist framework, the idea that education and the market are cooperating promoters of individual well-being may then be hard to resist. But will the subjective account do?

One much-discussed problem is that the satisfaction of *some* informed major preferences seems to have no bearing on one's well-being. Suppose I want people living two centuries hence to lead lives of great personal fulfilment. Let us take it that this is indeed what happens. How can something which occurs in the twenty-third century affect my well-being in the twenty-first (Griffin, 1986: 23; Sumner, 1996: 126)?

Could one cope with this problem by ruling out desires for happenings after one's death? Perhaps. But another difficulty may be more recalcitrant. It is not inconceivable that someone may want most of all in life to engage in some activity which many of us would call bizarre or trivial. John Rawls (1972: 432) famously invented a person whose greatest joy was in counting the blades of grass in city parks. Or take people always glued to patchinko machines, television game shows or computer games. In practice there may well often be pathological reasons why people do some of these things. But let us imagine we are talking about rational, informed choices. Would we be willing to say that these people are leading flourishing or fulfilled lives?

Insofar as we have doubts, is this because we are working with some richer notion of the contours of a flourishing life? If so, does this cast doubt on the idea, implicit in subjectivism, that the only authority on the prudentially good life can be the individual himself or herself?

Doubts like these can urge one in the direction of objectivism. O'Neill is, as already stated, an objectivist. He holds that an individual's well-being is objectively rooted in human nature, 'in the development of her characteristically human capacities' (O'Neill, 1993: 73). The inspiration for this is Aristotelian. He describes his view as:

> an Aristotelian conception of well-being according to which well-being should be characterised not in terms of having the right subjective states, as the hedonist claims, nor in terms of the satisfaction of preferences as modern welfare economics assumes, but rather in terms of a set of objective goods a person might possess, for example friends, the contemplation of what is beautiful and wonderful, the development of one's capacities, the ability to shape one's life, and so on.
>
> (O'Neill, 1993: 3)

O'Neill's adherence to an objective list of personal goods enables him to support the existence of a network of non-market institutions and practices alongside the market. These have to do, among other things with the promotion of science and other forms of knowledge, the arts, respect for the natural world, friendship (see, e.g. O'Neill, 1993: 88–89, 143). Education plays a vital role in developing the specific human capacities involved in such pursuits. It 'increases the well-being of the agent since it widens her powers to realise significant goods and achievements' (1993: 80).

O'Neill's position faces several difficulties. First, what are these 'characteristically human capacities'? In the long quotation above O'Neill's examples include capacities for friendship, the contemplation of what is beautiful and wonderful, and the ability to shape one's life. All these are certainly phenomena absent in other animals. But, notoriously, there are also capacities absent in other animals and found only in humans like the capacity to enjoy another's suffering. Is the development of this capacity an aspect of a human being's flourishing?

No doubt any item which makes a contribution to human flourishing – enjoyment of art, say, or physical pleasure, or having a deep personal relationship – must be the kind of thing that human beings can desire and for which we have a capacity. But this is not to say that an objective list of values can be *read off* from a list of our characteristically human capacities.

Does this latter term exclude capacities we share with other animals, like capacities for physical pleasure? O'Neill's 'characteristically human capacities' only include more high-flown items like the contemplation of beauty and the ability to shape one's life – items of which other animals are incapable. But why should the pleasures of food, drink, sex and exercise not count towards a flourishing human life?

O'Neill's example of 'the ability to shape one's life' also brings up another problem. He is talking about the value which he refers to elsewhere as 'autonomy' (O'Neill, 1998, chapters 5, 6). There are grounds for thinking that autonomy is a peculiarly modern ideal of personal fulfilment, which, although it had its seeds in ancient Greece, has come to prominence especially with the rise of liberalism and modern industrial societies over the past four centuries (see Raz, 1986, chapter 14). How valid is it, then, to read this value into *human nature itself*?

If these difficulties strike home, O'Neill may be not so much deriving values from human nature as giving an account of human nature which fits values independently posited. If this is so, the objectivity of his list of goods is in doubt.

In his 1998 book O'Neill modifies his position on human well-being. He still holds on to an objectivist account dependent on Aristotle, but denies that 'the objective standards of the good are ahistorical and fixed' (p. 51). He is attracted now by

> the kind of historicised Aristotelianism one finds in Kant, Hegel and Marx, which with Aristotle claims that it is the exercise of human powers and capacities that is constitutive of human well-being, but argues that these develop historically and are not determined by some fixed biological fact... On this account there is an objective standard of well-being given by our human powers, but this is not a given standard.
>
> (ibid.)

O'Neill says that he would endorse this view, but only given major qualifications – that passive as well as active powers are taken into account, that human nature is not infinitely plastic, and that it is not to be assumed that later is better, that is, that historical progress is inevitable (p. 52).

This modification certainly takes the edge off the two criticisms of O'Neill's 1993 position, but it faces a further difficulty of its own. What criteria are there for identifying when the historical changes which produce alterations in the objective standard of well-being occur? O'Neill clearly rejects any developmentalist account, such as that found in Kant (ibid.: 52), which implies that later is better. He still wants to hold on to a notion of historical development, but in the absence of the criteria just mentioned, we have no reason for embracing this.

All this has consequences for the issue raised earlier about the relationship between educational institutions and the market. If O'Neill's argument for an objective account is unconvincing, which way shall we move? In the interests of keeping education and the market as separate spheres, we could look for another, less porous, objective account. Or we could see if subjectivism could meet the objections levied against it above (thereby reviving the possibility of education and the market as co-promoters of personal well-being).

Is there a third way? The subjectivism with which we have been dealing has been individualistic, in that a person's well-being is taken as a function of the satisfaction of *his* or *her* wants. Could there be a subjectivism of a more inclusive sort, dependent on *many people's* rather than an individual's major informed desires?

Let us go back to Rawls's grass counter and the thought that satisfying his passion *just couldn't* make him better off. The problem with him seems to be that we cannot make any sense of him: his preference is so bizarre that it does not fit into any picture we have of what makes a human life go well. Our touchstone here is not some objective account of the good based on human nature. It is, rather, what *we* desire, where the 'we' refers to a more delimited collection of people than humanity as a whole. Let me explain.

The bizarreness of the grass counter is that he has no time for any of the ordinary pleasures which many people in, say, contemporary Britain would see as part of what makes our life worth living – things like physical exercise, socialising, eating and drinking, sex, being entertained, deep personal relationships, living autonomously, a degree of self-understanding, love of the arts, including their popular versions, love of the natural world. The grass counter is unmoved by any of these pleasures and commitments.

It should be clear that the people mentioned do not constitute a tightly-knit group. The group they constitute, if indeed it can be called a 'group', has ragged edges. Internally, it is not all of a piece, some values being shared across the whole spectrum, others not. Some people will be more *au fait* with poetry, mountaineering, classical music or the subtleties of intimate relationships than others. But there is no clearly-bounded élite which has a monopoly of the more recondite fulfilments. The people in question shade gradually into those who – perhaps being cut off by poor education from more reflective and contemplative activities – would see the good life more Marbellastyle in terms of a villa in the sun, sex, sangria and a handy golf course.

This loose group of people exists not only in Britain, but across much of the contemporary world. It also, most importantly, has a history. It includes not only contemporary inhabitants of modern, liberal societies, but their ancestors, too, stretching back to the origins of such societies over the past four or five hundred years. It has been over these centuries that such values as autonomy, depth in personal relationships, the pursuit of self-understanding and an understanding of the world, love of the arts and of natural beauty have become articulated as important goals of human life – in addition to its more ordinary pleasures.

There is an indebtedness here to more ancient thinking, such as that of the Greeks. The group has honorary members in Socrates and Plato. It cannot be understood except in terms of the breakdown of the medieval world order and the recovery of Greek ideals from the Renascence onwards. New values have had to be forged to fit an increasingly secular world and changing views about man's place in nature and the meaningfulness, if any, of an individual human life. Our being in the world has over these centuries become an object of increasing fascination to us – a disposition which has found expression not only in the arts, in contemplation of nature, in science, and in scholarly forms of self-reflection like philosophy, history and psychology, but at a more everyday level in self-examination and in the mutual explorations of intimate relationships, these finding literary embodiment in the new poetry of the late eighteenth century and beyond, the novel, biography and autobiography.

At first the new values were the province only of the leisured classes, and no doubt of only few of them, but as more of us have risen above the level of subsistence, not least in the twentieth century, they have filtered down into the population at large, often in more popular forms, the poorest-off being the least touched by them.

The items I have mentioned are roughly those found in O'Neill's objective account. But they do not derive from human nature, either in itself, or modified through historical development, but from what the roughly delineated group of people just mentioned thinks and desires.

The individual on his or her own is not the final authority on what counts as his or her flourishing. There is a centuries-long continuos tradition of thought about this topic to guide us. In this tradition all the various goods mentioned are elements which could be included in a flourishing life.

This position has affinities with that of John Stuart Mill (1861, chapter 2) in *Utilitarianism*. Notoriously, he argued that mental pleasures constitute goods higher in value than physical pleasures, because this is what those who have had experience of both would claim. I think it is true that there are people relatively untouched by the post-Renascence values, whose experience is broadly confined to what were grouped together above as 'ordinary pleasures'. It is also true that there are those who are also at home among the profounder satisfactions. I suspect (from experience) that very few who are well acquainted with the latter would willingly jettison all interest in them for the sake of ordinary pleasures alone. So far all this is compatible with Mill's position. Mill also goes on to claim that those who have experienced both mental and physical pleasures tend to prefer the former and that these are therefore more desirable than the latter. Here, it seems to me, Mill goes too far. As has often been said, he cannot legitimately derive the conclusion that mental pleasures are qualitatively superior from empirical facts about preferences. Further, to say that those who know both pleasures markedly prefer mental ones makes things too black-and-white. There may be scholars and poets who live for scholarship and poetry alone and have little room for physical pleasures. But there are plenty of other intellectuals and artists for whom sports or sex or carousing are activities pursued with passion.

We need not follow Mill into arranging personal goods into a hierarchy to agree with him that those who have wider experience of the range of goods within the tradition are in a better position to make judgements about what constitutes human flourishing than those who lack this.

Mill was a liberal. He also held that some people are better placed than others to make judgements about the components of personal well-being. (This is not to say that they are well-placed to judge in detail about specific individuals.) Some may see a paradox in such 'liberal élitism' (see Skorupski, 1992), but if they do, are they right to do so?

Is this third solution – the *non*-individualist subjectivist account – really viable? It faces two challenges. First, could not the superior judges simply be better at discerning objective values – that is, values which pre-exist their preferences for them? Second, could not their judgements simply reflect their own idiosyncrasies and thus provide no basis for a more general notion of well-being?

In this increasingly speculative and schematic part of this chapter, I would like to suggest a model for prudential judgements which might avoid these two difficulties. I have in mind judgements of artistic value (see Budd, 1995: 38–43). Here we also have grounds for saying that some people are better placed than others to make such judgements. They must have had extensive experience of works of art, across the board or in a particular mode. They must have reflected on the features, general or specific, which add to or subtract from artistic value. They must be prepared to substantiate their judgements by reference to these features, as found in particular works. No doubt there will be disagreements among them, but there exists at the same time an intersubjective discourse of artistic judgement which seeks to resolve these differences where possible, or to reveal different weightings among values which may help to account for them. The enterprise of revising, refining, extending, deepening judgements of artistic value is ongoing.

Such judgements are neither idiosyncratic nor about features of works which can be perceived in the straightforward way that colours can be perceived. They require evaluation in the light of reflection and are subject to others' critical assessment. In this way they are intersubjective judgements rather than straightforward perceptions of objective features of the world.

The social practice of making and challenging judgements of artistic value is not culturally confined. As we know it in Europe, it is certainly a cultural *product*, having developed with the rise of aesthetics as an autonomous domain in the eighteenth century. But its discourse is universal in intention and also in practice. This is shown by, among other things, its capacity to engage and sometimes fuse with other traditions elsewhere in the world.

If there is a model here for prudential judgements, it must also be sensitive to differences between the two spheres. Prudential judgements are about valuable features of human lives, not works of art. Their object is therefore less delimited, more amorphous. It is also, partly for that reason, something on which a less tightly defined group than a community of artistic judges can be expected to have views and contribute to a fuller delineation of human flourishing. As suggested above, nearly all of us in our kind of society will have *some* thoughts on what makes for a flourishing life; while amongst us there will be those of wider experience and greater reflectiveness whose views often carry more weight.

It should be clear by now that this account of personal well-being does not confine prudential values to a particular community. New personal goods have come into being over the past four or five hundred years, originating in many cases in Western Europe. But this is a point only about origins, not about any limitation on scope. As with the sub-class of aesthetic values mentioned above, once in existence the new values have been able to transcend their original social confines. That is why I have been cautious about labelling the widening number of people with this broader approach to well-being a tightly-definable 'group'. The values in question are theirs, certainly, in that they hold them; but this does not mean they are not potentially values which anyone in our world can hold.

This is only the briefest of sketches of an alternative. But if it can be adequately defended, what might be the implications for the aims of education and the relationship between education and the market? This is a big subject and I can only put up one or two signposts.

First, it means an end to an individualistic framework on personal well-being. Individuals are not the final authority on their flourishing, but can only defer to the accumulated wisdom described above. This is not to say that any authority will force them to lead such and such a life. We are still working within a liberal framework, if not an individualist-subjectivist one. People will be free, indeed encouraged, to make their personal weightings among the handed-down values (which come down to them with views attached about the relative importances – in general – of different values). They will also be encouraged to join in the ongoing social process of assessment and reassessment parallel to that in the arts, mentioned above.

Over time all this should give parents, teachers and educational policy-makers greater *confidence* in judgements about well-being. There is a source on which they can draw – and indeed on which they have already drawn throughout their lives. They should be able, gradually, to leave behind the uncertainties which have tended to beset us all in an age when the philosophical study of personal flourishing has been in its infancy, having had little attention in the Judaeo-Christian culture from which we in Britain, as elsewhere, are rapidly disentangling ourselves (Griffin, 1996: 66–67).

In that part of their endeavour concerned with personal well-being, schools and families should direct pupils, *inter alia*, towards the intrinsic goods within the tradition mentioned. These would no doubt include among other things such items as close personal relationships, a love of beauty in art and nature, understanding of oneself, human beings, and the world they inhabit, self-directedness and simple bodily pleasures, including the pleasures of physical exercise.

The aims of the English/Welsh National Curriculum to do with the child's well-being should become less the well-meaning but unargued list of items which they are now and more a philosophically and historically informed set whose rationale is fully stated, public and revisable. How good a shot could be made at this at first, given the remark just made about the infancy of the philosophy of well-being, is another question. But a first shot is perhaps better than no shot at all. The education system cannot be as aimless throughout the next century as it has been throughout the last.

More generally, teachers and parents should wholeheartedly encourage children to engage in activities subserving these ends. They would not be favouring their own idiosyncratic preferences, but inducting children into time-tested values. They should also leave children free to reject elements in this tradition in favour of values which lie outside it, such as obedience to God. Does this mean that the (on the whole secular) values of the tradition are privileged? There would be nothing wrong about teachers' encouraging a commitment to art or friendship. What could it be? But encouraging wholehearted devotion to a personal God is problematic, as the religious clauses of the 1944 Education Act and subsequent guidelines for religious education in English schools testify. Love of works of art is directed to objects about whose existence there is no doubt; but whether the same can be said about love of God is moot. This said, there is everything to be said for *revealing* this value to the pupil, in case he or she wishes to adopt it.

On this view the education system would not be all of a piece with the market. Schools, colleges and the market would not all be reinforcing the same meta-ethic, leading people to think that their flourishing consists in the satisfaction of their major desires, whatever these may be. Education would be driven by an independent set of values. The values of the market would have to be reassessed – and altered or abandoned accordingly – in the light of wisdom already accumulated within the culture about what makes for a flourishing human life.

Note

This chapter is a substantially revised version of a keynote presentation to a symposium on *Economy, Public Education and Democracy* held at Ascona, Switzerland, in September 2000 and organised by the Pedagogical Institute of the University of Zürich.

References

Budd, M. (1995) *Values of Art* (London, The Penguin Press).

DfEE/QCA (1999) *The National Curriculum* (handbook for teachers) (London, Department for Education and Employment and Qualifications and Curriculum Authority).

Griffin, J. (1986) *Well-being* (Oxford, Clarendon Press).

Griffin, J. (1996) *Value Judgement* (Oxford, Clarendon Press).

Mill, J.S. (1861) *Utilitarianism, Liberty and Representative Government* (London, Everyman).

Moore, G.E. (1903) *Principia Ethica* (Cambridge, Cambridge University Press).

O'Neill, J. (1993) *Ecology, Policy and Politics: Human Well-being and the Natural World* (London, Routledge).

O'Neill, J. (1998) *The Market: Ethics, Knowledge and Politics* (London, Routledge).

Peters, R.S. (1966) *Ethics and Education* (London, Allen and Unwin).

QCA (1999) *The Review of the National Curriculum in England: The Consultation Materials* (London, Qualifications and Curriculum Authority).

Rawls, J. (1972) *A Theory of Justice* (Oxford, Clarendon Press).

Raz, J. (1986) *The Morality of Freedom* (Oxford, Clarendon Press).

Skorupski, J. (1992) Liberal elitism. In D. Milligan and W.W. Miller (eds) *Liberalism, Citizenship and Autonomy* (Aldershot, Avebury).

Sumner, L.W. (1996) *Welfare, Happiness and Ethics* (Oxford, Oxford University Press).

PART III

POLITICS AND EDUCATION

CHAPTER 8

LIBERAL VALUES AND LIBERAL EDUCATION

J. Mark Halstead

In J. Mark Halstead and Monica J. Taylor (eds) *Values in Education and Education in Values (1996)*, London: Falmer Press, pp. 17–32

For most of the last thirty years, theoretical approaches to educational values have typically begun with an analysis of the concept of education. However, I shall argue in this chapter that the best way to come to understand the educational values of any society is to examine the broader framework of values in that society. This chapter therefore begins with an account of liberalism, which, it is argued, provides the theoretical framework of values that comes closest to the actual political and economic circumstances that prevail in Western societies generally. In the second section, the influence of fundamental liberal values on the dominant concept of education in the West will be explored. The chapter concludes with a brief discussion of some of the challenges to this dominant form of liberal education that have arisen both from within and from outside the fundamental framework of liberal values.

Fundamental liberal values

Although it is, of course, acknowledged that many different versions of liberalism exist, it is not relevant to the purposes of the present chapter to discuss the arguments between these different versions in any detail, or to discuss their historical origins. The understanding of liberalism which I shall adopt will be as broad as possible, though it will be necessary to establish the boundaries of liberalism by contrasting it with non-liberal world views such as totalitarianism. The chapter is written in the belief that liberal values are to be found in a wide range of political perspectives from conservatism (in spite of attempts by Dworkin, 1978: 136ff, Scruton, 1984: 192ff; and others to treat liberalism and conservatism as totally different world views) to certain forms of socialism (cf. Freeden, 1978: 25ff; Siedentop, 1979: 153). Where it is necessary to concentrate on one typical form of liberalism, I shall focus on the particular strand which can be traced from Kant to contemporary philosophers like Rawls, Dworkin, Hart, Ackerman and Raz, and in the area of education to liberal philosophers such as Peters, Hirst, Dearden and Bailey, because this strand seems to me to be the most influential one in contemporary liberal thought.

Core values: freedom, equality, rationality

Liberalism is generally considered to have its origin in conflict, but this conflict is variously depicted. Gaus (1983: 2f) depicts it as being between individuality and sociability, while Ackerman (1980: 3) sees it as a conflict between one individual's control over resources and another individual's challenge to that claim. In the present chapter I shall argue that there are three fundamental liberal values:

1   individual liberty (i.e. freedom of action and freedom from constraint in the pursuit of one's own needs and interests);
2   equality of respect for all individuals within the structures and practices of society (i.e. non-discrimination on irrelevant grounds);
3   consistent rationality (i.e. basing decisions and actions on logically consistent rational justifications);

and that the primary conflict exists between (1) and (2) (cf. Ackerman, 1980: 374ff; Norman, 1982). In fact, some liberals have argued strongly that the first value is the more fundamental (Hayek, 1960; Berlin, 1969) and others have made out an equal strong case for the second (Dworkin, 1978; Gutmann, 1980; Hart, 1984: 77f). However, I want to argue that it is precisely the tension between the first two values which gives rise to the need for the third. It is with these three fundamental liberal values and their inter-relationships that I shall be mainly concerned in this section.

Though they may be understood in a variety of ways (see below), there seems to be fairly widespread agreement among liberals that these are the most fundamental values, and that liberal ethical theory is based on them. Thus the principles of impartiality and tolerance are linked to the second and third values, and the principle of personal autonomy (Raz, 1986: chapters 14 and 15) to the first and third. The interaction between all three values provides the basis for the just resolution of conflict and the rule of law.

It is when we proceed beyond the three fundamental values that the different versions of liberalism part company. The first parting of the ways comes between those who believe that *good* is of prior importance and therefore justify actions and decisions in terms of their consequences, and those who believe that *right* is of prior importance and therefore justify actions and decisions in terms of a set of moral duties. The dominant view in the former category is utilitarianism, which maintains that the justice of institutions may be measured by their capacity to promote the greatest happiness of the greatest number; classical exponents of utilitarianism include Bentham (1948) and Mill (1972a), and it has found a modern upholder in J.C.C. Smart (Smart and Williams, 1973). The latter category has produced a range of different views, depending on how the moral duties are conceived. An initial distinction may be made between *intuitionism* (which involves the attempt to fit a set of unrelated low-level maxims of conduct together into a consistent whole, and thus may be considered the nearest philosophically respectable approximation to 'common sense'; cf. Raphael, 1981: 44f; Benditt, 1982: 81ff) and *distributive justice* (which involves the claim that the plurality of moral duties must be conceived hierarchically). There are two main approaches to distributive justice: that of libertarians such as Hayek, Friedman and Nozick who emphasize equality of opportunity within the market place and the individual's right to a fair reward for his talents and labour; and that of egalitarians such as Rawls, Dworkin and Gutmann, who emphasize (among other things) civil and moral rights, social welfare and meeting the needs of the least advantaged. To pursue the differences between these conceptions of liberalism, however, would take me beyond the very limited brief of this chapter, and I want now to return to a consideration of the three fundamental liberal values.

The framework of values can be classified initially by considering what is *excluded* by the three fundamental values. The first value, that of individual liberty, clearly excludes a totalitarian emphasis on communal unity to the extent that it endangers individuality; thus liberalism is broadly incompatible with Marxism. (This does not mean, of course, that everyone opposed to totalitarianism must be a liberal, as Solzhenitsyn's criticisms of liberalism make clear: see Walsh, 1990: 228ff.) The second value, that of the equality of respect, excludes the hierarchical ranking of individuals according to which some have a greater claim to freedom than others. Thus liberalism rejects slavery, for example, or Nazi claims to superiority over Jews (cf. Ackerman, 1980: 6). The third value, that of consistent rationality, excludes arbitrariness, inconsistency and the failure to take account of relevant factors (cf. Taylor, 1982). It rules out the uncritical acceptance of dogma, whether based on authority or revelation, and equally it refuses to drift into the sort of relativism which insists that cultures, for example, can only be understood from within and on their own terms (cf. Hollis and Lukes, 1982).

There is considerable scope, however, for different understandings of the three fundamental liberal values:

- Individual *liberty*, for example, may involve freedom to satisfy one's desires (as in Benthamite utilitarianism: cf. Bentham, 1948) or to realize one's rationally determined interests (as in Kant, 1948), or simply to be oneself by being free from constraint. It may, but need not, involve the construction of a life-plan (Rawls, 1972: 407ff; cf. Gaus, 1983: 32ff).
- *Equality* of respect focuses on one's dealings with others (Peters, 1966: chapter 8). It is understood in a fairly minimal way by some libertarians to imply formal equality of opportunity, but is sometimes expanded (especially by modern liberals) into a stronger form of equality, such as attempts to equalize life prospects or to distribute wealth and power more equitably (cf. White, 1994).
- Consistent *rationality* may, on a utilitarian view, involve no more than the rational appraisal of utility (i.e. what will promote happiness and reduce happiness), which is taken to provide the basis for the just resolution of conflict. A Kantian view of consistent rationality, on the other hand, is much richer, as it not only provides the basis for the just resolution of conflict, but also is an end in itself (the 'search for truth') *and* enriches our understanding of the first two liberal values: thus the freedom of the individual is understood in terms of rational autonomy and the will (which itself may provide the basis for certain supererogatory virtues such as generosity and humility), and the equal right of all other individuals to similar freedom provides the basis for an ethical system which includes respect for persons, promise keeping, refraining from deceit, tolerance, openness, fairness and freedom from envy. Even those who argue that liberalism is grounded in agnosticism about moral issues (e.g. White, 1983) are committed to the principle of consistent rationality, in that they insist on remaining sceptical only because no good reasons have as yet been provided to justify a change of view.

Rights

Rights are central to liberalism, particularly in its distributive justice mode. They may be analysed in terms of content, status, origin, context, or the grounds on which they are justified. They are usually prefixed by some sort of defining adjective: moral, political, legal, social, natural, human, constitutional, civil, individual, religious, women's, children's, and so on. In this section, however, I shall distinguish only two types of rights, which I shall call moral rights and social rights.

By *moral rights* I mean those rights without which the three fundamental liberal values cannot be achieved. Examples of these are the right to life itself, the right not to be enslaved, the right not to be brainwashed. These come closest to the status of absolute rights, though there has always been a debate among liberals as to whether there really are any absolute rights (Gewirth, 1984), for it is not difficult to imagine situations where one set of *prima facie* rights may be in direct conflict with another (McCloskey, 1985: 133ff).

By *social rights* I mean those rights which are established by rational debate as the most appropriate means of ensuring the just resolution of conflict and general human well-being. These rights are open to negotiation even among liberals, and may have to be fought for, even though they involve claims based on liberal ethics. They are often defined by law; examples include the right to education, the right to low cost housing, the right to free medical care or to a minimum income. Often these rights are to do with the definition of roles and relationships and the distribution of power (e.g. women's rights, parents' rights). Sometimes the rights are little more than a rhetorical expression of desires and needs, or a preference for particular social goals, such as students' rights and animal rights (cf. Jenkins, 1980: 241f). A right is only a claim or a demand unless it is built into the social structure and there is an apparatus for implementing it. As Jenkins points out, rights are not usually invoked except to redress injustice (ibid.: 243).

Typically, no one conception of the good life is favoured in liberalism, and a vast range of life-styles, commitments, priorities, occupational roles and life-plans form a marketplace of ideas within the liberal framework (cf. Popper, 1966). Liberalism makes an important distinction between the private and public domains (Hampshire, 1978), though Devlin (1965) and others have disputed the validity of this distinction. Thus, for example, religion is seen as a private and voluntary matter for the individual (though the practice of religion is a moral right based on the fundamental liberal value of respect for the freedom of the individual). Certain forms of human behaviour, however, are ruled out in principle by reference to freedom, equality and rationality; these include prejudice, intolerance, injustice and repression. Other forms of human behaviour are necessary in principle on a liberal view in certain contexts (such as impartiality), though ways of putting them into practice or even conceptualizing them are still hotly debated. In contexts where certain forms of behaviour are considered essential to a liberal perspective, a liberal theory can be developed. The liberal framework of values has produced in particular a political theory and an economic theory.

Democracy

The political domain has always been the central arena for liberal debate. Democracy is seen by liberals as the most rational safeguard against tyranny and a way of guaranteeing the equal right of citizens to determine for themselves what is in their own best interests. It provides a clarification of the role of the state and the law (Benn and Peters, 1959; Duncan, 1983). The state is not an end in itself but 'exists to regulate the competition among individuals for their private ends' (Strike, 1982b: 5). It provides the means of protecting the public interest and ensuring social justice (Miller, 1976). The law exists to maintain order in society, by protecting persons and property (Jenkins, 1980) and to prevent harm (Mill, 1972b).

Key liberal causes include human rights, free speech, opposition to censorship, racial equality, and opposition to the enforcement of morality through the criminal law (Hart, 1963). The liberal state is expected to show official neutrality on religious matters, together with a respect for individual freedom of conscience. As Fishkin points out,

> The state could not enshrine the religious convictions of any particular groups by public commitments and avoid the charge that it was biasing the market-place of ideas by giving certain metaphysical and religious claims, certain ultimate convictions, the stamp of state authority and legitimacy.
>
> (1984: 154)

Some major debates within liberal political theory include the extent to which democracy should entail representation, which may satisfy the protection of interests, or participation, which may contribute also to human development (Pateman, 1970, 1979; cf. Lucas, 1976); the extent to which political liberalism is part of a comprehensive liberal world view as opposed to an 'overlapping consensus' among different comprehensive views (Rawls, 1993); the extent to which nationalism is compatible with the liberal state (Miller, 1993; Tamir, 1993) the balancing of state power with civil liberties (cf. Dworkin, 1977: 206ff; Strike, 1982a); and the conflict between the right-wing emphasis on stability, non-interference, free enterprise, initiative and merit, and the left-wing emphasis on egalitarianism and the combating of social injustice.

Economic values

Liberal economic theory accepts the holding of private property as legitimate and supports the notion of the free market economy in which free markets provide the goods and services which consumers choose to buy, though the state may intervene to regulate the economy if necessary, to ensure free and fair competition and to prevent harm to others (Dworkin, 1978: 119; Gaus, 1983: chapter 7; Koerner, 1985: 315f; Ackerman, 1992: 9–10). Liberalism does not, however, require a particular stance with regard to any of the following debates: the debate between those like Hayek (1960) who continue to support the old liberal principle of *laissez-faire* and more modern liberals who emphasize the need for tighter government control, for example, in monetary policy or welfare distribution (Freeden, 1978: chapter 6); the debate between the supporters of capitalist free enterprise like Friedman (1962) and those who wish to see a significant redistribution of wealth and income, for example, by providing a minimum wage or by progressive taxes (Dworkin, 1978: 122); and the debate between those who emphasize the need for free enterprise and efficiency, and those who argue for an increase in industrial democracy (Gaus, 1983: 257–61). The relevance of economic liberalism to educational issues will be considered later.

The values of liberal education

Like liberalism, liberal education has a long history and a range of different meanings (Peters, 1977: chapters 3 and 4; Kimball, 1986). Its roots are often traced to ancient Greece, where liberal education involved the development of mind and the pursuit of knowledge for its own sake (Hirst, 1974a: 30–2), and to nineteenth-century thinkers like Mill, Newman and Arnold, with their emphasis on all-round development, the pursuit of excellence and high culture and their continuing belief in the humanizing effect of the liberal arts (White, 1986). It is the argument of this chapter, however, that the central strands of liberal education may be best understood in terms of the liberal framework of values outlined above. The vision of education which these values encompass has come to dominate Western educational thinking. All the values typically associated with liberal education – including personal autonomy, critical openness, the autonomy of academic disciplines, equality of opportunity, rational morality, the celebration of diversity, the avoidance of indoctrination, and the refusal to side with any definitive conception of the good – are clearly based on the three fundamental liberal values of freedom, equality and rationality, as, indeed, is the more recent emphasis in liberal educational thought on democratic values, citizenship and children's rights. Supporters of liberal education have gone so far as to suggest that it is the only justifiable form of education (Hirst, 1974b, 1985). For them, education *is* liberal education (Peters, 1966: 43).

Rationality

The development of the rational mind is at the very core of liberal education (Dearden, 1972; Strike, 1982b: 12); Hirst, for example, tells us that education 'involves a commitment to reason on the part of the educator, no more and no less' (1974b: 83f). The nature of rationality is much debated, but it is generally taken to involve having good reasons for doing or believing things (though what counts as a good reason is itself problematic; cf. MacIntyre, 1988). To make rationality a fundamental educational ideal, as Scheffler (1973: 60) points out, is 'to make as pervasive as possible the free and critical quest for reasons, in all realms of study'. The fostering of rationality in children requires that they be taught critical thinking (Siegel, 1988; Hirst, 1993) and open-mindedness (Hare, 1985). Together, these values involve teaching beliefs to children in a way that leaves the beliefs open to critical, rational evaluation, and they rule out any taking for granted of the truth of ideas that cannot be shown objectively to be true. Thus indoctrination is considered unacceptable in principle in liberal education (Snook, 1972; Thiessen, 1993). Critical openness involves impartiality and objectivity in assessing the validity of one's own beliefs and a willingness to revise these beliefs as new evidence, circumstances and experience comes to light (Hare and McLaughlin, 1994). Free critical debate and the critical examination of alternative beliefs are considered the best ways of advancing the search for truth. Open-mindedness is sometimes associated with neutrality, and implies that children should not be influenced towards any definitive conception of the good life. As Gutmann points out,

> If public schools predisposed citizens towards a particular way of life by educating them as children, the professed neutrality of the liberal state would be a cover for the bias of its educational system.
>
> (1987: 55)

The principle of neutrality has led some liberals to argue that moral education should develop the capacity for moral reasoning and choice without predisposing children towards specific virtues (see Chapter 1). Others, however, argue that there are certain moral values such as justice and equality about which liberalism can never be neutral (Dworkin, 1986: 441) and that moral education should be based on initiation into a rational morality built on these fundamental values (Hirst, 1974b, 1993: 187). The emphasis in liberal education on rationality has sometimes been criticized as emotionally empty and lacking a balanced sense of personhood (cf. O'Hear, 1982: 127f), but many liberals are careful to avoid construing a commitment to reason too narrowly. The dispositions and emotions are not ignored, and, as Hirst points out, there is 'much more to a person than the activities of reason' (1974b: 83).

Personal autonomy

Linked to the fundamental liberal values of freedom and rationality is the development of personal autonomy. Bailey (1984) describes a liberal education as one which liberates individuals from the restrictions of the present and the particular, so that they can become free choosers of what is to be believed and what is to be done. This is in line with Dearden's classic definition of autonomy:

> A person is autonomous, then, to the degree that what he thinks and does in important areas of his life cannot be explained without reference to his own activity of mind. That is to say...to his own choices, deliberations, decisions, reflections, judgements, plannings or reasonings.
>
> (1972: 453)

Kleinig points out that, in addition to choice, autonomy involves 'personal control' and 'initiating agency' (1982: 70). Thiessen identifies autonomy in terms of freedom, independence, authenticity, self-control, rational reflection and competence (1993: 118–19). J. White argues that autonomy is closely linked to personal well-being (1990). There are many things that are likely to contribute to the development of personal autonomy in children: a breadth of knowledge and understanding; an awareness of alternative beliefs and lifestyles; rational decision-making; the ability to think for oneself and rely on reason rather than authority; other desirable dispositions and social competences; self-knowledge and imagination. Personal autonomy as a fundamental educational ideal has been criticized as paying inadequate attention to human emotions and desires (Stone, 1990), as elitist (Halstead, 1986: 38; cf. Pring, 1996), as too 'masculine' a concept (Stone, 1990), and as conflicting with the goal of promoting morally desirable conduct (Lee and Wringe, 1993). However, I have argued elsewhere that we should not construe personal autonomy too narrowly as involving lonely agents 'in an emotionally empty state of rational reflection who have no feeling of what it is to be a person among other persons' (Halstead, 1986: 53). An enriched understanding of autonomy must take account of emotions, needs, attitudes, preferences, feelings and desires, as well as community structures and social interdependence (Kleinig, 1982: 71, 76).

Equality of respect

Reference to community structures and social interdependence leads directly to a consideration of the remaining fundamental liberal value – equality of respect. This is a key value in liberal education, not least because abuse and disrespect generate friction in society (Beck, 1990: 10) and are impediments to the autonomous flourishing of individuals (White, 1994: 179). This value provides the foundation for educational policies opposing discrimination on irrelevant grounds such as the race, gender, ethnicity, nationality, religion, social class or sexuality of the individual. Equality of respect, of course, does not imply complete uniformity or identity of treatment or of achievement in every respect (White, 1994); on the contrary, equality implies the welcoming of diversity, as even Scruton acknowledges in his acerbic comment on liberalism, 'In the perfect liberal suburb, the gardens are of equal size, even though decked out with the greatest possible variety of plastic gnomes' (1984: 192).

Equality of opportunity, however, is implicit within equality of respect, though it is itself an ambiguous term: it is sometimes applied to genuine attempts to increase opportunities for disadvantaged groups and individuals to gain access to valued goals like higher education, but it is also used to justify a competitive approach in which certain opportunities are *formally* available to all, though the inequality among the competitors makes it much harder for some to succeed. At its simplest level, equality of opportunity in education is about the rights of individuals to have equal access to goods and resources, so that no future citizens are unfairly disadvantaged in terms of life chances.

Multicultural education and education for citizenship

I have argued so far that the three fundamental values of liberalism are central to the liberal vision of education as a political and moral enterprise. This becomes even clearer when we examine the response of liberal educationalists to the increasing pluralism in the Western world. This response includes the development of multicultural education and an increasing emphasis on education for citizenship and democracy.

Insofar as multicultural education is concerned with preparing children for life in a pluralist society by encouraging them to respect those whose beliefs and values differ from their own, to see diversity as a source of enrichment and to be open to a variety of ways of looking at the world, it is clearly a liberal approach (cf. Halstead, 1988: chapter 8). Multicultural education contributes to the development of rationality; encouraging children to go beyond the framework of their own culture and beliefs is an important way of helping them to develop lively, enquiring minds, imagination and a critical faculty. Multicultural education is also liberating and a means to the development of moral awareness. As Parekh points out, it is

> an education in freedom – freedom from inherited biases and narrow feelings and sentiments, as well as freedom to explore other cultures and perspectives and make choices in full awareness of the available and practicable alternatives... If education is concerned to develop such basic human capacities as curiosity, self-criticism, capacity for reflection, ability to form an independent judgment, sensitivity, intellectual humility and respect for others, and to open the pupil's mind to the great achievements of mankind, then it must be multicultural in orientation.
>
> (1985: 22–3)

Education for citizenship and democracy is based on the assumptions that in a culturally plural society all children equally need to be prepared for life as citizens of the democratic state and that democratic values are an 'indispensable bulwark against social coercion and manipulation' (White, 1991: 207). It is thus potentially a unifying influence in a plural society, though McLaughlin (1992) has rightly drawn attention to the tension that exists between the desire to develop a sufficiently substantial set of civic virtues in children that will satisfy the communal demands of citizenship, and the need to tolerate diversity within the liberal state. J. White argues that as a minimum citizens will need some knowledge and understanding of their own political situation and of the principles of democracy and 'a ready disposition to apply all this knowledge and understanding in the service of the community' (1982: 117). Others have placed more emphasis on the use of education to protect and promote human rights (Starkey, 1991). P. White and others have argued that democratic values should permeate through all the structures of the school, so that pupils have practical opportunities to participate in decision-making and to develop an awareness of the responsibilities of group life (White, 1983; Chamberlin, 1989). However, Gutmann (1987: 88–94) and Dunlop in this volume have expressed doubts about the wisdom of making schools into democratic institutions.

Criticisms of the liberal democratic vision of education outlined above, as I have already hinted, are not thin on the ground. It has been criticized in particular for neglecting human nature, basic human values like friendship and in particular the emotional dimension of human life (O'Hear, 1982: 127f; Dunlop, 1991). However, many of these criticisms, I have suggested, can be taken on board in an enriched understanding of liberal education, particularly if it takes account of the critiques of liberal values offered from a communication perspective (MacIntyre, 1981; Sandel, 1984; Taylor, 1990; Mulhall and Swift, 1992). Hirst, for example, now favours an understanding of liberal education as concerned to develop 'capacities for critical reflection across the range of basic practices necessary to any flourishing life within a given context' (1993: 98). But there are two particular kinds of criticism that are currently challenging liberal education at a more fundamental level. The first comes from within the liberal framework of values outlined in the first section, but offers a very different emphasis from the one traditionally associated with liberal education. The second comes from groups that reject the whole structure of liberal values. This chapter concludes with a brief examination of these.

Challenges to liberal education

Traditionally, liberal education has been thought to be opposed to strictly utilitarian ends. However, as Pring points out in Chapter 9, there has been over the last fifteen years a renewed emphasis on utilitarian goals for education, such as producing skilled manpower, developing work-related skills and competences and facilitating 'effective competition in the international marketplace' (McMurtry, 1991). In fact, the enterprise culture and free market approach now play a prominent part in school organization and management, and a not insignificant one in the curriculum. These changes are reflected in the language of school management, where parents are customers, the success of a school is judged in terms of its ability to attract customers, senior management teams devise frameworks of quality control, and performance indicators are used by external auditors to monitor progress and effectiveness. As Pring (1994: 18) points out, the new vocationalism 'uses the language of usefulness' and 'cherishes different values'.

What is happening is a clash between a particular version of economic liberalism on the one hand and political liberalism on the other for the control of education. It is a clash between those who want the curriculum to reflect economic relevance and the needs of industry and those who want it to promote personal autonomy and the pursuit of truth, between those who think the performance of a school can best be judged by quantifiable outputs and recorded in league tables and those who would judge a school in terms of the critical understanding, imaginative insight and human relationships it generates. This clash generates very real tensions for teachers who may feel that the interests of the school and the interests of the child are no longer in harmony and that they are trapped between the market values which schools are being forced to adopt and the values which they as educators wish to pass on to their pupils. Undoubtedly it is such tensions which lie behind the strong opposition there has been within the teaching profession to many of the recent educational reforms in the UK.

Although the growth of the enterprise culture and market values in education is thus strongly regretted by many liberals (Bailey, 1992), others express the belief that they are not as incompatible with traditional liberal education as is sometimes claimed. This is because broadly educated students with some knowledge of social problems and moral issues may ultimately be of more use to business and industry than students with specific work-related skills, and also because enterprise education may be seen as an extension of liberal education, in that it develops certain kinds of personal qualities and specific areas of understanding (cf. Bridges, 1992; Pring, 1996).

A more fundamental challenge to liberal education comes from those who do not share its basic values. In particular, the values of liberalism and liberal education are broadly incompatible with Marxism (cf. Harris, 1979; Matthews, 1980), radical feminism (cf. Graham, 1994), postmodernism (cf. Aronowitz and Giroux, 1991; Carr, 1995: chapter 9) and various religious world views, including the Roman Catholic (see Burns, 1992; Arthur, 1994) and the Islamic (see Halstead, 1995), which claim that liberalism lacks a moral and spiritual foundation. To those committed to such world views, liberal education may appear as just one more challengeable version of what is good for children. The Islamic world view, for example, which is based on values drawn from divine revelation, produces an approach to education which is at odds at several crucial points with liberalism. In Islam, the ultimate goal of education is to nurture children in the faith, to make them good Muslims, and children are not encouraged to question the fundamentals of their faith but are expected to accept them on the authority of their elders. How should liberals respond to such a view? Some consider it intolerable and suggest that the state should intervene to protect the rights of the children to be liberated from the constraints of their cultural environment and to grow up into personally autonomous adults (Raz, 1986: 424). The moral justification of such intervention according to liberal principles, however, needs to be tempered by considerations of the social disunity and conflict it would cause. The best hope for a way forward in this situation, in my view, lies with a more tolerant and culturally sensitive approach which combines values drawn from political and moral liberalism (including freedom of conscience, respect for diversity and the search for shared civic values) and values drawn from economic liberalism (including freedom of parental choice and diversity of educational provision; cf. Halstead, 1994), which would allow non-liberal forms of life (i.e. communities, traditions, cultures) to pursue their own vision of the good as they choose, either inside or outside the common school.

References

Ackerman, B.A. (1980) *Social Justice in the Liberal State*, New Haven, CT, Yale University Press.

Ackerman, B.A. (1992) *The Future of Liberal Revolution*, New Haven, CT, Yale University Press.

Aronowitz, S. and Giroux, H.A. (1991) *Postmodern Education: Politics, Culture and Social Criticism*, Minneapolis, MN, University of Minneapolis Press.

Arthur, J. (1994) 'The ambiguities of Catholic schooling', *Westminster Studies in Education*, 17, pp. 65–77.

Bailey, C. (1984) *Beyond the Present and the Particular*, London, Routledge & Kegan Paul.

Bailey, C. (1992) 'Enterprise and liberal education: Some reservations', *Journal of Philosophy of Education*, **26**, 1, pp. 99–106.

Beck, C. (1990) *Better Schools: A Values Perspective*, London, Falmer Press.

Benditt, T.M. (1982) *Rights*, Totowa, NJ, Rowman and Littlefield.

Benn, S.I. and Peters, R.S. (1959) *Social Principles and the Democratic State*, London, Allen and Unwin.

Bentham, J. (1948) *An Introduction to the Principles of Morals and Legislation*, Oxford, Blackwell.

Berlin, I. (1969) *Four Essays on Liberty*, London, Oxford University Press.

Bridges, D. (1992) 'Enterprise and liberal education', *Journal of Philosophy of Education*, **26**, 1, pp. 91–8.

Burns, G. (1992) *The Frontiers of Catholicism: The Politics of Ideology in a Liberal World*, Berkeley, University of California Press.

Carr, W. (1995) *For Education: Towards Critical Educational Enquiry*, Buckingham, Open University Press.

Chamberlin, R. (1989) *Free Children and Democratic Schools: A Philosophical Study of Democratic Education*, Basingstoke, Falmer Press.

Dearden, R.F. (1972) 'Autonomy and education', in Dearden, R.F., Hirst, P.H. and Peters, R.S. (eds), *Education and the Development of Reason*, London, Routledge & Kegan Paul.

Devlin, P. (1965) *The Enforcement of Morals*, Oxford, Oxford University Press.

Duncan, G. (1983) *Democratic Theory and Practice*, Cambridge, Cambridge University Press.

Dunlop, F. (1991) 'The rational-liberal neglect of human nature', *Journal of Philosophy of Education*, **25**, 1, pp. 109–20.

Dworkin, R. (1977) *Taking Rights Seriously*, London, Duckworth.

Dworkin, R. (1978) 'Liberalism', in Hampshire, S. (ed.), *Public and Private Morality*, Cambridge, Cambridge University Press.

Dworkin, R. (1986) *Law's Empire*, Cambridge, MA, Belknap/Harvard University Press.

Fishkin, J.S. (1984) *Beyond Subjective Morality*, New Haven, CT, Yale University Press.

Freeden, M. (1978) *The New Liberalism*, Oxford, Clarendon Press.

Friedman, M. (1962) *Capitalism and Freedom*, Chicago, IL, University Press.

Gaus, G. (1983) *The Modern Liberal Theory of Man*, London, Croom Helm.

Gewirth, A. (1984) 'Are there any absolute rights?', in Waldron, J. (ed.), *Theories of Rights*, Oxford, Oxford University Press.

Graham, G. (1994) 'Liberal vs radical feminism revisited', *Journal of Applied Philosophy*, **11**, 2, pp. 155–70.

Gutmann, A. (1980) *Liberal Equality*, Cambridge, Cambridge University Press.

Gutmann, A. (1987) *Democratic Education*, Princeton, NJ, Princeton University Press.

Halstead, J.M. (1986) *The Case for Muslim Voluntary-aided Schools: Some Philosophical Reflections*, Cambridge, Islamic Academy.

Halstead, J.M. (1988) *Education, Justice and Cultural Diversity: An Examination of the Honeyford Affair, 1984–85*, Basingstoke, Falmer Press.

Halstead, J.M. (1994) 'Parental choice: An overview', in Halstead, J.M. (ed.), *Parental choice and Education: Principles, Policy and Practice*, London, Kogan Page.

Halstead, J.M. (1995) 'Towards a unified view of Islamic education', *Islam and Christian–Muslim Relations*, **6**, 1, pp. 25–43.

Hampshire, S. (ed.) (1978) *Public and Private Morality*, Cambridge, Cambridge University Press.

Hare, W. (1985) *In Defence of Open-Mindedness*, Kingston and Montreal, Canada, McGill-Queen's University Press.

Hare, W. and McLaughlin, T.H. (1994) 'Open-mindedness, commitment and Peter Gardner', *Journal of Philosophy of Education*, **28**, 2, pp. 239–44.

Harris, K. (1979) *Education and Knowledge*, London, Routledge & Kegan Paul.

Hart, H.L.A. (1963) *Law, Liberty and Morality*, Oxford, Oxford University Press.

Hart, H.L.A. (1984) 'Are there any natural rights?', in Waldron, J. (ed.), *Theories of Rights*, Oxford, Oxford University Press.

Hayek, F.A. (1960) *The Constitution of Liberty*, London, Routledge & Kegan Paul.

Hirst, P.H. (1974a) *Knowledge and the Curriculum*, London, Routledge & Kegan Paul.

Hirst, P.H. (1974b) *Moral Education in a Secular Society*, London, Hodder and Stoughton.
Hirst, P.H. (1985) 'Education and diversity of belief', in Felderhof, M.C. (ed.), *Religious Education in a Pluralistic Society*, London, Hodder and Stoughton.
Hirst, P.H. (1993) 'Education, knowledge and practices', in Barrow, R. and White, P. (eds), *Beyond Liberal Education: Essays in Honour of Paul H. Hirst*, London, Routledge.
Hollis, M. and Lukes, S. (eds) (1982) *Rationality and Relativism*, Oxford, Blackwell.
Jenkins, I. (1980) *Social Order and the Limits of Law*, Princeton, NJ, University Press.
Kant, I. (1948) *The Moral Law* (tr. Paton H.J.), London, Hutchinson.
Kimball, B.A. (1986) *Orators and Philosophers: A History of the Idea of Liberal Education*, New York, Teachers College Press.
Kleinig, J. (1982) *Philosophical Issues in Education*, London, Croom Helm.
Koerner, K.F. (1985) *Liberalism and its Critics*, London, Croom Helm.
Lee, J.-H. and Wringe, C. (1993) 'Rational autonomy, morality and education', *Journal of Philosophy of Education*, 27, 1, pp. 69–78.
Lucas, J.R. (1976) *Democracy and Participation*, Harmondsworth, Penguin.
McCloskey, H.J. (1985) 'Respect for human moral rights versus maximising good', in Frey, R.G. (ed.), *Utility and Rights*, Oxford, Blackwell.
MacIntyre, A. (1981) *After Virtue*, London, Duckworth.
MacIntyre, A. (1988) *Whose Justice? Which Rationality?*, Notre Dame, IN, University of Notre Dame Press.
McLaughlin, T.H. (1992) 'Citizenship, diversity and education: A philosophical perspective', *Journal of Moral Education*, 21, 3, pp. 235–50.
McMurtry, J. (1991) 'Education and the market model', *Journal of Philosophy of Education*, 25, 2, pp. 209–17.
Matthews, M. (1980) *The Marxist Theory of Schooling*, London, Routledge & Kegan Paul.
Mill, J.S. (1972a) *Utilitarianism* (first published 1863), London, Dent.
Mill, J.S. (1972b) *On Liberty* (first published 1859), London, Dent.
Miller, D. (1976) *Social Justice*, Oxford, Clarendon Press.
Miller, D. (1993) 'In defence of nationality', *Journal of Applied Philosophy*, 10, 1, pp. 3–16.
Mulhall, S. and Swift, A. (1992) *Liberals and Communitarians*, Oxford, Blackwell.
Norman, R. (1982) 'Does equality destroy liberty?', in Graham, K. (ed.), *Contemporary Political Philosophy: Radical Studies*, Cambridge, Cambridge University Press.
O'Hear, A. (1982) *Education, Society and Human Nature: An Introduction to the Philosophy of Education*, London, Routledge & Kegan Paul.
Parekh, B. (1985) 'The gifts of diversity', in *The Times Educational Supplement*, 29 March, pp. 22–3.
Pateman, C. (1970) *Participation and Democratic Theory*, Cambridge, Cambridge University Press.
Pateman, C. (1979) *The Problem of Political Obligation: A Critical Analysis of Liberal Theory*, Chichester, John Wiley.
Peters, R.S. (1966) *Ethics and Education*, London, Allen and Unwin.
Peters, R.S. (1977) *Education and the Education of Teachers*, London, Routledge & Kegan Paul.
Popper, K.R. (1966) *The Open Society and its Enemies, Vols I and II*, London, Routledge & Kegan Paul.
Pring, R. (1994) 'Liberal and vocational education: A conflict of value', in Haldane, J. (ed.), *Education, Values and the State: the Victor Cook Memoral Lectures*, St Andrews, Centre for Philosophy and Public Affairs, University of St Andrews.
Pring, R. (1996) 'Values and education policy', in Halstead, J.M. and Taylor, M.J. (eds), *Values in Education and Education in Values*, London, Falmer Press, pp. 104–17.
Raphael, D.D. (1981) *Moral Philosophy*, Oxford, Oxford University Press.
Rawls, J. (1972) *A Theory of Justice*, Oxford, Oxford University Press.
Rawls, J. (1993) *Political Liberalism*, New York, Columbia University Press.
Raz, J. (1986) *The Morality of Freedom*, Oxford, Clarendon.
Sandel, M. (1984) *Liberalism and its Critics*, Oxford, Blackwell.
Scheffler, I. (1973) *Reason and Teaching*, London, Routledge & Kegan Paul.
Scruton, R. (1984) *The Meaning of Conservatism* (2nd edn), London, Macmillan.
Siedentop, L. (1979) 'Two Liberal traditions', in Ryan, A. (ed.), *The Idea of Freedom*, Oxford, Oxford University Press.

Siegel, H. (1988) *Educating Reason: Rationality, Critical Thinking and Education*, London, Routledge.

Smart, J.J.C. and Williams, B. (1973) *Utilitarianism: For and Against*, Cambridge, Cambridge University Press.

Snook, I. (1972) *Indoctrination and Education*, London, Routledge & Kegan Paul.

Starkey, H. (ed.) (1991) *The Challenge of Human Rights Education*, London, Cassell.

Stone, C.M. (1990) 'Autonomy, emotions and desires: Some problems concerning R.F. Dearden's account of autonomy', *Journal of Philosophy of Education*, 24, 2, pp. 271–83.

Strike, K.A. (1982a) *Liberty and Learning*, Oxford, Martin Robertson.

Strike, K.A. (1982b) *Educational Policy and the Just Society*, Urbana, IL, University of Illinois Press.

Tamir, Y. (1993) *Liberal Nationalism*, Princeton, NJ, Princeton University Press.

Taylor, C. (1982) 'Rationality', in Hollis, M. and Lukes, S. (eds), *Rationality and Relativism*, Oxford, Blackwell.

Taylor, C. (1990) *Sources of the Self*, Cambridge, Cambridge University Press.

Thiessen, E.J. (1993) *Teaching for Commitment: Liberal Education, Indoctrination and Christian Nurture*, Montreal and Kingston, Canada, McGill-Queen's University Press.

Walsh, D. (1990) *After Ideology: Recovering the Spiritual Foundations of Freedom*, New York, Harper Collins.

White, J. (1982) *The Aims of Education Restated*, London, Routledge & Kegan Paul.

White, J. (1990) *Education and the Good Life: Beyond the National Curriculum*, London, Kogan Page.

White, J. (1994) 'The dishwasher's child: Education and the end of egalitarianism', *Journal of Philosophy of Education*, 28, 2, pp. 173–81.

White, P. (1983) *Beyond Domination: An Essay in the Political Philosophy of Education*, London, Routledge & Kegan Paul.

White, P. (1991) 'Hope, confidence and democracy', *Journal of Philosophy of Education*, 25, 2, pp. 203–8.

White, R. (1986) 'The anatomy of a Victorian debate: An essay on the history of liberal education', *British Journal of Educational Studies*, 34, 1, pp. 38–65.

CHAPTER 9

THE POLITICS OF DIFFERENCE AND COMMON EDUCATION

Eamonn Callan

In David Carr (ed.) *Education, Knowledge and Truth* (1998),
London: Routledge, pp. 145–158

1

Many people believe that their culture is the core of the one life worthy of human beings or that those who belong to supposedly inferior cultures count for little or nothing.[1] I call such beliefs and the conduct they motivate 'chauvinism'. The word names a familiar evil, at work not only in the horrors of ethnic cleansing but also in the pettier bigotries that fuel so many social conflicts around the world.

A common idea in much postmodernist social thought is that the tradition of liberal politics we inherit from the Enlightenment is morally defunct because it is inherently chauvinistic. By 'the tradition of liberal politics' I mean a family of ways of thinking about good government and the good society. Liberalism is rooted in the ideal of free and equal citizenship, and although its adherents often differ about how that ideal is best interpreted, they agree that institutions and policies must be assessed on the basis of their contribution to the well-being of citizens rather than, say, the glory of God or the success of some transcendent group project. Liberals will also say that acceptable terms of social co-operation must include a framework of individual rights that secures for all such goods as liberty of conscience and privacy.

The cardinal values of the liberal tradition have powerful educational implications. For they imply that future citizens must learn to adopt the shared public morality that sustains the tradition, and if these values are indeed inherently chauvinistic, this should be evident in the education they support. Much of Iris Marion Young's influential and avowedly postmodernist critique of liberalism is levelled against the culturally assimilative education it entails.[2] Young is a useful focus for my purposes because she is always a lucid and often a perceptive social critic who tries to give some tangible form to what many others only gesture vaguely towards – the possibility of a society that would make cultural difference its sovereign value while moving decisively beyond the confining limits of liberal individualism. Against Young, I argue that so far as the allure of her 'politics of difference' depends on our antipathy to chauvinism, her political prescriptions cannot really be distinguished from the liberal tradition. That is so because a world without chauvinism depends on an education that would establish the moral discipline of liberal politics.

The charge of chauvinism against liberalism is typically enmeshed with sceptical claims about reason and knowledge as these have been construed within Western philosophy, and Young's argument is no exception in that regard. But I doubt that the current attraction of the postmodernist label can be dissipated merely by criticizing what its advocates say about the relation between language and the world, truth and power, the authority of reason or the like, however cogent the criticism might be. I suspect that such criticism is often resisted because people think something *morally* powerful is expressed through the postmodernist indictment of liberal modernity. To reject postmodernist strictures on reason, impartiality and kindred concepts is somehow to remain mired in chauvinism, or so the argument goes. Therefore, it becomes important to examine postmodernist politico-moral themes in a way that does not begin and end with the anti-rationalist polemic within which the themes are typically enunciated. I return to the problems of postmodernist antirationalism as my argument unfolds, but until Section 3, these will not be in the foreground. In fact, I hope to show that there is something true and important in postmodernist anti-rationalism. That is the rejection of something I call 'moral hyper-rationalism'. Moral hyper-rationalism is both closely related to chauvinism and a prominent vice in the imperfectly liberal polities in which we live. But liberal ideals and the education they would support are not discredited by debunking hyper-rationalism, and although a more thoroughgoing anti-rationalism undermines liberalism, it also lays waste to any ethical viewpoint that could take the problem of chauvinism seriously.

2

Young espouses an 'ideal of city life'. The city is her focus because existing cities intimate, albeit very imperfectly, the social relations that would flourish were the politics of difference to prevail against the homogenizing imperatives of liberal modernity. 'City life' signifies 'the being together of strangers'. To be sure, the city is a place where communities of different kinds proliferate. But there we also mingle with strangers whose identity is so utterly different from ours that whatever delight or insight our relations might afford, they cannot yield the dissolution of self and mutual transparency intrinsic to full-blown community. Furthermore, the 'eroticization' of difference in the city means that its cultural variety becomes internalized. Citizens learn to find the free play of difference both within and without, as their kaleidoscopic social world arouses a restless longing for the strange and the exotic (Young, 1990: 236–41).

Set aside for now the question whether 'city life' is a persuasive vision of the good society. Why do we need to forsake liberalism if we are as taken with the charms of urbanity as Young would like us to be? Her answer is that city life requires practices that are ruled out by assumptions of liberal politics. Prime among these assumptions is the idea that individuals have moral standing only in abstraction from group differences and, therefore, group rights or even policies that foster group identity have no role to play in a liberal society.

In liberalism as Young depicts it, difference is transcended in the civic sphere. The common viewpoint of citizens is fixed by an ideal of impartial, homogeneous reason that abstracts from the dense particularity of their lives. Young contends that this ideal is a figment because all thought is 'situated', shot through with the partialities that make us irredeemably different knowers and choosers. The real social function of impartiality is to seal a veneer of rectitude on the interests of those with power and privilege (Young, 1990: 114–15). What presents itself as impartial judgement 'reinforces oppression by hypostatizing the point of view of privileged groups into a universal position' (p. 112).

The politics of difference requires the creation of a 'heterogeneous' public: 'we require real participatory structures in which actual people, with their geographical, ethnic, gender and occupational differences, assert their perspectives on social issues within institutions that encourage the representation of their distinct voices' (Young, 1990: 116). The necessary institutions include a system of collective rights that would empower marginalized groups (pp. 240–1). Yet something should be salvaged from the detritus of liberalism. Basic individual rights must be protected against 'each majority's whims' (pp. 93–4). Young's depiction of liberal politics involves some distortion. But she is alert to something crucial even on some less uncharitable reading of the tradition than the one she gives. Liberal politics must include a project of cultural assimilation, a project that Young describes as 'the transcendence of group difference' (p. 157). Citizens must, as a rule, become alike in certain ways. They must receive a common education that furnishes whatever knowledge and instils whatever habits of thought and feeling that participating competently in the government of a free people requires. Under the conditions of pluralism that obtain in liberal democracies, many kinds of separate education will thrive alongside the common education that assimilates all to a shared civic perspective. Furthermore, liberal theorists, and ordinary citizens as well, may disagree about what measures a state can justly pursue in support of the assimilative process of common education. And of course, it is one thing to say that some assimilative process is necessary and quite another to suggest that *what* future citizens are assimilated to is chauvinism with a mask of impartial moral reason.

Although Young says little explicitly about the educational practices that would perpetuate that politics of difference from one generation to another, she evidently thinks they could not be assimilative. 'In public life [in the ideal city] the differences remain unassimilated' (Young, 1990: 241). But a glance at the distance between our world and city life shows that the latter is not a place where 'differences remain unassimilated'. Many existing differences that are constitutive of identity for us have disappeared in Young's ideal. That means the progress of the politics of difference from our fallen state to the utopia of city life must assimilate those whose lives are now marked by these pre-postliberal differences.

The relevant differences derive from the many conceptions of the good that do not revolve around a playful engagement with the exotic; instead, the good is conceived in terms of a creed or a fixed set of priorities, and although those who reject these are tolerated, even respected, alternative ways of life hold no attraction save as sources of temptation and distraction. The salience of such differences in our world should be obvious – religious diversity is only its most obvious manifestation. In city life, all this has been transcended because we have all become connoisseurs of cultural flux.

The exclusion entailed here is more than an oversight. City life cannot be rid of its latent assimilative agenda merely by saying that all of us will be welcome there, after all. The exclusion of credal and related differences from Young's city is implicit in her interpretation of the subjectivity proper to members of the heterogeneous public. Overcoming oppression demands a 'revolution' in the subject of political judgement because otherwise we confront differences with an amalgam of fear and loathing: 'Rather than seeking a wholeness of the self, we who are the subjects of this plural and complex society should affirm the otherness within ourselves, acknowledging that as subjects we are heterogeneous and multiple in our affiliations and desires' (Young, 1990: 124). Those who have not experienced the revolution in subjectivity that Young prescribes are still burdened with civically unsavoury ideas of inner wholeness, and so they, or at least their children, would require Enlightenment if they were to become morally qualified members of the heterogeneous public.

The assimilative thrust of Young's politics of difference extends further. A world populated exclusively by mercurial connoisseurs of difference might also be a war of all against all. So diversity must be tamed by the cultivation of certain moral uniformities. At the very least, the structures necessary to the politics of difference – for example a scheme of group rights – will have to be made stable, and that will presumably require that citizens learn to care about those whom the structures protect. But that, too, is not enough. Justice will depend on the public deliberation that proceeds within the structures Young endorses. The reliability with which deliberation serves justice hinges on the discernment and character of those who participate, which will in turn depend on the common education that all receive.

The task that faces Young's heterogeneous public is to overcome oppression. But the public must understand oppression in a more nuanced fashion than mainstream political theory has acknowledged. Young identifies five 'faces' of oppression – exploitation, marginalization, cultural imperialism, powerlessness and violence – whose significance is obscured by our inordinate preoccupation with the distribution of material or quasi-material goods. 'Objective' criteria mark the five faces of oppression (Young, 1990: 65). That is to say, the criteria can be either applied correctly or not, and if the heterogeneous public is to reason as it should, those who learn to apply them correctly had better be more numerous than those who do not. Whatever individual and group differences stand in the way of that outcome must be transcended if the politics of difference is to succeed.

If liberalism is chauvinistic, this should come to light once we juxtapose it with some more culturally accommodating way of conceiving the good society. Young's conception of city life and its politics of difference are supposed to provide the needed light. But the outlines of the contrast are becoming severely blurred. A common education that cultivates the moral discipline of citizenship is as essential to Young's vision as it is to the liberalism she abjures. The question we now face is whether the particular discipline that common education would impose under Young's ideal polity is preferable to what liberal common education would exact, given that an antipathy to chauvinism is our criterion of choice.

Before addressing that question directly, I want to distinguish it from another, vaguely similar question that might appear to be a serviceable substitute for the one I have posed. Will there be *more* cultural difference in city life than there is in liberal societies? The question is foolish. Suppose two societies are alike in all respects save this: in one a practice that instantiates a 'face of oppression' continues – a practice of child-rearing, say, that involves violence towards children. The same practice had died out in the other society. Where the practice continues, it is a focus of identity for a particular social group. Notice how preposterous it would be to say that the society that tolerates the oppressive practice is better because it contains 'more' difference. True, it does contain a wider cultural diversity. But this detracts from the goodness of the society according to the very criteria that Young says give us the measure of the society's goodness.

The foolishness of the question – which society contains *more* cultural difference? – is worth stressing because it is easy to think that once we take the sin of chauvinism seriously the question becomes important. If we forswear *any* judgement about other cultures, and conceive the good society simply as one that welcomed indiscriminately as many cultural differences as possible, then it might seem that we were as far away from the risks of chauvinism as we could get. This 'non-judgemental' pluralism is one current among others in Young's thought, and it provides a way of creating some contrast between a liberal polity and city life. But the contrast is created only by repudiating the resources of moral criticism that are necessary to the construction of any credible social ideal, liberal or otherwise. If we want a world without chauvinism, we need to learn to make whatever moral judgements its avoidance requires, and so far as some cultures are carriers of chauvinism, we need to condemn them. An antipathy to chauvinism and an indiscriminate embrace of difference are not just distinct attitudes – they are incompatible.

The problem of moral discrimination on which non-judgemental pluralism founders is not solved by the revolution in subjectivity that is central to Young's assimilative agenda. Although she writes as if learning to find a plenitude of suppressed desires within ourselves teaches us appropriately to respond to the differences that abound in our social environment, that merely displaces the problem of moral discrimination. Simone Weil said somewhere that if she entered a room of Nazis singing patriotic songs something deep within herself would make her want to join them. Weil rightly thought this was no reason to include Nazis within the scope of the cultural differences we should celebrate. The welter of desire within any psyche is as much in need of moral scrutiny as the flux of culture that flows without.

3

The common education intrinsic to the politics of difference teaches us to prize cultural differences. How much distance does this put between the education Young wants and what liberal politics would commend?

Two important issues in recent liberal theory (and practice) are these: whether free and equal citizenship can be adequately protected by a system of political rights that ignores differences of ethnicity and gender, for example, where these yield sharply divergent interests some of which will be systematically slighted under that system; and whether a polity that ignores the fragile condition of some minority cultures can treat all with the dignity appropriate to citizens, given the intimate connection of cultural affiliation to self-respect (cf. Kymlicka, 1989, 1995; Spinner, 1994; Phillips, 1995). These are complicated questions. The best answers might not always be the ones Young would give. But they are questions *inside* the wide spectrum of liberal discourse that a good common education would encourage future citizens to address. So long as the questions are pressed within that setting, group rights and cultural recognition are understood in terms of their possible contribution to 'the prosperity of individual human beings' (Raz, 1994: 163). In other words, the relevant rights and recognition might be endorsed because of the benefits they bring to people who would otherwise be unfairly disadvantaged; they will not be chosen because cultures have a moral significance that supersedes their importance for individuals. But since Young thinks that the claims of groups cannot justify the oppression of individuals, she is evidently on the side of liberalism here as well (Young, 1990: 174).

A real distinction does separate an education that would insist on the unassailable correctness of something like Young's views on what is needed to affirm cultural differences and a liberal common education that approaches these matters in a more Socratic spirit. The latter would present liberal politics as a fluid set of beliefs and practices that properly evolves in response to local contingencies, broader social changes and the challenge of criticism. Throughout the processes of re-invention, a thread of continuity is sustained by an abstract ideal of citizenship and a reverence for the dignity of individuals. The question of how hospitable the just society can be to group differences has been a prominent motif within the tradition since its inception, and liberal education in a Socratic spirit will question established orthodoxy on such matters without attempting to install some heterodox dogma in its place. But not only is an antipathy to chauvinism consistent with common education in a Socratic spirit; it is necessary if we are to combat chauvinism, or so Young herself would seem to imply. The identification of chauvinism by those who live under institutions that encourage it presupposes independence of mind, and Young believes we live under institutions that corrupt us in just that way (e.g. Young, 1990: 134–5).

However, Young might object to education in the Socratic spirit on the grounds that any appeal to the independence of mind proper to free citizens invokes the nefarious ideal of impartial moral reason. This takes us to the heart of the matter. If Young is really recommending a wholesale rejection of impartiality, she is driven to non-judgemental pluralism. Alternatively, if her argument is read as supporting a contextually sensitive interpretation of impartiality, its congruity with liberal conceptions of moral reason becomes obvious. Since non-judgemental pluralism is inconsistent with an antipathy to chauvinism, only the latter, liberal construal of her position can provide the basis for an acceptable common education. Therefore, the gap between a morally credible politics of difference and liberalism has vanished.

We deem judgements, laws, and so on, impartial when we think they are unaffected by bias – that is, by illicit preference for the interests of some individual or group. A preference for the interests of some may count as illicit according to either of two, potentially conflicting perspectives: the range of reasons that rightly informs moral choice or whatever considerations are defined as relevant to choice by the rules of a given institution. Corresponding to the moral and the institutional charge of bias, we have moral and institutional conceptions of impartiality.

This distinction brings into relief what should puzzle us about Young's rejection of impartiality. She cannot mean that the rules shaping institutions in existing, professedly liberal societies are tainted by moral bias towards many who are marked as culturally different, with the consequence that the impartial application of those rules is oppressive. Her case would then be a paradigmatic liberal argument about the conditions of equal citizenship and the failure of existing institutions to embody them. Young's target must be the *moral* impartiality to which liberals appeal if she is to open up any distance between her politics of difference and the liberal tradition she disavows. How is Young's argument to be understood if that is indeed her target?

I suggested that impartiality acquires a moral content when it is coupled with principles and ideals that tell us what is morally relevant to our choices. According to one line of thought within liberal modernity, moral impartiality is achieved by prescinding in some drastic way from the context of deliberation, isolating a sparse array of reasons that is the same always and everywhere (e.g. Kohlberg, 1981). Young treats this particular version of impartiality as if it were the only possibility. But this is in fact a rather grotesque misconception. Moral judgement is as susceptible to error through discounting the relevant as it is through heeding the irrelevant, and I am as likely to be tempted to make the first as the second mistake by illicit preferences for particular individuals or groups. Therefore, the ascent to a more abstract level of thought will sometimes betoken bias rather than the pull of moral impartiality on its best interpretation.

This is a crucial point for an adequate understanding of moral impartiality. Unduly abstract conceptions of impartiality will hide morally significant contingencies from view, including those that have to do with cultural differences.

Therefore, we should expect excessive abstraction to appeal to those who, for morally deplorable reasons, want cultural differences ignored. If I want to maintain the unjust disadvantages under which some group lives, I will want to find a way of talking about politics that dismisses their disadvantages as irrelevant, and hence my chauvinism can masquerade as impartiality. A better conception of moral impartiality will militate against that pretence by specifying values that bring what was occluded by excessive abstraction into the light of common deliberation. That is what Young seems to be trying to do when she talks of traditionally neglected 'faces of oppression'. But if all Young wanted were some more capacious, contextually sensitive understanding of moral impartiality, she would be making common cause with liberal theorists who make just the same point (e.g. Johnston, 1994). Young's willingness to take the further step and discard impartiality, root and branch, is what makes her politics of difference genuinely postliberal. But that step turns out to be self-defeating.

Adapting Theodor Adorno's argument against 'the logic of identity', Young claims that impartial moral reason is but one example of the more general pathology of Western thought that Adorno diagnosed. The pathology consists in the urge to 'think things together, to reduce them to a unity'. However, the reduction does violence to the richly variegated world on which the logic of difference is imposed: 'Reason, discourse is already inserted in a plural, heterogeneous world that outruns totalising comprehension.' Because the world 'outruns' our rational categories, what impartiality really does is to dichotomize rather than unify. 'Not satisfied then to admit defeat in the face of difference, the logic of identity shoves difference into dichotomous hierarchical oppositions: essence/accident, good/bad, normal/deviant' (Young, 1990: 98–9). I am not competent to decipher the mysteries of Adorno's critique of the logic identity. But the one small point I wish to make is independent of these.

All conceptions of impartial moral reason purport to tell us what matters in general to our decisions about how to live, including what is valuable or tolerable difference on the one hand and unacceptable deviance on the other. If all conceptions of that kind fall prey to the critique of 'the logic of identity', then impartial reason has no legitimate purchase on our lives. The trouble is that if we are consistent in our avoidance of what the critique condemns, we have effectively adopted non-judgemental pluralism. Any attempt to judge the practices of some group as chauvinistic will install those very dichotomies – good/bad, normal/deviant, etc. – that Adorno's critique has taught us to relinquish. Since an antipathy to chauvinism cannot be reconciled with non-judgemental pluralism, whatever reasons we have to reject chauvinism must also be reasons to reject Adorno's critique, at least on any reading of the critique which takes it to entail the rejection of moral impartiality.

Non-judgemental pluralism is a way of giving up on moral reason. Therefore, the deliberative task that face Young's heterogeneous public, who attempt to see and overcome the oppression in their midst, must succumb to silence if they are consistent in their rejection of impartiality. Nevertheless, there is something to Young's argument against impartial reason that I have yet to bring into clear view, something that is, I suggest, the most interesting reason why postmodernist anti-rationalism has come to seem so morally wholesome to many.

Suppose my general conception of impartiality is not marred by excessive abstraction. Nothing in the moral values to which I subscribe necessarily blinds me to morally significant particularities. But I assume that when my judgement is rid of bias and the other vices of unreason, I will agree with all other reasonable people about how to live. Inclusive agreement among reasonable people is the feasible goal of moral reason, and whenever we fall short of agreement, it must be because some of us are biased, irrational, uncivilized or the like. This is 'moral hyper-rationalism'.

Notice the attitude towards cultural differences that hyper-rationalism will support in the following circumstances. My cultural identity ties me to groups who have traditionally dominated my society. I am a conscientious person, and I try to judge impartially in the beliefs I form and the choices I make qua citizen. Nevertheless, the upshot of my efforts are convictions and choices that are generally typical of people with cultural affinities like my own. People who belong to more marginal groups in my society tend to see things differently. But if I am confident that I have succeeded in being impartial, I must be equally confident, by virtue of hyper-rationalism, that all who disagree with me are guilty of bias or some other culpable lapse of reason. To whatever extent I see cultural differences as causally implicated in our disagreement, I must also see minority cultures as sources of error and evil. Of course, this could all be badly wrong. Those who disagree with me are perhaps no less reasonable than I am. And in that event, my commitment to impartiality has modulated into chauvinism or something pretty close to it.

But the slide from impartiality towards chauvinism depends on hyper-rationalism, and we have good reason to resist hyper-rationalism. Why? The reasons are many and complex, but something of their cumulative force can be conveyed here (Rawls, 1993: 54–8). Moral concepts are subject to hard cases. Their application includes a range of cases where reasonable people can be expected to disagree. Second, to a degree we can never precisely determine, judgements reflect particularities of sensibility and individual history, as well as wider cultural differences and conflicts of interest, whose influence we cannot surmount with certainty, no matter how scrupulously we reason. Third, the moral concepts we use in shaping what we take to be a good society are linked to the many different ways of life that people rationally choose. The concepts we employ may be designed so as to be broadly accommodating to diversity – the concept of a right to freedom is the prime example of this. But it would be foolish to suppose that even the feasibly best society will be equally congenial to all worthwhile ways of life. A social world that is equally welcoming to Salman Rushdie and conservative Muslims is an impossibility. Not all good lives can thrive equally in a good society. Therefore, the moral concepts we employ in politics will be ethically selective, and this in turn will create room for reasonable disagreement about how judicious our selectivity really is.

All this suggests that much of our disagreement about how to live together is not to be explained by a propensity to bias or any other remediable failure of intelligence or goodwill. We are divided by reasonable as well as unreasonable disagreement. Even when the shared exercise of moral reason is laudably impartial, the inherent frailties of human judgement are such that we will often fall short of consensus. But hyper-rationalism tells me that when you and I disagree, only one of us can be reasonable, and since I cannot think that the reasonable one is you without ceasing to disagree, I cannot see your viewpoint as one that merits my respect. You *must* be biased or morally or intellectually derelict in some other way. So whenever political disagreement follows the fault lines of cultural differences, hyper-rationalism will marginalize whatever distinctive perspective minorities might have, and it will make any accommodation with them seem like a surrender to ignorance or worse. Furthermore, the harm wrought by hyper-rationalism will tend to escalate as any society becomes more culturally diverse, either through the fragmentation of established cultures or immigration. Increasing cultural diversity will tend to increase the scope of reasonable political disagreement. At the same time, hyper-rationalists will infer only that more benighted people now clutter their world, people whose views they must, after impartial consideration, simply dismiss.

But it is calamitous to think that due sensitivity to reasonable disagreement in politics and its entanglement with cultural differences mean we should abandon the ideal of impartiality. Recall that one reason Young gives for doing so is the fact that we all think and choose in ways coloured by culture. When that point is re-cast as an objection to hyper-rationalism, it makes good sense: it becomes a humbling reminder that just because our own best moral judgements are reasonable they may not be uniquely so. But if we take her point literally as a general repudiation of impartiality, it becomes a licence to stop worrying about the difference between our best judgements and our raw prejudices. The bias we hope to overcome in struggling towards our best judgement is really intractable because our partiality is relentless. To change one's mind is only to discard one bias for another. Respect for reasonable differences becomes impossible here because differences cannot be adjudicated on the basis of reason. So we are back to non-judgemental pluralism, and the disintegration of any discourse that could take oppression seriously.

I will not deny that hyper-rationalism is a sin that has loomed large in the history of liberal theory, to say nothing of the often sordid reality of politics in avowedly liberal societies. But a commitment to moral reason is fundamental to the liberal, and any other credible social ideal. And if the kernel of insight in arguments for a politics of difference is the imperative to respect reasonable disagreement, the insight is central to much contemporary liberal philosophy (e.g. Macedo, 1990; Rawls, 1993; Gutmann and Thompson, 1996). More important perhaps, the insight lies within the virtues of moderation and principled compromise that characterize ordinary liberal politics at its honourable best.

4

I have said much here and implied still more about the common education proper to a liberal democracy. What I have said and implied will be challenged by many who have little sympathy with the politics of difference. An education that encourages children to grapple with the sources of reasonable pluralism, for example, harbours an ideal of personal autonomy that may be corrosive of some established religious groups. Some liberals will say that the moral ends of common education should be set more modestly, securing minimal ends of mutual tolerance rather than more strenuous and controversial ideals of civic virtue. Still others will doubt that the liberal tradition, unless it is complemented or corrected through ideals of community and the common good to which the tradition has been intermittently hostile, can provide an adequate vision of the good society and the education it would support. I say nothing to resolve these disputes here, although I have said a lot elsewhere (Callan, 1997).

But serious collective deliberation about the content of common education, in which the objections I have just mentioned are pondered, is the very foundation of educational endeavour for a free people. Without that, the idea of a national curriculum, for example, can be no more than an arbitrary imposition. My efforts here have been directed at one style of contemporary thought that threatens to undermine serious thought about common education. When it is not a kind of crypto-liberalism, the postmodernist case for a politics of difference descends into non-judgemental pluralism. Unfortunately, a world in which we wallow in unassimilated otherness is a poor substitute for a society in which justice might be done. But postmodernism is not the only cultural threat we face to serious thought about common education. Another, vastly larger threat confronts us. I will end by saying a little about that threat and its curious relation to Young's ideal of city life.

Western modernity is a far less monolithic cultural epoch than the coarse-grained caricature of much postmodern social criticism might suggest. One powerful idea that runs through so many aspects of the world we have inherited is the instrumentalist conception of practical reason. According to that conception, reason tells us how to pursue our ends successfully, but it can say nothing about what those ends should be. So instrumentalism must be silent on the questions of what is a good society and a good common education to the extent that these are about what ends we should pursue. But it does entail that we would be foolish to look for an answer more rational than any other because instrumentalism says there is none.

Suppose for the moment that we accept instrumentalism. It does not follow that we are at a loss to answer questions about social order. For many of instrumentalism's contemporary devotees, the market is the institution *par excellence* that co-ordinates behaviour without presupposing that anyone's ends are more rational than anyone else's. A market in religion allows people to shop around for the church that meets their spiritual desires just as a market in television allows you to select the channels that you want. And if this works for religion and television, it will work for education. Let people choose the educational products they want in the market. Talk of common education is idle chatter or a means by which powerful groups impose their ends on others. By this train of reasoning, instrumentalism seems to lead to a radical diversification of educational provision, without a thought for the common education that might be forfeited thereby.

Instrumentalism will seem friendly to difference in another way. When instrumentalists have different ends, at least one source of conflict is dissolved by their shared recognition that ends are not amenable to reasoned assessment. They understand that their difference does not mean that one is right and the other wrong. Indeed, they may come to enjoy differences that in a less enlightened world would occasion distress or conflict. Diversity has its delights. A city with many different ethnic restaurants is nicer than one with just a few. A city with many different cultures is more charming than one with just a few, or so the connoisseur of difference might suppose.

This takes us back to the question I set aside in Section 2. I asked there if Young's city life is a persuasive vision of the good society. No doubt different readers will respond differently to that question. But I think those who will be enticed are at least latent instrumentalists. A world in which we unambivalently celebrate difference could not be a world where those differences are invested with any ethical meaning. It would have to be a place where differences were reduced to mere objects of desire, that only a fool would think were subject to reflective evaluation. But because many of the differences we find in our world, both within and across cultures, are ethically significant for us, enmeshed with rival understandings of good and evil, right and wrong, we cannot without bad faith respond to them with the welcoming embrace that connoisseurs of difference would evince. Postmodernism and instrumentalism might seem like strange bed-fellows, but in their hostility to moral reason they share much.

Liberal politics offers another accommodation of diversity, one that does not extirpate ethical difference for the sake of a convivial harmony. Without requiring us to surrender our divergent ethical beliefs, it asks us to adjust these in light of the fact of reasonable disagreement, and to live in mutual respect with those who disagree reasonably with us. There is much room for cultural difference in that world, and none for chauvinism. It is a world that depends on a common education that the siren song of instrumentalism/postmodernism would distract us from. It is also a world we do not yet have, and perhaps too few of us want it anyhow.[3]

Notes

1 A longer and better version of this chapter would say much about the concept of culture that is relevant to the charge of chauvinism. Very roughly, 'culture' in the sense that matters here signifies established systems of convention that constitute the institutions under which people live. See Kymlicka (1995: 76–9).
2 The explicit target of Young's case against liberalism is not education. But her emphasis on the way moral capabilities and perceptions are malformed in liberal politics makes her argument substantively an argument about education.
3 I am most grateful to Ken Strike for helpful comments on an earlier draft.

References

Callan, E. (1997) *Creating Citizens*, Oxford: Clarendon.
Gutmann, A. and Thompson, D. (1996) *Democracy and Disagreement*, Cambridge, MA: Harvard University Press.
Johnston, D. (1994) *The Idea of a Liberal Theory*, Princeton, NJ: Princeton University Press.
Kohlberg, L. (1981) *The Philosophy of Moral Development*, San Francisco, CA: Harper and Row.
Kymlicka, W. (1989) *Liberalism, Community and Culture*, Oxford: Clarendon.
—— (1995) *Multicultural Citizenship*, Oxford: Clarendon.
Macedo, S. (1990) *Liberal Virtues*, Oxford: Clarendon.
Phillips, A. (1995) *The Politics of Presence*, Oxford: Clarendon.
Rawls, J. (1993) *Political Liberalism*, New York: Columbia University Press.
Raz, J. (1994) *Ethics in the Public Domain*, Oxford: Clarendon.
Spinner, J. (1994) *The Boundaries of Citizenship*, Baltimore, MD: The Johns Hopkins University Press.
Young, I.M. (1990) *Justice and the Politics of Difference*, Princeton, NJ: Princeton University Press.

CHAPTER 10

RETHINKING DEMOCRACY AND EDUCATION
Towards an education of deliberative citizens

Tomas Englund

Journal of Curriculum Studies, 32, 2, 305–313, 2000

We can date the intellectually significant relationship between democracy and education to the appearance of John Dewey's early influential short texts at the turn of the 20th century and his famous *Democracy and Education,* first published in 1916. These texts have been given two different educational–philosophical interpretations, leading to the movements known as progressivism and reconstructionism. For several decades in the US, and in many other countries, progressivism was rhetorically powerful, but its influence on practice in schools has been difficult to evaluate. Reconstructionism had a first phase in the 1930s and a revival, as neo-reconstructionism, in the 1970s and 1980s; it was a dynamic movement in both of these periods, but more limited than progressivism in its influence. The limitations of both of these perspectives, became apparent as they encountered conventional social forces in schooling. In both cases, there was little congruence between either philosophy and how society at large worked. Conservative forces in particular constantly pointed out that these educational ideas were inconsistent with the expressed needs of society at large (Englund, 1986).

In recent years a third interpretation of Dewey's (1916) work, seeing it as *neo-pragmatism,* has evolved. The insights from this new understanding of his thought has not yet developed any distinct consequences for schooling, although there are numerous educational analyses inspired by it. I understand the main characteristic of neo-pragmatism to be its concern for communication as a democratic form of life, that is the development of communicative and deliberative capabilities for democracy. The idea of deliberative democracy as an educational process, where individuals bring different perspectives to an on-going communication, is one way to characterize this third interpretation. Of course, this too may be construed as a challenge to social forces, but it can be seen as meshing more easily with the development of democratic society at large.

In what follows I will develop my arguments for this idea of deliberative democracy as an educational process, by showing, first, the limits of progressivism and reconstructionism and, then, the possibilities and importance of the neo-pragmatic perspective. Specifically, I want to underscore implicitly the need to develop deliberative capabilities in schools.

Progressivism

Progressivism is a multi-faceted movement aimed at changing school practice. In addition to Dewey's ideas, the progressive movement advocated such specific curriculum methods as the project method of W.H. Kilpatrick while the child study movement, which appeared in many countries, was another offshoot of Progressivism. But many of these movements, and especially the child study movement, were heavily criticized by Dewey. Progressivist educational movements have also been heavily criticized from totally different angles, and during the 1950s progressivism became discredited, except perhaps in the UK, partly as a result of the attack from such traditionalist educational philosophies as essentialism and perennialism which arose to meet the challenge from progressivism. Dewey himself, in this struggle for the American curriculum, 'hover[ed] over the struggle rather than belonging to any particular side' (Kliebard, 1986: ix). During the restructuration years of the 1980s progressivist ideas were rejected politically and traditional schooling restored (cf. Telhaug, 1990).

Nevertheless, some critics rejected Dewey and his progressive disciples for seeing the process of upbringing and teaching as an end in itself: 'since growth is the characteristic of life, education is all the one with growing; it has no end beyond itself' (Dewey, 1985: 58). Randolph Bourne (1917; see also, e.g. Rugg, 1931: 209), with his early explicit criticism of Dewey's imprecisely defined instrumentalism, offered a key starting point for this criticism. Reconstructionists saw this process mainly as a means for creating a *better* society on the basis of specific criteria. Other critics, such as the revisionists of (educational) history of the 1970s and the protagonists of the new sociology of education, saw progressivism as adaptable to the forces of the integration of modern, capitalist societies. The critical stance against progressivism from the new sociology of education – education as social control – was further developed during the last decades by studies inspired by Foucault. The interest in social order and the organizing of a welfare society by a progressivist-inspired social science has become characterized as primarily 'disciplinary'. In sum, progressivist interpretations of the relationship between democracy and education have been regarded as vague in their method-orientation and practically weak in their strong individualism.

Reconstructionism

Dewey's attempts to dissociate himself from vulgar interpretations of progressivism did not help him much for his name is closely linked to progressivism, even in its vulgar interpretations. I do not see it as a paradox that Dewey was also an inspiration to the reconstructionist educational philosophy, a philosophy that aimed at strengthening the school's role for democracy. His *Democracy and Education* was a specific starting point for such a reconstruction:

> we are doubtless far from realizing the potential efficacy of education as a constructive agency of improving society, from realizing that it represents not only a development of children and youth but also of the future society of which they will be the constituents.
>
> (Dewey, 1985: 85)

The main proponents of reconstructionism (George Counts, Theodore Brameld, and Harold Rugg) emphasized the societal role of schools. For them progressivism was too one-sided in its interest in the individual; with democracy as their reference point they saw the mission of schools as one of asking children with critical questions about the on-going development of society. This democratic ideal of reconstructionism can be compared with what has been called 'participatory democracy' in the recent past. From this viewpoint the schools should contribute to the development of pupils' interest in societal questions by focusing on possibilities for everyone understanding the kind of issues involved in such questions and opportunities for discussion of controversial questions offering.

Reconstructionism was at its height in the late 1930s. Cremin (1961) pointed out that Harold Rugg's textbook, *Man and His Changing Society*, almost changed US lessons in social studies. However, by the end of the 1930s, Rugg's textbooks were under violent attack for being un-American, for posing open-ended questions rather than teaching unchanging moral values, and could not be sold. Reconstructionist ideas were revitalized after the Second World War as arguments for a propaganda-critical and citizen-preparing school, both in USA and in Europe, but again they were soon overshadowed by a rhetoric about the need for the schools to prepare societies for economic growth and for enhancing the labour market, in short, for economic efficiency. During the 1970s and the early 1980s there was again some renaissance of reconstructionist ideas, and citizenship education in schools was once again in focus, especially in Europe under such headings as 'political education' and 'politische Bildung'. However, the conservative political restructuring of society and education of recent years, seems to have made such concerns unfashionable. In the USA, the reconstructionist ambition had remained alive, but was marginalized to the social studies where it played a role in some textbook projects during the 1960s and 1970s. Interestingly, reconstructionist ideas have been recently promoted by such scholars as Henry Giroux (1988), who sees Dewey as a reconstructionist, and William Stanley (1992), who also gives a condensed analysis of the historical relationships influencing reconstructionism.

Reconstructionism viewed education as an instrument for change. If one reads Dewey from a perspective of neo-pragmatism, the emphasis is on communication. And, putting the progressivist to one side, these other approaches to reading his work are strikingly revealed in the following quotation (Dewey, 1985: 105), where Dewey as the reconstructionist is seen in the first part and Dewey as the neopragmatist in the second:

> Since education is a social process, and there are many kinds of societies, a criterion for educational criticism and construction implies a *particular* social ideal. The two points selected by which to measure the worth of a form of social life are the extent to which the interests of a group are shared by all its members, and the fullness and freedom with which it interacts with other groups.

Neopragmatism

This third, neopragmatic interpretation of Dewey's work is recent, in what is generally called the pragmatic renaissance. Dewey's work is analysed from the perspective of a broader philosophy of science and is labelled as a pragmatist – and his close connections to other well-known pragmatists, such as William James and Charles Sanders Peirce, are underscored. In this interpretation Dewey is seen as an advocate of education as communication. Education is just one aspect of a democratic form of social life that is communicative: 'Not only is social life identical with communication, but all communication (and hence all genuine social life) is educative'

(Dewey, 1985: 8). Consequently, this interpretation is not focused on education as such, but education is merely one of the spheres in which a communicative competence can be promoted by linguistic and other forms of interaction. This focus on communication and interaction also means that the work by the 'fourth pragmatist', George Herbert Mead, becomes more important (cf. Biesta, 1997).

The two central figures in the pragmatic renaissance are Richard Rorty and Richard Bernstein. Each puts Dewey and pragmatism in the context of a history of philosophy in which analytic philosophy has dominated the scene and, for a long time, stigmatized pragmatism. In his neo-pragmatic reconstruction, Rorty (1967) has accentuated 'the linguistic turn' as a central background; he has analysed how the language of Dewey aims at a sense of community and has stressed the potential of this point of view, pointing out the relationship between knowledge and *solidarity*. He has compared this emphasis to the language of Foucault, who, in Rorty's (1982) account, has tried to show how social science has worked as an instrument for the disciplining institutions, and emphasized the relationship between knowledge and *power*. And in *Contingency, Irony, and Solidarity* and in later works Rorty has created a hypothetical Dewey by driving his postmodern pragmatism further, making a strong distinction between the private and the public and dissociating him from all forms of universalism (cf. Shusterman, 1992; Kloppenberg, 1998; Westbrook, 1998):

> Abandoning universalism is my way of doing justice to the claims of the ironists whom Habermas distrusts: Nietzsche, Heidegger, Derrida. Habermas looks at these men from the point of view of public needs. I agree with Habermas that as *public* philosophers they are at best useless and at worst dangerous, but I want to insist on the role they and others like them can play in accommodating the ironist's *private* sense of identity to her liberal hopes. All that is in question, however, is accommodation – not synthesis. My 'poeticized' culture is one which has given up the attempt to unite one's private ways of dealing with one's finitude and one's sense of obligation to other human beings.
>
> (Rorty, 1989: 68)

Rorty's neopragmatic interpretation of Dewey can be contrasted to another neo-pragmatic tradition which stresses the strong link between the public and private or, rather, attempts to dissolve the distinction between them by emphasizing the need for a public philosophy (cf. Festenstein, 1997): 'The pragmatic legacy (which Rorty constantly invokes) will only be recovered and revitalized when we try to do for our time what Dewey did in his historical context – articulate, texture and *justify* a vision of a pragmatically viable ideal of communal democracy' (Bernstein, 1992: 253).

It is Bernstein who has taken his starting-point in Dewey's writings and interpreted him as a spokesperson for a society with critical, inquiring citizens testing different solutions in an open and respectful spirit. From the two reference points of 'critical citizens' and 'social action', Bernstein (1983, 1986, 1987) has constructed his neopragmatic alternative, strongly influenced by Dewey. Hilary Putnam has further developed the argument of the consistency between democracy and pragmatism, claiming that Dewey offered the epistemological justification of democracy, that is, he suggested that it rested on a specific epistemological conception, free individuals' common deliberation on different statements. Putnam (1991: 217) actually sounds like Dewey when he writes that 'democracy is not just a form of social life among other workable forms of social life; it is the precondition for the full application of intelligence to the solution of social problems'.

The postmodern questioning of the use of universal principles for reaching democratic agreements and common understanding is explicitly rejected by Richard Bernstein in his *The New Constellation* (1992) where, in the spirit of Dewey, he discusses the possibilities for reaching and acting in relation to democratic agreements. As a neopragmatist Bernstein shares the postmodern (Rortyesque) rejection of foundations, its fallibilism, contingency and pluralism; but he also points out that the pragmatic attitude is firmly established in social experiences and that our private selves cannot be loosened from our ethical responsibility. We always have to be ready to expose our private attitudes to critique and discuss them publicly with those who have other opinions, not necessarily in order to reach consensus but in order to understand and respect each other. In his comprehensive work Bernstein has evaluated many attempts to create models intended to develop these ideas and found Jürgen Habermas' writings among the most promising. I also believe that Habermas (1984, 1988) has given us some basic starting-points for an analysis of the relationship between society and education within a perspective of normative rationalization, that is, the transformation of the source of the sacred to communication as collective will-formation. In this perspective, what ultimately explains social integration is communicative and argumentative consensual processes. It is the good argument that creates validity, a validity that also has an integrative force.

Deliberative democracy as a neopragmatic model

Habermas' (1996) theory of communicative action, further developed into a model for deliberative democracy and a discourse theory of law and democracy, is perhaps also the most developed and well-known theory of deliberative democracy. The model is developed in relation to the liberal and the republican/communitarian traditions and in his analysis he has emphasized the different citizenship concepts of these traditions. Habermas (1996: 271) has also emphasized how the usual dichotomized conceptualization around citizenship rights within these traditions 'fail to grasp the intersubjective meaning of a system of rights that citizens mutually accord one another'.

Habermas' model integrates fragments from both the liberal and the republican/communitarian traditions in the idea of an ideal procedure for deliberation. The implications of the model for education are not explicit and Habermas can be interpreted in different ways. What can be said is that he places the realization of deliberative policy in the institutionalization of procedures, where an intersubjectivity on a higher level is expected to emerge; public discourses find a good response *only* under circumstances of broad participation. This in turn 'requires a background political culture that is egalitarian, divested of all educational privileges, and thoroughly intellectual' (Habermas, 1996: 490). Political autonomy cannot be realized by a person who fulfills his or her own private interests, but only as a *joint* enterprise in an intersubjective, shared practice. On this account, the deliberative project could be regarded as the continuation of the project of modernity.

Deliberative democracy as an educational process

Different models for deliberative democracy are explicitly based on the need for education in deliberative attitudes on the part of citizens who exercise the communicative power that is one of democracy's consequences (Gutmann and Thompson, 1996). The models of deliberative democracy also see the discursive creation of public opinion as an educative process. The obvious question is what is the part of the schools in these processes. Amy Gutmann, the author of *Democratic Education* (1987), and a co-author of *Democracy and Disagreement* (1996), ends *Democratic Education* with the following words:

> ...we can conclude that 'political education' – the cultivation of virtues, knowledge, and skills necessary for political participation – has moral primacy over the other purposes of public education in a democratic society. Political education prepares citizens to participate in consciously reproducing their society, and conscious social reproduction is the ideal not only of democratic education but also of democratic politics.
>
> (Gutmann, 1987: 287)

She argues that it is reasonable to try to develop everyone's capacity, and the opportunity, to question traditional authorities (e.g. parents and religious ideas) and to provide every student with the critical intellectual abilities needed to evaluate and judge different life forms, even those that differ from those of their own environment. In short, it is the task of the schools to elevate every individual out of his or her *private* life to a *public* world, with the possibilities of making one's own choice among different ways to the good life.

Gutmann is only one among many others writing in a liberal, virtue-oriented tradition who have pointed to the mission of the *public* schools to develop the deliberative virtues. The schools have, they say, to develop the capacities of children and youngsters to enter critical discussions where facts and values are simultaneously present, and to develop their moral and political capacity to evaluate and judge in public discussions (Kymlicka and Norman, 1995). She can also be seen as a representative of a balance between a *participatory* and a *deliberative* democratic view, developing with this latter view further together with Dennis Thompson (Gutmann and Thompson, 1996). Like participatory democracy, deliberative democracy emphasizes participation in democratic processes, but it accentuates the character of the processes. Thus advocates of deliberative democracy stress the presence of different views or arguments, which are to be negotiated, or put against each other in argumentation. Two or more different views on a subject are proposed by persons who confront each other, but with an openness in the argumentation: 'While acknowledging that we are destined to disagree, deliberative democracy also affirms that we are capable of deciding our common destiny on mutually acceptable terms.' (Gutmann and Thompson, 1996: 361). Compared to participatory democracy, deliberative democracy especially emphasizes responsibility and consequences, implying that socialization to citizenship and the exercising of a citizenship must be in focus. As Gutmann and Thompson (1996: 359) write,

> In any effort to make democracy more deliberative, the single most important institution outside government is the educational system. To prepare their students for citizenship, schools must go beyond teaching literacy and numeracy, though both are of course prerequisites for deliberating about public problems. Schools should aim to develop their students' capacities to understand different perspectives, communicate their understandings to other people, and engage in the give-and-take of moral argument with a view to making mutually acceptable decisions. These goals, which entail cultivating moral character and intellectual skills at the same time, are likely to require some significant changes in traditional civic education, which has neglected teaching this kind of moral reasoning about politics.

Robert Westbrook (1991: 138), the author of the most influential recent biography of Dewey, has asserted that the ideal of democracy and education which Dewey pursued would be characterized as a 'deliberative democracy':

> I think [deliberative democracy] captures Dewey's procedural ideals better than the term I used, 'participatory democracy', since it suggests something of the character of the participation involved in democratic associations...rooted in an expansive conception of the community of inquiry.

Bohman (1997: 322–323) adds that ideal proceduralism 'is the standard criterion of deliberative legitimacy, since it gives everyone an equal standing to use their practical reason in the give and take of reasons in dialogue'. If, as Bohman (1997: 322) suggests, the proper criterion for deliberative democracy is indeed 'equality as effective social freedom, understood as equal capability for public functioning', how should schools prepare for conditions where this criterion could be met? Deliberative conceptions of democracy 'must have demanding requirements of political equality, if they are not to favor the more virtuous, the better educated, or simply the better off' (Bohman and Rehg, 1997: xxiv).

Concluding remarks

A neopragmatic interpretation of Dewey's work creates new visions for the relationship between democracy and education. The idea of deliberative democracy as an educational process offers an image of a kind of communication where different perspectives are brought into ongoing meaning-creating processes of will-formation. To make curricular room for these kind of activities, where deliberative capabilities are developed, would be one way to realize a democratic conception of education implying a communicative rationality (cf. Englund, 1996, 1999).

References

Bernstein, R. (1983) *Beyond Objectivism and Relativism: Science, Hermeneutics, and Praxis* (Philadelphia, PA: University of Pennsylvania Press).
Bernstein, R. (1986) *Philosophical Profiles* (Philadelphia, PA: University of Pennsylvania Press).
Bernstein, R. (1987) The varieties of pluralism. *American Journal of Education*, 95(4), 509–533.
Bernstein, R. (1992) *The New Constellation. The Ethical-Political Horizons of Modernity/Postmodernity* (Cambridge, MA: MIT Press).
Biesta, G. (1997) George Herbert Mead's lectures on philosophy of education at the University of Chicago (1910–1911). Paper presented at the meeting of the John Dewey Society at the annual meeting of the American Educational Research Association.
Bohman, J. (1997) Deliberative democracy and effective social freedom. In J. Bohman and W. Rehg (eds), *Deliberative Democracy: Essays on Reason and Politics* (Cambridge, MA: MIT press), 321–348.
Bohman, J. and Rehg, W. (1997) Introduction. In J. Bohman and W. Rehg (eds), *Deliberative Democracy: Essays on Reason and Politics* (Cambridge, MA: MIT press), ix–xxx.
Bourne, R. (1917) Twilight of idols. *Seven Arts*, October, 688–702.
Cremin, L. (1961) *The Transformation of the School: Progressivism in American Education 1876–1957* (New York: Vintage Books).
Dewey, J. (1985) [1916] Democracy and Education. In Jo Ann Boydston (ed.), *The Middle Works, 1899–1924: Volume 9: 1916* (Carbondale, IL: Southern Illinois University Press).
Englund, T. (1986) *Curriculum as a Political Problem: Changing Educational Conceptions with Special Reference to Citizenship Education*, Uppsala Studies in Education 25 (Lund, Sweden: Studentlitteratur).

Englund, T. (1996) The public and the text. *Journal of Curriculum Studies*, 28(1), 1–35.

Englund, T. (1999) Does a new (teacher) professionalism need a new language? Paper presented at the Meeting of PACT (Professional Actions and Cultures of Teaching), Hong Kong, January 1999.

Festenstein, M. (1997) *Pragmatism and Political Theory: From Dewey to Rorty* (Cambridge, MA: Polity Press).

Giroux, H. (1988) *Schooling and the Struggle for Public Life: Critical Pedagogy in the Modern Age* (Minneapolis, MN: University of Minnesota Press).

Gutmann, A. (1987) *Democratic Education* (Princeton, NJ: Princeton University Press).

Gutmann, A. and Thompson, D. (1996) *Democracy and Disagreement* (Cambridge, MA: Harvard University Press).

Habermas, J. (1984/1988) *The Theory of Communicative Action*, 2 vols. (Boston, MA: Beacon Press).

Habermas, J. (1996) *Between Facts and Norms: Contributions to a Discourse Theory of Law and Democracy* (Cambridge, MA: Polity Press).

Kliebard, H. (1986) *The Struggle for the American Curriculum 1893–1958* (Boston, MA: Routledge).

Kloppenberg, J. (1998) Pragmatism: an old name for some new ways of thinking? In M. Dickstein (ed.), *The Revival of Pragmatism: New Essays on Social Thought, Law, and Culture* (Durham, NC: Duke University Press), 83–127.

Kymlicka, W. and Norman, W. (1995) Return of the citizen: a survey of recent work on citizenship theory. In R. Beiner (ed.), *Theorizing Citizenship* (Albany, NY: State University of New York Press), 283–322.

Putnam, H. (1991) A reconsideration of Deweyan democracy. In M. Brint and W. Weaver (eds), *Pragmatism in Law and Society* (Boulder, CO: Westview Press), 217–243.

Rorty, R. (ed.) (1967) *The Linguistic Turn: Recent Essays in Philosophical Method* (Chicago, IL: Chicago of University Press).

Rorty, R. (1982) *Consequences of Pragmatism* (Minneapolis, MN: University of Minnesota Press).

Rorty, R. (1989) *Contingency, Irony, and Solidarity* (Cambridge: Cambridge University Press).

Rugg, H. (1931) *Culture and Education* (New York: Harcourt, Brace and Company).

Shusterman, R. (1992) *Pragmatist Aesthetics: Living Beauty, Rethinking Art* (Oxford: Blackwell).

Stanley, W. (1992) *Curriculum for Utopia. Social Reconstructionism and Critical Pedagogy in the Postmodern Era* (Albany, NY: State University of New York Press).

Telhaug, A.O. (1990) *Den utdanningspolitiske retorikken* [The new rhetoric of educational policy] (Oslo: Universitetsforlaget).

Westbrook, R. (1991) *John Dewey and American Democracy* (Ithaca, NY: Cornell University Press).

Westbrook, R. (1998) Pragmatism and democracy: reconstructing the logic of John Dewey's faith. In M. Dickstein (ed.), *The Revival of Pragmatism. New Essays on Social Thought, Law and Culture* (Durham, NC: Duke University Press), 128–140.

PART IV

EDUCATIONAL POLICY

CHAPTER 11

WHAT'S THE GOOD OF EDUCATION?

Joseph Dunne

In P. Hogan (ed.) *Partnership and the Benefits of Learning* (1995),
Dublin: ESAI, pp. 60–82

Introduction

It is encouraging, that many of the responses to the Green Paper, *Education for a Changing World*, lamented the absence from it of any coherently articulated philosophy and that the opening chapter of the *Report on the National Education Convention* affirms that 'the provision of an adequate philosophical rationale... remains a priority'.[1] In an age when there tends to be a specialised provider of every service, it would be a neat division of labour if philosophers could be called on for the provision of this 'rationale' – if their expertise could be relied on to sort out otherwise bedevillingly vague, or contentious issues of values, fundamental assumptions, and overall aims. It would be no compliment to philosophy – and no service to education – compliment to philosophy – and no service to education – however, if these bothersome issues were assigned to it only in order to clear the ground for an unencumbered consideration of all the other, apparently more tractable and 'real' considerations: strategic planning, efficient management, adequate resourcing, effective delivery and so on. The first task of philosophy, indeed, is to question any such convenient separation of ends and means or of value issues and technical ones. For while this separation allows an advertence to aims or values to be granted a privileged status at the beginning of official documents this can all too easily turn out to be the dubious privilege of a purely aspirational, not to say ceremonial role; they may not then be seen as carrying any implications for, or as having any power to penetrate, the functional or technical issues which are addressed in the subsequent discussion.

In this preliminary marking out of the ground, I will offer an interpretative comment on the two major documents we have had so far, the Green Paper and the Convention Report, as well as on the debate which occurred in the interval between them. Thus I may find an opening into a more satisfactory philosophical engagement with this debate. It was a notable feature of the Green Paper that in a quite bold and vigorous way it inserted education within a wider matrix, especially an economic and social one. The overall sense of its message to educators was: the school is not a cultural oasis; the environments and worlds that we live in and that schools willy nilly are part of, are changing rapidly and inexorably – so that in our understanding and practice of education we must situate it realistically within some wider sense of where this social and economic change is taking us and what it will require of our pupils if they are to negotiate it in ways satisfactory and enhancing to themselves and to society.

Now much of the critical response to the Green Paper sprang from a belief that its understanding of the broad context was in fact too narrow – that its concern with the economy and the labour market occluded other, more humanistic, concerns (especially spiritual and artistic ones). Or, put somewhat differently, that the Green Paper's too partisan and unreserved espousal of a productivity-driven society and its 'enterprise culture' seemed to want to harness education *in the service* of this society and culture rather than to see it as, in some respects at least, in unavoidable conflict with it. Critical responses to the Green Paper from many diverse sources, then, were motivated by a sense that in some strands of its thinking it had *colonising* ambitions towards education (casually betrayed in its language – most conspicuously perhaps in its renaming a school principal as 'chief executive' – but also in its restriction of the wider community to be represented on school boards to the business community); and that it therefore needed to be resisted in defence of the autonomy or, perhaps better, the *integrity* of education.

If this was the thrust of a great deal of the response to the Green Paper it seems to me that the later Convention Report reflects it in a particular way; in a certain withdrawal from the wider arena of discussion and a more focused preoccupation with education as a distinct and autonomous sphere. Curiously, however, this intramural move does not seem to lead to a very close focus on what is really specific or proper to education; a great deal of the discussion is about issues such as administration, management, planning, control, accountability and quality assurance. These issues do, of course, come into play in important ways in education and there is no reason why they should not feature in discussions and reports. They are not, however, unique to education – a fact which is evidenced by the curiously content-neutral language (now in very wide currency) which they seem to attract. Moreover, there is a danger that preoccupation with them can replace attention to fundamental issues about the identity of education – without which they themselves cannot be adequately approached.

These fundamental issues do not mainly arise in intramural reflection, and if we want to defend the integrity of education we can do so only by first acknowledging how deeply and perplexingly it is challenged, not primarily by the economist ideology which forms a definite strand of thinking in the Green Paper, but rather by the reality of the kind of society in which we live and must try to educate (and of which the Green Paper happens to take an up-beat view). If, as so many people have said, a philosophical dimension has been signally missing from the debate, this is mainly because we have not given sufficiently close and vigilant attention to the real predicaments that face educators in an advanced industrial, or, increasingly, post-industrial, society such as our own. The philosophical task as I see it – and of course it is a task for all of us and not just for philosophers – begins with a recognition of just how deeply problematic education is in our society. In what follows I try to analyse the nature of these problems and to articulate an approach that may be helpful in grappling with them.

The burdens of contemporary schooling

In one sense schools are curiously sequestered zones, with their spatial aloofness from the workaday and domestic environments, their routine exclusion of 'outsiders', their suspension of the ordinary rhythms of experience, their adherence to a strict timetable, their paraphernalia of uniforms and other rituals that lend them a strange continuity with an ancient academy, not to say a medieval monastery. And yet, of course, despite the almost timeless icon of the schoolhouse, or the archetypal images of teacher and pupils, our schools have very vulnerable borders with the 'outside world'. To be sure, they still, as ever, introduce children to the basic literacies, to competencies in the notational and symbolic systems of the society, and beyond that initiate them in some systematic way into disciplines of knowledge. On these tasks the school has a pretty exclusive franchise and they still seem to define its proper and inalienable function. And yet, clearly, to focus only on this function is to neglect the complexity of the school's role in a modern society.

Consider first, then, the way the school is asked to carry the burden of what society still officially considers sacred even though it may not be prepared to do much or suffer much on its behalf – other than to project responsibility for it onto the schools; I am thinking here of Irish (the Irish language) and of religion (mainly the Catholic religion). Or consider, next, issues which surely are experienced in society as very real; increasing crime and delinquency, drug abuse and various other forms of abuse that reveal large cracks in the civic, and familial, fabric. When these problems are discussed is it not again the school which is so often looked to as the source of a solution – if, that is, is it not seen as itself a cause of the problem ('there's no discipline anymore in schools')? Or consider, then, other issues that periodically come on the agenda of social concern. There is the environment and matters to do with pollution, conservation and the promotion of a green consciousness and life style. Or new senses of how oppressions have been rife – though often largely unrecognised – and can no longer be tolerated. Issues of gender equity come to mind here but also development issues, new senses of global interdependencies and of the responsibilities of the richer countries of the North to the poorer ones of the South. Or the stronger awareness of the need for ways of tackling prejudice and dealing with difference, that has found expression in, for example, programmes of anti-racism, conflict-resolution and peace studies. Or, again, an awareness of the power of the media in our lives, which has given rise to media studies, not to speak of the power of digital technologies to refashion pedagogy. Or, finally (though the list could go on), a new awareness not exactly of sex, I suppose, but of the importance as well as the dangers associated with sexuality in contemporary society, that has prompted calls for more adequate programmes of sex education. Take all these together and you have a big bundle of priorities accumulating at the school door, with claims for entry being made on behalf of all of them – and meanwhile with the exit door firmly closed on anything that might be dismissed in order to accommodate them.

But that is not all. Consider next the imperatives laid on the school by the state. Any state must expect its schools to perform a strong socialising function – to equip young people with kinds of knowledge, skill and conviction that will fit them for citizenship as it is defined in that state. For a democratic state one might expect that the crucial requirement of schools would be that to educate young people in those civic virtues (such as a deliberative concern for the public good, a sense of tolerance and of social responsibility) without which the more external marks of democracy become empty forms. In fact, however, democratic states do not always seem to put a premium on principled education for citizenship: In Ireland, the fate of civics, as well as of various efforts to establish a coherent programme of social and political education, illustrates this neglect. It is a very different function that schools take on as their primary role in advanced industrial democracies – and perhaps nowhere with such extreme efficiency as in Ireland. They take on the function of social selection, of assigning people, on the basis of their performance on (usually centralised) examinations, to the various occupational slots – with corresponding levels of income and status – that are available in the society. Education thus becomes the primary means whereby individuals can promote their self-interest, their private economic gain. The democratic state's concern with this transaction is to increase the fairness of the playing pitch on which it is conducted; hence, the prominence in the Green Paper of issues concerning equity.

Education, production and the economy

We come close here to what is perhaps most problematic for a modern educational system: the extent to which it is implicated in the functioning of the economy. This fact imposes an instrumental role on education which (though many lament it) may be essential and not merely accidental to a *modern* education system. A brief historical advertence will help to bring this fact into focus. Our most venerable picture of a non-instrumental type of education, one that would be pursued simply for its own sake, comes to us from ancient Greece. A salient fact about classical Athens, however, is that it was not a democracy. In a sense, of course, it was the birthplace of democracy, giving as not only the name but the ideal of this form of politics. But it was not a democracy in a sense which we could now accept, quite simply because of its drastic restriction on the range of citizenship: only a small fraction of the adult population were citizens. This elite among its other privileges, could benefit from a liberal education – but only because the work of production and reproduction was done by the disenfranchised majority, which included slaves, skilled craftsmen and women. If we now aspire not only to universal suffrage but to mass education this is surely because our egalitarian conscience is more developed than was that of the Greeks. But this aspiration would have remained just that – an aspiration – if something else had not intervened, namely, a huge shift in the nature of knowledge and of its role in society. This shift has really only occurred in the last century, indeed with decisive influence in Ireland only in the past few decades.

A great extension of the democratic ideal and a big move towards some sense of universal rights was certainly ushered in by the eighteenth-century Enlightenment; and yet when Thomas Jefferson, who was quintessentially an Enlightenment man and one of the founders of the new American Republic, founded the University of Virginia he was unabashed in asserting that its doors should be open only to 'a handful of geniuses'. If we now regard this as unacceptable this is not necessarily because we espouse egalitarian values more strongly than Jefferson did; what makes the crucial difference is the fact that now, far more than then, knowledge has actually become power (as Bacon, nearly two hundred years before Jefferson, had already anticipated) – ultimately the power to produce and transform. It is primarily this change in the role of knowledge that underlies the huge change in the scope of access to education. So long as knowledge stood apart from production, no society could afford to have more than a small minority devoted to the pursuit of knowledge through education; for it needed as many hands to the wheel as it could muster. And if by contrast our society tries to provide something like universal education, this is not because it is any less concerned than earlier societies with the imperatives of production; it is simply that the productive person now is the educated person. The realisation of this fact in Ireland was most conspicuously evidenced in the title of perhaps the single most influential policy document in the history of Irish education, *Investment in Education*.[2]

The relationship between education and the economy has become a reciprocal one, with dependency running in both directions. On the one hand, the productiveness of the economy depends on the educational system for the supply of a skilled workforce (what is increasingly called 'human capital'). On the other hand, the educational system depends on a productive economy for funding on the scale which is required by a modern democratic system of schooling – even one as relatively under-resourced as our own. This interlocking of education with the productive and economic sphere circumscribes the autonomy of education, rendering problematic the ideal of a humanistic education without utilitarian purpose. For if schools were to break the tie in one direction by defining an agenda of their own which was not, at least in some important respects, responsive to the needs of production, they would themselves be casualties of the tie broken from the other direction; because of their ceasing to feed the goose there would no longer be the golden egg which feeds themselves.

The points system

A major consequence of the phenomenon I have just been analysing presents itself in the most concrete and real way in every student's experience and every parent's or ordinary citizen's perception of education nowadays. Its most manifest presentation is in the competitive Leaving Certificate examination and the points system based on it. This system dominates the consciousness of students, the work of teachers, and the attitudes of parents in post-primary schools. It determines entry to third level education of every kind. And it has even exerted an influence downward on primary schools in the pressure which has been felt in the senior classes to succeed in entrance examinations to secondary schools. It is the focus of huge media attention twice yearly, as a great public ritual is enacted of preexam speculation and prediction turning, paper by paper, to post-exam analysis and debriefing – and all of this to be succeeded a few months later by the appearance of results and the labyrinthine process of assigning, through the exact and impassive medium of numbers, a whole generation of young adults their most tangible life-chances.

If this is the most public – one might say the most blatant – aspect of Irish education, one cannot conclude from the Green Paper or the Convention Report that it is very significant. In her opening address to the Convention, the chairperson, Professor Donnelly, said to the assembled delegates. 'It is not only what you are aware of which is interesting, but what you have forgotten.' These words of the chairperson's might be taken to invite a deconstructive reading of the Report, with attention not so much on what is said in the text as on what is not said – what is absent or 'forgotten'. If the forgotten participants of the Convention were the pupils (who remained absent, while so many other 'partners' – at least forty different groups or representative interests altogether – were present) perhaps the forgotten issue, not only in the Convention Report but more seminally, and less understandably, in the Green Paper, is the points system. In the section on assessment in the latter, it is only testing in the primary school and evaluation of the new Junior Certificate that merit attention,[3] while the single most obtrusive – and, I want to argue, most problematic – feature of our whole educational system is passed over in silence.

The points system is the most clear-cut line at which education meets up with the socio-economic system. Through Leaving Certificate results this wider system uses the education system to select people for progressive towards the various job opportunities that it makes available: the progression in the first instance for an increasing proportion of students is into and through third level education and the different courses which, with varying degrees of specificity, provide more immediate access to these occupational slots. There are very large questions to be asked about the relationality of this selection mechanism from the viewpoint of the partner which it most clearly serves, that is, employers. It is rational to the degree that those selected for different occupational pathways are indeed more suitable for these occupations than others who desire them but are excluded. And this will be the case if exam performance is indeed a good indicator of potential accomplishment for the job (or in other words a good predictor of future actual accomplishment) so that we correctly infer that proficiency in exams will translate into adeptness on the job. There must be large questions about this – when many hugely heterogeneous types of slot use the one same instrument of selection, and no attempt is made, through specific tailoring of different tests, to ensure in each case a strong correlation between what is tested and what is required on the job.

There are questions here which are important for the overall effectiveness of our society as well as for the happiness of many persons within if – not only those who fail on this basis to find any employment but also perhaps many others who succeed only in finding work that is less congenial than they might otherwise have found. But I shall not follow out these questions here. I propose rather to look at another question, or set of questions, which arise at the same contact point, but which focus on the effects of this arrangement not on the socio-economic system, but rather on the other partner, namely education. What are the effects on education of the fact that it is now the decisive agency in determining people's economic futures?

The fact that the selection process occurs only when post-primary schooling is already completed does not prevent it from having a huge effect on the nature and significance of school experience itself. The most obvious effect is that by greatly raising the stakes in education, for many students (and their parents) it solves at a stroke the whole problem of *motivation*. It supercharges the significance of one's school performance, now cashed out in terms of exam results, making it almost redundant to ask, why study? why work? why bother? For a significant number of other students, of course, it may open a gaping motivational hole: why bother when it is already so clear that in *this* race one is an also-ran. The question that arises here is whether or not the effect of all this is beneficial to education. What this arrangement adds, from the viewpoint of education, is a set of extrinsic rewards. This addition does nothing to enhance the quality of education, however, unless it alters *in a positive way* the students' relation to what I want to call the *intrinsic* goods of education. In fact what is all too likely to happen is that these external rewards, precisely because they are so powerful, rather than acting as helpful incentives, can subvert or displace the intrinsic goods by becoming themselves the end; and then education has in a sense gained the world, but in doing so, has lost its own soul.

Education and equity

To judge whether or not this is in fact now the case in Irish education, we need to understand what these intrinsic goods of education are – or, in other words, to have a tolerably clear and defensible answer to the fundamental question posed in the title of this chapter, 'what's the good of education?' I want to go on to suggest an approach to answering this question. But before doing so, let me clarify matters here by indicating a few points which I am *not* committed to arguing. I am not suggesting that there should be no evaluation or assessment of educational achievement. And though I would argue that a great deal of emphasis in education should be on self-evaluation, that is, on helping the learner to assess her own progress – *as part of the learning process* – I am not rejecting in principle any system of assessment by others, inside or outside the school, at the end of post-primary schooling. Neither do I deny the need for a rational system of selecting people for available opportunities in work and in third level education – a need that is clearly more acute when there are significantly fewer opportunities than there are aspiring candidates. Indeed, given that these two processes – of educational assessment and of social selection – have come to coincide so much, and notwithstanding the fact that I have just been pointing out problems that stem from the way they coincide at present, I see great difficulty in arguing that, without radical changes in our socio-economic structures, they should be decoupled.

For, in our existing society, it is easy to imagine undesirable consequences of such a decoupling. If school attainment were no longer to function as a determinant of a person's chances on the job market then it would be replaced in this function by something else. Different employers as well as third level institutions, for instance, might devise their own entry tests. In that case, however, schools would be under enormous pressure to incorporate preparation for these tests (or at least for those of them in which success was highly prized) into their own agenda – alongside their now more restrictively defined educational work. If schools were to succumb to this pressure the problem which the restriction had been intended to solve would now have simply reappeared in a new guise. But, even if schools were successfully to resist this pressure, a different and surely undesirable consequence would be likely to follow: preparation for these tests would devolve on to the market, with 'academies' of various kinds springing up to cater for it. It is one of the less desirable aspects of the points system that it has already spawned a plethora of these institutions – increasingly, in recent years, not just as adjuncts to, but as replacements for school. But if the work of schools were to be marginalised in the selection process these entirely private institutions, conferring huge advantage on those who could afford to attend them, would be at a far greater premium. And, in terms of social equity, such a development is unconscionable.

It is already a huge challenge to our society to bring about greater economic and social justice and in particular to break the cycle of poverty which tends to perpetuate disadvantage from one generation to the next. Any commitment by the state to meet this challenge could hardly set aside the educational system in which the state itself already has a huge financial stake. There are already very formidable barriers to realising the ideal of 'equality of educational opportunity' even within the state sector – and quite apart from the growth of private enterprise in the field of general education. Many of these barriers are deeply entrenched in existing class structures and social patterns that make it extraordinarily difficult for schools on their own to exert much leverage on them. Hence, the depressing evidence that even when schooling has replaced more traditional mechanisms as the dominant agency of social selection, it confirms the biases of these earlier mechanisms: children from poorer families still tend to do less well in school and to remain poorer themselves as adults.[4] Despite all this, however, schooling policy, in tandem with other socio-economic policy, needs to address the problem of educational 'underachievement' due to disadvantage; and in this regard it might be said that one of the more commendable features of the Green Paper is its emphasis on equity. The point I make here, though, is that equity in education can hardly be divorced from a fuller economic and cultural equity throughout society. And, if this is so, it is hard to see how educational assessment and social selection could be entirely sundered from each other.

Equity may be granted to be a necessary corollary of any ultimately defensible education; but it still remains a formal concept insofar as it concerns the *distribution* of goods – where the latter can be characterised and vindicated as goods, however, only by invoking some other, substantive sense of 'good', which is not contained in the notion of equity itself. And here a more radical perspective might be introduced into our analysis. For it could be argued that the whole constellation of rewards, in terms of jobs, status and income, which is on offer through the points system, and the distribution of which is the focus of conventional discussions of 'equity', is itself gravely deficient in the 'good'. This is the case because of the undesirable nature of the work enshrined in many existing jobs, in terms either of social impact or of import for the individuals who do it, and because of the dubiousness of 'taken-for-granted aspirations, reward criteria and understandings of success and happiness [and]...existing rules by which status, wealth and power are allocated'.[5] Given these defects of our established socio-economic structure, a concern to render 'equitable' the mechanism for selecting people for differential slots within it may appeal to a thin notion of fairness but hardly to any strong conception of justice.

Even if one inclines (as I do) to this more radical analysis, one must still acknowledge that it is the present system, deeply entrenched, and pervasive in its effects, that individuals involved in education – pupils, their parents and their teachers – must now contend with. And it is hard to argue that, individually, they ought to act as if it did not exist – or that, so long as it does, it is not preferable that an admittedly limited and compromised ideal of 'equity' should not be pursued. For the work done in many jobs is socially valuable as well as personally rewarding and, moreover, many of the things that can be acquired only through money are also substantive goods or at least necessary conditions for the enjoyment of substantive goods (only a particular kind of saint or mystic could, without hypocrisy, deny this).[6] It is hard to expect, then, that if access to these goods is tied to opportunities that depend on educational success, albeit within a stratification that is not systematically justifiable, this fact will not greatly influence altitudes to education itself. Despite this, however, I still want to argue that these opportunities are, and should be recognised to be, *external* to education. I say they are external because I take it that a person might enjoy them and still not be an educated person; while, conversely, a person without them, or with them only to a very limited degree, might be a truly educated person. But if this is so it invites once more our fundamental question, which surely requires fuller analysis: what is the educated person, or what are the goods *internal* to education?

'Internal goods' and 'practices'

The form of this question should not suggest that it is amenable to an essentialist answer, or that an ahistorical analysis will yield an idea of education, valid beyond every cultural development and difference. Still, I shall try to articulate a set of concepts that may be firm enough to give some coherence and justification to the endeavours of 'educators' – while being open enough to comprehend, or at least not in principle to exclude, the density and variability of the concrete conditions in which 'education' has to be brought to life. First of all, what I'm calling an internal good arises only in the context of a practice that a person becomes engaged in. A practice is a coherent and invariably quite complex set of activities and tasks that has evolved cooperatively and cumulatively over time. It is alive in the community who are its insiders (i.e. its genuine practitioners), and it stays alive only so long as they sustain a commitment to creatively develop and extend it – sometimes by shifts which at the time may seem dramatic and even subversive. Central to any such practice are standards of excellence, themselves subject to development and redefinition, which demand responsiveness from those who are, or are trying to become, practitioners. We may look at this relationship to standards of excellence in the characteristic activities and tasks of a practice as a submission that imposes a discipline; but this discipline enables or empowers people, in a very real sense of that sometimes abused or, at least, overused word. For through real engagement with, and in, a practice a person's powers are released, directed and enlarged. The denotative range of 'practice' in this sense may be illustrated by examples as various as cabinet-making, physics, farming, chess, computer-programming, metal-work, history, rearing a family, music-making, drama-production, soccer and weaving.[7]

Engagement in the characteristic tasks of a practice, which embody standards that challenge one insofar as they are beyond one, leads, when it goes well, to the development not only of competencies specific to that practice but also of moral qualities that transcend it – that characterise one not just as a practitioner in that domain but as a person in life. To really engage with a practice in the sense of striving to realise the goods intrinsic to it – and not just to treat the practice as a means for attaining external goods (external in that they might equally be achieved by other routes, for example, money, status, reputation) – is to acquire, in doing so, qualities such as honesty and humility (in admitting the shortcomings of one's attempts), as well as patience and courage in sticking at a task, even when it does not offer immediate gratification, and a sense of justice and generosity in cooperating with others in projects that require a kind of partnership which overrides the rivalries of individuals precisely insofar as it responds to the demands of the practice itself. And it is a noteworthy fact about what might be called the economy of a practice – when we stay on the inside of it – is that it is not an economy of scarcity. In other words, if one person really comes to excel, this need not be at the cost of other people's chances to develop *their* talents. Every achievement of excellence enriches all who participate in or care about a practice; it can be an occasion for admiration or even celebration as well as sometimes, of course, for attempts at emulation.

The case is otherwise when we look to the *external* goods or rewards which can attach to success in the practice. When it comes to distributing *these* goods, whether they be money or jobs, especially in a society that finds it increasingly difficult to create jobs, there is scarcity, everyone cannot be a winner. And this remains the case even if we make great progress in terms of equity in *education*. Extending educational provision – when at the same time real job opportunities remain severely limited – clearly does not increase the number of winners. At most what it achieves, when our focus now is on external rewards, is, firstly, inflation of the educational currency, (so that Leaving Certificate becomes equivalent to what an Intermediate Certificate was a decade or two earlier, or what a primary degree will be a decade or two later); and, second, not more equality but rather inequality with a different base, a stratified society still, but stratified now on the basis of scholastic achievement, or attainment in exams. To be sure, this basis may be less questionable in a modern democracy than the earlier basis of (unmedicated) family background and inheritance; but it is still a basis for inequality of a type which is itself very questionable.

The notion of an internal good, and its distinction from an external good, may need some further clarification – if only to forestall any impression that practices are closed, esoteric spheres, accessible and of benefit only to specialists or professionals. In the first place, competencies and virtues acquired and exercised by practitioners are not the only internal goods of practices; also to be included among the latter are more objective achievements, for example, a well-made cabinet, wholesome food, a melodious tune, increased knowledge of the past of a local area of community, or a well-designed experiment – which are internal goods of the practices of cabinet-making, farming, music-making, history and chemistry, respectively. Second, to say that a broadly conceived good is internal to a practice which has become professionalised is not to imply that the professionals have any exclusive competence, let alone concern, with respect to the achievement of that good. At the level of a very general characterisation, health, for example, is a good internal to the practice of medicine; but it does not follow from this that the role of the doctor (or nurse or other 'health care professional'), or the institution of the hospital, has any monopoly in the enterprise of protecting or improving health. (And, *mutatis mutandis*, the same of course is true with respect to education, teachers and schools).

Third, there are important practices which, even though they contain possibilities of great virtuosity, are nonetheless available with real integrity at quite modest, even rudimentary, levels of accomplishment. Examples of such practices are writing, reading or playing a musical instrument. It seems likely that many people have been greatly short-changed in their education, precisely because they were introduced to these activities not as practices, but rather as sites where decomposed drills, exercises and 'micro-skills' were rehearsed as means, while a taste of the whole activity as an end was continually deferred or displaced. There are approaches, however, through which small children can come to experience these activities in their wholeness; they then participate in them in a way which is personally meaningful to themselves – and in which, incidentally, the continuity between their engagement and that of 'great masters' (a very heterogeneous grouping) is very real.[8] Fourth, there is a sense (and this, incidentally, was the original sense)[9] in which the concept, 'practice', designates a whole area of activity which is precisely non-specialist in that no one can be excluded from participation in it. The practice I speak of is the practice of living, more especially living as a member of a community (or increasingly, of several distinct communities) and as a citizen of the polity. Here, 'good' takes on its widest and most contestable connotations, and its realisation calls for capacities of deliberation and judgement and for the exercise of moral and civic virtues. Education in more particular practices should, I believe, contribute to the cultivation of these capacities and virtues, but perhaps the most significant contribution of schooling in this respect – positively or negatively – lies in the 'hidden curriculum' or ethos of the school, the ways in which it constructs the role of 'pupil' with respect to issues of authority, responsibility and decision-making.

'Practices' and education

Having introduced the notion of a 'practice' and having attempted to forestall some possible misgivings about it, I shall now try to outline more positively the kind of help it may offer in understanding education. I have stressed standards and also the difficulty – and, because of the difficulty, the discipline – involved in responding to them and thus becoming a practitioner. This may seem an over austere view which, if taken up in education, would be at odds with our current concerns that children be happy, well-adjusted and, perhaps above all, have high self-esteem. It needs to be pointed out, though, that the discipline involved in real learning is not a suppression of desire. For the desire of the person must be awakened and drawn out, and, as it were, drawn in by the goods that the practice has to offer – so that one comes to care about these goods and even to love them. This is true of a child learning to play chess, make things with wood, play football. There are indeed restrictions in all of these; castles just can't be moved diagonally, a nail hammered only in a particular way will go in straight, and only if one's foot, eye and whole body are finely disposed in balance, coordination and timing can one dribble, cross or volley. But these restrictions can be accepted for the sake of the immense, almost limitless possibilities that are opened up by chess, woodwork or football as practices. These possibilities can come to lure the learner, to attract and as it were to captivate him – so that he willingly, even joyfully, submits to the demands that they make.[10] And it is in giving himself to the pursuit of structured possibilities of this kind, embodied in practices, that he finds himself. For it is his own powers that are extended through his pursuit and realisation of the possibilities offered by the practice. And this is a way to a real, deeply grounded 'self-esteem'.

In extending this analysis of a practice to a consideration of education, it may be noted that in its range of application, 'practice' is inclusive. In itself, it provides no basis for discriminating between 'cognitive' and 'practical' (or 'manual') domains – let alone for privileging one above the other. And so, in making this the core concept in our understanding of education, we give no hostages to the kind of 'academic' bias which traditionally has dominated curricular policy in schools – a bias that may be particularly acute in a country like Ireland which, for historical reasons, lacks strong traditions in the crafts and trades, but that in any case goes back to the Greek philosophers and has been powerfully reinforced in the modem era by the baleful influence of Descartes's wholly distorting split between mind and body. Young people can surely be educated through engagement with a practice such as woodwork, metalwork or music-making, when such an engagement involves the following: release from the tyranny of the ego through a focusing and concentration of energies on goods that transcend themselves (thereby paradoxically enabling them to discover and realise themselves); release from a vacant present through partnership in a tradition that is richly alive in the present, stretches back into the past and, partially through them, can be extended forward into the future; the achievement of competencies which are ones of the whole person and which, just because they are rooted in the body, do not for that reason call any less into play qualities of creative insight, judgement and expression, which only a terribly limited cognitive psychology could fail to recognise as qualities of *intelligence*. In looking at education into a practice in some such way as this I would also, of course, want to see it as being *in itself* in a very strong sense a *moral education* insofar as, properly conducted, it involves, as I have already suggested, the learning not only of skills but also of virtues.

There is one other point here: the competencies learned, as I have stressed, are enabling ones and therefore give a kind of resourcefulness and *mastery*. But genuine education into a practice will also develop qualities of appreciation and *receptivity*. The whole frame of modern culture – inscribed most deeply in the project of exploiting technically the resources of modern science – has tended to be one of control, mastery and domination. The intended domination has been of the earth and its resources in the first place but more and more of our own living, too. It is becoming ever clearer, however, that this aspiration to technocratic control does not have within it the wisdom to bring about conditions that make our social and personal lives more just or fulfilling; to the contrary, in its unidimensional approach to finding solutions, it often relocates, adds to, or even creates, the problems. This has not prevented it, however, from offering to our culture a beguiling and deeply influential ideal-image or hero-type: the expert (invariably male) who is invulnerably in charge, who can set his goals confidently and manage things, other people, and even himself, effectively in order to deliver success. Such a type seems to provide the ideal of the educated person in important sections of the Green Paper, in the chapter on 'Broadening Education', under the heading, 'Educating for Life', the first aim for students is: 'An ability to manage oneself and to make the most use of personal resources.'[11] It is clear from the language here that a deeply technocratic and instrumental orientation has been imported into the attitude to oneself that education is to promote. And the point I wish to make here is that the educational value of 'practical' subjects would be greatly diminished if they were to succumb to this technicist ideal; and that an important element in their being genuinely educative is that they should open students to a sense of admiration, and sometimes even of awe, at the possibilities and also, of course, the historical achievements in a practice.[12]

It would be a mistake to suppose that the 'practical' subjects are the only beneficiaries if the notion of practice is made central to our conception of education – by being rescued from the prejudice which has relegated them to second class status. For the more traditionally valued academic subjects benefit at least as much – if only by being extricated from the superficial understanding of their supposed virtues which was the obverse side of the condescending attitude to 'practical' subjects. The sort of things that I have said about 'practical' subjects should be true also of 'academic' subjects such as history, physics, English literature or biology. In each case it is an ongoing practice that students need to be introduced to – a practice that embodies its own ways of conducting inquiry, asking fruitful questions, imagining or empathising with characters or situations, devising plausible hypotheses or interesting interpretations, sifting and weighing evidence, making creative connections or shifts of perspective, identifying and reflecting on basic assumptions, becoming sensitive to different contexts, making critical judgements. All these (and much more besides) involve activities that are specifically patterned in each practice, though clearly there are common or overarching types of activity that allow one to speak in the general terms I have just used. It is these activities, with the criteria and standards built into them, that students need to learn. Apart from them, facts, concepts, or propositions make no sense; and only through them – in discussion and cooperation with others – can students be enabled to think and thereby to come into the full exercise of their own minds.

Teaching and learning in the light of practices

While I do not claim that the notion of a practice can by itself answer all significant questions about education, it does carry some strong implications for the conduct of teaching and learning which are worth a brief elaboration. Emphasising practices would combat the tendency endemic in schooling in almost in all cultures towards a 'recitative script', with the expectation that teachers will 'instruct and assess' and that pupils will 'absorb and regurgitate'. Instead, the expectation would be that teachers are practitioners in different domains who find ways of introducing pupils to the practices, and inviting them to become themselves practitioners at the level of proficiency to which at each stage they can aspire.[13] Pupils would be involved in activities and tasks, and in the conversations and discourses that arise in attempting to perform them. Teaching/learning would involve a strong element of apprenticeship in that students would *do* history or *do* physics and the teacher, as well as arranging opportunities for this to happen, would provide significant modelling of what in each case it entails. These activities, with the materials, texts and tools that go with them, would provide a medium between teacher and pupils in relation to which each could be agents (cognitively as well as in other respects).

It is through participation in conversations that arise in the context of focused tasks that people truly develop their repertoires of thinking, feeling, speaking and acting as well as reading and writing. Creating contexts that elicit and sustain such conversations is the great challenge to schools. And the great art for teachers is to be responsive not only to the opportunities and demands of the specific practice but also to the needs, aptitudes and difficulties of particular pupils.[14] It is the latter requirement that makes them teachers, that is to say people competent not only in the specific practices that give substance to education, but also in the peculiar practice that is *teaching itself*. This double requirement gives a paradoxical character to what is perhaps the essential interaction in educative teaching, namely, 'instructional conversation'. 'Instruction' and 'conversation' appear contrary, the one implying authority and planning, the other equality and responsiveness. The task of teaching is to resolve this paradox. To most truly teach, one must converse; to truly converse is to teach.[15]

For pupils, the fact that they are recipients of instruction through being at the same time participants in conversation, and apprentice practitioners, gives an integrating character to their learning. Insofar as they are drawn actively into the open texture of a practice they more readily take what Howard Gardner calls 'risks for understanding' rather than relying on 'correct answer compromises'.[16] And in this mode of learning their newly acquired knowledge is not only integrated by the structure of the practice itself (which in some cases, for example, in mathematics or in physics, can reach rarefied levels of abstraction); it is also integrated into their own developing cognitive/emotional structures. And this latter fact acts against one of the most limiting aspects of much school learning, its frozenness in one compartment of the mind, so that it does not interact with other areas of schooled knowledge, let alone illuminate aspects of non-school experience. This is one of the great difficulties of teaching: how to enable students to 'bridge' between the 'official' knowledge of the school and their own informal, personal or 'life-world' knowledge so that the latter is enriched and challenged by the former.[17] For students are hardly educated unless what they learn in school penetrates their ways of thinking and feeling and informs their reading not only of books but also of their own experiences and worlds.

Stressing the need for 'schooled knowledge' to animate and inform out-of-school experience is not reducible to a point which resounds in the Green Paper, echoing comments on education from other sectors: that schools should take their cue, so to speak, from the existing or emerging society and bend their efforts to serving its needs. The point I wish to make, rather, is that education should indeed equip people to address their present society – and of course the shape of their own lives within this society – but that it will not adequately do this unless it enables them to reflect critically on this society by offering them fuller perspectives on the human good than they find instantiated in its institutions and practices. The life and death of Socrates, perhaps the first exemplary teacher in our Western tradition, is testimony to this point. Anything less might be an education of consumers and even of producers, but not of citizens.

Conclusion

In concluding the chapter, I am aware that there are important issues, implicitly raised by my own analysis, which I have not addressed. Here are a few: What historical forces shape the emergence – and decline – of practices? What criteria should govern the selection of some practices for inclusion in the content of education – and the exclusion of others? By whom, and through what process, are these criteria themselves to be determined? In what respects will these criteria differ for pupils from different places and backgrounds or of different ranges of age and aptitude? How could existing school subjects be reconceived as 'practices' and how hospitable would the latter be to curricular integration or to interdisciplinary initiatives? Would an emphasis on practices bring into relief radical alternatives to existing 'subjects'? How substantial a reorganisation, indeed redefinition of school would be necessary in order to accommodate practices as the central endeavours of the institution? And, very crucially (as the point at which internal goods are most vulnerable to external pressures), what modes of assessment are most congruent with the characteristic fabric of practices?

While I have not attempted to answer these questions, I hope that I have provided a conceptual context which gives them point and pertinence as questions. The answer I have attempted to sketch to the wider question posed in the title of the chapter is not intended to offer anything like a blueprint that might then be systematically implemented; practices cannot be established through the medium of a technicist logic. It is largely for this reason that, over a long period, many successive waves of 'school reform' in many countries have come unstuck. Without a willingness to enter the core reality of a practice, they have sought, in 'top-down' fashion, to specify 'outcomes' and have conceived the task of effective management as one of getting teachers to maximise these outcomes and making them accountable for doing so. It is a hopeful sign that the ineffectiveness of such a model of change and the need for alternatives to it is now more widely recognised (conspicuously, indeed, in the Convention Report); and that this recognition is accompanied by a greater appreciation not only of the difficulty of changing schools but also of the great need to do so.[18]

So long as we entrust huge responsibility for education to schools, any adequate approach to educational reform needs to ensure that these are learning institutions for all who are involved in them – teachers, administrators, and parents, as well as pupils. Nothing I have said implies that education should be conceived as the narrow preserve of specialists; clearly, it is too important to every citizen for this ever to be the case. At the same time, it follows from the stress I have put on practices that teachers, as the practitioners who are most centrally engaged in education, are the ones on whom the achievement of its goods most heavily depends; and it follows from this that their good as practitioners should be a paramount consideration in all educational decision-making. This good is not well provided for when teachers are permanently isolated in their own classrooms as 'deliverers' of a prescribed curriculum. Perhaps their greatest need is proper opportunities for the kind of focused conversation about their own activities as teachers that they, at their best, make available to their pupils in their learning activities. There are hopeful signs that, despite the contrary pressures, spaces for such 'conversations' have been growing in recent years (in this respect the National Education Convention itself was a welcome initiative). It is only from such conversations, rooted in and faithful to the texture of educative practice, that reform in assessment procedures as well as in modes of school organisation can come. The burden of my chapter has been not so much to suggest ways of bringing about such reform, as to sketch a conception of the internal goods of education which might help us to identify what is to count as genuine reform. If educators do not attend vigilantly to these goods there is no shortage of other functions that will be pressed upon them. When they do attend to them, education acquits itself as education *and* best serves the wider society – even if there is much in this society to block a proper recognition of this fact.[19]

Notes

1 *Report on the National Education Convention*, Dublin: National Education Convention Secretariat, 1994, p. 7.
2 *Investment in Education*, Dublin: Stationery Office, 1965.
3 Ireland, *Education for a Changing World*, Green Paper, Dublin: Stationery Office, 1992, pp. 174–178.
4 See, for example, C. Whelan and B. Whelan, *Social Mobility in the Republic of Ireland: A Comparative Perspective*, Dublin: E.S.R.I., 1984; P. Clancy, *Who Goes to College*, A Second National Survey, Dublin: Higher Education Authority, 1988; and C.M.R.S., *Education and Poverty: Eliminating Disadvantage in the Primary School Years*, Dublin: CORI Education Commission, 1992.
5 The quotations here are from an exceptionally acute essay, D. O'Sullivan's 'The Ideational Base of Irish Educational Policy', in D. Mulcahy and D. O'Sullivan, eds, *Irish Educational Policy: Process and Substance*, Dublin: Institute of Public Administration, 1989, pp. 264–245.
6 A rejection of just this kind of mysticism seems to be essential to the 'affirmation of ordinary life', which Charles Taylor claims to be one of the defining characteristics of modernity, in *Sources of the Self: The Making of the Modern Identity*, Cambridge: Cambridge University Press, 1989.
7 Perhaps the most seminal elaboration in recent philosophy of the concept of a 'practice' – to which my discussion here is much indebted – is in Alasdair MacIntyre's *After Virtue*, London: Duckworth, 1981, especially chapter 14. See also W. Carr, 'What is an Educational Practice?', *Journal of Philosophy of Education*, 24, 1990, pp. 15–24.
8 This point is developed a little in a later section, 'Teaching and Learning in the light of Practices'. Examples worth noting here of approaches to the teaching of the three activities mentioned are Donald Graves' approach to writing, various approaches to 'paired reading' or 'shared reading', and the Suzuki approach to musical performance. See D. Graves, *Writing: Teachers and Children at Work*, London: Heinemann, 1983; K.J. Topping and G.A. Lindsay, 'Paired Reading: A Review of the Literature', in *Reading Papers in Education*, 7(3), 1992, pp. 1–50, and S. Suzuki, *Nurtured by Love: A New Approach to Education*, New York: Exposition Press, 1969.
9 I refer here to the Greek concept of 'praxis', and more particularly Aristotle's analysis of it. See J. Dunne, *Back to the Rough Ground: Phronesis and Techné in Modern Philosophy and in Aristotle*, Notre Dame and London: University of Notre Dame Press, 1993.
10 On this point, see R.K. Elliot, 'Education, love of one's subject, and the love of truth', *Proceedings of the Philosophy of Education Society of Great Britain*, 8(1), 1975, pp. 135–153; and Paddy Walsh, *Education and Meaning*, London: Cassell, 1993, pp. 164ff.
11 *Education for a Changing World*, Green Paper, Dublin: Stationery Office, 1992, p. 85.
12 The limitations of the technicist approach, and in particular the significance of the distinction between 'Technique' and 'Practice', is the major theme in Dunne, op. cit.
13 For a much fuller and more nuanced articulation of this point, see G. Gaden, *On the Participant's Engagement with his Activity and the Value of Specialisation in Post-Primary Education*, N.U.I., Ph.D. dissertation, 1985.
14 The latter responsiveness, which is at the heart of educative teaching, is well elucidated by Martin Buber under the rubric of 'inclusion' in his essay, 'Education', in *Between Man and Man*, London: Fontana, 1969.
15 R.G. Tarp and R. Gallimore, *Rousing Minds to Life*, Cambridge: Cambridge University Press, 1988, p. 111.

160 *Joseph Dunne*

16 See H. Gardner, *The Unschooled Mind: How Children Think and How Schools Should Teach*, London: Fontana, 1993.

17 The distinction I make here between two kinds of knowledge, and the importance as well as the difficulty of respecting both of them while bridging the gap between them, is a significant theme in writings in educational psychology and in philosophy. In educational psychology, see, for example, L. Vygolsky on the distinctions and relations between 'scientific' concepts and 'everyday' concepts in *Thinking and Speech*, Collected Works, Vol. 1, New York: Plenum, 1987 Margaret Donaldson's similar points on 'disembedded' knowledge and knowledge 'supported by human sense' in *Children's Minds*, London: Fontana, 1978, especially chapter 7, and H. Gardner's outline of evidence on the widespread inability of students in the USA to deploy specific domains of 'school' knowledge in informal contexts when its relevance is not explicitly signalled to them, op. cit., chapters 8 and 9. In philosophy and sociology, the 'life-world' is an important concept for phenomenologists such as E. Husserl and A. Schutz; and recently the need for the enlightenment of the life-world by more formal 'discursive' knowledge – as well as the danger of its being 'colonised' by the latter – is a major theme in J. Habermas, *The Theory of Communicative Action*, 2 Vols., Boston: Beacon Press, 1984 and 1987. A closely related issue concerns the mediation between the 'theoretical context of dialogue' and the 'real' context of people's life-experience in P. Freire's attempt to construct a pedagogy that is both faithful to experience and facilitative of transformative insight, *Pedagogy of the Oppressed*, Harmondsworth: Penguin, 1972.

18 For recent writing on this point by influential authors, see A. Hargreaves, *Changing Teachers, Changing Times*, London: Cassell, 1994, and M. Fullan, *Changing Forces: Probing the Depths of Educational Reform*, Lewes: Falmer Press, 1993.

19 Without imputing responsibility to them for any of the views expressed here, I want to acknowledge the helpfulness to me in preparing this chapter of conversations with Peter Archer, John Doyle, Gerry Gaden, Tom Kellaghan, Frank Litton and Father Fergal O'Connor, O.P.

CHAPTER 12

IMAGINING FUTURES
The public school and possibility

Maxine Greene

Journal of Curriculum Studies, 32, 2, 267–280, 2000

The 'facts of the case'

To project a vision of what public education in the USA might become in the twenty-first century is to move back and forth between the predictable and the possible. Changes wrought by technology, by demographic shifts around the world (the movements of refugees, the diasporas), by decolonization, by the new pluralization in tension with media-imposed uniformity, make it impossible to think in terms of continuities in the histories of schools. New populations being initiated into a democratic way of life in the USA come from backgrounds and hold expectations that were seldom taken account of in time past. The perceived absoluteness of value systems and moral codes has changed with a growing regard for diversity and, at once, the discovery of 'otherness'. Notions of liberalism and what is called 'neo-liberalism' have altered, especially in the light of what appears to be a newly coherent US conservatism. And in the USA obligations to the poor or unfortunate in the shape of social support systems have become problematic for many people. Yet under the surfaces of a prosperous, self-confident social order in the USA there exists undeniable social suffering, resulting 'from what political, economic, and institutional power does to people, and, reciprocally, from how these forms of power themselves influence response to social problems' (Kleinman *et al.*, 1996: xl). All such changes affect, in some measure, conceptions of education as well as conceptions of democracy.

Defining the possibilities of schools and the purposes of a system of US public education is therefore an uneasy task. Familiar certainties have slipped. Upsurges of optimism with regard to technical and economic advances have become more startling. Yet the tendency to ignore the growing gulfs between rich and poor is all-pervasive, and ethnic and racial prejudices are seemingly insuperable. No serious consideration seems to be given, perhaps especially among public school curriculum-framers, to the traditions that should be kept alive, of the 'conversation' Michael Oakeshott (1962: 199) saw as the bearer of liberal education. Conversation, he said, is an 'unrehearsed intellectual adventure':

> …Education, properly speaking, is an initiation into the skill and partnership of this conversation in which we learn to recognize the voices, to distinguish the proper occasions of utterance, and in which we acquire the intellectual and moral habits appropriate to conversation. And it is this conversation which, in the end, gives place and character to every human activity and utterance.

Such a 'conversation' raises questions that need attending to: the matter of the canon; the fixation on the West; the suppression of colonialist perspectives; the exclusion of women's voices, working class voices, the voices of the oppressed.

In the search for a vision of education, what is called 'reality' must be understood to be interpreted experience. Interpretations and perspectives on the world are bound to differ. Children's poetry and paintings now give some idea of how young people look upon schoolrooms and schoolyards and the surrounding streets. Teacher research offers a viewing of contemporary schools by those held central to what happens there. On occasion, renderings of parents' responses to what they see and hear are made public. Through partnership arrangements, the voices of artists, scientists and local businessmen are heard. Reports come from various levels of administration. Stories of classroom veterans often conflict with those starting out on teaching careers. Voices come these days too from kitchens, courtrooms and the waiting rooms in welfare offices. Immigrant voices come from the so-called 'borderlands' (Anzaldua, 1987) as they tell stories of tyrannies and massacres. They try to say what it means for their children to learn in a free country. Some are hypnotized by images of success. Fundamentalists of all religions make themselves heard, men and women intent on their own orthodoxies. The children of all such families are the newcomers today, each of whom, as Hannah Arendt (1958: 177–178) put it, inaugurates a new beginning as she or he brings into the social grouping something 'which cannot be expected from whatever may have happened before'.

The poet, Derek Walcott (1987: 79), gives an implicit warning to the theorists at odds with one other, empirical scientists, psychologists of various perspectives, curriculum designers, management specialists, social scientists and philosophers. 'To have loved one horizon is insularity', he wrote, 'it blindfolds vision, it narrows experience'. Monological naming and seeing, and one-dimensional thinking is so appealing so much of the time. Against that is what critic Mikhail Bakhtin (1981: 288–300) called *heteroglossia*, becoming more aware of the diversity of horizons in the discourse, and of the danger of reducing what is known to a single consciousness, rather than a multiplicity of voices in any gathering of persons.

The work of US schools used to be an expression of a consensus, a set of agreements on the nature of adult society and what ought to be transmitted to the upcoming generation. The diversity of voices, horizons and opinions from the outside was distracting, at odds with the culture of public schooling. The task of the American school was to assimilate those who were different, to enable them to stand on common ground. Schools would wall out the polyphony of the ever-changing culture; something better, something more democratic, something more 'American' would counteract the heterogeneity that seemed to many to threaten the existence of community.[1] Such a stance is no longer possible. The multiplication of dissonant voices and the proliferation of what used to be called 'antisocial' sub-cultures, the languages, the costumes, the symbolic codes and gestures cannot be denied their reality nor their intrusive power. Music identified with popular culture – rock, rap, hip-hop and the rest – must be granted its integrity and its importance in expressing widely shared concerns in young people's lives. That some of it is marred by sexism, racism, unwarranted spurts of violence and hate may mean a need for critical understanding rather than censorship and disapproval.

The implications for curriculum and for an approach to older traditions are multiple. It will be both necessary and interesting to involve students in the shaping of curricula, especially those geared to the teaching of the many modes of literacy now required for making sense of a changing world. It may be that the 'conversation' described by Oakeshott can be expanded, again with the help of young people, not only to include those voices so long excluded, but the popular and folk arts as well. Street theatre, varieties of graffiti, murals: all may be absorbed, as the population becomes all the more multicultural, as intermarriage increases, and as new immigrants exert more influence over television and film.

Collaborations now vaguely anticipated will become commonplace. Churches, neighbourhood groups, clubs, informal organizations of many kinds may be playing parts in the construction of new traditions and new curricula. At once, differences among diverse groups, gangs, coalitions and the rest will have to be confronted and, when possible, resolved.

American young people are presently often called upon to make the kinds of choices their elders seldom had to confront: the use of drugs; birth control and the problem of abortion; decisions with regard to handguns; the predicament of foster children or abandoned children; child abuse; the disintegration of numerous families. Questions about birth control, sex education and single motherhood are questions that radiate outward; but most schools do not treat such matters as relevant to the larger issues of literacy. Schools of the future, no matter what their origin or allegiance, will be called upon to do more than what is loosely called 'community service'. Young people need to be coached, at the very least, in the skills required to cope with institutions, agencies of various kinds, family illnesses, the complexities of 'welfare-to-work' regulations. To do this well may mean to integrate certain of these concerns, as well as students' ability to cope with losses and catastrophes (and the kinds of learning, including film, that they entail), into interdisciplinary curricula. For example, writing about a notorious assault on a woman jogger in Central Park in New York City a few years ago, Deborah Meier (1995: 61), once a New York principal, stresses the importance of addressing the children's reaction to something that had happened nearby and to the teachers' fears and angers as well.

> The events unfolded in such a way that adolescents in East Harlem were perceived as a threat to decent middle class joggers. It was easy for kids to fall into the trap set by reporters and the general climate and respond as though they were defending the alleged attackers and distancing themselves from the victim.... Our [school's] size, our simple and flexible schedule, the advisory system, and our collegial organization made it feasible to address the crisis together and immediately.

In a New York school like Central Park East, there was no problem in making what occurred part of a subject of study. Clearly, the tensions and violence that mark much of urban life could become relevant issues in social studies or in the arts and the humanities. Rigour and quality of research need not be sacrificed when problems close to students' lives force a recognition that students and teachers both need help in reading the surrounding culture, in naming what is lacking, in identifying what might be done in efforts to transform.

Until a community discovers how to make technology serve its articulated needs, there will be no knowing whether or not it serves the human cause. Preoccupations with testing, measurement, standards and the like follow from a damaging approach to children as 'human resources', their supposed malleability and the belief that they can and should be moulded in accord with the needs of the technological society. Assessments are important if they do more than simply sort people out for places on a hierarchy. Standards are important if they connect with learners' own desires to appear as the best they can be, to achieve in response to what they hope to be. Extrinsically imposed they can deny the human effort to reach further, to imagine possibility.

Similar things might be said about the uses of television in recent US history. The rendering of demonstrations, marches, sitins and of the attacks on civil rights workers surely helped to change public opinion about the civil rights struggle. The federal government might not have felt it politically expedient to intervene if public attention had not been drawn to the struggle. Television images may have fuelled flames of racial hatred in some places, as they brought ancient prejudices and fears to the surface. The focus on such events as the assassinations of President John F. Kennedy and Martin Luther King helped bring into being a number of cultural myths, widely shared experiences that helped create (at least for a while) common memories, if not a common world. Similar responses to the deaths of John Lennon, Elvis Presley, Princess Diana and John F. Kennedy, Jr have helped to draw public mourning away from centres of benign and romantic power to what is described as 'celebrity culture', something that calls for attention from the schools.

Seeking role models of authentic excellence and not celebrity for its own sake, teachers and students in all their diversity may be drawn to reflect on the standards or norms that become summonses in their lives – what is attainable, what is only glitter and show, the contemporary Jay and Daisy Gatsby (Fitzgerald, 1991: 104):

> The truth was that Jay Gatsby of West Egg, Long Island, sprang from his Platonic conception of himself. He was a son of God – a phrase, which, if it means anything, means just that – and he must be about his Father's Business, the service of a vast, vulgar and meretricious beauty. So he invented just the sort of Jay Gatsby that a seventeen-year-old boy would be likely to invent, and to this conception he was faithful to the end.

Gatsby's was not merely a dream of wealth and status. It was accompanied by unembarrassed racism, anti-Semitism and a fearful 'carelessness'. Jay and Daisy 'were careless people...they smashed up things and creatures and then retreated back into their money or their vast carelessness or whatever it was that kept them together, and let other people clean up the mess they had made' (Fitzgerald, 1991: 187–188). For all the sentimental, romantic, and sometimes pietistic hopes of certain educators, the common dream and dominant hope of the contemporary American is for personal wealth and prominence, if not for a kind of boundless security.

The sociologist–philosopher Pierre Bourdieu (1999) is among those who believe that television is today largely responsible for identifying 'reality' with economic reality. The media, he argues, imposes an acceptance of the claim that democracy can best be insured by the so-called free market economy. The free market, along with worldwide monetary controls, globalization and the insistence that social spending must be cut in order to prevent inflation and economic decline, are all ascribed an objective existence, bringing with them an increase of the 'social suffering', the erosion of social services, support for health and education, and new explosions of nationalism and chauvinism.

Yet, even if we were to take for granted the need for such cuts and controls, television disseminates a myth of liberal triumphs. The suppression of the Sandinistas in Nicaragua, the so-called winning of the Cold War, the apparent withdrawal of a few of the worst modern tyrants, the 'victory' over Saddam Hussein, have each been used to justify the control by the International Monetary Fund, in some fashion linked to neoliberalism. If photographs of starving children and homeless adults and corpses spread upon roadways no longer appear on television, we are somehow convinced that peace and security have been won in those countries. Distancing, abstractness, wishful acceptances take over, even when current events are talked about in schools. For all the talk of global citizenship, multiculturalism, social justice and the rest, an untroubled positivism (an unexamined split between facts and values) has taken over in too many classrooms. Reflectiveness and critical inquiry by children will be increasingly difficult if this particular mode of 'carelessness' is not allayed.

These then may well be called 'the facts of the case' at the end of the twentieth century.

Coming together in the name of 'something to pursue'

Discussing the role of the disciplines in US scholarly life, John Dewey wrote that, for all the effort put forth in the sciences, social sciences and philosophy, the results were not adequate when measured against the energy exerted. What is wrong, Dewey (1931: 11) argued, lies

> ... with our lack of imagination in generating leading ideas. Because we are afraid of speculative ideas, we do, and do over and over again, an immense amount of specialized work in the region of 'facts'. We forget such facts are only data; that is, are only fragmentary, uncompleted meanings, and unless they are rounded out into complete ideas – a work which can only be done by hypotheses, by a free imagination of intellectual possibilities – they are as helpless as are all maimed things and as repellent as needlessly thwarted ones.

The claim about the incompleteness of mere facts remains important, as does the linking of imagination to possibility.[2] Yet teacher educators and school administrators do not think speculatively despite all the work towards fruitful conceptions of active learning, critical questioning and the construction of meanings. There is almost no mention of imagination or of its relation to notions of the possible. No attention is paid to Dewey's idea of the incompleteness of meanings when not rounded out by the imaginative projection of possibilities.

'The Possible's slow fuse is lit by the Imagination' (Dickinson, 1960: 688–689), but there are no single views of the possible, any more than there are ways of measuring what it signifies in anyone's imagination. Imagination summons up visions of a better state of things, an illumination of the deficiencies in existing situations, a connection to the education of feeling, and a part of intelligence. Mary Warnock (1978: 202–203) evokes Derek Walcott's view of the enlargement of experience and the need for more than one horizon:

> The belief that there is more in our experience of the world than can possibly meet the unreflecting eye, that our experience is significant for us and worth the attempt to understand it ... this kind of belief may be referred to as the feeling of infinity. It is a sense that there is always more to experience and *more in* what we experience than we can predict. Without some such sense, even at the quite human level of there being something which deeply absorbs our interest, human life becomes perhaps not actually futile or pointless, but experienced as if it were. It becomes, that is to say, boring. In my opinion, it is the main purpose of education to give people the opportunity of not ever being, in this sense, bored; of not ever succumbing to a feeling of futility, or to the belief that they have come to the end of what is worth having.

On the importance of having something worth pursuing, Warnock (1978) quotes a few lines from the British poet William Wordsworth's *The Prelude* (1805), subtitled 'The growth of a poet's mind'. The poem is studded with accounts of moments when the boy and then the man feels himself to be in touch with something larger, something that activates his imagination and moves him to reach beyond himself. Writing about 'School-Time', recalling horseback riding with his friend through the countryside, Wordsworth recaptures such moments and asks 'who shall parcel out/ His intellect, by geometric rules,/ split like a province into round and square?'. No one can predict the experiences of wideawakeness, of insight that at least allow a young person to drink the visionary power. Remembering, he 'retains an obscure sense of possible sublimity'. And then, aware of growing up, aware of his 'growing faculties', he feels they have something to pursue.

There is something vitally important to education in the idea that the consciousness of growing, becoming different, can be tied to some memory of feelings of wonder, of recognition, that can counteract the feelings of futility Warnock (1978) speaks of feelings that so often block any intention to learn. A practitioner too can respond imaginatively to educational deficiency. Thinking about a small school in which people come together in community, a teacher may be provoked into a critique of a large, bureaucratic, depersonalized urban school that had never occurred to her or him before coming on an example of the way schools ought to be. The thought of the difference between a school caught in the lockstep of 45-minute periods and one allowing for flexible time periods for, say, social studies and the humanities may sharpen the teacher's feelings of frustration at inflexibility and move her or him to call for change. There are many instances of images of the possible calling attention to what is lacking that break through the boundaries laid down by the taken-for-granted.

When we think of the boredom in US high schools and the nihilism that can and has led to fearsome violence, we need to explore the ways there are of overcoming senseless fury at existing conditions, feelings of pointlessness, even despair. All this argues for an encouragement of imaginative reaching out that finds responses in the community. It argues for an opening of spaces for dialogue, for shared memories, for a coming together in the name of 'something to pursue'.

Clearly, the creation of communities in classrooms may be one of the most difficult and yet the most essential undertakings in the schools of the future. The fascination with cyberspace communications rarely leads to those face-to-face relationships that enable persons to be open to one another. Nor does it lead to the active empathy, made possible largely by imagination, which draws young people together. It is not simply a passive intuition of what others are feeling but individuals moved to be there for each other in times of difficulty, confusion, suffering, making more likely a sharing of what Alfred Schütz (1961: 220) called 'a common vivid present, our vivid present'. A 'we-relation' is established when people communicate in such a fashion that, by means of their communication, they feel as if they are experiencing an occurrence together. 'Living in our mutual vivid present', Schütz wrote, we are directed towards the thought to be realized in and by the communicating process. 'We grow older together.' We grow through the cultivation of our capacities as the poet did; we grow as we choose the projects by which we create our identities.[3]

To educate for the mode of associated living that is called community, teachers must think about what is involved in inventing the kinds of situations where individuals come together in such a way that each one feels a responsibility for naming the humane and the desirable and moving together to attain them.[4] For the community is of great relevance for our thinking about schools of the near future and the formation of what Dewey (1954: 184) called 'an articulate public'. El Puente is a school in Williamsburg, the largest Latino centre in New York City, concerned with building a movement focused on the development of the whole human being and the whole community (Rose, 1995). Frances Lucerna and Luis Acosta, who founded the school under the aegis of the New Vision Schools in the city, are opposed to the kind of bureaucracy that places more value on standards and benchmarks 'that are outside ourselves, outside of both our individual and collective experience'. Where subject learning is concerned, Frances Lucerna (Rose, 1995: 211) says:

> Look what's happened to reading, writing, and arithmetic...these 'basics'. We don't see them any longer as life skills. They're subjects to be taken, subjects outside our experience. They're not seen as essential to our knowledge of the world, but that if young people know that if they can read, if they can write, if they can understand algebraic codes – if they see that they can use those skills, use them to bring about change in their own lives or in the lives of their families, or in their communities – well, then, there's no stopping them.

Through the use of those skills, the students mapped their community, launched a newspaper, undertook one campaign on vaccination, and another on lead and lead poisoning. Bridges were built between the community and the school. Diverse young people and their parents came together, each from her or his location, to pursue something they all thought worth pursuing. They were not like the young Wordsworth hearing the blasts of wind below the mountain crag and feeling in touch with something larger that awakened a 'visonary power'. But, feeling the changes in themselves and those around, they were able to extend the grasp of consciousness beyond Williamsburg to the city itself and, at length, develop a vision of what urban life might be if communities worked together and social suffering was, in some manner they were trying to imagine, healed.

Such people are beginning to grasp the Deweyan idea that democracy means a community-in-the-making. Through the building of a community the ground may be laid for an articulate public empowered and encouraged to speak for itself, perhaps in many voices, within classrooms (and corridors, and school yards) people look forward to seeing, across spaces where there can be dialogue and exchanges of all kinds in which persons can speak in their own idioms, avoiding the formulaic, the artificial and the 'sound-bite'. For democracy, Dewey (1954: 184) argued, 'is a name for a life of free and enriching communion. It had its seer in Walt Whitman'.

The voice of the artist in imagining the possible

Poets help us to penetrate the darkness and the silences and move on to visions of possibility. The nineteenth century US poet, Walt Whitman (1931: 46) presented himself as the comrade of all sorts of people, as a learner, a teacher (of the 'simplest...of the thoughtfullest'), as a novice, a farmer, an artist, a gentleman, a rowdy, a fancy-man, a physician, resisting 'anything better than my own diversity'. In *Song of Myself* (1931: 53), he called to the stage the forgotten, the disabled and the oppressed, all of whom were to become cherished members of the community:

> Through me many long dumb voices,
> Voices of the interminable generations of prisoners and slaves,
> Voices of the diseas'd and despairing and of thieves and dwarfs,
> Voices of cycles of preparation and accretion,
> And of the threads that connect the stars, and of sombs,
> and of the fatherstuff,
> And of the rights of them the others are down upon....
> Through me forbidden voices....

William Carlos Williams[5] (Rosenthal, 1956: 46–47) spoke oftentimes about the need to imagine, to 'invent', as in *A Sort of a Song*:

> Let the snake wait under
> his weed
> and the writing
> be of words, slow and quick, sharp
> to strike, quiet to wait,
> sleepless
> —through metaphor to reconcile
> the people and the stones.
> Compose. (No ideas
> but in things) Invent!
> Saxifrage is my flower that splits
> the rocks.

Silence often afflicts those wanting to write or to speak. Tillie Olsen (1978: 6) wrote of 'the unnatural thwarting of what struggles to come into being, but cannot. In the old, the obvious parallels: when the seed strikes stone, the soil will not sustain; the spring is false; the time is drought or blight or infestation; the frost comes premature'. Out of such recognition may come the envisaging of a better state of things, an imagining of the possible. Other voices demand attentiveness by school people. James Baldwin (1972: 285) described the profound impact of Martin Luther King's tragic murder after all the acts of faith demanded by all the marches and petitions when Dr King was alive:

> One could scarcely be deluded by Americans anymore, one scarcely dared to expect anything from the great, vast, blank generality, and yet one is compelled to demand of Americans – and for their sakes, after all – a generality, a clarity, and a nobility which they did not dream of demanding of themselves.... Perhaps, however, the moral of the story (and the hope of the world) lies in what one demands, not of others, but of oneself.

There is a bitter futuring here, the other dark side of possibility. How, striving to create a vision of what the schools should be, do we cross the gulfs? How do we overcome the 'blank generality'?

The African American novelist Ralph Ellison (1952: 579) signals another possibility:

> So why do I write, torturing myself to put it down? Because, in spite of myself, I've learned some things. Without the possibility of action, all knowledge comes to one labeled 'file and forget', and I can neither file nor forget. Nor will certain ideas forget me; they keep filing away at my lethargy, my complacency.

It is not that the artist offers solutions or gives directions. He nudges; he renders us uneasy; he makes us (if we are lucky) see what we would not have seen without him. He moves us to imagine, to look beyond. And at the end Ellison (1952: 581) speaks in a language school people like the founders of El Puente understand, along with enough others to give us models and a kind of hope:

> In going underground, I whipped it all except the mind, *the mind*. And the mind that has conceived a plan of living must never lose sight of the chaos against which that pattern was conceived. That goes for societies as well as for individuals. Thus, having tried to give pattern to the chaos which lives within the pattern of your certainties, I must come out, I must emerge.... Even hibernation can be overdone, come to think of it. Perhaps that's my greatest social crime, I've overstayed my hibernation, since there's a possibility that even an invisible man has a socially responsible role to play.

To be responsible in that fashion, we realize, the individual has to win recognition. In his prologue, before flashing back to his life story, the narrator explains that he is invisible 'simply because people refuse to *see* me'. And then:

> That invisibility to which I refer occurs because of a peculiar disposition of the eyes of those with whom I come in contact. A matter of the construction of their inner eyes, those eyes which they look through their physical eyes upon reality.
> (Ellison, 1952: 3)

In any quest for educational purpose, for people to overcome invisibility, they must do something about their own and their colleagues' 'inner eyes' so they can reconceive or reconstruct or reinterpret what they look upon as reality. It may be a matter of conceiving a plan of living once again, a project through which we can choose ourselves.

Encounters with the arts

'Human association' writes Bernard Barber (1992: 5), a US sociologist,

> depends on imagination: the capacity to see in others beings like ourselves. It is thus through imagination that we render others sufficiently like ourselves for them to become subjects of tolerance and respect, sometimes even affection. Democracy is not a natural form of association; it is as extra-ordinary and rare contrivance of cultivated imagination. Democracy needs the arts.

They are 'civil society's driving engine, the key to its creativity, its diversity, its imagination, and hence its spontaneity and liberty' (Barber, 1998: 109). If the cultivation of imagination is important to the making of a community that might become a democratic community, then the release of imagination ought now to be one of the primary commitments of the public school. One of the primary ways of activating the imaginative capacity is through encounters with the performing arts, the visual arts and the art of literature.

Art works being merely present in the school building are not sufficient nor are some of the partnerships now in existence between US schools and cultural institutions. If an aesthetic education is to be fully realized, children need varied reflective encounters: Ibsen's *The Doll's House*, Miller's *Death of a Salesman*, with classical ballets like *Swan Lake* or *Giselle*, with modern works like those choreographed by

Mark Morris or Twyla Tharp, with various jazz pieces, with novels like Don DeLillo's *White Noise* or Toni Morrison's *Beloved*, with the poetry of Adrienne Rich, Mark Strand, Robert Pinsky and with musical works ranging from Bach's to Philip Glass's and Steve Reich's. Such encounters make possible an education of feeling; an education in critical awareness, in noticing what there is to be noticed. By making Monet's paintings of *Rouen Cathedral* objects of her or his experience a student will discover through looking at several versions with their changing colours and transient light that the phenomena of the visible world are themselves always fluid, always in process and signifying differently. To realize that, in one rendering, the cathedral looks delicate, lacy, in a certain fashion feminine, and that (through rendering at another time of day) it looks grey, rocky, unforgiving and still starkly beautiful, is to see new possibilities in experience and to attend to the world around with eyes wide open, refusing the fixed and unchangeable.[6] What could be more important than a consideration of the unfinished in our classrooms? There would always be something still to ask still to inquire into, still to know, still to understand.

The arts hold no guarantee as to true knowledge or understanding, nor should they replace other subject matters in middle school and high schools. They should become central to the curricula and include exhibitions and live performances, thus adding to the modalities by means of which students make sense of their worlds. With aesthetic experiences a possibility in school, education will be less likely merely to transmit dominant (usually middle class and sometimes usually patriotic) traditions. Experiences with the arts and the dialogues to which they give rise may give the teachers and learners involved more opportunity for the authentic conversations out of which questioning and critical thinking and, in time, significant inquiries can arise. People's conscious lives of opinion and judgement 'often proceed on a superficial and trivial plane', Dewey suggested. Then:

> But their lives reach a deeper level. The function of art has always been to break through the crust of conventionalized and routine consciousness. Common things, a flower, a gleam of moonlight, the song of a bird, not things rare and remote, are means with which the deeper levels of life are touched so that they spring up as desire and thought. This process is art. Poetry, drama, the novel, are proofs that the problem of presentation is not insoluble. Artists have always been the real purveyors of the news, for it is not the outward happening in itself which is new, but the kindling by it of emotion, perception, and appreciation.
>
> (Dewey, 1954)

Exposure to works of art and the nurture of the capacity to engage with them are what make it possible for us to notice the flower, the moonlight, the songs of birds. Noticing requires more than merely taking note or recognizing. It demands responsiveness to colour and to texture and, oftentimes, to design. It requires a release of imagination, a moving beyond mere facts and the cultivation of a dialogical community, important though that is. It requires a space and a community where diverse views can find expression and diverse hopes take form, energized by shared art experiences. Shared objects of concern will be discovered as the deeper levels of life are touched, as they find expression in desire and thought. To ponder about the future of the school can only be to explore such moments, to expand the spaces where deepening and expanding conversation can take place and more and more meanings emerge.

Conclusion

With reminders of incompleteness and possibility in mind, listen to Merce Cunningham, a great contemporary dancer–choreographer, now in his eighties. For him, too, the questions remain open and the future continues to reveal itself, in process of being made. He is speaking here about breaking through the boundaries of the ordinary and what it means to think of dance as a transformation of life.

> Take nothing else but space, you see how many possibilities have been revealed. Suppose you now take the dimension of time. Our eight dancers can be doing different movements, they may even to them to the same rhythm which is all right – but there is also the possibility that they can be doing different movements in different rhythms, then that is where the real complexity comes in, adding this kind of material one on top of and with another. One may not like it, but it seems to me anyway that once one begins to think this way, the possibilities become enormous. One of the points that distinguishes my work from traditional choreographies, classical and modern, is certainly this enlargement of possibilities.
>
> (Lesschaeve, 1991: 18)

He is suggesting what it might mean to refuse the conventional ways of dealing with what had been for so long taken for granted about time and space, and the body's self-identification in relation to time and space. Doing so, he was opening new pathways for dancers as well as choreographers; he was provoking those willing to pay heed to resist 'insularity', to conceive things as if they might be otherwise.

Although Merce Cunningham (Lesschaeve, 1991: 73–74) was not concerned about education in the usual sense, he had something to say about children. When asked if he had ever thought of working with children, he said he would have liked it but never thought it would be practical. Then:

> I was looking out the window one morning and there were several children out there. They were skipping and running about playing, little kids, and I suddenly realized they were dancing, you could call it dancing, and yet it wasn't dancing. I thought it was marvelous. There was no music. They were skipping or stopping the way children do, and falling down. I asked myself what it was. Then I realized it was the rhythm. Not the immediate rhythm, for each one was doing something different, but the rhythm of each was so clear because they were doing it completely, the way children do.

There are implications for those of us wondering about the future of US public schools. There is the metaphor of looking through the window. There were children expressing what might have been their desires and thoughts through their skipping and their stopping, their reaching out for their own language. There was their 'doing it completely', in the mood Dewey was describing when he wrote about imagining intellectual possibility. And there was Cunningham seeing something he had never thought of before. He thought it was 'marvelous'. Out of the dread, out of the inequalities, out of the contradictions and the cruelties and the misunderstandings, there may be a vision of the 'marvelous'. The dialogue, the wonder, the openings: we can only trust they will continue on.

Notes

1 We can see this with painful clarity in the US fiction of the early twentieth century: Sherwood Anderson's *Winesburg, Ohio*, Edith Wharton's *The House of Mirth*, Theodore Dreiser's *Sister Carrie* and Ernest Hemingway's short stories. The rebellious one, the one Anderson called a 'grotesque' were not only in some manner destructive of themselves; by example, or through the disturbances they caused, they appeared to endanger the community.

2 Given the advances, particularly in the mathematical and natural sciences since 1931, it is doubtful that Dewey would make the same arguments with regard to all or most of the disciplines.

3 Dewey (1916: 404), always concerned about escaping from the 'dominion of routine habits and blind impulse' and about 'the accentuation of consciousness' that occurs when we are faced with an interruption in the ordinary flow of things, or when we confront novelty or something unexpected, had in mind what he thought education should become. Dewey (1916: 408) emphasized the 'conscious deliberating and desiring' that identified the engaged practitioner. 'The self is not something ready made but something in continuous formation through choice of action . . .' Indeed it is a matter of interest, he said, and interest signifies an active identification of the self with a certain object or project. Dewey's vision obviously had to do with persons, old and young, moved into wide awakeness and the making of life choices. Action, not merely behaving, signifies a sense of agency, an ability to begin something new in the light of untapped possibility. Imagining, choosing, people develop a consciousness of an enlargement of experience, a making of more and more connections, a tapping into funded meanings as new possibilities present themselves.

4 At moments like these in classrooms, individual young people may come to a realization that their uniqueness, like their individual integrity, is a function of active participation in a community, a neighbourhood, an organization. Witness the examples of high idealism in this country: the Civil Rights movement, peace movements, actions to institute the fair treatment of immigrants, projects to insure research on AIDS and related illnesses, movements for equity on behalf of homosexuals and the disabled. A school that succeeds in making a social emergency (like the building of an unwanted incinerator, the dumping of dangerous garbage, the absence of clinics for the poor) a subject of serious study may be on the way to full and creative membership for all involved.

5 William Carlos Williams was a medical doctor who wrote stories, poems and critical essays (see Williams, 1956).

6 There is, as Herman Melville suggested in *Moby Dick*, a great power in what is incomplete, as there is a challenge to any all encompassing system (like the system called 'cetology' or the classification of whales). It cannot be completed, says the narrator (1981: 148), or perfected:

You cannot but plainly see that I have kept my word. But now I leave my cetological System quite unfinished, even as the great Cathedral of Cologne was left, with the crane still standing upon the top of the still uncompleted tower. For small erections may be finished by their first architects; grand ones, true ones, ever leave the sopestone to posterity. God keep me from ever completing anything. This whole book is but a draught of a draught. O Time, Strength, Cash, and Patience.

References

Anzaldúa, G. (1987) *Borderlands: The new mestiza = La frontera* (San Francisco, CA: Spinsters/Aunt Lute).

Arendt, H. (1958) *The Human Condition* (Chicago, IL: The University of Chicago Press).

Bakhtin, M. (1981) *The Dialogical Imagination* (Austin, TX: University of Texas Press).

Baldwin, J. (1972) *No Name in the Street* (New York: Doubleday).

Barber, B.R. (1992) *An Aristocracy of Everyone* (New York: Ballantine Books).

Barber, B.R. (1998) *A Place for Us* (New York: Hill and Wang).

Bourdieu, P. (1999) *The Act of Resistance* (New York: The New Press).

Dewey, J. (1916) *Democracy and Education* (New York: Macmillan).

Dewey, J. (1931) *Philosophy and Civilization* (New York: Minton, Balch).

Dewey, J. (1954) *The Public and Its Problems* (Chicago, IL: Swallow Press).

Dickinson, E. (1960) The gleam of an heroic act. In T.H. Johnson (ed.), *The Complete Poems of Emily Dickinson* (Boston, MA: Little Brown).

Ellison, R. (1952) *Invisible Man* (New York: Signet Books).

Fitzgerald, F. Scott (1991) *The Great Gatsby* (New York: Simon and Schuster).

Kleinman, A., Das, V. and Lock, M. (1996) Introduction. In *Social Suffering* Daedalus: Proceedings of the American Academy of Arts and Sciences, 125(1), xi–xx.

Lesschaeve, Janet (1991) *The Dancer and the Dance: Merce Cunningham in Conversation with Jacqueline Lesschaeve* (New York: M. Boyars).

Meier, D. (1995) *The Power of Their Ideas* (Boston, MA: Beacon Press).

Melville, H. (1981) *Moby Dick* (Berkeley, CA: University of California Press).

Oakeshott, M. (1962) *Rationalism in Politics and Other Essays* (London: Methuen).

Olsen, T. (1978) *Silences* (New York: Delacorte Press/Seymour Lawrence).

Rose, M. (1995) *Possible Lives* (Boston, MA: Houghton Mifflin Co.).

Schütz, A. (1961) *Collected Papers: Vol. 1: The Problem of Social Reality*, (ed.) Maurice Natanson (The Hague, The Netherlands: Nijhoff).

Walcott, D. (1987) Tomorrow, tomorrow. In D. Walcott, *The Arkansas Testament* (New York: Farrar, Strauss and Giroux).

Warnock, M. (1978) *Imagination* (Berkeley, CA: University of California Press).

Whitman, W. (1931) *After Warnock* (New York: Aventine Press).

Williams, W.C. (1956) in M.L. Rosenthal, *The William Carlos Williams Reader* (New York: New Directions).

Wordsworth, W. (1990) The prelude: Book II. In William Wordsworth, *Selected Poems*, (ed.) Sandra Anstey (New York: Oxford University Press).

CHAPTER 13

THE LIMITS OF AESTHETIC SEPARATISM[1]

Literary education and Michael Oakeshott's philosophy of art

Kevin Williams

Westminster Studies in Education, 25, 2, 163–173, 2002

Introduction

Most teachers probably believe that literature can teach their pupils something about life. This view is intuitively plausible and it has also been endorsed by philosophers from Plato to the present day. Eamonn Callan (1997), for example, sees in literature an avenue to enable children to understand and appropriate their political traditions with 'generosity and imagination' (Callan, 1997: 122). Martha Nussbaum (1995) claims that the novel is capable of prompting 'empathy and compassion in ways highly relevant to citizenship' (Nussbaum, 1995: 10) and she actually envisages what seems to me a very questionable connection between this genre and 'the Enlightenment ideal of the equality and dignity of all human life' (ibid.: 46). Nonetheless, I do believe that through teaching literature we can also teach young people about life. This connection between literature and life is even more salient where teachers use literary texts in the area of civic/political education. Yet there is a view of literary education that would be hostile to the use of literary texts with any such didactic intent. But before examining this view and its supporting epistemology in the writings of Michael Oakeshott, it will be helpful to provide an example of what is involved.

Enabling young people to understand the distinction between nationalism and patriotism is an important aim in civic education. Nationalism is a defensive sentiment that defines itself in opposition to the outside world by excluding those who are said not to belong to a particular ethnic or cultural community. Patriotism, by contrast, is self-confident in respect of the outside world and capable of embracing all who are willing to be part of the community making up the nation. This conception of patriotism has nothing to do with nationalism and its associated notions of blood and soil and racial purity. The following two texts offer a basis for an exploration of this distinction and provide one example of the potency of literature in civic education.

The first is Frank O'Connor's short story, 'Guests of the nation' (O'Connor, 1968), which shows how excessive national sentiment can be destructive of the ties that bind us to other human beings. During the Irish War of Independence

1919–1921, a group of Irish republicans is holding two British soldiers hostage and a bond of friendship and human solidarity develops between captors and captives. Yet when ordered to execute their captives/friends, the republicans do so, albeit with great reluctance. The desolation of the narrator following the act derives from a form of national sentiment that can destroy all that is wonderful, morally and psychologically, in our relationships with other human beings. It is the fruit of the kind of nationalism that we all rightly fear and abhor.

By contrast, the second text, Roddy Doyle's essay, 'Republic is a beautiful word' (Doyle, 1993), offers an account of patriotic, rather than nationalistic, sentiment. It is a non-fictional work that deals with the author's reaction to the Republic of Ireland's participation in the World Cup in Italy in 1990. Use of the word 'republic' serves to restore acceptability to a word that has been tarnished through association with the kind of murders described in the O'Connor story and with outrages perpetrated by the Irish Republican Army (IRA) in the latter part of the twentieth century. Doyle writes: 'It was one of the great times of my life, when I loved being from Dublin and I loved being Irish' (ibid.: 21). Three years afterwards the feeling is still present in him. 'The joy and the fun and the pride. Adults behaving like children. ... The excitement and madness and love' (ibid.: 21). I believe that this kind of patriotic sentiment has the potential to unlock borders between people and is one that many educators would feel that they can endorse.[2]

These two texts, one a work of fiction and the other a non-fictional essay, are being treated as resources in teaching about civil life. Yet, as was stated previously, there is a view of literary education that would preclude a teacher from making such a direct link between imaginative literature and life even in the context of a lesson in civic education. This view is expressed very trenchantly by James Gribble (1983). 'It is widely assumed by English teachers', he writes, 'that literature is just a semi-fictional way of analysing moral and social problems' (Gribble, 1983: 158).

> In many schools, works of literature are used as adjuncts to social studies, and books allegedly 'about' old age, the environment, the family and so on are discussed. It is implicit in such courses that works of literature are viewed as sources of knowledge on matters of public or personal concern.
>
> (ibid.: 5)

Gribble refers to someone who presented *Romeo and Juliet* to police cadets 'as a study in juvenile delinquency' (ibid.: 5). He criticises the 'way "topic-based courses" ... tend to draw on literature as merely a form of social documentary' (ibid.: 158). This practice derives from a view of truth in literature as 'the accurate portrayal of aspects of the world or of human life' (ibid.: 12). This view can lead many readers of literature to

> believe that they gain knowledge and understanding from works of literature. ... It is common to find literature courses in schools organized around themes such as 'the family', 'authority', 'race relations', etc., and some teacher education programmes include courses such as 'Children in Literature'. One assumption of such courses is that works of literature will develop knowledge and understanding of the nature of authority, the family, children and so on.
>
> (ibid.: 12)

Gribble argues that there is great danger in the use of literature as what he calls 'source material' in classes of 'social studies or social biology' (ibid.: 158). This is because it involves an attempt to 'tear the "thought" out of the delicate "organic" structure of a work of literature' and any such attempt will 'destroy' the aesthetic quality of the thought (ibid.: 158). On account of the 'embodied' nature and the 'intricate unity' of good literature, Gribble argues that we must never view it as 'a form of expression reducible to, and thus comparable with, other forms of expression or communication' (ibid.). Therefore he announces that his 'own tendency is to take the risks of some form of aestheticism' (ibid.: 155) rather than to accept that works of literature could be studied in other than aesthetic terms. By this he means that he would prefer to take an extremely formal approach (i.e. a concern with form) to the analysis of literary texts rather than to give any impression that the thoughts or ideas of the writer can be considered on their own terms apart from their aesthetic embodiment.

A comprehensive epistemological position that supports this view is to be found in the work of Michael Oakeshott, whose authority is invoked by Gribble (1983: 61). Oakeshott expressly denies that literature offers 'thoughts about the world in general and about the conduct of life' (Oakeshott, 1981: 243) and rejects the possibility that it can 'give a special kind of moral education' (ibid.: 240). This is because, for Oakeshott, the aesthetic marks a unique area of human experience that absolutely resists reduction to any other terms. This aesthetic theory is clearly very hostile to the use of literature with any kind of didactic intent. I call the theory 'aesthetic separatism' because it seeks to separate literature from life. If it were sustainable, this theory would exclude any role for literature in moral or civic education and require the extremely formal approach referred to above in the teaching of literature. In this chapter, I propose to challenge this theory of art and the philosophy of knowledge that informs it and also to disclose in Oakeshott's work evidence of a more nuanced and defensible theory of literary education. To this end it is necessary to explore Oakeshott's epistemology in some detail, especially the relationship between what he calls 'practical experience' (Oakeshott, 1978: 247–321, 1981: 206–212) and aesthetic experience.

The epistemological separatism of Michael Oakeshott

According to Oakeshott, experience offers itself in terms of five discrete and autonomous modes: the mode of practice or practical living and the modes of scientific, historical, philosophical and aesthetic experience. The activities, practices, or forms of life that make up these modes are described in a memorable metaphor as 'voices' in the 'conversation of mankind' (Oakeshott, 1981: 197–247). The notion of the practical as a distinct mode of experience serves therefore to distinguish the ordinary world of human affairs from the scholarly and aesthetic/contemplative forms of understanding or experience. Much of the distinction between the practical and the other modes is well captured in the distinction between the Greek and Latin words *ascholía/negotium* which mean work or business, that is, work done as a means to an end, and *scholé/otium*, which mean leisure, that is, activity enjoyed for its own sake.

Delight as the criterion of the aesthetic

Let us dwell further on his account of the relationship between the world of practical endeavour and that of aesthetic experience. In *Experience and Its Modes*, aesthetic experience is described by Oakeshott as an aspect of the world of practice. Here he writes that music, art and poetry and 'all that we mean by beauty' are ultimately 'wholly taken up with practical life' (Oakeshott, 1978: 296–297). And so he concludes that the 'most thoroughly and positively practical life is that of the artist or the mystic' (ibid.: 296). But he entirely revises this view and, later, in the preface to *Rationalism in Politics*, he writes that the essay, 'The voice of poetry in the conversation of mankind', is a 'belated retraction' of the 'foolish' inclusion of mysticism and art in the practical mode of life (Oakeshott, 1981: vii). In this essay he identifies aesthetic experience as a distinct and autonomous activity which consists in contemplating or 'delighting' in works of art. Poetic, by which he means artistic, experience consists in creating and responding to images simply and exclusively for the sake of the delight they give us. Creating and enjoying works of art are solely and exclusively experiences in responding to images of delight. In his posthumously published words, he writes of the 'poetic' as a 'dream enjoyed for its own sake' (Oakeshott, 1995: 32).

> The world for the poet is not material to be used for satisfying wants, it is something to be contemplated. ...Poetic imagination is not a preliminary to doing something, it is an end in itself.
>
> (ibid.: 32–33)

Therefore we can say that within the terms of Oakeshott's account of the matter, aesthetic experience, in an exemplary and pre-eminent sense, is characterised by its intrinsically valuable or non-instrumental nature. More even than with the scholarly forms of knowledge represented by science or history, art exists for its own sake or on its own account, rather than for any instrumental reason. 'A poem should not mean/but be', Archibald MacLeish's famous lines from *Ars Poetica*, would be an excellent epigraph for Oakeshott's theory of art.

We should note also a contrast between the delight that characterises aesthetic experience and pleasure, a term that belongs to the language of practical experience. In the language of practical experience, the pleasurable is contrasted with the painful and associated with desire as opposed to aversion. In the world of poetic experience even the pity and fear prompted by the depiction of a tragic situation such as that of King Lear provoke aesthetic delight rather than feelings of sadness. Pleasure is also associated with entertainment, distraction or diversion that belong to the world of practical endeavour rather than to that of art. For Oakeshott the world of aesthetic experience is absolutely discrete, self-sufficient, and autonomous and offers neither 'wisdom' nor 'entertainment' (Oakeshott, 1981: 237).

As this is a fairly severe theory of aesthetic experience, it is not surprising to find that Oakeshott acknowledges that the enjoyment of such experience is an uncommon occurrence. All departures from practical experience are, he writes, 'excursions into a foreign country' (Oakeshott, 1978: 296, also 1981: 222), but access to the universe of aesthetic experience is particularly difficult to achieve. It is described as 'a momentary release, a brief enchantment' and as 'a sort of truancy, a dream within the dream of life, a wild flower planted among our wheat' (Oakeshott, 1981: 247), and 'every backward glance' to the world of practical experience is 'an infidelity at once difficult to avoid and fatal in its consequences' (ibid.: 242). How, then, do we come to 'absolve ourselves' (ibid.: 143) from the world of practical activity and enter the world of aesthetic experience? The mode of practical experience includes what Oakeshott calls 'ambiguously practical activities which intimate contemplation' (ibid.: 244). This includes any activity which we engage in for the pleasure of it rather than for an extrinsic purpose such as a reward, and it also includes relationships of friendship, love and affection. These relationships are 'dramatic, not utilitarian' (ibid.: 177, 244) and those involved are concerned only with enjoying one another's company and not with any considerations of usefulness. Oakeshott believes that the cultivation of moral character, where 'doing is delivered, at least in part, from the deadliness of doing' (Oakeshott, 1975: 74, see also 1981: 245), also intimates the world of aesthetic experience. Our moral sentiments or achievements in what he calls 'self-enactment' (Oakeshott, 1975: 70–81) are 'private and self-sufficient' (Oakeshott, 1981: 245). By this he means that where an action does not have the positive consequences that we intend, our moral integrity cannot be impugned on this account. As regards the aesthetic mode of experience, Oakeshott argues that this finds embryonic form in those moments of lethargy where we take lazy delight in the images that flow into our minds. This is why memories can be a 'fruitful spring of poetic images' because when we are indulging in memories 'we are already halfway released from the practical world' (ibid.: 232, n. 2). (He distinguishes between contemplating which involves dwelling upon a memory and simply remembering, which is a feature of the practical world.) The poetic mode is not, however, lethargic but asserts itself only when the urgency of practical desire and ambition have abated, when 'practical and scientific imagining have lost their authority' (ibid.: 222). Aesthetic experience is, therefore, a leisurely 'non-laborious activity'; it is a 'playful and not businesslike' activity (ibid.: 221).

Art and the languages of human inquiry

I find Oakeshott's account of the relationship between the world of aesthetic experience and the worlds of history and science intriguing. He believes that it is mistaken to understand works of art as 'contributions to an inquiry into the nature of the real world' (ibid.: 230) and susceptible of being shown in some sense to be 'true' (ibid.: 229). He claims that the impulse of aesthetic, as well as scientific and historical, activity lies in wonder. The wonder experienced by the scientist or historian has, however, a restless quality that passes into curiosity, inquiry, speculation and research. By contrast, the wonder associated with aesthetic experience provokes only delight (ibid.: 146, 216–223). According to his theory, creating or appreciating a work of art offers a satisfaction of a very different character from that associated with the construction of an explanatory account of human experience. Furthermore, unlike in the case of a piece of scientific or historical inquiry, a work of art provides no detachable conclusions that can be translated into the language of practical activity. (Here he is referring only to the results, outcomes or conclusions of scientific and historical inquiries because he maintains that actual research in science and history cannot be translated into the language of practical life.) Quite commonly, scientific investigation yields results or information that can be exploited in devising technological inventions. Historical study can also furnish conclusions that can be detached from the activity of research that went into establishing them. For example, historically authenticated conclusions about the development of the institution of private property might be used to make a point in a political debate.

Works of art, by contrast, do not have a connection to the world of practical life. A work of art is absolutely divested of its aesthetic quality when introduced into the world of practice. A politician who, for example, accuses an opponent of 'vaulting ambition which o'erleaps itself' (*Macbeth*, Act 1, Sc. vii, line 27) is speaking the language of practical life rather than of poetry (Oakeshott, 1983: 18–19, 38–39) because he or she is treating art as capable of yielding an outcome or end-product. When invoked in the engagements of practical living, the aesthetic integrity of an image is absolutely dissipated; what is left is 'merely what is unpoetic'

(Oakeshott, 1981: 243). This is because in art, form and content, activity and outcome are absolutely inseparable; in art '*what* is said and *how* it is said' are indistinguishable (ibid.: 246). For this reason, as we have seen, Oakeshott believes that literature cannot furnish us with detachable 'thoughts about the world in general and about the conduct of life' (ibid.: 243) or 'give a special kind of moral education' (ibid.: 240).

Aesthetic experience and personal integration

Unsurprisingly, Oakeshott's view of art has been subject to much criticism. Colin Falck criticises Oakeshott's attempt to dissociate the cognitive from the affective aspects of aesthetic experience, and he argues that Oakeshott's view of poetry would apply only to such poetry as that of Mallarmé (Falck, 1963: 72). Howard Davis wonders whether one can impose 'a single form of experience on to such a heterogeneous and expanding "object" as art' (Davis, 1975: 66). More to the point of this discussion he asks whether Oakeshott's universe of aesthetic discourse is 'sufficiently "stable" a Mode of Experience' (ibid.: 65). Davis's point is that it is hard to see how we can entertain the artistic expression of emotions, thoughts and ideas without reference to the languages, both natural and metaphorical, of practical life from which they are constructed. Regrettably, Oakeshott fails to make sufficiently explicit the connection between the mode of practical experience and the modes of human understanding and of art. The discrete, autonomous and disjoined nature of his epistemological categories makes it hard to discern how precisely he conceptualises the relationship between the world of practical experience and the other universes of discourse. In correctly identifying contemplative delight as a feature of aesthetic experience, Oakeshott then, implausibly and restrictively, seeks to make delight the sole criterion of the aesthetic. His philosophy of art suffers, therefore, from an 'overeconomy of concepts', which comes from his having 'insufficiently multiplied essences' (Auspitz, 1976: 266, 288). (This criticism is made in another context but it also has application to his theory of aesthetic experience.)

The separatism that seeks to make delight the sole criterion of the aesthetic is inconsistent with a common conception of the relationship between literature and life, and indeed, truth. In a famous passage, Jane Austen, for example, speaks of the power of the novel to communicate 'the most thorough knowledge of human nature' as well as the 'happiest delineations of its varieties' (Austen, 1987: 22). In a similar vein, Monk Gibbon, in his novel/autobiography, *The Pupil*, argues that it is the aspiration of 'serious novelists ... to make some contribution to the greater understanding of human nature' (Gibbon, 1981: 62). Such novelists seek to offer to their readers 'truth' rather than mere 'verisimilitude'; he describes them as the 'giants of their profession' whose 'insight is matched by their powers of invention' (Gibbon, 1981: 62). Marcel Proust also thought of himself as a searcher after truth. 'I very much wish to finish the work I've begun and to put in it those truths that I know will be nourished by it and that otherwise will be destroyed with me' (quoted in White, 2000: 31). Alain de Botton's book on Proust (de Botton, 1998) owes some of its popularity to the psychological truthfulness de Botton discloses in his work. Proust, he writes, 'offers us a picture of human behaviour that initially fails to match an orthodox account of how people operate, though it may in the end be judged to be a far *more* truthful picture than the one it has challenged' (ibid.: 108). Seamus Heaney endorses this conception of the relationship between literature and truth; he has written persuasively of the poet's 'truth-telling urge'

(Heaney, 1988: xvi) and of the 'necessary function of writing as truth-telling' (ibid.: 97). Of course, affirming a relationship between literature and life is not to be committed to a didactic view of literature. This is the view famously expressed by John Milton in his description of *Paradise Lost*, in the introductory lines of the poem, as an attempt to 'justify the ways of God to man'. Daniel Defoe expresses a similar view in the description of *Moll Flanders* as 'a work from every part of which something may be learned, and some just and religious inference is drawn, by which the reader will have something of instruction, if he pleases to make use of it' (Defoe, 1980: 30). The intention of its creator does not define the meaning of a work of literature and this meaning is never reducible to its author's proselytising intent.

This defence of the relationship between literature and life is not based merely on the authority of distinguished writers. If literature and life are not related, then it is hard to see how the sensibility acquired through engagement within the world of aesthetic experience can inform and enrich the quality of practical experience. It is difficult to see how experience organised within the terms of Oakeshott's rigorously discrete epistemological categories can cohere in the sensibility and character of the human person. In particular, Oakeshott fails to explain how the sensibility acquired through engagement within the world of aesthetic experience can inform and enrich the quality of practical experience. Reading *Hard Times*, for instance, may provide aesthetic pleasure but in some readers it may also provoke feelings of increased sympathy towards others and perhaps hostility to uncontrolled market economics. For readers who have these feelings, their encounter with the novel has implications for their moral lives. Nonetheless, it is in principle possible to appreciate works of art and make no connection between art and life, and obviously people of aesthetic sensibility can be cruel and heartless in the manner of Gilbert Osmond in *The Portrait of a Lady* by Henry James, or indeed of some Nazi officers. Yet there does seem something unusual about the psychological make-up of such people.

Although Oakeshott appears to want us to believe that what we learn in one mode can be 'completely evaded or forgotten' (Greenleaf, 1966: 95) within the other modes, there is also evidence that he seems aware of some relationship between aesthetic experience and the conduct of our lives within the world of practical experience. For example, he contrasts the quality of moral sensibility likely to be developed by young people in the English-speaking world through exposure to Shakespeare and that likely to be acquired by young French people through study of Racine (Oakeshott, 1981: 243). Moreover, in writing about education, he draws attention to the potential of literature to enhance and celebrate 'human self-understanding' (Fuller, 1989: 40). Unfortunately, however, he does not pursue the implications of these insights. The failure to make the connection between his aesthetic theory and education is quite surprising in view of Oakeshott's affirmation that his general epistemology 'springs from reflecting upon teaching and learning rather than from reflecting upon the nature of knowledge' (ibid.: 57). If he had dwelt on the implications of his remarks about education, this would have allowed him to clarify aspects of his theory of art and would probably have led him to qualify its separatism.

Means, ends and didactic intent

How can we reconcile this eloquent testimony to the power of literature in education with the separatism of the aesthetic theory? It can seem unfair to apply an aesthetic theory to educational practice when it was not conceived with teaching and learning in mind. Yet I think that what animates his strictures about didacticism in art derives from a fear that the presence of didactic intent will have a corrosive effect on the rich educational purposes of literary education. The pre-eminent of these purposes is to nourish the imagination or, to adapt a phrase of Oakeshott's from a slightly different context, to introduce young people to a world of 'wonder and delight' (ibid.: 40). He rightly fears that didactic intent may subvert the properly educational purposes of teaching literature and reduce literary works to a means for purveying 'truths' in what he describes as ' "lessons" learned' or as 'hackneyed and unrecognized quotes from Virgil, Dante and Shakespeare' (Oakeshott, 1983: 19, n. 3). What he seems to have in mind is something like the situation in China as described by Colin Thubron where everything 'politically and ethically – is *settled*' and where consequently works of fiction are conceived as *romans à thèse* and serve as mere 'instruments of education' (Thubron, 1988: 187). Indeed, in a Western context, we even find the philosopher, William Galston (1991), echoing Plato's notion of literature as providing noble lies or moralising fables to induce allegiance to the polity on the grounds that children can best be brought to accept the 'core commitments' of a liberal polity through exposure to a 'pantheon of heroes' who offer to them 'noble, moralizing' narratives (Galston, 1991: 243–244). This kind of didacticism is anathema to Oakeshott, as it is to most educators, and this is what he is rejecting in arguing that literature cannot 'give a special kind of moral education' (Oakeshott, 1981: 240). What he wishes to affirm is respect for the integrity of literary works and the necessity to maintain what I propose to call a certain pedagogic detachment or distance in teaching literature. By detachment or distance I mean the attitude that allows literature to speak to the learners in its own terms, unencumbered by any proselytising intent or ulterior purpose on the part of the teacher. In achieving this detachment, much will depend on the manner in which literature is treated by the teacher. Pedagogic tact will be required to avoid an instrumental and reductionist approach and to ensure that the encounters that young people have with literary works are sensitive to their complexity.

In rejecting the encroachment of instrumentalism, there remains something to be said about the relationship between means and ends in the teaching of literature. Literary education has multiple purposes and those that relate to life (e.g. enhancing understanding, sensitivity and tolerance) are not extrinsic to teaching literature. In other words, they are not related to teaching literature in instrumental terms or in terms of using a means to achieve an end. It is as inappropriate to speak in means–ends terms of benefits of literary study as it would be to speak of the activity of sailing as a means to the pleasurable end of enjoyment. The exhilaration, the sense of mastery, well-being and closeness to nature which a person gets from sailing are not ends to which certain physical arrangements are the means. From the enthusiastic and practised participant's point of view such feelings are what sailing is for him or her; they are not ends that are instrumentally related to participation in the activity itself. Likewise, for example, an understanding of the corrosive power of ambition is not the end to which watching a performance of *Macbeth* is the means, any more than an understanding of the beliefs and loyalties, the fears and commitments of Northern Irish Unionists is an end to which a performance of *Observe the Sons of Ulster Marching Towards the Somme* by Frank McGuinness is the means. In the same way, feelings of increased sympathy towards others, an appreciation of, and a sense of outrage at, the destruction wrought by misguided patriotism are not ends, results, consequences or effects which may or may not follow a sensitive reading of Frank O'Connor's short story 'Guests of the nation'. To read the fictional 'Guests of the nation' is to come to a deeper understanding of the malign potential of national sentiment, just as to read Roddy Doyle's non-fictional essay, 'Republic is a beautiful word', is to enter vicariously into the joys of generous-spirited patriotic feelings. Responding to novels and plays actually means enjoying insights and having experiences. (This, of course, is not to suggest that all readers will respond in the same way or have the same kinds of experiences.) Accordingly, responding to literature involves the enlargement of understanding and sympathy as a feature, rather than as an effect, result or by-product of our reading.

Shaping the civic imagination

On account of this capacity to cultivate sympathy and what Oakeshott calls 'human self-understanding' (Fuller, 1989: 40), I would argue that literature can make a significant contribution to civic education. Syllabi in civic and political education quite properly place much emphasis on factual and theoretical knowledge but this aspect of education is likely to be more productive if it acquires a human dimension that allows teachers to focus on the concrete and the particular, and this is precisely the dimension provided by literature. The difference between abstract theory and literature as conduits of human understanding is captured in Goethe's distinction between theory and life itself. '*Grau, theurer Freund, ist alle Theorie,/Und grün des Lebens goldner Baum*' ('Grey, dear friend, is theory all/And green the golden tree of life') (quoted in Grant, 1990).[3] Of necessity there is a grey quality in theoretical work but literature does offer something of the 'green' of life's 'golden tree'. Literary images have a power to reach young people in a way that more theoretical and abstract arguments may fail to and also to provide a source of imagined experience that can serve as an accessible and sustaining form of civic glue.

This power is acknowledged in one of the standard justifications for the teaching of Greek and Latin. This was to gain access to the potential of the great literature of Greece and Rome to provide civic instruction. There is a wonderful short story by Rudyard Kipling (2000) entitled 'Regulus' that illustrates how both in theory and in practice this great Ode of Horace's was taught in this perspective. The story shows how the Ode actually provides the boys with images of courage and forbearance that they apply in their own lives. In the twentieth century, *Lord of the Flies* and *Animal Farm* are examples of well-known novels that, as well as being engaging works of literature, could also serve as vehicles of civic learning. For further illustrative purposes, I wish, however, to consider a recent novel, *The Poisonwood Bible* by Barbara Kingsolver (1999) that I recommend for use in the context of civic education. This novel can be used to address the theme of inter-cultural understanding with a view to enabling young people to engage in what I call cultural decentring. Kingsolver provides a memorable analysis of the possibilities of this cultural decentring in her imaginative representation of contrasting attitudes towards encountering other cultures.

An American family arrives in the Congo in the early 1960s because the father wishes to pursue his mission of evangelising the natives. Husband, wife and eldest daughter are unable to make any kind of imaginative connection with African culture. Reverend Price subscribes to a rigid and stern Protestantism that makes no allowance for any deviation from a strict theological and moral code. He fails entirely to exhibit any understanding of, or sympathy towards, native religion and culture and cannot comprehend the antagonism displayed by natives towards Christianity. When informed that the village chief is worried that he is trying to 'lure' the villagers into 'following corrupt ways' and leading them 'down into a hole, where they may fail to see the proper sun and become trapped like bugs on a rotten carcass' (Kingsolver, 1999: 146–147), he attributes the chief's concern to perverseness on his part. His wife, although not committed to his mission, explains that it is 'all so clear to him that the words of Jesus will bring grace to their lives' but that the 'people here have such different priorities from what we're used to' (ibid.: 277). In a discussion with a young Congolese interpreter, she reaches 'the limits of mutual understanding', when the latter tries to explain that white people seem to them to have a 'strange color' and do not have 'proper skin' (ibid.: 297). The eldest daughter, Rachel, cannot understand why, when Africans built their houses with crates, they 'leave the writing part on the outside for all to see' but, she comments, 'you just have to try and understand, they don't have the same ethics as us. That is one part of living here. Being understanding of the differences' (ibid.: 480).

The attitudes of these characters are contrasted with those of Brother Fowles, Reverend Price's predecessor as missionary, and of Leah, the middle daughter. Brother Fowles, who has gone native and has even married a Congolese, has, he tells the Price family, 'come to love the people here and their ways of thinking' (ibid.: 280). He resonates to their sense of religion.

> Everything they do is with one eye to the spirit. When they plant their yams and manioc, they're praying. When they harvest, they're praying. Even when they conceive their children, I think they're praying. ...I think the Congolese have a world of God's grace in their lives.
>
> (ibid.: 278)

Christian missionaries were, he explains, not required to teach them to pray and worship as 'they already knew how to make a joyful noise unto the Lord a long time ago. ...They're very worshipful. It's a grand way to begin a church service, singing a Congolese hymn to the rainfall on the seed yams' (p. 278). Like Brother Fowles, Leah becomes assimilated into Congolese life. Her assimilation is conveyed by her learning the native language, Lingala, and even assuming a different personality in it. In English she is described as 'sarcastic', whereas in Lingala she is said to sound 'sweet and maternal' (p. 490). She expresses her appreciation of difference as follows: 'Everything you're sure is right can be wrong in another place. Especially *here*' (p. 572).

This novel, and the other texts referred to above, offer what Oakeshott would describe as 'images of a human self-understanding' (Fuller, 1989: 40) that extend beyond 'the narrow boundaries of the local and the contemporary', and beyond 'what might be going on in the next town or village, in Parliament or in the United Nations' (ibid.). Like other accomplished works of literature, I believe that they offer a store of images that may endure in consciousness of young people long after most of what they have learned at school has dropped into the deep well of human forgetfulness. This is why it is perfectly appropriate in civic education to draw on the resources of literary texts. And if we read Oakeshott's aesthetic theory in the context of his writings on education, it is clear that he too accepts that literature can play a role in shaping the civic imagination of the young generation.

Notes

1 This chapter has greatly benefited from the comments of the editor and the Journal's anonymous referees on an earlier draft.

2 It is worth noting that this sentiment is less limited to the inhabitants of one small corner of this earth and thus less circumscribed in its remit than one might imagine. For example, it is expansive enough to include the Pope, a Pole, whom Doyle dislikes intensely and with whom as an atheist he has no religious affiliation. Yet when the Pope met the team – 'I couldn't fight down the lump in my throat as the lads in their tracksuits lined up to meet him. They were all Catholics, the reporter told us. Great, I thought; and I wasn't messing. It was strange' (Doyle, 1993: 20). It also includes Nelson Mandela who, on his arrival in Dublin to accept the freedom of the city, was greeted by crowds chanting 'Ooh Ah Paul McGrath's Da' (Paul McGrath was a black Irish soccer star) (ibid.: 21).

3 I have slightly changed Grant's translation.

References

Auspitz, J.L. (1976) Individuality, civility and theory: the philosophical imagination of Michael Oakeshott, *Political Theory*, 4, pp. 261–294.

Austen, J. (1987) *Northanger Abbey, Lady Susan, The Watsons, Sanditon* (Oxford, Oxford University Press).

Callan, E. (1997) *Creating Citizens: Political Education and Liberal Democracy* (Oxford, Clarendon Press).

Davis, H. (1975) Poetry and the voice of Michael Oakeshott, *British Journal of Aesthetics*, 15, pp. 59–68.

De Botton, A. (1998) *How Proust Can Change Your Life* (London, Picador).

Defoe, D. (1980) *Moll Flanders* (London, Penguin).

Doyle, R. (1993) Republic is a beautiful word, in: N. Hornby (ed.), *My Favourite Year: A Collection of New Football Writing* (London, H., F. & G. Witherby).

Falck, C. (1963) Romanticism in politics, *New Left Review*, January/February, pp. 60–72.

Fuller, T. (ed.) (1989) *The Voice of Liberal Learning: Michael Oakeshott on Education* (New Haven, CT/London, Yale University Press).

Galston, W. (1991) *Liberal Purposes* (Cambridge, Cambridge University Press).

Gibbon, M. (1981) *The Pupil* (Dublin, Wolfhound Press).

Grant, R. (1990) *Thinkers of Our Time: Oakeshott* (The Claridge Press, London).

Greenleaf, W.H. (1966) *Oakeshott's Philosophical Politics* (London, Longman's, Green).

Gribble, J. (1983) *Literary Education: A Revaluation* (Cambridge, Cambridge University Press).

Heaney, S. (1988) *The Government of the Tongue* (London, Faber & Faber).

Kingsolver, B. (1999) *The Poisonwood Bible* (London, Faber & Faber).

Kipling, R. (2000) *The Complete Stalky and Co.* (Oxford, Oxford University Press).

Nussbaum, M.C. (1995) *Poetic Justice: The Literary Imagination and Public Life* (Boston, MA, Beacon Press).

Oakeshott, M. (1975) *On Human Conduct* (Oxford, Clarendon Press).

Oakeshott, M. (1978) *Experience and its Modes* (Cambridge, Cambridge University Press).

Oakeshott, M. (1981) *Rationalism in Politics and Other Essays* (London, Methuen).

Oakeshott, M. (1983) *On History and Other Essays* (Oxford, Blackwell).

Oakeshott, M. (1995) Work and play, *First Things*, July/August, pp. 29–33.

O'Connor, F. (1968) Guests of the nation, in: F. O'Connor (ed.), *Modern Irish Short Stories* (London, Oxford University Press).

Thubron, C. (1988) *Behind the Wall: A Journey Through China* (London, Penguin).

White, E. (2000) *Proust* (London, Phoenix).

CHAPTER 14

INCLUSION vs FAIRNESS

Robin Barrow

Journal of Moral Education, 30, 3, 235–242, 2001

Once upon a time, there was a corrupt world in which Nasty people took advantage of Decent people. The Nasties wanted all the good things in society for themselves and, since they had the power, there was nothing the Decent could do about it. The Nasties simply ignored the claims of the Decent and this went on for several centuries, although it is a fact, curiously unremarked by historians, that during that time some Decent people somehow became Nasty, and a few Nasty people somehow sank to the level of Decency.

Then one day, by some quirk of fate, the rulers, despite being Nasty, realised how immoral this state of affairs was and elected Affirmative Action as their President. Affirmative Action decreed that henceforth all goods would go to the Decent rather than the Nasty. Affirmative Action did his job so well that, after a while, everybody called him her and all the Decent people took advantage of the Nasty people. The Decent people wanted all the good things in society for themselves, and, since they had the power, there was nothing the Nasty could do about it. The Nasties wanted to re-elect Affirmative Action, so that she could look after their interests. But the Decent people said that she had done her job, and shot her. *Sic transit . . .*

The fundamental point about affirmative action is that while it may be justified, it has to be justified in particular cases. It plainly cannot be regarded as an inherently moral principle: it involves, by definition, giving benefit or advantage to certain people on the strength of such generic characteristics as gender, race, colour or whatever and, by the same token, disadvantaging certain other people, regardless of their legitimate claims, because of their gender, race or colour. This is not only morally offensive in itself (unless justified in particular cases by *further* argument) involving as it does stereotyping, visiting on children the sins of the fathers and discriminating against people on irrelevant grounds; it also instantiates the very 'crimes' (such as sexism and racism) that it is a response to. I repeat that this is not to say that it cannot be justified, perhaps as the lesser of two evils, perhaps as politically necessary, or perhaps to realign the balance. Furthermore, even if the argument for it in a particular case is of the politically expedient variety, that does not mean that it cannot also be the morally right thing to do in the circumstances.[1] But what it does mean is that any instance of affirmative action is in itself morally wrong, and has to be justified as none the less morally appropriate by means of a further, distinct argument relating to a particular context.

I begin by reference to affirmative action because it is by now a fairly well-discussed concept and a familiar phenomenon in one shape or another, because it directly invokes consideration of the principle of fairness or impartiality, and because it is an example of a principle which, since it can be justified on occasion, is widely and wrongly presumed to be a moral principle, despite being in fact and in itself the very opposite: an immoral principle; and, I wish to argue, the notion of inclusion shares these three characteristics. Despite being generally and unthinkingly intuited as a self-evidently good thing in our democratic age (even exclusive schools or clubs tend to be careful where they advertise, and nobody would risk publicly proclaiming that he thinks some people should be excluded from a particular setting or context by dint of who they are), the notion of inclusion or being inclusive is at best normally natural and is likely on many occasions to offend the principle of fairness. This may be said of the idea of inclusion in a wide variety of contexts (e.g. clubs, sporting teams, any meritocratic organisation), but I shall focus on the idea of inclusion in an educational context, specifically the state schooling system. (I confine myself to the schooling system in order to take the harder case: the schooling system is generally agreed to be a good that should be available to virtually all, whereas higher education is regarded by many as a limited good such that the case for inclusion would be harder to make. I confine myself to state schooling because, for reasons of space, I want to avoid entering into arguments about freedom of choice, although ultimately they too are relevant.[2])

Let us turn at this point to the fundamental principle of fairness. By this I mean the contention that it is morally wrong, in itself, to treat individuals differently without providing relevant reasons for so doing. This principle has been knocked about a good deal over time, particularly in recent years when liberalism has been either explicitly and viciously repudiated, particularly by totalitarian ideological regimes, or sneeringly patronised as a paternalistic wet dream. It has been pointed out that at best the principle is general and without substance: everything depends upon what constitutes a relevant reason, and that in turn depends upon context and has to be established by independent reasoning. It has been argued (distinctly from and in fact missing the point of the first objection) that, on the contrary, it can be morally right to discriminate. It has been said that it is simply inadequate to hide behind a general procedural principle such as this in the face of real substantive moral issues facing us in Rwanda or Kosovo: the important thing to do (the *morally* important thing) is to stop the mayhem, bloodshed and torture, and if that means riding roughshod over fine considerations of who gets treated how, so be it. It has been pointed out that a procedural morality may, in missing the essence of what morality is all about, be as good as no morality at all.[3]

These objections differ in kind and plausibility. The general thesis that justice is more than procedural is one that I heartily endorse. It is both intellectually depressing and experientially tragic to watch institutions increasingly reduce questions of ethical conduct to questions of due process, by reference to policies and rules that may themselves be plain barmy, not to say unjust. Ultimately any moral system has to be grounded in some substantive view of goodness and/or rightness; but that does not prevent a purely formal procedural principle being a vital part of a coherent moral viewpoint. I also agree that there can be occasions when it is morally justifiable to proceed unfairly in the short term, either by necessity or for the sake of the longer term. This is to say nothing more, although it is extremely important and not always consciously acknowledged, than that moral principles can clash and that what it is morally best, necessary, or justifiable to do in a particular context can involve ignoring a particular principle. Thus while it may be said that 'it can be morally right to discriminate', to concede as much does not in any way invalidate the principle that in itself discrimination is wrong.[4] Finally, to reiterate, the principle of fairness is indeed a formal one: what behaviour it actually enjoins cannot be determined except by reference both to other substantive moral values and to the various facts of a particular situation.

None of the above alters the fact that the principle of fairness or impartiality is absolutely fundamental to any coherent moral philosophy; (logically there has to be a distribution principle, and there is not a more undeniably valid one); nor is it the case that the principle is somehow vacuous. On the contrary, even with the qualifications implicit in the previous argument, this is a most powerful weapon in the fight for justice: almost every morally offensive act of the century, considering for the moment only the stage of national events, can be condemned on the grounds of gross partiality or unfairness, notwithstanding the qualifications considered. It is not the *only*, nor by any means the most emotive, objection to, for example, the race laws of the Nazis that they contravened this principle, but for those whose task is dispassionately to map out the moral arguments for and against various types of conduct it is a complete and sufficient condemnation.

Inclusion, I take it, is merely the fashionable phrase for a concept that has long been familiar to us, and that in the educational context is closely allied to such concepts as mixed-ability classes and mainstreaming. For present purposes, I shall focus on inclusiveness in respect of the deaf and those with learning disabilities, given the nature of the points I wish to make. Inclusion or inclusiveness, and let us not mince words here, as a principle of school practice, might very obviously lead to or involve unfairness or an offence against the principle of impartiality. If, for example, a class is designed for students with certain prior knowledge, skills and understanding, such that the skill and understanding in question become the relevant criteria for admission, to take in those who do not meet these criteria straightforwardly involves unfairness: people are being treated in the same way for no good reason, which is as partial as treating people differently for no good reason. (The principle is generally couched in terms of treating people the same except where good reasons can be given for differential treatment, but it should more properly be stated as the principle that treatment of people should be based upon relevant reasons.)

The first thing to sort out is whether any particular argument for inclusivity is designed to be an empirical or a moral argument (or both). There is all the difference in the world between arguing that deaf people should be taught in normal classes because they will be provided with a better education, because they will gain in some other way or because other pupils will gain in some way and, on the other hand, arguing that it is morally desirable that they be included. The difference is particularly evident in the quite different ways that one would need to assess the validity of either claim. In the former kind of case, even though some value judgements (e.g. 'better education', 'gain advantage') and some real conceptual issues (e.g. 'what is a better education?') arise, the heart of the claim remains the empirical assertion that if we proceed in a certain way it will be more conducive to a certain effect than if we do not. In the latter case, the issue is unaffected by empirical data, since the claim is not that inclusion is the mechanical cause of moral good, but that it is in itself morally right to adopt this policy, whatever the consequences in educational or any other respects.

The empirical claims might seem to present something of a challenge in the context of an argument such as this, since they may be very many (and varied) and it would be beyond the scope of a short chapter to study and assess them. In fact, relying on arguments I have advanced elsewhere, I think that it can be established that this is not the case (or) at the very least that there is no reason to accept it.[5]

My argument in outline is this: a claim such as that 'deaf people will benefit educationally from being taught in the normal classroom' is usually both supported and challenged by various different studies or research programmes. That is to say, there are very few significant empirical claims in education that are plainly and incontestably supported by all research into the matter. This seems to me no accident. The reasons that research findings tend to be so contradictory and inconclusive are many and various, but they certainly include conceptual inadequacy. To establish this claim, for example, the researcher would need to provide an articulation of 'educational benefit' that was not only full and clear, but that was also widely shared. Generally speaking, such articulation is not forthcoming, in its place some kind of operational definition is provided, either explicitly or implicit in the research instrument(s), and in either case invariably some observable criterion, such as success in public examinations, is used. Second, there is the problem of moving from correlation to cause and effect: yes, these deaf children have done well, but was it *because of* the classroom context? Closely connected to this is the general problem that human action and diversity is such that it is difficult to conceive of a research programme that could control for all conceivable variations. Third, behind the edifice of empirical research in education lies the totally unquestioned assumption that there are answers to the questions as framed. However, suppose the fact of the matter were that some deaf people will benefit educationally from being taught in the normal classroom in some circumstances, some in others, and some not at all. It seems evident that the sum of our current research knowledge is consistent with this conclusion and that, if it happens to be true, our empirical research can go on for ever seeming to shed light on the issue but actually doing nothing at all.

What I am suggesting is that for the sorts of reason referred to in the previous paragraph, we actually are in no position to say (notwithstanding what individual researchers claim) whether teaching deaf children in normal classes is educationally preferable to teaching them in classes exclusively designed for the deaf, whether it is educationally preferable for the non-deaf, or whether it is easier or more difficult for teachers. The most we can do is seek to report (more fully and more accurately than researchers usually do) on particular cases; but even the conclusion from a large number of individual studies that inclusion works for the deaf does not yield the conclusion that a particular teacher of the deaf (who is unique and has not been studied) would be more successful (on terms that we will assume have been agreed) if he opened his classroom to the non-deaf.

If my general contention that we do not have any conclusive evidence and are not likely to obtain it on such matters is correct, surely we may go further and say that on the face of it the current enthusiasm for increased inclusivity is counter-intuitive. If education is about anything specific, as distinct from just another word for 'upbringing', then its nature must give rise to some criteria that are relevant to people's capacity for it. For the sake of argument, let us say that education is about developing understanding in relation to certain basic disciplines and subjects. (It is important to stress that my argument here is not dependent on this particular definition, only on there being some definition.) One of the reasons I am focusing on the deaf is that it is a relatively clear concept, notwithstanding the fact that there are obviously degrees of deafness. What counts as legally deaf may be arbitrary to some degree and therefore contentious, but it would be mere obstructionism to maintain at this point that we do not have any clear grasp of what constitutes deafness. Given, then, that we know what both 'education' and 'deafness' mean, does it really seem plausible to suggest that the average teacher would be as good at teaching Shakespeare (mathematics or whatever) to both the deaf and the non-deaf? If so, would that be by using the same methods in either case, or by being equally proficient in two distinct methodologies? When it comes to the inclusive classroom, does it seem plausible to assume that this average teacher is likely to do a better or even as good a job as he would focusing on one style of teaching appropriate to one group, when trying to cope with different groups needing different approaches?

It is the sense that such contentions are counter-intuitive, and the view that the research does not and cannot show that the teacher is likely to (let alone necessarily will) do a better job teaching deaf and non-deaf together, that leads me to the conclusion that the main force behind arguments for inclusion is not empirical, but ethical. One quasi-moral consideration might be some reference to caring or respect. Thus, the argument might run, it is not really a question of whether the deaf (or the non-deaf) will gain a better understanding of Shakespeare; it is a question of treating them with respect, of refusing to make them feel different or marginalised. This line of reasoning, with its failure to distinguish between morally appropriate and morally inappropriate differential treatment, is lamentable. If the deaf and the non-deaf are to be protected from feeling different, we have moved into cloud-cuckoo-land. Of course they are different. The trick is to make sure that acknowledging difference is not confused with patronising and that it is not regarded as marginalising. The mistake is to confuse acknowledging difference with lack of respect.

This is where the force of my earlier observations about affirmative action and fairness comes into play. It is *not* fair (or just or equitable) to base one's treatment of people on irrelevant criteria, and it is not fair or just, or even sensible, to refuse to recognise differences that may constitute relevant differences in relation to important matters. The fact of the matter is that, on the face of it, being deaf or not being deaf is a very relevant consideration in relation to the most effective and suitable ways of educating a given individual. That being so, it is certainly not *in itself* morally right to adopt a policy of inclusion with regard to the deaf.

Thus far I have argued that at least in cases where the distinguishing characteristics are fairly straightforward, such as deafness or blindness (distinctions which are not helped by patronisingly understated and inaccurate euphemisms such as 'aurally challenged' or 'hearing impaired'), there is no clear evidence of any advantage to them or anyone else of a policy of educational inclusion. I have then ventured to suggest that not only is there no good evidence to support the contention, but it is in fact a most implausible hypothesis. I have then argued that there is no obvious moral merit in refusing to acknowledge such difference, and that a policy of inclusion has no self-evident moral virtue. On the contrary, on the face of it, it is in itself an unfair policy, involving a refusal to discriminate on seemingly relevant criteria.

The question is more complicated if we turn to other learning disabilities such as dyslexia. The complexity here, however, arises not from a problem in ethics, nor from a different empirical situation, but from the logically prior difficulty of the concept itself. The question of what constitutes dyslexia, or what it is, is simply more vexed than the question of what deafness is. This leads to practical difficulties in determining whether an individual is dyslexic (and indeed in determining how to determine whether someone is dyslexic). It also opens up the possibility that whereas deafness and blindness, at least in extreme cases, are natural phenomena, by contrast dyslexia might be a cultural phenomenon. That is to say, dyslexia might be the name for something which, like 'cultivated' or 'boorish', is defined by changeable cultural standards.

The general point here is that difficulty in pinning a concept down enhances the difficulty of deciding when a difference is a relevant disability. Before arriving at that judgement in the case of dyslexia, there is a question of what it is; once the meaning is clear, there is the further question of whether it is truly a disability, and if so of what sort: is it, for example, a neurophysiological problem? A psychological one? Next there is the issue of whether it is a natural phenomenon or a social construct. The word 'stupidity', for example, might be used to refer to some physical problem; but it might also be used to pick out a lack of valued understanding, in which case it would label a socially constructed shortcoming, the stupid person in one society quite possibly being the wise in another.

The extent and variety of the problems in relation to arguments about inclusion, only some of which have been alluded to in this chapter, make it quite impossible, within those same confines of space, to draw any firm conclusion on the merit or demerit of inclusion in general. One can only say that the fundamental questions, once one has arrived at a proper and thorough understanding of the characteristic in question, are whether it will be better (in the sense of more effective) for individuals with that characteristic (deafness, dyslexia) to be included in the classroom with those without it and whether it will be better for the latter. In seeking to answer these questions one must place them in the context of relevant factors such as the abilities of teachers and the purpose of the exercise (namely, educating people). One may well then face a straightforward insoluble dilemma if, for example, one were to conclude that it is better for one group, but worse for another. The only thing that is clear is that the view that 'inclusion' is somehow morally incumbent on us is quite false.

Some might characterise my position, perhaps also some of my language and argument, as 'tough-minded', and that in no particularly flattering sense. Accepting a crude distinction between the 'tough'- and 'tender'-minded, and assuming it to be referring broadly to the traditional/progressive dichotomy in education, one must ask this question: tough on what? In other words in respect of what are we supposed to consider the rival merits of tough and tender minded approaches? In the context of discussion of inclusivity there is a widespread tendency to assume that the point at issue is tough or tender attitudes to people, and by extension, tough or tender treatment of them. So, before one realises it, one may find oneself typecast as a 'send the difficult ones to Borstal' campaigner; but I am writing as an educationalist. It seems to me that as *educators* our first duty (and it is actually a moral duty) is to be tough-minded about and on behalf of education, rather than about or on behalf of social problems.

Thinking in those terms my conclusion is that there is no universal answer to the question of inclusion. We should take each individual issue on its own and seek to resolve it on educational grounds. I suspect that such an approach would lead to more difference in education than we currently have or aspire to.

Notes

1 On this distinction between an action being morally good and morally right or morally justified, see further Barrow, R. (1990) *Utilitarianism*, Hants, Edward Elgar.
2 I also want to avoid the question of religious schools.
3 I provide no specific references here, since I regard all these points as commonplace, but that does not mean that they can be ignored.
4 Actually the word 'discriminate' can lead to further problems. To some the connotations of the word are negative, inasmuch as they use the word to mean what others would refer to as 'unjustified discrimination'; to those others, of course, discrimination

is neutral, meaning merely the making of distinctions that are there to be made. Perhaps there are even some for whom 'discrimination' is in itself necessarily positive since it refers to recognising differences that are there to be (i.e. that ought to be) recognised. I must admit that in a chapter on this topic in *Injustice, Inequality and Ethics* (1982) I effectively used the word in this third way. When I say in the text above that 'in itself discrimination is wrong', I mean, of course, that treating people differently for no good reason is wrong.

5 See, for example, Barrow, R. (1984) *Giving Teaching back to Teachers*, Sussex, Harvester Wheat-sheaf; *Understanding Skills* (1990) London, Ontario, Althouse Press; and, more recently, 'Controversial and Conservative' (2000), *University of Regina, Distinguished Visiting Speakers Series, No. 1*, 'Educational Leadership: did behaviourism ever die?' (2000), *Prospero*, and 'The Poverty of empirical research in moral education: beyond John Wilson' (2000), *Journal of Moral Education*, 29, pp. 313–321.

PART V

THE MORAL DIMENSIONS OF TEACHING

CHAPTER 15

EDUCATION AS A MORAL PRACTICE

Richard Pring

Journal of Moral Education, 30, 2, 101–112, 2001

Introduction

It is 23 years since Lawrence Kohlberg addressed a conference at Leicester University. It had a profound influence on many who attended the conference, and upon me in particular. The work of Kohlberg and his colleagues brought together a rigorous research agenda with a carefully thought-out philosophical position within the area of moral development. Furthermore, it saw the close connection between the individual efforts of teachers (carefully informed by a research-based pedagogy) and the wider social context and ethos of the school. Hence, the research on, and the practice within, the 'Just Community School'. In an age where these connections are too frequently missing – where teachers are blamed for educational failings as though the moral climate of school or system have no relevance or where 'effectiveness' is pursued in the absence of educational ideals or moral purposes – it is refreshing to recall an age when philosophy, psychology and sociology were brought together in an 'interdisciplinary colloquium' which the AME so conscientiously tries to promote.

Of course, the Kohlberg enterprise has not been without its critics, but I take that as a compliment rather than as cause for rejection. Knowledge and understanding grow through criticism. What was articulated then (the stages of moral development, the identification of the 'logic' to the moral thinking which characterised the deliberations of young people at different ages, the painstaking attempts to find measurable indicators, the analysis of such key concepts as 'fairness' and 'universalisable principles', the location of moral development within a mainstream philosophical tradition, the interlinking of rational deliberation with dispositions to appropriate action, the need to embody the values of individual morality into the morality of the school) remain the touchstones of further theorising, research and practical development. All knowledge is provisional, but it is a sign of the strength of the foundation studies that they need constantly to be returned to for further inspiration.

It is within that spirit, therefore, that I write this chapter. The main theme is this. The aims and practice of moral education, as inspired by Kohlberg and his colleagues, should not be confined to a section of the curriculum – as though but one of the fragments which makes up the total mosaic. Rather are such aims and practice central to what I would regard as an 'educational practice'. Indeed, I shall argue that education itself is a moral practice, part of the 'humane studies' or humanities rather than the social sciences. Ideally the 'practice' should be in the hands of moral educators (who themselves should manifest the signs of moral development) rather than in the hands of managers, trainers or 'deliverers' of a curriculum. The fact that increasingly (as I shall illustrate) the language of education is one of managing, training and delivering serves to emphasise the urgency of my thesis.

The danger of not recognising this is twofold.

First, the actual practice of education (the rituals of daily schooling, the assemblies and classes, the rules and regulations, the purposes served, the sponsorships sought, the acceptance of outside pressures and instructions) becomes detached from a moral perspective. There remains no driving and unifying ideal, no coherent set of values from which to engage morally and critically with the powerful agencies which seek to use 'education' for their own material or political ends.

Second, and closely connected with the point above, one drives a clear logical distinction between the ends of education and the means of achieving those ends. This is illustrated amply in so much literature about, and research into, the 'effective school'. Severing educational from moral discourse results in a theory of effectiveness which ignores the question 'Effective for what?' But *moral* activities require no justification beyond themselves. 'Justice' may be adopted or carefully engineered, as the most effective way of winning support, but it no longer is (though no doubt resembling) the virtue of justice. 'Educational practice' brings together a wide range of activities which *embody* the values and the moral aims which they are intended to promote. The ends, as it were, are inseparable from the means of attaining them. The enhancement of 'rationality' as a distinctively human quality (or of justice and fairness) is embodied in the very procedures and subject matter of teaching.

In pursuing this thesis, I divide the chapter into four sections:

1   I shall start with two examples of teaching.
2   I shall then bring out from these two examples the moral characteristics of the activity of teaching.
3   The significance of this is then illustrated through the current impoverishment of the concept of teaching, and through the interest now being shown in citizenship education.
4   Finally, by way of conclusion, I shall point to the need to preserve 'teaching as a moral practice'.

Two examples of teaching

In the ancient synagogue of Prague, now a museum to the victims of the Holocaust, there are some remarkable examples of poetry and of paintings of children aged 10–16, very few of whom were to survive. The children had been deported to Terezina, a garrison town about 50 kilometres from Prague. The conditions were appalling, and there was a daily coming and going of prisoners – to destinations which could only be guessed at.

A teacher, Fiedl Brandejs, somehow managed to keep these children together in a makeshift schoolroom. She was a brilliant art teacher and she insisted upon high standards of technique, perspective, use of colour even within these conditions. Art, as anything else, had its standards, and these had to be as rigidly applied. Activities, after all, are characterised by the standards of truth, correctness, validity, appropriateness without which there would be no struggle to improve, no searching for the most precise account, no refinement of one's feelings as they are embodied in one's best endeavours.

These children saw what the adults did not see – butterflies outside the window, rainbows in the sky, green fields beyond the gates, merry-go-rounds on which children played, dinner tables for family and friends, autumn leaves blown by the wind. On the other hand, their poetry gave a different picture – fear, sadness, unbelief at the inhumanity of their conditions.

The Butterfly

The last, the very last,
So richly, brightly, dazzlingly yellow.
Perhaps if the sun's tears would sing
against a white stone...

Such, such a yellow
Is carried lightly 'way up high'.
It went away I'm sure because it wished
to kiss the world goodbye.

For seven weeks I've lived in here,
Penned up inside this ghetto
But I have found my people here.
The dandelions call to me
And the white chestnut candles in the court.
Only I never saw another butterfly.

That butterfly was the last one.
Butterflies don't live in here,
In the ghetto.
          (Pavel Friedmann, b. 7.1.21; d. 29.9.44)

None the less, the human spirit in one sense grew, not as a result of their poetry and painting, but through and in it. The arts were, to use Susan Langer's phrase, 'embodied meaning'. That embodiment of meaning, that struggle to make sense, was made possible by an inspired teacher. But in one sense that teacher was not seeing herself to be doing anything exceptional. She was, through the arts, enabling those young people to make sense, to refine their feelings, to embody the human emotions of hope and sadness, love and fear. She remained an *educator* to the end. However, we must note one key feature of this educational task, namely, the transaction that took place between each of those children and herself who, as it were, matched the particular situation of the young people (their feelings and aspirations) to those cultural resources which she, the teacher, was able to make accessible. In the absence of language, one cannot make sense, and the arts are a kind of language which makes that possible (see Frankova and Povolna, 1993).

The second example is as follows. In England, in the early 1970s, the school leaving age was raised from 15 to 16 years. Great was the anxiety among teachers and the community. Reluctant learners, disillusioned adolescents, alienated young people would hardly welcome yet more of what they had clearly failed at. One proposed solution was the provision of vocational courses – learning the skills of plumbing and decorating would (it was thought) be seen to be more relevant to their future and thus more motivating.

It was, however, the vision of Lawrence Stenhouse and, indeed, of a very fine civil servant, Derek Morrell that, properly taught, the humanities and the arts were as relevant to such young people, and could be perceived as such by them, as any vocational studies. The concerns of young people, as they seriously reflect and argue about the present and future are the very stuff of literature, drama, history and the arts – the use of violence, the prevalence of injustice and poverty, the relations between the sexes, the imposition of authority, the prevalence of racism, the fear of war, the consequences of jealousy or revenge or ambition, the pursuit of nationalism. Furthermore, the complex values which permeate the discussion and understanding of such issues divide society. There is little consensus. It is a test of the maturity of a society or a social group that they can address such issues openly, with passion certainly but with a respect for those who have different views.

The Humanities Curriculum Project sought to offer the means whereby the humanities, the arts and the social studies might provide the resources and the evidence upon which the young people might explore those matters of deep personal concern on which, however, there was often disagreement between them and their parents, friends and acquaintances. The essence of the curriculum lay in this exploration, seeking answers even when there were not certain conclusions, and testing out those tentative conclusions against evidence (see Stenhouse, 1975).

The classroom, therefore, was the arena in which the teachers were able to share their common humanity with the pupils and their common uncertainty in the face of significant and personal problems. Hence, the teacher's main task was to mediate to the young people the products of what others had said and achieved through the humanities, social studies and the arts – the different 'voices in the conversation of mankind'. Crucial to such mediation was the carefully structured discussion of issues in which differences of opinion would be respected, minority views protected, rationality promoted and discussants helped to defend their arguments in the light of evidence.

Central to the justification of the humanities and the arts is their relevance to the young people's understanding of their humanity and in particular of the values through which that humanity is defined. That understanding leads to a recognition of the way in which values permeate not only the provisional conclusions reached but also the procedures through which they are always open to scrutiny, criticism and further development.

In these two examples the teacher was helping the young people to make sense, to develop a serious and authentic response to the real, sometimes threatening and practical situations in which they found themselves. This 'making sense' is not something which can be 'imparted'; it requires deliberation, reflection, reconciliation of conflicting views, solutions to value conflicts. Nor is it the preserve of the academically able, for I am not talking of anything esoteric. The humanities, not skills training or vocational courses, are in this respect central to the education of all young people as they are deliberating seriously about decisions and issues which concern them deeply.

Teaching as a moral practice

To teach is to engage intentionally in those activities which bring about learning. Thus, I can teach by example, by instruction, by explaining, by structuring experience, by writing a suitable text. All sorts of activities can count as teaching. What they have in common is (a) the intention that learning occurs, (b) some connection between what the teacher says and does and that which the student is intended to learn, and (c) some connection between what the teacher says and does and the mental state of the learner. Thus, a person could not be said to be teaching if the lecture on nuclear physics made no connection with the level of understanding of the young audience or if the content of the lecture made no logical connection with the intended learning outcomes.

However, this is a rather dessicated definition of a 'teaching act'. Teachers are members of a profession. As such they have been initiated into a social practice with its own principles of conduct and values. These are frequently implicit, but they embody a commitment to helping young people to learn those things which are judged to be worthwhile. Of course, views differ on what is worthwhile, or what sort of books or activities are more worthwhile than others. Teaching, then, reflects the very moral divisions of the wider society – and teachers, in making choices about the content of learning or about the ways of promoting learning, are inevitably caught up in the moral debate.

Although the social activity of teaching inevitably reflects the moral divisions within society, that activity is concerned with the learning of those concepts, ideas, principles, understandings which enables the young person to make sense of the world. There may be many other worthwhile things to do in life; but the values that teaching is centrally concerned with are those of understanding or making intelligible the experiences one has and of making accessible yet further understanding and experiences.

Such 'making sense' has, of course, many dimensions – those of the physical world made intelligible through the basic concepts of science, those of the social world, those of the aesthetic world and those of the moral – the values and ideals through which certain actions and styles of life are evaluated and seen to be worthwhile.

Such valuing would take seriously the understandings, perceptions, valuings of others – whether through literature, drama, history, theology and so on. These are embedded within the traditions we have inherited, constantly refined through criticism and new experiences. The profession of teaching is the custodian of such traditions – not in a clear or inert sense (not as archivists or librarians), but in the sense of critical engagement. The teacher, in helping the learner to make sense, both respects what is inherited and at the same time helps the learner to engage critically with such a tradition.

Jacob Neusmer in his book *Conservative, American and Jewish* (1993) expresses admirably the essential nature of those moral traditions and the custodial role of educators in relation to them.

> Civilization hangs suspended, from generation to generation, by the gossamer strand of memory. If only one cohort of mothers and fathers fails to convey to its children what *it* has learned from its parents, then the great chain of learning and wisdom snaps. If the guardians of human knowledge stumble only one time, in their fall collapses the whole edifice of knowledge and understanding.
> (Sacks, 1997: 173)

Teaching, therefore, is more than a set of specific actions in which a particular person is helped to learn this or that. It is an activity in which the teacher is sharing in a moral enterprise, namely, the initiation of (usually) young people into a worthwhile way of seeing the world, of experiencing it, of relating to others in a more human and understanding way. In so doing, it is a transaction between the *impersonal* world of ideas embodied within particular texts and artefacts and the *personal* world of the young person as he or she struggles to make sense, searches for value, engages in discovery, finds ideals worth striving for, encounters ideas. That transaction between the impersonal and the personal is conducted through the interpersonal relation of teacher with learner. Whatever the temptation of government to manage learning (thinking 'in business terms'), there can be no avoidance of that transaction – of that essentially moral judgement of the teacher over what is worth learning and what are the worthwhile ways of pursuing it.

The impoverishment of teaching

How we see and understand the world depends on the concepts through which experience is organised. Those concepts are 'embodied' within the words, language and metaphors which we have inherited and use. Change that language and you change the way of conceiving things; you change the evaluations as well as the descriptions, the relationship which you enter into as well as goals which you are seeking.

In its attempts to transform the teaching profession in the United Kingdom into a more efficient and effective force, the government sought advice from Allen Odden, whose book (with Kelly) *Paying Teachers for What They Know and Do* provides the basis for doing this (Odden and Kelly, 1997). Odden and Kelley argue that the traditional way of paying and rewarding teachers is out-dated. Management and compensation in other employments reflect much more what the employees can do and have achieved in terms of devolved responsibility and remuneration. Teaching should be rather like that: greater recognition, through an appropriate funding mechanism and through the devolving of management responsibility, of what teachers can do and have achieved. There is, in their view, an urgency to move in that direction because:

> the tax-paying public, the business community, and policy-makers still pressure the education system to produce results and to link pay – even school finance structures, more broadly – to performance.
>
> (p. 11)

The pressure arises from the felt need to raise standards, to improve 'productivity' in relation to these standards, and to hold teachers accountable (both positively where they have succeeded and negatively where they have failed) for their professional work. To enable this to happen, there needs to be much greater precision in what teachers are expected to achieve – productivity targets; but this in turn requires the setting of *reasonable* targets – the clear statement of what good teachers of subject X and level Y should be able to achieve. There should be professional development to enable teachers achieve these targets. To help with that, the British government imported further advice from the United States. This time the firm Hay/McBer was paid £4 million (or $6 million) to spell out what were the characteristics of a good teacher, thereby enabling appropriate teaching targets to be set (Hay/McBer, 2000).

Odden and Kelley's argument has been influential both within and outside the United States. Certainly it has had a profound effect upon the British government which, with the advice of Odden, is now swiftly introducing 'performance-related pay' to schools in England and Wales. The government Green Paper, *Teachers: Meeting the Challenge of Change* (DfEE, 1998), followed by a 'technical consultation document' on pay and performance management, spell out a new pay and reward structure, connected positively with a 'new vision of the profession', including professional development.

The performance-based management of education takes on a distinctive language through which to describe, assess and evaluate an 'educational practice' and thus the professional engagement within it. It draws upon new metaphors, and through these metaphors the concept of the profession of teaching changes. Teachers and 'their managers' perceive what they are doing differently. Hence, according to the civil servant responsible for implementing these changes, we must 'think in business terms' – and thus draw upon the language and practices of the business world. That means that we look at the changes for the improvement of standards as a 'quality circle' in which one defines the product, identifies the means for producing that product, empowers the deliverer, measures the quality, empowers the client and develops partnership between the clients, the deliverers and the managers of the system such that there might be a continuous review of targets and means for achieving those targets. The 'product' is defined in terms of a detailed, outcomes-related curriculum. The 'process' (or 'means' for reaching the targets) is spelt out in terms of 'effectiveness' in the production of this 'product'. The changed management structures 'empower the deliverers' of the 'process' to satisfy the needs of the respective 'stakeholders'. The 'measurement of the quality' of the 'product' is provided through a detailed assessment (a 'testing against product specification'). 'The empowering of the clients' comes about through the creation of choice, which is achieved through the availability of public data on effectiveness and through competitiveness amongst the 'deliverers of the product' so that the clients can exercise choice. And 'partnerships' are created for 'stakeholders', 'deliverers' and 'clients' to work together in developing the 'effective processes' for producing the 'product' (which is generally defined by someone external to the 'process'). The management of the whole process is conducted by the cascading down from above of 'productivity targets'.

The language of education through which we are asked to 'think in business terms' – the language of inputs and outputs, of value-addedness, of performance indicators and audits, of products and productivity, of educational clients and curriculum deliverers – constitutes a new way of thinking about the relation of teacher and learner. It employs different metaphors, different ways of describing and evaluating educational activities; but, in so doing, it changes those activities into something else. It transforms the moral context in which education takes place and is judged successful or otherwise.

The effect of this new language is not a matter for empirical enquiry alone, for that which is to be enquired into has become a different thing. So mesmerised have we become with the importance of 'cost efficiency', 'value for money', 'productivity' and 'effectiveness' that we have failed to see that the very nature of the enterprise – of an 'educational practice' – has been redefined. Once the teacher 'delivers' someone else's curriculum with its precisely defined 'product', there is little room for that *transaction* in which the teacher, rooted in a particular cultural tradition, responds to the needs of the learner. When the learner becomes a 'client' or 'customer', lost is the traditional apprenticeship in which the students are initiated into the community of learners. When the 'product' is the measurable 'targets' on which 'performance' is 'audited', then little significance is attached to the 'struggle to make sense' which characterises the learning of what is valuable.

Think, however, in terms of a different set of metaphors. Oakeshott (1972), in his essay 'Education: its engagement and its frustrations', speaks of education as the introduction of young people to a world of ideas which are embodied in the 'conversations between the generations of mankind'. Through that introduction the young learner comes to learn and appreciate the voices of poetry, of philosophy, of history, of science. There is an engagement with ideas, a struggle to make sense, a search for value in what often appears dull and mundane, an excitement in intellectual and aesthetic discovery, an entry to a tradition of thinking and criticism. As in all good conversations (especially one where there is such an engagement with ideas and where the spirit of criticism prevails), one cannot define in advance what the end of that conversation or engagement will or should be. Indeed, the end is but the starting point for further conversations.

Teaching, therefore, becomes a 'transaction' between the teacher and the learner in which the teacher, as in the case of Fiedl Brandejs, mediates the different voices of poetry and of art, to those who are seeking to take part. That conversation between the generations, embedded within literature, drama, oral traditions and narratives, artefacts, social practices, works of art and so on speak to the needs and aspirations of the young people, but at different levels and in different ways. The art and skill of the teacher lie in making the connections between the *impersonal* world of what is bequeathed to us in libraries and so on and the *personal* world of the young people, thereby creating an *interpersonal* world of informed and critical dialogue. The fruit of such efforts will be reflected in thoughts, beliefs and valuings which are diverse, unpredictable and sometimes slow to mature.

The problems are reflected in the latest attempts to bring citizenship onto the curriculum (Crick Report, 1998). At first glance, this seems eminently sensible. To live intelligently and responsibly in a democracy requires certain skills, qualities, attitudes and understandings. To participate in government requires an inclination to do so and some understanding of the issues. It requires, too, the ability to engage with other people, whom one might disagree with, in attempting to arrive at agreed solutions to problems. Citizenship would seem, therefore, to be the very sort of 'subject' which ought to be taught in schools. And so citizenship will soon be a compulsory part of the curriculum, and teachers are being trained specially to teach it.

According to Crick and Porter (1978), whose report provided the basis for this policy, 'citizenship' is 'the knowledge, skills and attitudes needed to make a man or woman informed about politics and able to participate in public life and groups of all kinds, both occupational and voluntary, and to recognise and tolerate diversities of political and social values'. The concepts which the students of citizenship need to master are those of 'power', 'freedom', 'rights', 'justice' – what Crick earlier referred to as the key words of 'political literacy', without which one would simply not be able to understand the political life and context within which one lives. There needs also to be, of course, relevant knowledge, about government, for instance. There are procedural skills, too, concerned with discussion and argument.

However, upon reflection it would seem that the 'outcomes' of a citizenship course are the very skills, understandings and qualities which should arise from the study of the humanities and the social studies. In Bruner's (1966) *Man: A Course of Study*, learning was structured around three major questions: What makes us human? How did we become so? How might we become more so? Answers to these questions are, of course, the very stuff of the humanities, the social studies and the arts, as student and teacher explore together, albeit in the light of what others have said, what it is to be human. Such an exploration (seeking solutions to problems, listening to advice and even criticism, articulating one's views in the light of evidence) requires certain procedural skills and attitudes towards argument and evidence. It is difficult to disassociate such qualities and skills from what we pick out as an *educational* practice within arts, humanities and social studies or from what we would recognise to be as a moral enterprise.

Picking out citizenship as a subject in its own right reflects a failure to recognise this. It is to accept a limited and impoverished understanding of teaching. It fails to see it as a 'practice' whereby young people (mainly) are introduced to the qualities and understandings which we have inherited (through literature, drama, history, the arts, etc.) and which prepare the next generation of young people to live a fully human life both as individuals and as citizens. It looks at the rest of the curriculum (now 'delivering targets' set by government) and finds that such a curriculum is not helping young people address the moral and social issues, questions of personal identity, matters of value on which society is divided but which need to be tackled. In other words, it fails to see that all teaching, when conceived as a moral practice concerned with values and conceptions of what it is to be human, necessarily is a preparation for citizenship broadly conceived.

Preserving teaching as a moral practice

Teaching can be very narrowly conceived as any intentional attempt to impart learning – the learning of specific skills or particular facts. Not all teaching is, therefore, necessarily educational; but teachers are, generally speaking, members of a profession. They have a role within the wider society of helping young people to learn those things which society (whether the civil society or that or religions or social groups) believes to be worthwhile. The teaching of literature and the sciences, of drama and the arts, of history and social studies assume that these studies somehow enhance the quality of life. Such teaching draws upon the rich cultural resources with which they are familiar through their own education, training and experience and endeavours to make them accessible to the students for whom they are regarded as valuable.

In that sense there are two levels of narrative. There is the 'impersonal' level – the narratives within science or history or literature wherein ideas are preserved, developed, criticised within a public tradition. But there is the 'personal' level at which young people try to make sense of the world and the relationships around them and at which they find, or do not find, valuable forms of life to which they can give allegiance. This personal narrative is where young people seek to understand who and what they are, partly, of course, in relation to other people and to the wider society. Teaching, as illustrated in the work of Friedl Brandejs or in the Humanities Curriculum Project or in Bruner's *Man: A Course of Study*, is where these two narratives are brought together, and it is the mark of the good and inspired teacher that this is enabled to happen. Teaching, then, enables that learning to take place in which the young person finds values in a range of activities which are of human importance and do so through being put in touch with what others have said, done and achieved. They become part of a wider learning community in which questions of value have been and continue to be explored. They learn that there is no end to this exploration.

Teaching, therefore, requires the recognition that all young people, even though academically not very able, have the capacity for what can be described as 'moral seriousness': that is, the capacity to think seriously about their relationships, about the kind of future (including jobs) they want to pursue, about loyalties and commitments. Both developing and supporting that sense of 'seriousness' seem to be a central task of the profession of teaching. It requires, on one hand, roots within those traditions of thought and experience through which such questions have been posed and explored by others elsewhere. But it requires, too, a respect for the authentic voice and feelings of the young persons as they struggle to make sense of their place within society. In making the connections between the two levels of narrative, the teacher provides the wider perspective, questions the perhaps rather limited vision, points out other possibilities. In doing so the teacher is, through the different elements within the overall curriculum, deliberating about the ends and purposes of education, not simply about the most effective means of attaining someone else's ends.

The danger is that, as we adopt a very different language of teaching – a language which for the sake of increased productivity and improved standards as conceived by those who think in business terms – this essentially moral purpose and character of teaching will be lost. The role of the humanities and the arts will be diminished. Teaching will become a purely technical matter of hitting targets.

During the brief period when I met Kohlberg at Harvard, I was advised to visit a school in outer Boston whose principal had been much influenced by Kohlberg's work. Moral education required a reappraisal of the moral practice of teaching, and this in turn required a reappraisal of the moral ethos of the school. The principal was reading poetry, which she had written at the age of 11 when parted from her mother and twin sister, to an attentive group of 17-year-old high school students. Again, it was through poetry that they, seriously and attentively, were seeking to make sense of aspects of being human which too often can be swept on one side.

It was a large school, with therefore a sizeable intake of new teachers every year. To these teachers, the principal wrote the following letter.

> Dear Teacher,
>
> I am a survivor of a concentration camp. My eyes saw what no man should witness:
>
> Gas chambers built by learned engineers.
>
> Children poisoned by educated physicians.
>
> Infants killed by trained nurses.
>
> Women and babies shot and burned by high school and college graduates.
>
> So, I am suspicious of education.
>
> My request is: Help your students become human.
>
> Your efforts must never produce learned monsters, skilled psychopaths, educated Eichmans.
>
> Reading, writing, arithmetic are important only if they serve to make our children more human.

I wish to argue that what makes sense of the curriculum, in educational terms, is that it is the forum or the vehicle through which young people are enabled to explore seriously (in the light of evidence and argument) what it is to be human. Such an exploration has no end. That is why teaching should be regarded as a moral practice.

Note

This is the text of the 13th Lawrence Kohlberg Memorial Lecture, delivered at the 26th annual conference of the Association for Moral Education, University of Glasgow, Scotland, July 2000.

References

Bruner, J. (1966) 'Man: a course of study', in: J. Bruner (ed.), *Towards a Theory of Instruction*, pp. 73–101 (Cambridge, MA, Harvard University Press).

Crick, B. and Porter, A. (1978) *Political Education and Political Literacy* (Harlow, Longman).

Crick Report (1998) *Education for Citizenship and the Teaching of Democracy in Schools*, Initial Report (London, QCA).

Department for Education and Employment (DfEE) (1998) *Teachers: Meeting the Challenge of Change* (London, DfEE).

Frankova, A. and Povolna, H. (1993) *I have not seen a butterfly around here* (Prague, The Jewish Museum).

Hay/McBer (2000) *Raising Achievement in our Schools: model of effective teaching*, interim report to DfEE (London, DfEE).

Oakeshott, M. (1972) 'Education: its engagement and its frustrations', in: M. Fuller (ed.), *Michael Oakeshott and Education* (New Haven, CT, Yale University Press).

Odden, A. and Kelly, C. (1997) *Paying Teachers for What They Know and Do* (California, Corwin Press).

Sacks, J. (1997) *The Politics of Hope* (London, Jonathan Cape).

Stenhouse, L. (1975) *Authority, Education and Emancipation* (London, Heinemann).

CHAPTER 16

PATHS OF JUDGEMENT
The revival of practical wisdom

Richard Smith

Educational Philosophy and Theory, 31, 3, 327–340, 1999

The ascendancy of technicism, of technical or instrumental rationality, is sufficiently marked in education, in the English-speaking world at least, to need little illustration. The assumption that the main values of the education system can be characterised in terms of efficiency and effectiveness, and that learning to teach is a matter of acquiring competencies; the growth of what Power (1997) calls the 'audit society', the proliferation of performance indicators – these latest and peculiarly insidious manifestations of technicism present a formidable challenge to richer, more humane and in the end more *educational* conceptions of education and, *mutatis mutandis*, of other forms of public service. The work this challenge should inspire seems to me among the most important that philosophers of education can undertake at the present time.

Dunne (1993: 369) writes that 'What is important . . . is that in the educational community – which rightly is the *whole* community – a discourse should be available in which the nature of teaching as a practice can be articulated and thereby *defended*'. Many, including Dunne himself, have suspected that the idea of practical reason or wisdom, the Aristotelian phronesis, might play an important part in that discourse, and phronesis variously interpreted has been enjoying something of a revival, perhaps to be dated to the work of Hans-Georg Gadamer and certainly stimulated by MacIntyre's *After Virtue* (1981). I share that suspicion, and in this chapter I sketch a conception of practical judgement or practical reason, for the most part using the former phrase as likely to prove rhetorically and politically more handy. This conception is not exactly the Aristotelian phronesis. That term and related concepts such as *techne* and *praxis* do not translate into our language and world without bringing certain distortions with them, as I shall indicate. However, I shall borrow from Aristotle where he is insightful, as so often he is. By liberating a modern sense of practical judgement from too close a marriage to phronesis and its problems I argue that we stand to gain much, especially for our understanding of teaching.

Those impressed by the claims of practical judgement (or wisdom, or reason) need to confront a number of questions. Dunne (1993) helpfully sets out five of these at the end of his book. The first question is that presented by the problem of freedom. Does practical judgement offer us a recognisable picture of the kind and extent of human freedom we have, especially given that the modern world, comprehended by science and dominated by technique, appears to present us with less unconditioned opportunities for its exercise than Aristotle could have imagined?

Second, practical judgement may seem too complicit with established ways of life to offer anything significant to critique of them. It can appear to comprise a cautious set of virtues within a markedly conservative system. Where the first question suggests that practical judgement implies an unrealistically extensive conception of freedom, the second can be read as the claim that Aristotle's account of the voluntary agent falls too short of what the 'free subject' needs in order to take, not the view from nowhere, but the view from elsewhere. Taken together, then, these two questions are demanding ones. Third, there is the question of how practical judgement can make claims to objectivity and truth in the face of the spectres of relativism and subjectivism – and do so without collapsing into a discredited form of foundationalism. Fourth, it may seem too close to and to need distinguishing from indefensible notions of common sense or flair. The fifth question is whether an account of practical judgement helps us to describe teaching as a coherent practice and defend it from the technicism which in its various forms threatens to reduce and distort it.

In sketching some answers to these questions I draw attention to several neglected aspects and implications of practical judgement. I do no more than indicate a basis for applying the practical judgement to teaching, not just because of limitations of space but for other reasons I discuss briefly in the last section. There, too, I turn to the puzzling question, as it seems to me, of just what an account of practical judgement is an account *of*, and quite what it means to offer such an account or provide such a picture.

A Martian view

The need for an account of the 'rationality of practice' of teaching which supplies an alternative to prevailing technicist versions grows ever more pressing. Reynolds, for example, begins a presentation called 'Better Teachers, Better Schools', on the UK Teacher Training Agency's website, as follows:

> Were a Martian educationalist to arrive in Britain today, I am confident that what would most surprise him or her is that we have no applied science of teaching, that we have no plans to generate one and that many people are happy with this situation. Teaching is the core technology of what teachers do. It is more and more prescribed as politicians and others start to, quite rightly, intervene in the teaching methods that are used. It is the distinct area of teaching that provides for me the most likely explanation for why educational reforms in Britain have hitherto always failed, namely that in pulling the 'lever' of the school we have missed pulling the 'lever' of the teacher.

Here the aspiration to formulate an 'applied science of teaching' with a 'core technology of what teachers do' is matched by talk of pulling the teacher's lever, presumably to make her operate, for all the world as if teachers were a primitive kind of machine. Reynolds believes that schools should become, like aeroplanes and nuclear power stations, 'high reliability organisations' where failure in even the smallest percentage of cases is as unacceptable as it would be for air traffic control regularly to lose a plane or two. We are all familiar with the ambition to spell out the business of teaching in terms of procedures and competencies such that there is no room left for error. Cause (teacher behaviour) and effect (pupil learning) are to be conjoined with sufficient scientific glue to defy the most incompetent or (the older fantasy) bolshy practitioner.

In the recent UK Green Paper, *Teachers Meeting the Challenge of Change* (DfEE, 1998), technicism begins to parody itself, in general adulation of all things technical and technological. The first chapter acknowledges that 'At the heart of what teachers do will remain the good, well taught lesson.' This is said to have proved its worth, or rather its 'effectiveness'. The paragraph (para. 8) continues:

> Throughout this century teachers have had to choose between prioritising the needs of larger groups or following up the diverse needs of individuals. Now for the first time they can do both.

How is this millennial vision to be accomplished? 'New technology can add new dimensions to lessons, improving both effectiveness and presentation...'. In the same chapter (para. 8) there is rapturous talk of 'electronic registers, assessment and recording systems, software for managing budgets, search facilities for computerised records'. Thus technicism passes beyond even the celebration of skills and effectiveness, the elevation of means above ends. These at least left open the possibility that there were ends, somewhere, to which the means were leading. Now the means appear to have kicked free of ends altogether and whirl, beatified, in a technological utopia[1]: a Green Paper which is less a vision of teaching (still less of education) than a kind of educational Argos catalogue, including a new electric kettle for the staff-room (para. 9).

Practical judgement

This, then, is the kind of discourse that drives us to look for a different, coherent set of concepts and ideas truer to the nature of the activity of teaching in particular. To some (e.g. Carr, 1987; Dunne, 1993) Aristotle's phronesis has seemed a promising source for such an alternative rationality of practice. However, there are notorious difficulties with Aristotle's account. I shall touch on some of these briefly (cp. Mackenzie, 1991).

Some activities or professions which might seem to us pre-eminently the realm of phronesis, such as medicine or seamanship, Aristotle regards as matters of *techne*. The distinction between *poiesis* and *praxis*, often supposed to map onto *techne* and phronesis, respectively, does not work as we might want it to. Medicine employs *techne* and operates in the realm of *poiesis*, according to Aristotle, producing an end – health – towards which medicine is the means. Of course a great deal of teaching also works like this. I try every ethical means available to get my students to see why talk of the 'rights' of animals or future generations is problematic. But this is instrumental thinking and appears to take my teaching out of the realm of phronesis. *Poiesis* is further complicated by a specialist application to certain of the arts, when it is actually contrasted with *techne*; at the same time the Greeks seem to have thought of the arts as generally the province of *techne*, as matters for the use of technique, yet this would hardly make them models of what we would now call instrumental or technical reasoning. Worst of all, Aristotle seems to say quite explicitly (*Nicomachean Ethics*, 1112b11) that we deliberate not about ends, τελη, but about τα προς τα τελη, translated by Ross as 'means'. This is a crux: if 'means' is the correct translation then we have here a picture of instrumental reason, and the account of phronesis becomes incoherent. Much ingenuity has been spent on attempts to rescue the preferred Aristotelian picture.[2]

Rather than go further into textual analysis of Aristotle I shall from here on talk of 'practical judgement'.[3] Of the two other possible terms 'practical reasoning' risks seeming to suggest a technical, almost algorithmic, process, an axiom system or decision procedure such as some have tried to make of the practical syllogism.[4] Despite that risk I shall nevertheless suggest that the metaphor of the syllogism sometimes serves to draw our attention to important features of practical judgement. (This is a good example of where we can use Aristotle when he is helpful and part company with him when he is not.) 'Judgement' usefully connects the cognitive and affective and captures something of the importance of the discernment of particulars in practical judgement, as well as its ethical character, of which more below. I return to practical *wisdom* at the end of the chapter. The distinctive nature of practical judgement – and this, too, is to follow Aristotle – is that it is attentive to the particular case and is pre-eminently flexible. It is characterised by *attentiveness*, which is my version of Aristotle's *aisthesis* (some commentators, for example, Dunne and Wiggins, translate this as 'situational appreciation'). Attentiveness involves a sensitive attunement to what we usually think of as the object of apprehension, rather than the more dominating kind of 'grasp' which instrumental or technical reason practises. Technical reason generally lends itself to planning while it is more typical of practical judgement that it is exercised in the course of 'hot action'. The attentiveness in practical judgement means that one is constantly open to further experience and the possibility of modifying one's judgement.

Practical judgement has, unlike technical rationality, a significant and irreducibly ethical dimension. There are two aspects to this. When a person exercises practical judgement the question of her character, of what kind of person she is, is always at issue. It is never simply a matter of what 'skills' she is exercising or what rules she is following. In chairing a meeting, for example, she encourages one colleague to hold the floor but another to be brief. Now she attempts a summary of where the meeting has got to, but now she allows ideas to go backwards and forwards without intervening. At one point she lightens the atmosphere with a joke, at another reminds colleagues of inexorable external pressures. All this flows to a large extent from the sort of person she is: generous and good-humoured, or tense, defensive and impatient. Later her colleagues are as likely to remark on her character as on her skill at chairing meetings.

The other aspect of the ethical nature of practical judgement can be seen by again examining the distinction commonly made between practical judgement and technical reason. Technical reason produces goods (the vase or the chair or the dinner), the ends to which doing or making (Aristotle's *poiesis*) is the means. These ends are specified by considerations external to the process of doing or making. As good technical reasoners we want a jar of a certain sort (a perfume flask of the right size, suitably painted, with a stopper that fits) rather than one produced in a particular way. If the product meets our requirements we do not generally stop to enquire whether it was made by an unhappy craftsman concerned only to pay his bills or one practising pottery in the spirit of Zen. Where we exercise practical judgement, by contrast, we see the good to be realised as something to be sought *through* the action and not as an independently specifiable aim. Lasch (1984: 254–255), clearly following MacIntyre's analysis in *After Virtue*, writes:

> Instrumentalism regards the relation of ends and means as purely external, whereas the older [Aristotelian] tradition, now almost forgotten, holds that the choice of the means appropriate to a given end has to be considered as it contributes to internal goods as well. In other words, the choice of means has to be governed by their conformity to standards of excellence designed to extend human capacities for self-understanding and self-mastery.

The good manager, say, chooses means which extend her colleagues' 'capacities for self-understanding and self-mastery' by encouraging open and honest discussion and democratic decision-making, rather than ruthlessly driving the meeting towards a predetermined conclusion. The good politician does not simply pursue certain ends (re-election, a lower public borrowing requirement, more nurses in the hospitals) while being indifferent to means. He is concerned to win the argument by open and honest debate, as opposed to corruption and what we now call 'spin'. The good teacher similarly does not adopt *any* means to achieve improved results. There are values that are internal to the practice of the school: good teaching by its very nature goes about its work in adherence to values and ethical norms (e.g. collegiality, respect for pupils, justice and truth), equally concerned with those internal values and norms as to achieve 'external' ends such as more examination passes and a good Ofsted report.

This is an attractive picture particularly since it offers a way of counteracting the criticism that teaching and other public services have been too much in the grip of a 'producer culture' concerned with its own members' benefits and conditions of service, to the detriment of the consumers of education whose interests ought to be put first. The 'phronetic' model of teaching expresses the development of teachers' 'capacities for self-understanding and self-mastery', in Lasch's words, as intrinsic to the nature of the practice.[5] (There is, incidentally, no obvious reason why this should be peculiar to teaching or the professions. The carpenter, office cleaner or shop worker can also go about their jobs in ways either conducive to the development of such capacities or damaging to them.)

It may be helpful at this point to summarise: the defining features of practical judgement include flexibility, attentiveness (understood as including alertness and sensitivity), matters of character and experience, and the ineliminability of ethical considerations. An extended example will illustrate these features and show their interconnections.

John is hill-walking, mostly following established paths but sometimes striking out across open country with map and compass in order to enjoy particular views or climb certain peaks. His flexibility consists partly in his readiness to adapt to conditions. If Great Gable is covered in mist he is prepared to leave it off his itinerary, even though it is a peak he particularly wanted to 'bag'. In fact his flexibility extends to re-thinking what he is about altogether. Perhaps there is something foolishly macho about peak-bagging, and a circuit of rolling countryside is just as satisfying, in a different way, and will do less damage to over-visited areas. He is attentive to map and compass and their relation to the terrain, and to signs that suggest the weather may be closing in. Such signs help him re-shape his ends.[6] Nor is this responsiveness a purely cognitive thing. The inviting aspect of that valley, in this weather, heartens him to walk more miles than he would usually attempt. He does not take such instincts as wholly authoritative yet he accords them respect, being dimly aware that extending his emotional experience in this range is one of the things that he comes to the hills *for*. The mountains around him have to be met on their own terms and are not to be mastered. The use of bolts and ropes to force a way up seems at odds with being fully alive to this particular place as opposed to any indifferent route that presents the same technical difficulties. Clambering safely around that crag requires having a feel for its distinctive kind of rock, lichens and mosses and not simply the deployment of a general skill of rock-climbing.

John knows, somewhere below the level of explicit consciousness, that he cannot take for granted being the sort of hill-walker he likes to be. The frame of mind conducive to his sort of hill-walking has to be worked for. Staying overnight at a pub helps make it the right experience, even though in practical terms he could perfectly well drive out, walk and drive home in the same day. Some companions respect and enhance the right spirit: others, though congenial enough people, will somehow infuse a mood of sight-seeing or officer training. John's hill-walking requires that he attends to being the sort of person he needs to be if, in turn, walking the hills is to refresh his soul. This is what I mean by saying that a person's character (rather than simply their skills) is at stake in matters of practical judgement. As for experience, John could certainly not enjoy the hills so easily without the years of experience behind him, yet he knows this can equally stale the freshness of each new visit, covering it with the patina of previous expeditions, or tempting him into recklessness. The voice of one's experience is to be listened to with some caution.

The *ethical* quality of this relationship with the natural world is there in John's respect for its otherness. But it is also there in his insistence on seeing how hill-walking fits into his other commitments and engagements and re-shapes them, rather than allowing hill-walking to be a self-contained and self-sufficient business. Ethics, it is sometimes said, is the system of thinking that embraces and unites all merely partial systems: in my example ethical thinking is concerned with the shape of a life and its component parts, and not only that but with the life of the natural world and what it means for the individual to be embodied within it. If the fundamental ethical question is Socrates's 'How should a life be lived?' then John's is an ethically rich life.

All of these features of practical judgement will appear in different ways in what follows. It would not be difficult to give a similar picture of teaching, emphasising flexibility and attentive alertness to the particular occasion. Take as a familiar example the child who interferes with a neighbour's work. The child may be bored, frustrated, envious or awash with unfocused feelings of aggression. Explanatory knowledge is not to the point here, as if there were some general principle, to the effect that bored (etc.) children interfere with their neighbour's work, of which this was an instance, with the conclusion no doubt to be drawn that more 'effective teacher behaviours' (improved lesson clarity, instructional variety and time management: these examples are taken from Reynolds, op. cit.) will generate more 'time on task' and prevent such incidents arising. The significant difference here is, of course, between the idea that lesson clarity is a good thing and the idea that we could turn such a truism into a highly reliable technology that would largely release us from the need for attention to the particular and unique case.

Attentiveness

It is when we see how extensive and complex the work of 'attentiveness' is that we can understand why practical judgement is seldom significantly a matter of *inference*. In all kinds of cases it is in our perception of the meaning of things, or in the 'thick descriptions' we allow them to fall under, that truth or error lies. Stealing is wrong: here is a wealthy-looking house, so I shouldn't steal from it – but the burglar reasons that 'it hardly counts as thieving if they leave the back door unlocked'. Or the car driver, who would formally defend thinking that follows the syllogism 'one should stop at a red light: here is a red light, so stop' drives on through, later justifying his action on the grounds that the syllogism clearly should not apply if it might mean braking dangerously abruptly. Here we are in the realm of the 'ethics of belief', where self-deception, wishful thinking, selective blindness, prejudice and precipitancy – characteristic weaknesses in our modes of attention – cause us to cast the world in one light, under one description, rather than another.

On a deductivist view which emphasises practical *reasoning* the challenge here is largely a matter of will, for the *inference* is clear and so the difficulty is to act in accordance with it. On my account what is at issue is rather the quality of our attention. As Iris Murdoch's narrator says in *The Black Prince* (p. 189), getting things wrong, even horribly wrong, is often 'the product of a semi-deliberate inattention... We never allow ourselves quite to focus on moments of decision... we allow the vague pleasure-seeking annoyance-avoiding tide of our being to hurry us onward until the moment when we announce that we can do no other'.

Here practical judgement presents us, as Dunne (1993) notes, with 'the need to develop even greater moral sensitivity rather than a closed deductivist code' (p. 310). And that moral sensitivity, *contra* Dunne (p. 308), must extend to careful attention to the formulation of the minor premise of the practical syllogism. 'Stealing is wrong: this is someone else's property, therefore it is wrong for me to take it' can indeed be revisited in light of the perception that the property's owner seems to have lost all interest in and all rights over it (a neglected dog, say), whatever the dangers of wishful thinking in such a case. This murky area is where we live a great part of our moral lives. To put it epigrammatically, we are denizens of the minor premise. The quality of our moral lives is often a matter less of our principles or the soundness of our reasoning than of how we see the ordinary world around us. 'The selfish self-interestedly casual or callous man sees a different world from that which the careful scrupulous benevolent just man sees' (Murdoch, 1992: 177). Moral enlightenment, which we might also call wisdom or a kind of knowledge, comes through 'a refinement of desire in daily living, and involving a clearer perception, including literal perception, of the world' (ibid.: 175). Iris Murdoch thinks of this as an essentially Platonic account, but it is the connection between knowledge and 'the refinement of desire' that lies at the root of Aristotle's remark that we can speak of choice indifferently as deliberative desire or desiderative reason (*Nicomachean Ethics*, 1139b4–1139b5).

Thus we see how practical judgement is connected with the idea of truth. The phronimos sees clearly, truly, because she attends to the world as it is and not through the distorting mists of self-deception or fantasy. Here, too, is an accurate picture of one kind of human freedom, as consisting partly in the often long and difficult struggle – neither the dramatic leap nor the inevitability of false consciousness – to rid ourselves of characteristic forms of (moral) blindness. Reason works here in partnership with desire without committing us to an objectionably foundationalist theory. A response to Dunne's first and third challenges might proceed along these lines.

Among the things that we must be alert to is *language*. The teacher implicitly reasons: it is important to be firm with recalcitrant pupils, and here is a recalcitrant pupil. But recalcitrance, high spirits, independent-mindedness and a host of other conditions keep close company and discrimination requires linguistic resources as well as resources of other kinds. Consider the importance of the words that teachers use to talk of their less able pupils. The prevailing language of education (standards, competencies, time on task, quality, modules to be delivered...) may betray our best efforts in practical judgement unless we are prepared to challenge it. We need both to seek more responsive language and to come at education through different genres of language (e.g. poetry and the novel). The dreary jargon of official documents and the mind-numbing paperwork generated in the proper desire to guarantee accountability and other goods may prevent us from attending to the features of our experience which they cannot express, in the end causing that experience to be less available to us. A great deal of the work of practical judgement occurs precisely at the point where particular forms of words are settled upon (this is a *lazy* pupil rather than one without the confidence to commit herself, say) and the outcome of the process of reasoning is thus largely pre-empted. This again is why talk of practical *judgement* often seems more helpful than talk of practical *reason*.

The importance of being alert and attentive to the particular case, which an analysis of practical judgement foregrounds, must not, however, persuade us that there is no place for general principles, even for technical rules. O'Neill (1993: 118) writes that 'one of the mistakes of defenders of practical judgement is to set up an *opposition* between "moral and aesthetic judgements" and the "technical" rule-governed rationality of science'. We cannot, as O'Neill notes, be exercising practical judgement reflectively and sensitively without rules. Professions and organisations properly set out procedures for various exigencies. The teacher to whom a child discloses abuse knows, or should know, what steps to follow; the lecturer whose student repeatedly misses tutorials sets established wheels in motion, and Teaching Quality assessors rightly expect to see such a procedure set out and communicated to students at the beginning of a course. Such rules and procedures give us the time and room to exercise practical reason where it really matters.

True though this is, it enables us to reassert the credentials of practical judgement on two grounds. First, judgement is needed to decide if this is a case for the application of the procedures. We hesitate, for example, over the child's reluctance to go home 'because Uncle Bob is there tonight', perhaps unsure whether this is a case where we should gently press a line of questioning. A high degree of sensitivity to this particular child seems essential if we are to know whether the rules and procedures are relevant. Second, judgement needs to be brought to bear on the rules and institutions themselves. From time to time they need to be challenged, revised and reorganised, and often that will be in the light of our awareness of particular cases for which they are inadequate.

Complicity

Much can be learned about practical judgement from cases where it goes wrong. Ishiguro's novel, *The Remains of the Day*, tells us much about practical judgement and its characteristic flaws, especially in the context of work and professional life. The butler, Stevens, has long been exercised by the question of what makes a first-class 'gentleman's gentleman'. His hypothesis is that it lies in 'dignity', a high professionalism which is not shed like a persona at the moment the butler comes off duty. He has glimpsed the limitations of technique, contemptuous of butlers whose eminence consists in a series of 'technical flourishes' (p. 42), and approving the refusal of the Hayes Society, a kind of guild for butlers of the first rank, to publish criteria for membership beyond 'that the applicant be possessed of a dignity in keeping with his position' (p. 33). Not for him mere technicist or instrumental thinking:

> We were ... an idealistic generation for whom the question was not simply one of how well one practised one's skills but to *what end* one did so; each of us harboured the desire to make our own small contribution to the creation of a better world.
>
> (p. 116)

Many of the elements of practical judgement are in place here. As a butler Stevens is the very model of attentiveness. Yet his attentiveness is misdirected: he attends to his master's guests while his own father is dying upstairs. His respect for his first employer, Lord Darlington (to us clearly a pre-war Nazi sympathiser), is based partly on an appreciation of his *amateurism* in the world of politics, as if

Darlington's rejection of professionalism automatically guaranteed his own wisdom and good judgement and as if amateurism could be equated, as Darlington claims, with honour (p. 103). Here the *phronimos* does indeed resemble a version of the 'English gentleman'. Practical judgement comes down to flat intuition ('when one encounters them [the "great" butlers] one simply *knows* one is in the presence of greatness', p. 44), and the flexibility that is the hallmark of practical judgement becomes accommodation – Stevens's to whatever Lord Darlington judges is best and the latter's accommodation of his German friends' political aims, which turns in the end into appeasement. Here practical judgement leans towards complicity, but precisely because one of its key elements, attentiveness, is wrongly developed, its ambit too narrow a conception of the moral life and moral responsibility.

Other examples from literature enable us to understand the nature of internal ends or goods of practices. They are not *unconditional* ends-in-themselves. A lawyer, for example, aims to win the case for her client. That is her 'external end'. To achieve it she will need to be well read in the law, persuasive, alert, prudent. When she is absorbed in the ethos of her practice these qualities become internal to her professional and personal being and we lose the sense that they are there merely or essentially to win this case or even cases in general. But if they become ends in themselves to the extent that their connection with wider ethical values and ideals is severed, the lawyer becomes not a model of practice but a caricature. Tulkinghorn, the lawyer in Dickens's *Bleak House*, never could see what the figure of Allegory on his ceiling was pointing to, for his being was wholly contained in his role. His lawyer's professionalism had become a substitute for his ethical being-in-the-world rather than an expression of it. Letwin (1982) writes of two of Trollope's fictional lawyers, Dove and Chaffanbrass, that each lacks any 'sense for the connection between his work and his understanding of himself' (p. 120). Grey, by contrast, another lawyer, sees a law-case 'as part of a larger context of obligations... his personality is neither determined not exhausted by his occupation' (pp. 120–121). The mark of a gentleman, concludes Letwin, is 'an ability to work conscientiously without losing himself' (p. 122). It is, of course, necessary not to be distracted here by unfortunate gender-and class-connotations of the word 'gentleman'. The guiding virtue of the gentleman-as-phronimos[7] has nothing to do with breeding or 'flair'. It is that essential aspect of the ethics of belief, the discrimination necessary to perceive the world accurately:

> Discrimination is displayed by recognising that the same sort of action may have been inspired by different motives, by an ability to acknowledge ideas and purposes alien to oneself, by care to distinguish between malice and error, disagreement and depravity.
>
> (p. 68)

These examples show us attentiveness in action and the rounded phronimos in the modern world: active in practical matters, governed by standards of excellence, possessing and respecting genuine skills, whether of craft or profession, and with the self-knowledge to check any tendency for absorption in profession or craft to become obsession or self-indulgence.

Everyday virtues

Dunne's fifth challenge was to show how practical judgement makes possible an account of teaching more satisfactory than that set out in the terms of the prevailing technicism. This chapter has made only limited progress in meeting this challenge, and not only because of shortage of space and the need to begin by describing and emphasising certain features of practical judgement.[8] Proper execution of the project, it might seem, would require something like very extensive descriptions of teaching, taken from a variety of sources including practitioners' own stories of their work: the very thickest of 'thick descriptions', a kind of anthropology of teaching and its daily virtues and practices. Then it might be possible to show how such descriptions correspond with practical judgement and its elements.

There are difficulties with that project, even though something like it is what seems to be attempted, with some distinction, by a number of 'action-researchers'. Technicism has now been so successful in colouring the very way many teachers understand and articulate their practice that one is conscious of being selective in fastening onto those stories that still preserve a different and older understanding of teaching. Furthermore, by re-shaping our sense of what such stories and accounts are *for* technicism has more and more ensured that they will take technicist forms and foreground technical skills. Where our careers are dominated by the need to demonstrate possession of competencies, to show mastery of the techniques required to teach the numeracy or literacy hour, or to prove that we have what it takes to be promoted into the ranks of Advanced Skills Teachers, it is an unusual narrative and a brave life that does not respond appropriately. Against this leviathan, driven by the imperatives of security and status, it seems a puny thing merely to describe teaching in a different way, and urge that it be seen like *this*: to speak an alternative language, offer fragments of novels or autobiography, and urge people to consider whether they do not preserve truths lost in the language of techno-instrumental rationality. Yet this, together with the careful drawing of the framework of humane alternatives to the technicist model – and, crucially, a mapping of the connections between such a framework and the 'thick descriptions' of practice – is perhaps all that philosophers of education can attempt here.[9]

To put the matter like this is to revert to an issue touched on at the end of the first section. Quite what, when we give an account of practical judgement, are we doing? To give an account might be a matter of telling a story: then the story we require is one that is internally coherent, clearly set out in its principal elements, consistent with our best understanding of the facts of human experience. But I have twice above, and deliberately, written of 'the rationality of practice', as if something grander and more systematic were at stake, or something that allowed us to make firm, if novel, connections with ideas of knowledge and truth. I raise that possibility not in order to disavow it wholly (we cannot do without truth and knowledge, even if these days they seem more elusive than ever), but to suggest that there is another way of understanding things here. In the attentiveness of good practical judgement, its sensitivity, flexibility and attunement to experience, perhaps there lies the possibility of doing justice to the diversity of particulars in our homogenising world, characterised as it is by relentless standardisation, frequently in the name of educational standards. Poster (quoted in Peters, 1996: 170) writes that the problem raised by such explorers of our postmodern condition as Lyotard is 'not to find a defense of rationality but to enable cultural difference to emerge against the performativity or rationality of the system'. If the 'performativity of the system' – this latest twist of technicism – is what now most stands in the way of ameliorating the human condition through education then perhaps it is not defences of rationality, cast in any traditional sense, that we most need.

We have been here before. The middle of the nineteenth century was marked by a technicism that sprang from Utilitarian roots as well as by a vigorous debate on the nature of work. Dickens satirises the technicism in *Hard Times*, famously in the school instituted by Mr Gradgrind and his system for bringing up his own children. When he wants to create the very antithesis of this, Dickens invents a travelling circus, known for its horse-riding. In his discussion of the novel, Leavis (1983: 263–264) writes:

> Representing human spontaneity, the circus-athletes represent at the same time highly-developed skill and deftness of kinds that bring poise, pride and confident ease...Their skills have no value for the Utilitarian calculus, but they express vital human impulse, and they minister to vital human needs...[The circus brings] the spectacle of triumphant activity that, seeming to contain its end within itself, is, in its easy mastery, joyously self-justified.

Deftness, then; confident mastery that is not opposed to skills but incorporates and transcends them; activity that seems (*seems*: the circus must pay its way) done not for the sake of an external end (entertaining the public) but 'to contain its end within itself'. Charles Taylor (1992: 383) writes that 'the life of instrumental reason lacks the force, the depth, the vibrancy, the joy which comes from being connected to the élan of nature', qualities which, moreover, the 'instrumental stance... constitutes a bar to our ever attaining' (ibid.). Above all the horse-riding expresses a sense of the *vitality* that is lost in regimes of utilitarianism or perfomativity. And that vitality seems, if not in any clear-cut way, connected with the ethical qualities of the circus community:

> There was a remarkable gentleness and childishness about these people, a special inaptitude for any kind of sharp practice, and an untiring readiness to help and pity one another, deserving often of as much respect, and always of as much generous construction, as the every-day virtues of any class of people in the world.
>
> (Hard Times, chapter 6)

Their virtues, we note, deserve 'generous construction': we are to understand them with the same flexible, attuned sympathy that they bring to bear on each other. Dickens seems to be showing us here, in contrast with 'the bullying formalities and dry precision assertions of the Gradgrind set' (Craig's introduction to the novel, 1969: 33) something very like practical judgement taken to its highest pitch of virtuosity and, in its strong connections with moral goodness and a way of life at peace with itself, something worthy of the name of practical wisdom.

When Tom Gradgrind robs the bank where he is employed and looks for refuge it is the horse-riding that hides him, in return for Mr Gradgrind having 'stood by' one of their own people, Sissy Jupe. Gradgrind finds his son in the circus ring, dressed as a 'comic blackamoor', 'in a preposterous coat, like a beadle's, with cuffs and flaps exaggerated to an unspeakable extent; in an immense waistcoat, knee-breeches, and a mad cocked hat...'. It is the circus and its people, and their combination of playfulness and practical wisdom, that allow difference to emerge against the inflexible regularities of the Utilitarian system:

> Anything so grimly, detestably, ridiculously shameful as the whelp in his comic livery, Mr Gradgrind could never by any other means have believed in, weighable and measurable fact though it was. And one of his model children had come to this!
>
> (Hard Times, chapter 7)

Notes

This chapter started as a paper read to meetings in Leeds and Cambridge of the Philosophy of Education Society of Great Britain; more recently a version was read to the 1999 Annual Conference of the same Society at Oxford. I am grateful to all those, too numerous to name, who made comments and suggestions.

1 This phrase, and some of the line of thought here, were suggested by Nigel Blake.
2 For example, by reading Aristotle as saying here that we do not deliberate about ends but about what constitutes ends: that we do not deliberate about whether we want happiness or justice but about what exactly these things are. Wiggins (1978: 145) observes that 'the difficult problem in practical reasoning is not "what will be causally efficacious in the promotion of these concerns?" but to see what really qualifies as an adequate and practically determinate specification of that which is here to be heeded or realised or safeguarded'. But if this is what Aristotle has in mind then he has chosen an odd way to say it.
3 I shall, however, use the expression 'the *phronimos*' from time to time as less cumbersome than 'the person of practical judgement'.
4 Wiggins (1978: 150, n. 1) helpfully reminds us that 'the role of a philosopher of praxis... is not to codify some "logic" of overall appreciation of practical situations. It is rather to describe, elucidate and amplify the concerns of human life, and to make transparent to theory the way in which these concerns necessitate, when they do necessitate, the actions or decisions in which they issue'.
5 Contrast the current tendency to try to raise the status of the profession by more pay in return for acquiring Advanced Skills: an extrinsic reward for embracing technicism.
6 Richardson (1997) supplies a detailed analysis of how we can think about and re-shape our 'ends' through the use of practical reasoning or judgement.
7 Letwin's analysis, though of the greatest philosophical sophistication and insight, makes virtually no reference to Aristotle and none to phronesis or practical judgement. Perhaps this is a strength and not a weakness.
8 The project continues as a book provisionally entitled *Teacher Training: Policy, Philosophy and Power*, Falmer Press, in preparation.
9 Some people, I find, worry that this work will seem irrelevant to or even offend those educationists who focus rather on instrumental matters, effectiveness and value-for-money. They may be reassured to some degree by the verses from which the title of the chapter is taken:

I wisdom dwell with prudence...
I lead in the way of righteousness,
In the midst of the paths of judgement:
That I may cause those that love me to inherit substance;
And I will fill their treasures.

(*Proverbs* 8: 12–21)

References

Aristotle (1969) *Nicomachean Ethics*, D. Ross (trans.) (Oxford, Oxford University Press).
Carr, W. (1987) What is an educational practice?, *Journal of Philosophy of Education*, 21(2).
Department for Education and Employment (DfEE) (1998) *Teachers Meeting the Challenge of Change*, Green Paper (London, HMSO and at http://www.dfee.gov.uk/teachers/greenpaper/index.htm).
Dickens, C. (1969) *Hard Times*, D. Craig (ed.) (London, Penguin).
Dunne, J. (1993) *Back to the Rough Ground: 'Phronesis' and 'Techne' in Modern Philosophy and in Aristotle* (Notre Dame, Indiana, University of Notre Dame Press).
Ishiguro, K. (1989) *The Remains of the Day* (London, Faber).
Lasch, C. (1984) *The Minimal Self: Psychic Survival in Troubled Times* (London, Picador, Pan).
Leavis, F.R. (1983) *The Great Tradition* (London, Penguin).
Letwin, S.R. (1982) *The Gentleman in Trollope: Individuality and Moral Conduct* (London, Macmillan).
MacIntyre, A. (1981) *After Virtue* (London, Duckworth).

Mackenzie, J. (1991) Street phronesis, *Journal of Philosophy of Education*, 25(2).

Murdoch, I. (1975) *The Black Prince* (London, Penguin).

Murdoch, I. (1992) *Metaphysics as a Guide to Morals* (London, Chatto & Windus).

O'Neill, J. (1993) *Ecology, Policy and Politics* (London, Routledge).

Peters, M. (1996) *Poststructuralism, Politics and Education* (Westport, CT, Bergin & Garvey).

Power, M. (1997) *The Audit Society: rituals of verification* (Oxford, Clarendon Press).

Reynolds, D. (n.d.) Better Teachers, Better Schools, http://www.teach-tta.gov.uk/speech.htm

Richardson, H.S. (1997) *Practical Reasoning about Final Ends* (Cambridge, Cambridge University Press).

Taylor, C. (1992) *Sources of the Self* (Cambridge, Cambridge University Press).

Wiggins, D. (1978) Deliberation and practical reason, in: J. Raz (ed.), *Practical Reasoning* (Oxford, Oxford University Press).

CHAPTER 17

MORAL LANGUAGE AND PEDAGOGICAL EXPERIENCE

Max van Manen

Journal of Curriculum Studies, 32, 2, 315–327, 2000

Introduction

In recent years there has seen a search for an ethics-sensitive language of teaching and an epistemology of practice that is guided by an interest in the child's experience and in the relational sphere between teachers and their students. Sockett (1987, 1993), van Manen (1991), Goodlad *et al.* (1991), Noddings (1992), Jackson *et al.* (1993) and others have argued that the most unfortunate fact about contemporary discourses and practices of education is that they have tended to become overly rationalistic, scientistic, corporatist, managerial and narrowly results-based. They argue that we need to ask what it would mean if teachers were treated as moral agents with a practical professional language. A professionally acknowledged moral language would allow teachers to think about their daily practices as essentially pedagogical interactions. Sockett (1997) has pointed out that 'education does not have a sophisticated moral language, and the specific tasks of teaching and of understanding education are made extraordinarily difficult by this vacuum.' As a result of this vacuum, he argues, it is difficult to name the problems that we have, to break out of our primitive discourse, to hold profound conversations, and to teach a moral language to children and students.

Common examples of a practical pedagogical language are easily found in the ordinary life-worlds of parents and children. In an online (Ouders Online) parent forum, a mother poses a question:

> My problem is that I find it very difficult to pass the care for my family to someone else. I don't mean just for an evening but for several days. (Are they enjoying good company? Are they feeling okay? Are small conflicts properly resolved? Are they eating regularly and enough? Are they getting clean towels?) I know this is a problem of being a worrywart, but do others recognize it and what can I do about it? (My husband is a dear father, but he is often away and is not as close to the home front as I am; he simply does not experience this 'problem' the way I do.)

A second mother responds to the online question:

> I do not know if there is a real solution to your query. But you can probably make it somewhat easier for yourself...by beginning to look for situations that are not problematic. You are struggling with the process of letting go that begins in part already right at the birth of your first child.

The second mother seems to recognize the worrying experienced by the first. It is not just the mother finds it difficult 'to pass the care', she really has a problem with 'letting go'. Next, the second mother gives suggestions for dealing with the problem in some appropriate manner. Indeed, this is often how it goes in life. Language is the way of accessing and understanding experience. By naming and renaming experience, we bring it to awareness, (re)interpret it and come to particular understandings or misunderstandings. The example simply illustrates that finding a language to describe our experience is a critical requirement for addressing and understanding our pedagogical predicaments. And, in passing, it points up a dimension of caring that educators intuitively should understand but on which they rarely seem to reflect.

In education we now hear calls for 'caring schools', 'caring teachers', 'caring curricula', 'caring pedagogies', etc. 'Care' becomes a critical term of a morally attuned professional language, expressing vocational commitments and passing on 'the tradition of service' (Schervish *et al.*, 1995). Such moral professional language appears especially highly developed in the health sciences where there is an extensive literature where theorists call for a sophisticated science of care (Watson, 1985; Morse *et al.*, 1990). In education, too, there seems to be growing interest in care (Jarrett, 1991; Prillaman *et al.*, 1994; Deiro, 1996; Eaker-Rich and van Galen, 1996). But if we want to understand how caring is actually experienced, then conceptual models and professional discourses are not always the best references. We may need to bypass conceptual and cognitive models in favour of more literary and imaginary sources that stay attentive to ethical experience.

Since in literature, as in all art, the image has not yet been reduced to the concept, it is useful to work with narratives that are emotionally complex and that offer us some understanding of the meaning of care-as-worry that is unmedicated by conceptualization. Through some recognizable anecdotes and literary quotations, I will explore the experiential subtleties of the moral vocabulary of care in terms of our responsibilities to our children as parents and as educators. Next, I will relate these moral sensibilities to the question of the unique sense of pedagogical responsibility, especially as suggested in experience-based ethics.

Experiencing care-as-worry

When I ask people for concrete examples to illustrate the caring of their parents, I receive various anecdotes. A 30-year-old woman told how her mother had come to stay with her for a few days in the big city. When in the evening she returned home from late night shift-work, she found her mother still up. Surprised, the daughter said, 'Why didn't you go to bed? You knew I would be late.' 'Yes', her mother answered, 'but I wanted to make sure that you got home all right.' 'But, Mom, this is my life. What do you think I have been doing for the last 10 years!' 'Yes, yes', the mother answered, 'I can't help it. I just like to know that you are okay.'

For many parents, care seems to consist of fretting and fussing and worrying and generally making a nuisance of oneself for the sake of one's children. Of course, kids at times hate this in their parents, but in the back of their minds, they also know that it would be much more terrible if there was no one to worry about them. Recently, a Canadian radio station broadcasted an interview with street children in Canada. One street-kid said,

> What is most terrible being on the street is that there is nobody who has dreams about you. Ordinary kids have parents who worry about them. Nobody, neither my father nor my mother ever worried about me, ever had a dream for me.

Of course, we should not think that caring is something that comes naturally with being a mother or a father. Children may have 'caring' parents but still end up in government care. A 14-year-old foster girl said, 'You know what I am afraid of? I am afraid that if I would die no one would really care.'

It seems that when we try to recall particular moments of caring it is often the intense experiences that stand out. But the qualities of these experiences seem characteristic also of the more mundane and common moments of caring. The following is an excerpt from the diary of Judith Minty (1982: 215–216). It is a story that could have been told by many parents:

> My son, my middle child, the handsome one, the worst student, the one most admired by his peers, came home from football practice tonight sick, with a bellyache, half crying.
>
> Thirteen years old, short for his age, he pedals off on his bike at 5 p.m. drags back into the house around eight every night...
>
> A half-cold dinner waits for him in the kitchen. I rush him out there so that he can eat, shower, and rifle through the pages of his homework before he groans into bed... And I don't forget to remind myself that if most of his friends are playing football and he isn't, then there is no one to occupy his time, nothing to do between school and bedtime.
>
> But tonight is different. He eats little, says he is sick. I tell him it was the peanut butter sandwich he ate before practice. I tell him that big Scott M across the street throws up after every practice if he eats less than two hours before. My son trudges upstairs to suffer alone.
>
> After his shower he goes to his room, where he thinks no one can hear him. But I hear him crying. I don't worry too much. He is the one who moans when he has a minor cold. Briefly, I think of appendicitis, but brush the thought away. I also think about those other times he has cried because something he couldn't cope with what was gnawing at him. I will wait awhile, see what develops.

In this recognizable family situation, we hear a mother worrying. But this is not the kind of worrying that we commonly regard as self-indulgent and useless. The kinds of things the mother does is the ordinary stuff of parenting: the things parents do and think. This worrying is not a side-effect of parenting: it is the very life of it. A mother is involved in taking care of her son. In everyday life-situations, caring is lived as a worrying attentiveness.

And Judith Minty knows this. She says, 'I don't worry too much' – but of course the point is that she does worry. Saying this to herself is as much a manner of keeping herself in check as it is a way of assuring that she should not let her own feelings and needs overshadow those of her son. She seems to know that worry can be both a way of staying in touch with her child and a way of dwelling too much on her own anxieties. She chooses the former. She worries and waits (Minty, 1982: 216).

> When he comes downstairs, I ask him if the practice went badly today, was the coach after him? No, he just feels sick. I tell him no television – he needs to lie down in his room. The others come [his sisters].... [We talk but I] hear my son in the distance, still crying behind closed doors.
>
> I am reading in my bed. He appears. I put my book down. He sits at the foot of my bed, still young enough to weep in public, and tries to start. The others hover, then vanish. They know this is his crisis.

'Lorie [his sister] is going to leave soon', he finally manages to blubber out. I tell him no, that she won't be going to college for years yet. [He says] 'I don't want anything to change'.

Parental care is rarely an explicit fretting and more often a lingering awareness, a heedful attunement. While talking to her daughters or reading, the mother at the same time remains aware of her son's presence in the background. Did she do the right thing?

Worry, it seems, is the *active* ingredient of parental attentiveness. Worry – rather than duty or obligation – keeps us in touch with the one for whom we care. Worry is the spiritual glue that keeps the mother or father affixed to the life of their child. So when Judith Minty's (1982: 216–217) son finally comes to talk to his mother, she expects that he will open up to her:

> The crack begins to open. 'Do you want to stay just the way you are?' [I ask.] Of course he does, and nods, and then it all comes spilling, tumbling out, a waterfall full of worry and sadness and tears. As he tells it, I remember how, when he was ten, he worried about what would become of us when the sun burned itself out; how, when he was nine, he worried about having to fight in Vietnam. This tough boy-child, whom we worry about with his D+ 's and C− 's has a different depth to him than our others.
>
> What will happen to him if his father dies, if I die? What will he do if he lives to be 103 and there is no family left? . . .
>
> We laugh that when he is 103, [his younger sister] Annie may be 101 and Lorie 105. I tell him that when he goes away to college, I expect him to come back now and then. We talk about change, how people make plans to do things when they grow up, how I will miss him, but won't be lonely. And we talk about the new family that he will have when he leaves his old family.

Notice how nicely the worrying mother takes away the worries of her child, how she indicates her worry as a mother (that she will miss him), but that he need not worry about that either. Finally Minty (1982: 217) reflects to herself:

> Have I done a good job? I don't know. He is not crying any more. He tells me he has been thinking about this for a week and hasn't been able to eat much. We both laugh and agree that the not-eating part was probably good for him. (He had put on too much weight.)
>
> It is much later now. He is sleeping. Everyone is sleeping. I hope his spirit sleeps well.

When everyone is sleeping, the mother is still awake, thinking about her child. In some sense, this wakefulness to one's child is characteristic of the life of parenting. To have children means that one will never be able to just sleep. Caring for one's children is a kind of worrying mindfulness. (In several languages this worrying dimension is much more pronouncedly felt by the speakers of different languages, but this is not the place to expand on this curious cross-cultural phenomenon.) I conclude that this caring–worrying is really a very human response to vulnerability in others, it is what philosophers such as Emmanuel Levinas (1993), Jacques Derrida (1995) and Knud Løgstrup (1997) have described as the moral ground of human existence.

Worry as caring responsibility

The French philosopher Emmanuel Levinas (1993, 1998) has insistently proposed that caring responsibility can only be understood in its most basic modality if we can somehow transcend the intenational relation toward the world that accompanies all modes of being and thinking. He has shown that it is only in the direct and unmediated encounter with the other that we can gain a glimpse of the meaning of the ethical impulse that he describes as the human responsiveness to the appeal of the other who needs my care. Usually we think of other people as selves who are in the world just as we are in the world as selves. And so we are cohabitants, fellow human-beings who live in reciprocal relationships. In these relations, each of us cannot help but see others as objects of our personal perception and thinking. But this is not the only possibility. It also may happen that the other person bursts upon my world and makes a claim on me outside of my own intentional cognitive orientation. In other words, it is also possible to experience the other in the vocative: as an appeal. This is especially true of situations where we meet the other in his or her vulnerability, as when we happen to be handed a hurt and helpless child, or when we suddenly see a person fall in front to us. What happens then is this: I have felt a response that was direct and unmediated by my intentions or thinking.

This kind of experience alludes to the originary caring encounter. And thought comes too late, according to Levinas (1981), in this situation. What happens is that this person in distress, this child in need, has made an appeal on me already. I cannot help but feel responsible even before I may *want* to feel responsible. In his earlier book, Levinas (1979) describes the phenomenon of the involuntary experience of ethical responsibility as fundamental, not only to the experience of human relationship, but also to the experience of the self. To meet the other, he (1979: 187–253) argues, is to see this person's face, is to hear a voice summoning me. This is the call of the other. A demand has been made on me, and I know myself as a person responsible for this unique other. This relation with the other is non-reciprocal (in some sense a non-relational relation). Indeed he states this predicament even more provocatively, arguing that the other is not only someone I happen to meet, but this person calls me to responsibility. Stronger yet, this person takes me hostage, and in this gesture, I have experienced also my own uniqueness because this voice did not just call. I do not need to look around to see if it was meant for me. The point is that I felt responsive, I am the one, the voice called *me*, and thus took *me* hostage (Levinas, 1981: 44).

Hostage? Is this not just a metaphorical way of speaking? Not if we recognize this experience in our own life: is this not precisely what happens to us when we are claimed by our sick child or by someone in need? The strange thing is that here is this vulnerable child who exercises power over me. And I, the big and strong adult, am being held hostage by this small and weak person who relies on me. If, as a parent, I am careless (meaning: free of worry), then I may inadvertently expose him or her unduly to risks and dangers. For example, I fail to keep my eye on my child when he or she wanders astray. Thus, the paradox is that a care-less parent is not necessarily uncaring but unworrying. Levinas (1998) points out that in relation to the face we come closer to the other. At the same time, it is the face that makes the distance between the self and other irreducible, infinite. In caringly worrying for this person, I cannot reduce this care-as-worry to the care of the self, as described, for example, by Foucault (1986). Indeed, it is especially the face that takes on caring-meaning for us. Many will recognize this phenomenon. What is meaningful in the face is the command to responsibility.

In a recent tele-commercial by the Save the Children Fund, the woman from the agency holds up a child of poverty and then she says to us, the television viewers, 'Look into these eyes and do what you would do if you were face to face.' At the very moment she utters these words, the child turns and stares directly into the camera. Now, no matter what we think of these kinds of commercials, if we really looked into this child's eyes and if we did not just click to another television channel, then we may have experienced an uncanny sensation. The child's eyes look at us so immediately that, before we knew what happened, they burned us, as it were. What did we see? We saw in this face a vulnerability, a strange accusation – an accusation of a guilt of which we know ourselves innocent. And yet, we felt this guilt, this indebtedness: We have experienced responsibility. This is what Levinas talks about as being addressed by the otherness of the other. In this experience, I do not encounter the other as a self who is in a reciprocal relation with me as a self. Rather, I pass over myself and meet the other in his or her true otherness, an otherness that is irreducible to me or to my own interests in the world (Levinas, 1993: 44).

The strange thing is that the more I care for this other, the more I worry and the stronger my desire to care. By desire, Levinas does not mean a personal want or need. Wants and needs differ from desire. I may always have wanted to buy a cottage at the lake, and now that I finally am able to afford my dream, I feel satisfied; or I may find that I am disappointed and that my want was not as worthwhile as I thought. At any rate, my want has been stilled. But desire that lives in my relation of care reaches beyond anything that might bring satisfaction and thus acquiesce in the desire. For example, love is desire in this sense. Think of the lover who asks his loved one, 'Do you love me?' And his love says, 'Yes, you are my love and only love.' The question is: What happens to desire? Chances are that a week later, a day later, or maybe even five minutes later the lover may again feel the desire to ask and say, 'Yes, but do you *really* love me?' And again his love responds, 'Yes, I really do love you.' This example illustrates that true desire cannot be stilled. No answer can forever satisfy. In fact, desire feeds on itself and fans itself – think of the great love tragedies. Similarly, caring responsibility increases in proportion to the measure that it is assumed. The more I care for this person, the more I worry, and the more I worry, the stronger my desire to care.

What is also peculiar about this ethical experience of caring responsibility is that it singles me out. It addresses each person uniquely. When the voice calls, then it is no use to look around to see if it was meant for someone else. No, here is this child in front of me, and I look this child in the face. Before I can even think about it, I already have experienced my responsiveness. I 'know' this child calls upon *me*. It is undeniable: I have experienced the appeal. And this experience is a form of knowing. I am called. I am being addressed – or to use a Levinassian (Levinas, 1998: 133–153) phrase: 'I am the one who is charged with responsibility.' What makes Levinas's insights so unique is that he is the only philosopher who offers us an ethic of caring responsibility that is not founded in ethics. That is why he calls it pure ethics. In a sense, this is not yet philosophy, not yet politics, not yet religion, not yet a moral judgement. He shows us that in the encounter with the other, in this greeting, in this face, we experience the purely ethical before we have involved ourselves in general ethics as a form of thinking, reflecting and moral reasoning (Levinas, 1998).

Experiencing responsibility in the face of the unique

Several authors have clarified and explored the ramifications of this distinction between caring as general ethics and caring as pure ethics (Rée and Chamberlain, 1998).

Some of these discussions have evolved around the biblical parable of Abraham and Isaac in Genesis 22. For example, Søren Kierkegaard (1983) portrays Abraham as the great God-fearing man who was commanded by God to sacrifice his only son. The horror is that Abraham was indeed prepared to sacrifice his beloved Isaac in the face of and in defiance of any ethical standard. This horror is difficult to alleviate. Yet, in Abraham's predicament we may sense the tension between two demands of caring responsibility. First, there is the demand experienced in the call that has singled *me* out as uniquely responsible. And, second, there is the demand of the community that we must always be able to justify and account for our responsibilities, duties and tasks in some kind of ethical manner. The first demand is explicated in the famous *Fear and Trembling* by Kierkegaard (1983); the second demand is articulated by the French philosopher Jacques Derrida (1995) in his remarkable text *The Gift of Death*.

Would it not have been easier for Abraham if he had at least tried to explain God's strange command to his wife and son at the outset of the journey? Kierkegaard (1983: 82–120) shows that this would have been impossible. The absolute responsibility that Abraham felt towards God could not, and cannot, be justified in any system of ethics or by any moral principle. If anything, child sacrifice is a mad, murderous and scandalous act, and Abraham would only have met total scorn and disbelief. So it was Abraham's fate that he had to carry this unbearable burden, this terrible secret, all by himself. Abraham had heard God's call, and he felt it was his responsibility to heed this call.

In re-reading Genesis 22, one may wonder: What would have been the significance of the fact that it was a second voice, the voice of an other, who called Abraham and who commanded him to stop and not raise his hand against his son, the son he loved so deeply? Abraham might have been confused. Why did not God call to him directly as he had done when he asked for the sacrifice? But then, the Bible (King James version) says, the angel called from heaven a second time:

> And the angel of the LORD called unto Abraham out of heaven the second time,
> And said, By myself have I sworn, saith the LORD.

And indeed the other, every other who calls upon me as true other, calls me with the voice of God. And the voice says, 'Thou shalt not kill!' (Levinas in Rötzer, 1995: 64). The ultimate other is God. And so, without intending to be sacrilegious, I like to think that this is how it went: Abraham tied his son to the sacrificial stake as the Bible said he did. He sharpened his knife as he must have done. Then he raised the knife and, at that moment, as he looked Isaac in the face, he heard the voice call his name. And the voice said, 'Lay not thine hand upon the lad.' Thou shalt not kill. Of course, it was not Isaac who uttered those words, but they arose from Abraham's originary acknowledgement of the ethical encounter of the face, the face of his own son.

So who called Abraham with the voice of the ultimate other? The point is that this is already an intellectual question, a religious ethical question perhaps. We might just as well say that pedagogy called him. Or that it was Isaac's face, the face of any child for whom the parent holds a unique and inexpressible caring responsibility.

Both Caravaggio and Rembrandt have depicted the sacrificial biblical scene in their paintings. The treatment of Isaac's face is especially striking. In Caravaggio, Isaac's face is contorted with dread and fright, and the Angel's face is expressive with appeal. But in spite of these very different expressions, what is most remarkable is the uncanny likeness of the two faces. Abraham is held from killing his son by staring into the face of his son. Strangely, in Rembrandt's painting, Isaac's face is completely covered over by the clutching grip of Abraham holding him down. It is as if Rembrandt, the famous master of portraiture, did not know what to do with the face of Isaac. And so he covered up the face completely. But both Caravaggio and Rembrandt anticipate Levinas in their understanding of the significance of the face as the ethical experience of responsibility for the other, and in particular for one's child.

The reason that Caravaggio and Rembrandt could show us the ambiguous role of the face is that Abraham's situation is not at all exceptional. In fact, it powerfully portrays our modern or postmodern predicament: our ambiguous relation to our own children. Derrida (1995) has put it very well: in a real sense we can kill our children (i.e. their uniqueness) in many different ways, and all of us, men and women, are like Abraham holding the knife over those who are dear to us. How do we do this? And what does Levinas mean when he says, 'Care for the death of the other is the beginning of the acknowledgement of the other?' (Levinas in Rötzer, 1995: 65.)

We need to be sensitive to the uniqueness of the other. And the uniqueness of each person comes into sharp relief against the fact of his or her individual mortality. Ironically, we are given this mortality right at birth. Therefore, Derrida (1995) calls this 'the gift of death' since it is our own mortality that belongs to each of us more uniquely than anything else imaginable. Whatever else can be taken away from us, there is one thing that belongs to us so essentially that nobody can take it away, and that is our own death. I may give my death in sacrifice to someone else, and yet even that supreme gift cannot be substituted for their own death. Thus, it is the non-substitutional uniqueness of the other that I must preserve and not kill by betraying it to the general. And yet, Derrida (1995: 69) claims, this is precisely what we do every day:

> By preferring my work, simply by giving it my time and attention, by preferring my activity as a citizen or as a professorial and professional philosopher, writing and speaking here in a public language . . . I am perhaps fulfilling my duty. But I am sacrificing and betraying at every moment all my other obligations: my obligations to the other others whom I know or don't know . . . also those I love in private, my own, my family, my son, each of whom is the only son I sacrifice to the other, every one being sacrificed to every one else in this land of Moriah that is our habitat every second of every day.

It seems that we constantly betray the call of caring responsibility in our efforts to be caring in the general sense of duty, as in our professional practice. Derrida (1995: 78) articulates the dilemma in such a way that his confession of failing to be responsive to the call of his own son becomes an unsolvable predicament:

> what can be said about Abraham's relation to God can be said about my relation without relation to *every other* (*one*) *as every* (*bit*) *other* [*tout autre comme tout autre*], in particular my relation to my neighbour or my loved ones who are inaccessible to me, as secret and transcendent as Jahweh . . . Translated into this extraordinary story, the truth is shown to possess the very structure of what occurs every day. Through its paradox it speaks of the responsibility required at every moment for every man and woman.

In a way, Derrida seems to let himself and us off the hook in our unique responsibility to care for the other as other. On the one hand, he suggests that we need to heed this call. On the other hand, his deconstructionist strategy aims to show that we must constantly fail since we cannot possibly be responsive to every other who is out there and who also makes an appeal to our caring responsibility. Since we can only worry about one thing at a time, we cannot worry about everyone and everything. So why worry? Why care in this deepened sense? Indeed, even as a teacher, one would have to agree with Derrida. We cannot really see how we could worry for each child in our charge.

Does that mean that we must flee into the ethical domain of a professional responsibility that says that we must subsume our caring behaviours under some general moral code? The problem with Derrida's approach is that he has already fled into language and ethics when he deconstructs the prereflective occurrence of the caring encounter. The point is that in everyday life the experience of the call of the other, of care-as-worry, is always contingent and particular. It can happen to anyone of us anywhere, anytime. Every situation like that is always contingent. I can only be here and now. In this home. In this classroom. In this street. Thus, it is the singularity of this person, this child who addresses me in my singularity.

Caring for the faceless

I am inclined to suggest, somewhat tongue-in-cheek, that care-as-worry can be likened to an illness, a chronic condition of worrying for this other person who is dear to me, whom I love, or for whom I happen to feel responsible. And indeed, this condition of care-as-worry is truly somewhat like an affliction. Existentially, the vulnerability of the other tends to be experienced as, what we might call, ethical pain – ethical pain that is symptomatic of the worrying condition engendered in the encounter with this other person who has made a claim on me. Many parents, many teachers, many nurses, many physicians and other professional carers would readily agree that this worrying is painful and troubling. But it is also necessary. Why? Because worrying keeps me in touch with the presence of this other. Or as Levinas (Rötzer, 1995: 62) says, 'The presence of the other touches me.' And now the ethical has entered my life, I feel I should do something, that something is demanded of me (Løgstrup, 1997).

Again, we can check the truth of care-as-worry against our own experience as a parent where pain, fear, illness, discomfort, anxiety endured by my child may hurt me even more than it hurts the child. In other caring relations, too, this can be our experience. A teacher may feel a special responsibility for this or that child. And this care-as-worry is often expressed as, 'I have to let him know that he is doing okay.' Or, 'I need to keep a special eye on her.' Administrators who regulate the practices of educators need to understand that caring in a deeper sense can only occur where contexts, structures, teacher–student ratios and schedules provide opportunity for the occurrence of genuine caring relations, even though these cannot be controlled or predicted.

Effective practice is not the primary reason to remain open to the ethical demand. Also important is that caring in this deeper sense is the source for understanding every other kind of caring. Of course, care-as-worry cannot be legislated, managed, or controlled. But the sporadic and spontaneous occurrence of this originary kind of care provides the basis for understanding the more practical caring responsibilities that we do expect from professional educators on a routine basis. As I was completing this chapter I was invited to join several junior and senior high school graduation celebrations. Here is a fragment from a farewell speech by a junior high school teacher to her home-room students:

> I will miss you. And I will think about you, how you are doing. I will miss the good discussions we have shared during class. I will miss the thoughtful and also the embarrassing questions in health. I will miss the penbook letters about novels. The poems you have written. And yes, I will miss even the arguments we have had about why it is a good thing in this day-and-age to study old-fashioned grammar...
>
> Our home room has indeed been like a home. We have been like a family. And, of course, families have their difficulties and differences. I have admired how you, the students, have looked after one another, how you have shown sensitivity to personal vulnerabilities and strengths.
>
> Like in any home squabbles did abound. Yet there were many of those special moments that will leave their traces – you know, those are the moments that an insight occurred, that a discovery came to mind, that a spontaneous chuckle, giggle or laughter broke up the class. Also the moments of a knowing look, a rolling of the eyes, or a quick clearing of the throat, and the occasional happening of a tear to the eye.
>
> I want to say to the parents how lucky they are for having such wonderful sons and daughters. You have been special to me, and I will carry you forever in my heart.

What struck me is that in private conversation the above teacher expressed apprehensions: she was worried about passing her students on to others, to senior high school teachers. Not uncommonly, teachers worry about particular students. A grade nine teacher said,

> For example, there is Michael and Alex. Michael and Alex visit me five times a day for chats between classes, during classes and at the end of the day. They never leave without saying good-bye. I do a lot of listening. Everyday I know what is going on in their lives. These are kids who thrive on personal contact. And now they are leaving I wonder: Who will take my place? Will there be some teacher in that large impersonal high school whom they can talk to?

It is because a teacher feels addressed by the 'faces' of particular students, about whom he or she worries, that the teacher can remain sensitive to the sometimes 'faceless' multitude of all the other students for whom he or she is responsible. The point is that this deeper sense of care-as-worry is the source for understanding and nurturing the more derivative varieties of care that occur and are theorized and called for in our research literature and professional practices. Only by remaining attuned to our sense of unique responsibility can we insert into our professional ethical practices the general responsibility of caring in all its various modalities that our vocations require. For the cynics and the pragmatically minded, this may still be an unrealistic or a 'heavy' idea. Caring as worrying seems a burdening responsibility. But so it is a burden. It may not always be pleasant or delightful, but as Levinas (Rötzer, 1995: 61) says, it is good: 'It's the experience of the good, the meaning of the good, of goodness. Only goodness is good.'

References

Deiro, J.A. (1996) *Teaching with Heart: Making Healthy Connections with Students* (Thousand Oaks, CA: Corwin).

Derrida, J. (1995) *The Gift of Death* (Chicago, IL: University of Chicago Press).

Eaker-Rich, D. and van Galen, J. (1996) *Caring in an Unjust World* (Albany, NY: SUNY Press).

Foucault, M. (1986) *The Care of the Self* (New York: Pantheon Books).

Goodlad, J.I., Soder, R. and Sirotnik, K.A. (eds) (1991) *The Moral Dimensions of Teaching* (San Francisco, CA: Jossey-Bass).

Jackson, P.W., Boostrom, R.E. and Hansen, D.T. (1993) *The Moral Life of Schools* (San Francisco, CA: Jossey-Bass).

Jarrett, J.J. (1991) *The Teaching of Values: Caring and Appreciation* (London: Routledge).

Kierkegaard, Søren (1983) *Fear and Trembling: Repetition*, trans. Michael V. Hong and Edna H. Hong (Princeton, NJ: Princeton University Press).

Levinas, E. (1979) *Totality and Infinity*, trans. Alphonso Lingis (Pittsburgh, PA: Duquesne University Press).

Levinas, E. (1981) *Otherwise than Being or Beyond Essence*, trans. Alphonso Lingis (The Hague, The Netherlands: Martinus Nijhoff).

Levinas, E. (1993) *Outside the Subject*, trans. Michael B. Smith (London: Athlone Press).

Levinas, E. (1998) *Entre Nous: On Thinking-of-the-Other*, trans. Michael B. Smith and Barbara Harshav (New York: Columbia University Press).

Løgstrup, K.E. (1997) *The Ethical Demand* (Notre Dame, IN: University of Notre Dame Press).

van Manen, M. (1991) *The Tact of Teaching: The Meaning of Pedagogical Thoughtfulness* (London, ON: Althouse Press).

Minty, J. (1982) From the diary of Judith Minty. September 19, 1972. In L. Lifshin (ed.), *Ariadne's Threat: A Collection of Contemporary Women's Journals* (New York: Harper & Row), 215–219.

Morse, J.M., Solberg, S., Neander, W., Bottorff, J. and Johnson, J.L. (1990) Concepts of caring and caring as a concept. *Advances in Nursing Science*, 13(1), 1–14.

Noddings, N. (1992) *The Challenge to Care in Schools* (New York: Teachers College Press).

Ouders Online Available: <http://www.ouders.nl/forum/1f00613.htm> (in Dutch; visited September 3, 1999).

Prillaman, A.R., Eaker, D.J. and Kendrick, D.M. (eds) (1994) *The Tapestry of Caring: Education as Nurturance* (Norwood, NJ: Ablex).

Rée, J. and Chamberlain, J. (eds) (1998) *Kierkegaard: A Critical Reader* (Oxford: Blackwell).

Rötzer, F. (1995) *Conversations with French Philosophers*, trans. Gary E. Aylesworth (Atlantic Highlands NJ: Humanities Press).

Schervish, P.G., Hodgkinson, V. and Gates, M. (eds) (1995) *Care and Community in Modern Society: Passing on the Tradition of Service to Future Generations* (San Francisco, CA: Jossey-Bass).

Sockett, H. (1987) Has Shulman got the strategy right? *Harvard Educational Review*, 57(2), 208–219.

Sockett, H. (1993) *The Moral Base for Teacher Professionalism* (New York: Teachers College Press).

Sockett, H. (1997) Caveat emptor: children and parents as customers. <http://www.quasar.ualberta.ca/cpin/papersframe.htm>

Watson, J. (1985) *Nursing: The Philosophy and Science of Caring* (Boulder, CO: Colorado Associated University Press).

CHAPTER 18

ETHICS BEFORE EQUALITY
Moral education after Levinas

Paul Standish

Journal of Moral Education, 30, 4, 339–347, 2001

I

Emptiness, indeed nihilism, is a characteristic of so much contemporary discourse regarding morality and moral education. This is found in facile notions of teaching right and wrong.[1] It is apparent in a common understanding of values and of values education. It is evident in the prevalence of rights-talk, with its sacrosanct assumptions about equality. It is there in the mantra of standards.[2] Why should I call this nihilism, why see it as a kind of emptiness? Because these different ways of thinking about moral education or about matters related to it have in common a certain conception of human being, of subject–object relations, in which values are grafted onto, or otherwise attached to, an original subjectivity. I shall explain this more fully in terms of the targets of my argument below.

This chapter examines this contemporary discourse in the light of remarks of Jean-François Lyotard and, especially, of Emmanuel Levinas. I want to call upon Levinas' account of the primacy of ethics – of my absolute responsibility in the face of the other, of the asymmetry of my relation to the other – in order not only to move beyond the carping that I might otherwise be accused of here, but also to adumbrate an idea of human being that might show the potential of such a shift in thinking. This invokes of sense of the importance of receptivity, a receptivity that releases the ethical from the limitations of moral reasoning (where the central figure is the autonomous free agent) but that also goes well beyond the terms of current accounts of virtue ethics.[3]

The targets of my argument manifest problems of two related forms. To begin with there is the tendency to see the ethical as a segment of human experience that can leave more or less untouched other segments. Ethics is a part-time business: it is the stuff of dilemmas – of earnest discussions on radio shows or classroom debates – covering such issues as abortion, capital punishment, euthanasia, etc. (Note incidentally the pretentiousness that such discussions sometimes encourage. Many teachers of adolescents will be familiar with the way that discussions of such issues can take on an air of unreality: it is perhaps a combination of the relative remoteness of these matters from the lived experience of most students, the abstract nature of the discussion, and peer group pressure that inclines many students to adopt attitudes for debate that may have little bearing on the rest of their lives. Note also the potential trivialisation of these matters resulting from commercial or media influence – for example, in such television shows as *Oprah*, or in a game such as *Scruples* where players have to select from multiple choice options concerning such matters as fidelity – 'What would you do if...?') The segmental character of ethics is seen, although the vocabulary swirls around unstably, where people say such things as 'Surely you shouldn't bring religion into politics!' Or politics into sport. Or politics into religion. Or morality into business or professional practice...and so on. There goes with this a tacit idealisation of objectivity as freedom from value, where the accusing tone of 'Aren't you bringing values into this?' or 'You shouldn't be judgemental' is evidence of a kind of subjectivism: to wit, the only values there can be are ones that are personal; and no one is in a position to pass judgement on the values of another. Of course, the motivation behind these ways of thinking is not difficult to see when one considers the various illegitimate ways in which values have been imposed on people, but this does not make such a position any more defensible or coherent.

The related set of problems here concerns the assumption that human beings are fundamentally isolated individuals in quasi-contractual relationship with society (i.e. with others). Such individuals have needs and desires, and these are, other things being equal, to be satisfied. Indeed it is the authenticity of my feelings that gives authority to my judgements – so *you* are in no position to judge *me*! Such individuals also have rights, which can be (often rightly) the occasion of much clamour, and responsibilities, which have recently been the source of rather more concern. But responsibilities here take off, as it were, from their logical correlation with rights. Both are typically focused on relatively specific matters, such that they could, for example, be entered in a list ('These are your rights...'). It goes without saying that such rights are (again rightly) central to the concerns of equal opportunities policies.

If some of what is described here is less typical of the thinking of those engaged directly in aspects of moral education but rather a backdrop of popular thinking against which such education takes place, it should not be supposed that (moral) philosophy has itself been free from these ways of thought. The picture of the individual in a contractual relationship with others is clearly derived in part from Thomas Hobbes, and it continues to be a salient feature of the moral philosophy of the modern (Anglophone) world. Similarly, the modern sense of ourselves as beings with inner depths, attunement to which is the requirement of authenticity and reference to which is a source of authority, derives most clearly from Rousseau. A critical factor in Rousseau's profound and revolutionary thought is the way that this relocation of authority in the inner self lays the way, to our immense benefit, for a principle of equality, and indirectly, and to our cost, for the subjectivism mentioned above.

It is in this light that the attempt in phenomenology to understand things in terms of how they come to appear (to us as human beings) reinforces what has become the presumption in favour of the primacy of ontology over ethics, so that, the danger is, ethics comes in somehow after the event. It is this too that must be opposed. 'To be or not to be' is *not* the question: this can only be a distraction from the ghost that rumbles under the stage, the ghost to whom we are inevitably, inescapably, always obligated.[4] Levinas points to a generalised responsibility.

In what follows I want to isolate two quotations, from Lyotard and from Levinas, and to explore the ways that these might unsettle the kinds of views considered above.

II

In *Postmodern Fables* Lyotard imagines the effects of globalisation in terms of a megalopolis that spans the globe, a megalopolis where all have been absorbed into an endless suburbia, a social structure with no other. In this dystopia, needs are satisfied, rights are exercised, and, with phone-ins or focus groups answering to all occasions, everyone's views can be expressed. All are represented. But, Lyotard urges us to see, a second existence of privacy, silence – of a silence and privacy beyond the scope of representation – must be prior to the assertion of rights. A background silence is necessary for rights to be articulated:

> If humanity does not *preserve the inhuman region* in which we can meet this or that which completely escapes the exercise of rights, we do not merit the rights that we have been recognized. Why would we have the right to expression if we had nothing to say but the already said? and how can we have any chance of finding how to say what we know not how to say if we do not listen at all to the silence of the other within? *The silence is an exception to the reciprocity of rights, but it is its legitimation.* The absolute right of the 'second existence' must be well recognized, since it is that which gives the right to rights. But as it escapes rights, it must always be content with an amnesty.[5]
>
> (Lyotard, 1993, 1997: 121–122)

Lyotard can speak favourably of the *inhuman* here because the idea of the human is loaded with precisely those (Western) commitments to the individual, to rights, to representation, and to the metaphysics of presence that run through the problems identified at the beginning of this chapter. The human, thus understood, is not a context free category or essence but a construct of those ways of thinking and those values delineated above – with all their shortcomings.

Let us consider in relation to this quotation a remark by Levinas, from some 30 years before, from *Totality and Infinity*. In Levinas' usage, *happiness* is to be contrasted with *desire* in that happiness relates to needs and wants that can be satisfied – in other words to the more or less naturalistic ethics that is familiar in the viewpoints being criticised here (the realm of politics, as Levinas sometimes puts this); desire, in contrast, relates to an aspiration to what is infinitely higher and beyond reach but which can constantly beckon (the realm of the religious):

> the distance that separates happiness from desire separates politics from religion. Politics tends toward reciprocal recognition, that is, toward equality; it ensures happiness. And political law concludes and sanctions the struggle for recognition. Religion is Desire and not struggle for recognition. It is the surplus possible in a society of equals, that of glorious humility, responsibility, and sacrifice, which are the condition for equality itself.
>
> (Levinas, 1961, 1969: 64)

Neither Lyotard nor Levinas is against rights, it must be clear; neither is against equality. Their concern is rather with what is under threat where the framework of values of which they are typical holds sway. In their remarks here, there is a symmetry in the phrasing that I want to draw attention to. '*The silence is an exception to the reciprocity of rights, but it is its legitimation*', writes Lyotard. 'The absolute right of the "second existence" must be well recognized, since it is *that which gives the right to rights*' (italics added). For Levinas, 'It is the surplus possible in a society of equals, that of glorious humility, responsibility, and sacrifice, *which are the condition for equality itself*' (italics added).

Levinas wants to overturn the primacy of ontology, even where this is conceived in terms that overcome the subject – object dichotomy (e.g. in Heidegger). He wants to do this by showing that fundamental to our being, indeed prior to our *being*, is our responsibility to the Other.[6] Paradigmatically, in Levinas, this is a responsibility to other people, though we shall consider shortly how far this can be extended to a generalised responsibility towards other living things and towards non-living things. Levinas characterises this responsibility in terms of the contrast between our awareness of things through sensible experience and the epiphany of a face. Where sensible experience is our starting point, it is understandable that we can construct a story of that experience in terms of the receiving of data, the stimulation of affect, and the objectification of the world as we gradually grasp the objects in it. In contrast, when confronted with the face I see something that necessarily goes beyond anything my senses can determine. For what I see to be a face something must be revealed of the interiority of the Other – perhaps no more than that interiority is there. That interiority always exceeds any possibility of knowing that I may have. Moreover, for the face to be a face, it must reveal a being whose ultimate vulnerability and need puts me always in a position of obligation. This, Levinas will claim, is a responsibility that will deepen the more that I answer to it; and this is wholly other to any calculus of want and satisfaction, of need and fulfilment. Levinas famously quotes *The Brothers Karamazov*: 'Each of us is guilty before everyone for everyone, and I more than the others.' Before the Other I am individuated in my obligation – this is not something I can pass up or pass on – and before the Other my obligation is absolute. As John Llewelyn puts this, 'Ethical Desire is not the correlate of satisfaction. It is Absolute relation that disturbs all correlation, bad conscience that provokes consciousness, the itch of the other under my skin. Every apology *pro vita mea* is ever increasingly lame' (Llewelyn, 2000: 121–122).

All this can seem wildly implausible, or hyperbolic to say the least. But might it not give us pause to consider how far this very sense of implausibility is itself the product of our being steeped in those assumptions of modernity that are at issue here, assumptions so deep that we do not notice them? How difficult it is for us to think of the world other than in terms of inert matter to which we subsequently attach value, and how difficult for many *not* to think that it might be most rational to view others initially in terms of the cold light of 'objectivity', before particular obligations and attachments are taken into account!

There is, perhaps, a further factor that can make more plausible the evocation of the face. In developmental terms, is not the growing awareness of the face of the mother (the first Other) crucial for the child's becoming a person, and for the subsequent awareness of things? The mother's face is present to the child not merely as a source of sensations but as an interiority the nature of which is quintessentially the call to the child for response and responsibility. (It is relevant here, surely, that the child's initial awareness of things in the world, which partly takes off from this awareness of the mother, is animistic.)

Levinas is emphatic that the Other teaches me, and this teaching involves the sense of this unscalable height and mysterious depth, and of the Other as both 'holy' and humble. The face, as interrogative, presents itself to me in discourse. It is to this that I now turn.

III

Let us say: I am as nothing before the Other. The height or the distance that confronts me is infinite, beyond measure. Is this not scandalous to modernity? To be condemned surely as poetic licence? (It is this sense of scandal that Kierkegaard wanted to excite.) In that scandalised reaction are there not grounds once again for a suspicion of the repressions of modernity's all-too-rational thought? And is not the suspicion of the poetic[7] suggestive of a language too preoccupied with the representational and the indicative, a language where active and passive, subject and object, transitive and intransitive are too neatly dichotomised?

In an earlier book that also pursues Levinassian themes, John Llewelyn explores the significance of the disappearance of the middle voiced forms of verbs, as found, for example, in Ancient Greek, verbs that are something between the active and the passive (Llewellyn, 1991). Thus, the active

> *Luei ton hippon*   He unties the horse.

is to be contrasted with the middle-voiced

> *Luetai ton hippon*   He unties the horse and in doing so affects himself.

Of course, the clumsy and inadequate nature of this second translation very much proves the point: that there is something lacking or suppressed in the dominant forms of our language. Perhaps the curious interchangeability of the phrases 'she married him' and 'she got married to him' and 'he married her', with their merging of the active and passive, is partially suggestive of what is at stake here. While our own conception of language is dominated by the indicative mood, we might ponder forms of language that defy categorisation as indicative or interrogative or subjunctive, or that seemingly give greater prominence to a different mood. (Llewelyn connects the imagination, so crucial in our ethical lives, with the subjunctive mood especially – the imagination that ponders what *may be*, and that thinks perhaps: *let it be so*.) Can we think of the child's proto-language or first words as being primarily subjunctive in mood? Or think of the language of other tribes as giving greater priority to the subjunctive? Then is the presumption in favour of the indicative in our own language perhaps something that may inhibit that exercise of the imagination and stifle our ethical lives?

Llewelyn regrets that Levinas is so struck by the need to do justice to the human being that he fails to do justice to the non-human being. Yet there is in ordinary lives the potential to relate to things in richly ethical ways, a potential that is covered over by our ways of speaking and our inhibition of a certain kind of imagination. Llewelyn is attracted to an idea that might be drawn from Heidegger of a responsibility that is incumbent on us in our relationship to the non-human. Such a responsibility is not something that I can sign up to by recognising, for instance, the arguments of the Green Party; it is not wholly or even primarily a matter of choice. Rather it needs to be understood in terms of the mutual appropriation of man and Being, in Heidegger's terms – of the way the world comes to be not as the object of scientific research but as the place of *dwelling* (from which a scientific understanding can only be a subsequent abstraction). Perhaps that child's proto-language or the language of the 'primitive' tribe more vividly realises this; and perhaps, as Wittgenstein recognised, this insight is constantly vulnerable to misunderstanding when it is exposed to the spectatorial scrutiny of the Western world (see, e.g. Wittgenstein, 1979). In a lyrical, difficult, richly allusive passage, the source and sense of which I elaborate below, Llewelyn gestures towards the Heideggarian and poststructuralist ideas in play here. Initially, let these words speak for themselves:

> The ordinary mortal shares with the poet who is 'struck by Apollo' and whose 'eye too many' is dazzled by the fire of the sky the responsibility

of loyally remembering the extraordinariness of ordinary beings, whether they be human beings or not: 'the jug and the bench, the footbridge and the plough...tree and pond too...brook and hill...heron and roe deer, horse and bull...mirror and clasp, book and picture, crown and cross', where the book may be the Book or may not, its word the word of the prophet or the word of the poet, where the cross may be the cross of the Word, of the Trinity, or may not, because the cross of the word B̶e̶i̶n̶g̶, the quaternity, and the burden of ontological responsibility it carries with it, are prior to theistic and atheistic faith as well as to rational onto-theology and onto-atheology.

(Llewelyn, 1991: 141)

The suspicion of the poetic, which was recognised at the beginning of this section, is shown here to have consequences that affect our ordinary lives – and that is, let us make no mistake, the morality of our ordinary lives. But the sensibility or response in question here has less to do with a heightened sense of *being* than with the *responsibility* of remembering the extraordinariness of ordinary things – of their otherness to us and ultimate unfathomability even as they are part of our ordinary world. This goes beyond, and perhaps against Levinas, in that this loyal remembering is directed towards things 'whether they be human beings or not'. These particular things – 'the jug and the bench...' – Llewelyn finds in the closing paragraphs of Heidegger's essay 'The Thing' (in Heidegger, 1971). Such things are discovered, Heidegger shows us, not as items among the innumerable 'objects' in the world, or amid the 'measureless mass of men as living beings'. They depend upon a dwelling with things. This dwelling is characterised by a reverence for things that is poetic in kind, where the poetic implies something both about language itself (and the dangers of an excessive emphasis on the indicative or representational), and about the *poeisis* of bringing things forth into being. With Heidegger's turn from the project of fundamental ontology, the direct description of being,[8] the word 'Being' is crossed through with two intersecting diagonal lines. The notion of being is displaced by the idea of the fourfold of earth, sky, gods and mortals – the quaternity mentioned in this passage, that is, a quaternity graphically gestured by the four points of this cross. These are the dimensions of the world in which our lives are lived out. They are dimensions without which things as things cannot be understood. For what is (something so simple as) a jug? Is it a three dimensional object, inert matter, of a certain weight and shape? In one sense there is no doubt, of course, that it is. But this is how the jug is understood in abstraction, by way of a reduction of language that can, if it is imagined to be somehow fundamental, obscure more than it reveals. This is not how the jug is understood in the context of lived experience. For then the jug holds the water that slakes the thirst after the day's work; it pours the wine shared at the family meal. The jug focuses a practice in such a way that what it means must be something more than the physical description offered above can possibly convey: that physical description effects a kind of etiolation of the thing. What the jug means, the way it is understood, is tied to the practices of which it is a part, in all their fourfold richness. In contrast to the reductiveness that threatens to deny this richness, the language of poet and prophet, in proximity here, suggests a way of thinking beyond rational ontology or rational theology, beyond also the idolatrous deification of Being, in that a responsibility is realised to what cannot be directly named or represented: this is a responsibility to what *may be*, to a way of being that is *always still to come*.

IV

One of the quotations with which Levinas prefaces *Otherwise than Being or Beyond Essence* (1981, 1978) is the remark of Pascal: '... "That is my place in the sun." That is how the usurpation of the whole world began' (Pascal's *Pensées*, 112). Ethical naturalism, the satisfaction of need and want, is here implied to lead to an avaricious or grasping relation to the Other. Its usurpation takes over the space in which the sense of mystery and reverence might be felt, and this is effected through its presumption that that space is reckonable and graspable. The emptiness of so much of our language of morality and moral education is to be understood in this way. In part it may be true that these problems are to be associated with the absence of a religious ethos in the common school, but it would be wrong to see them simply in those terms, or to imagine that the religious school is necessarily free from these vices. If the secular school makes the assumption that religion is an optional extra, this is as fallacious as the conception of ethics as part-time.

There are, on the strength of these arguments, implications for classes in moral education but it may be, it surely is the case, that what would constitute the best moral education would necessarily exceed such bounds. Only a brief indication of what this might entail is possible here. The sense of unattainable height and the sense of mystery that are so strongly evident throughout Levinas' work point to a kind of perfectionist education. Just as my attempt to answer to my obligation to the Other only deepens that obligation, so too a student inspired by the sense of what is infinitely high might find that her deepening knowledge of a subject only intensifies her aspiration, her desire. The point here is not just the character that this might give to the academic life but rather its total defiance of attempts ultimately to categorise and contain. It is what this models for the learner. We can see behind this perhaps some sense of the subjunctivity that subtends our practices and thoughts, where to do or think anything at all we must first *let things be* (this as this and that as that), and let them be in certain relations and practices that are the unfounded conditions of our lives.[9] The precious fragility of this for ethics!

Education at its best (indeed, as properly understood, I would like to say) must be suggestive of the good life and of the compelling and absolute obligation that this imposes on us. Its vision must be such as to expose the limitations of performativity (of clear objectives that must be hit, of competencies to be attained, efficiently and effectively), where things are geared ultimately to secure my (or someone's) place in the sun. Think for a moment what that models for the learner! Placing ethics before equality, education must expose the limits of totality through its sense of infinite responsibility.

Notes

1 Such notions are found in the tendency to blame teachers for whatever misdemeanours of the young have most recently captured the attention of the popular media. Sometimes such attitudes are exploited by politicians; sometimes they are evident in educational policy. This aspect of contemporary conceptions of moral education is examined in Smith and Standish (1997).

2 The term 'standards' often functions to stop debate rather than as its fitting subject. The emotive force that the term currently commands, and the hollowness that this masks, is addressed in Blake *et al.* (2000).

3 Examples in modern educational theory of the emphasis on moral reasoning are to be found in the restatement of liberal education in the work of R.S. Peters, Paul Hirst, R.F. Dearden and John Wilson, and of course in the work of Lawrence Kohlberg. Their emphasis on the centrality of the value of rational autonomy has been a main

preoccupation of a certain strand of contemporary moral philosophy. An energetic advocate of virtue ethics in education is David Carr, while Carol Gilligan's response to Kohlberg is also to be understood very much in these terms.

4 This is the ghost of Hamlet's father, whose murder he is obligated to avenge. The sound Hamlet hears comes from *below* the stage on which he stands, the stage which, in his preoccupation with the nature of his being, with 'What a piece of work is man...?', he imagines to be the ground of his being. Obligation is prior to being.

5 The amnesty here should perhaps be understood as an amnesty from litigations. By litigations Lyotard means the application of rules of judgement in which what is being judged is compelled to submit to the terms of those rules. Of course, such litigations are a normal part of our lives, and it could hardly be otherwise. Lyotard is concerned to show ways in which such application can, however, do violence to what is being judged by forcing it into terms that do not do justice to its nature.

6 The capitalisation of 'Other' denotes a relationship of a different order from the kind of otherness that is definitional of items in a categorisation. This Other is different from me not in virtue of any perceivable characteristic or quality but because of its invisible interiority.

7 The suspicion of the poetic has ancient roots. It is there in Plato's banishment of the arts, though this is complicated by deep and surely self-conscious irony given the literary character of Plato's own writing. It is there in modern ideals of objectivity, where language is conceived as a potentially pure instrument of communication.

8 To clairfy the terminology here, Heidegger's concern in his earlier work, in *Being and Time* especially, is with *Sein* rather than *Seindes*, which is typically represented by translators in terms of a contrast between 'Being' and 'beings'. That is to say, he is concerned not with the properties of things, with what they are like, but with the nature of their *being*, with what it is to be.

9 The phrase 'let things be' echoes Heidegger's *Gelassenheit* (see Heidegger, 1966), but what is at stake here is subtly different. This implies no necessary traditionalism or conservatism, still less a resignedness to what cannot be changed. It does acknowledge the way in which our deliberations always rely on a background that can only ever be examined piecemeal. That background is one of provisionality, of taking things this way or that through our accustomed practices. It could never be the scene of foundational activity. It is understood appropriately in terms of subjunctivity.

References

Blake, N., Smeyers, P., Smith, R. and Standish, P. (2000) *Education in an Age of Nihilism* (London, RoutledgeFalmer).

Heidegger, M. (1971) *Poetry, Language, Thought*, trans. A. Hofstadter (New York and London, Harper & Row).

Heidegger, M. (1996) *Poetry, Language, Thought*, trans. J.M. Anderson and E.H. Freund (New York, Harper & Row).

Levinas, E. (1961, 1969) *Totality and Infinity: An Essay on Exteriority*, trans. A. Lingis (Pittsburgh, PA, Duquesne University Press).

Levinas, E. (1978, 1981) *Otherwise than Being or Beyond Essence*, trans. A. Lingis (Pittsburgh, PA, Duquesne University Press).

Llewelyn, J. (1991) *The Middle Voice of Ecological Conscience: A Chiasmic Reading of Responsibility in the Neighbourhood of Levinas, Heidegger and Others* (London, Macmillan).

Llewelyn, J. (2000) *The HypoCritical Imagination: Between Kant and Levinas* (London and New York, Routledge).

Lyotard, J.F. (1993, 1997) *Postmodern Fables*, trans. G. van Den Abbeele (Minneapolis, MN and London, University of Minnesota Press).

Smith, R. and Standish, P. (eds) (1997) *Teaching Right and Wrong: Moral Education in the Balance* (Stoke-on-Trent, Trentham Books).

Wittgenstein, L. (1979) *Remarks on Frazer's* Golden Bough, Rush Rhees (ed.), trans. A.C. Miles, revised by Rush Rhees (Doncaster, S. Yorks, The Brynmill Press).